The
Rattle of the North

AN ANTHOLOGY OF ULSTER PROSE

edited by
Patricia Craig

THE
BLACKSTAFF
PRESS

———

BELFAST

First published in 1992 by
The Blackstaff Press Limited
3 Galway Park, Dundonald, Belfast BT16 0AN, Northern Ireland

This book has received financial assistance from The Arts Council of
Northern Ireland, under the Cultural Traditions Programme, which aims to
encourage acceptance and understanding of cultural diversity.

Typeset by Textflow Services Limited

Printed by The Guernsey Press Company Limited

British Library Cataloguing in Publication Data
The rattle of the North: an anthology of Ulster prose.
I. Craig, Patricia
828.08

ISBN 0-85640-464-0

CONTENTS

INTRODUCTION by Patricia Craig   1

1

A.T.Q. STEWART
from *The Narrow Ground*   15

EAMONN MCCANN
from *War and an Irish Town*   20

JAMES STEVENS CURL
from *The Londonderry Plantation 1609–1914*   29

MARIANNE ELLIOTT
from *Wolfe Tone: prophet of Irish independence*   37

T.W. MOODY
from *Ulster Since 1800*   45

PATRICK SHEA
from *Voices and the Sound of Drums*   51

A.T.Q. STEWART
from *The Narrow Ground*   54

2

MARY DELANY
from *The Autobiography and Correspondence of
Mary Granville, Mrs Delany*   65

THE REVEREND SAMUEL BURDY
from *The Life of the Late Reverend Philip Skelton*   71

WILLIAM DRENNAN/MRS MCTIER
from *The Drennan Letters*   75

JOHN GAMBLE
from *A View of Society and Manners in the North of Ireland*   80

WILLIAM CARLETON
from *Autobiography of William Carleton*   90

BENEDICT KIELY
from *Poor Scholar* 98

SHAN F. BULLOCK
from *The Squireen* 101

AMANDA MCKITTRICK ROS
from *Helen Huddleson* 104

KATHLEEN FITZPATRICK
from *The Weans at Rowallan* 107

ROBERT LYND
'The Orange Idealist' 113

FLORENCE MARY MCDOWELL
from *Other Days Around Me* 118

3

JOHN HEWITT
'No Rootless Colonist' 121

GEORGE A. BIRMINGHAM
from *The Red Hand of Ulster* 132

MAX WRIGHT
from *Told in Gath* 140

ROSEMARY HARRIS
from *Prejudice and Tolerance in Ulster* 152

BENEDICT KIELY
'The Night We Rode With Sarsfield' 158

SAM HANNA BELL
from *December Bride* 168

CAROLINE BLACKWOOD
from *Great Granny Webster* 172

4

ROBERT LLOYD PRAEGER
from *The Way That I Went* 183

FORREST REID
from *Apostate* 197

C.S. LEWIS
from *Surprised by Joy* 200

FLORENCE MARY MCDOWELL
from *Other Days Around Me* 205

E. ESTYN EVANS
from *Mourne Country* 209

E. ESTYN EVANS
from *Northern Ireland* 215

DENIS O'D. HANNA
from 'Architecture in Ulster' 218

W.F. MARSHALL
from *Ulster Speaks* 228

DENIS IRELAND
from *From the Irish Shore* 234

LOUIS MACNEICE
from *Zoo* 242

SEAMUS HEANEY
from 'The Sense of Place' 248

ROBIN BRYANS
from *Ulster: a journey through the Six Counties* 252

FRANK ORMSBY
'County Fermanagh' 261

5

SEAMUS HEANEY
from 'Mossbawn' 267

GEORGE J. WATSON
'Cultural Imperialism: an Irish view' 274

DENIS DONOGHUE
from *Warrenpoint* 287

PEADAR O'DONNELL
from *On the Edge of the Stream* 291

MICHAEL MCLAVERTY
from *Call My Brother Back* 296

JOHN O'CONNOR
    from *Come Day – Go Day*   301

ROBERT HARBINSON
    from *No Surrender*   308

BRIAN MOORE
    from *The Emperor of Ice-cream*   319

JOHN MORROW
    from *Northern Myths*   335

MAURICE LEITCH
    from *The Liberty Lad*   338

EAMONN McCANN
    from *War and an Irish Town*   341

C.E.B. BRETT
    from *Buildings of Belfast 1700–1914*   348

MICHAEL LONGLEY
    from 'Tu-penny Stung'   354

6

CAROLINE BLACKWOOD
    'Memories of Ulster'   359

C.E.B. BRETT
    from *Long Shadows Cast Before*   366

NAOMI MAY
    from *Troubles*   372

POLLY DEVLIN
    from *All of Us There*   379

SEAMUS DEANE
    from 'Why Bogside?'   394

ROBERT JOHNSTONE
    from *Images of Belfast*   401

TOM PAULIN
    from 'Paisley's Progress'   410

CIARAN CARSON
  'Question Time'   425
DENIS DONOGHUE
  from 'The Literature of Trouble'   431

BIOGRAPHICAL NOTES   444
BIBLIOGRAPHY   450
ACKNOWLEDGEMENTS   453
INDEX OF AUTHORS   456

INTRODUCTION

It is well known that conditions in the North of Ireland, from Plantation times on, were never sufficiently settled to foster literary activity, and that the development of the novel, in particular, was consequently retarded; for on-the-spot information about social life before the nineteenth century, you have to turn to poems, letters, diaries, travel writing, essays, political commentaries and such detailed family papers as the Hamilton and Montgomery manuscripts. Not all these categories provide suitable material for inclusion in an anthology of Northern Irish prose writing, though some do: for example, the earliest contributor I have chosen is Mrs Delany, wife of the Dean of Down in the mid-eighteenth century, who often stayed at the house called Mount Panther, near Dundrum (now a ruin on a hilltop), from which setting she dashed off letters to her sister in England discussing the flora of the Mourne district, the doings of various landed families in the area, and excursions as far afield as the Giant's Causeway (by which she was suitably affected).

It was a time of sharp social and economic divisions. While Mrs Delany and her guests eat gigantic meat meals, hurrying to get them down 'between church and church', a clergyman less decorous than Dean Delany, and armed with a club, is standing guard over meal sacks in a market town in County Tyrone. The inhabitants of parishes bordering on Pettigo, driven desperate by hunger, have designs on these meal sacks, and although the Reverend Philip Skelton is known for his generosity and humane temperament, he is also an upholder of law and order, and whatever civilised values he can find in the back end of Tyrone. His biographer, the Reverend Samuel Burdy (writing in 1792 about events of thirty or forty years earlier), presents Skelton as a very curious and interesting figure indeed – impatient, impetuous, learned, charitable and subject to what Burdy calls 'the hips', that is, hypochondria. *The Life of the Late Reverend Philip Skelton* is fashioned with the kind of artless charm we associate with eighteenth-century anonymous woodcuts or engravings for children's books, the same charm that occurs in the following lines by Burdy, describing some tinkers on the road near Ardglass:

1

There have I seen them with their wives and lasses,
Their smiling babies, and their little asses;
Each ass then carried on its useful back
Two pretty babies sticking in a sack.

Burdy was Rector of Kilclief parish in Down, at one time associated with Bishop Percy's circle at Dromore, and in the habit of commemorating small events in weak verse: for example, the failure to obtain sweet milk to lace his tea at Ballyhornan is the subject of one mock diatribe composed in doggerel.

At this time – the 1790s – while rhyming clergymen and others were disporting themselves thus, the country was well on the way to insurrection. The Society of United Irishmen had come into being to challenge misgovernment and inaugurate a new liberal era: we get the picture, or a part of it at least, in another celebrated correspondence (more topical than Mrs Delany's): that between Mrs McTier in Belfast and her brother Dr William Drennan in Dublin. 'Murders and assassinations are dreadful subjects, but common here': so reads the news from Belfast in 1797, prompting quotation of the line attributed to William Carleton in Seamus Heaney's poem 'Station Island': 'Oh holy Jesus Christ, does nothing change?' Things do, of course, even if, in retrospect, they seem to fall into a pattern: at one minute deadly, and at the next inspiriting. For all the disagreeable images associated with Northern Ireland – bigotry, aggressiveness, a backward-looking mentality, and so on – we find, in the literature of the last 200-odd years, continuous acknowledgement of its fascination and its virtues, including the virtue of egalitarianism which has always interposed itself between competing prejudices. It is true to say that an anti-sectarian drive has existed in Ulster as long as monolithic sects have been at one another's throats, and that the most persuasive social commentators are those who uphold it; most enduring literature shows at least a wish to be impartial about tribal matters, even if ideas concerning abuses and how to tackle them keep changing from author to author, and from one decade to the next.

Historical circumstances have always to be taken into account. For example, it is instructive to consider how the republican spirit prevailing in the North at the end of the eighteenth century began to look disruptive, rather than enlightened, once the failure of the United Irish uprising, and consequent union with Britain, had put it into a new perspective. The egalitarian impulse quickly found different outlets, some philanthropic and some literary. Because of this importance of context, in this anthology, in order to set the scene for much of what follows, I have started with a section given over to historical comment: Marianne Elliott, for instance, gets to grips with events in Belfast during the 1790s; Eamonn McCann offers a socialist analysis of both unionist and nationalist myth-making; and James Stevens Curl blends history and architectural history to illuminating effect. T.W. Moody provides 'A General Survey' (taken from a collection of talks originally broadcast in 1954, and published under the title *Ulster Since 1800*), which is just what it says, and as succinct and informative as it can be. A.T.Q. Stewart, in his striking and vigilant study *The Narrow Ground*, from which I have selected a couple of extracts, has the aim of providing as much insight as possible into 'the distinctive patterns of the past'. In his 'Sermons From Stones', he gives a mildly sardonic account of the stone-thrower's art, and at the same time tells us quite a lot about the tradition of rioting in Northern Ireland and its periodic eruptions. The idea seems to be that Ulster intransigence demands to be confronted head-on (you can't get away from it), but also that the sometimes complex ingredients of simplified sectarian hostility will repay investigation, since the more knowledge and understanding one gains, the greater one's tolerance will become.

If you think of the novel in Ulster during the nineteenth century, the name that comes to mind is that of William Carleton (born in 1794), a Clogher Valley peasant who experienced in his lifetime all the worst excesses of sectarian villainy, religious oppression, social miseries, bad landlords and so on, and didn't play down the effects of these disabling forces in his books. He wasn't under any misapprehension about the sources of blight in Northern Ireland: 'I have never entertained any ill-feeling against the people on either side; it is their accursed systems which I detest.' Their accursed systems: on the one hand, the Orange Order, and on the other a band of arsonists and cattle-maimers like the Catholic Ribbonmen (agrarian malcontents). Carleton lost no opportunity to denounce these bodies, along with anything else that brought on a sense of outrage (his scope was wide). His novels and stories are marked by an extraordinary

3

vehemence and gusto, with every emotion and every misfortune enacted to the full; without an exacting readership to monitor his plot-making (as W.B. Yeats and others have pointed out), Carleton was at liberty to turn the rural disaffection he saw all around him into the stuff of melodrama. But his achievement was immense, not least in the field of social history, in depicting the life of the townlands subsequently depopulated by the Famine. And when it comes to sectarian inflexibility, Carleton understood as well as anyone the scope this affords for farce and irony. There's a marvellous set-piece in his novel of 1847, *Valentine M'Clutchy*, in which a Protestant convert comes face to face with his Catholic counterpart. Gradually, a subtle shift in positions occurs, as the two men revert to their original faiths. It isn't long before they come to blows, with support from co-religionists of both persuasions. However, as it happens, 'the Catholics, ignorant of the turn which the controversy had taken, supported Bob and Protestantism; while the Protestants, ow-ing to a similar mistake, fought like devils for Darby and the Pope'. It is hard to think of a more telling indictment, or one more economically expressed.

If it's sectarian high jinks we're after, we might do worse than turn to Kathleen Fitzpatrick, author of a single work of fiction, probably written for children, and published in 1905 as *The Weans at Rowallan*. (It was reissued under a different title, *They Lived in County Down*.) The five weans of the title, in one high-spirited episode, resort to playacting to reform a drunkard, a Catholic-turned-Protestant who will shortly turn back again. It has long been understood that one effective way of putting the sectarian instinct in its place is to poke fun at it – not that it is always possible to follow this sensible precept. For some authors, such as Louis MacNeice, Maurice Leitch and Caroline Blackwood, the incorrigible busi-ness of inherited allegiances and hostilities in Ulster makes for a thor-oughly dispiriting atmosphere (though there's nothing dispiriting in the way they evoke it). And at times, especially, when some enormity has taken place, it is difficult to associate a comic mode with the desperate actions of ideologues – unless it's comedy of the blackest sort, like John Morrow's.

It does no harm to bear in mind that the Orange and Green ideologies may have something of the festive and regenerative about them: their

4

effect isn't invariably malign. There are sometimes things to commend in the tribal displays put on by one side or the other, whether it's the good behaviour of Tanderagee Orangemen in 1812 (as reported by John Gamble), or the singular exhilaration of the whole Twelfth phenomenon (as conveyed by Robert Harbinson). On the Catholic side – as we learn from Eamonn McCann and others – it was elating to possess such an exorbitant history (selectively taught), always characterised by devotion to the unimpeachable cause ('On our side is virtue and Erin,/On theirs is the Saxon and guilt', as Tom Moore put it). But what happens if you are Catholic, growing up in Portadown, with a Southern Irish father who has joined the RUC, and a taste for intoxicating, low-grade literature through which the peculiar virtues of an *English* outlook are being inculcated? Read George J. Watson's very thoughtful and animated essay ('Cultural Imperialism: an Irish view'), and find out. Reading: at the same time, in another part of the North, Seamus Heaney was ingesting the same material and finding it more enticing than anything contained in the Christian Brothers' periodical *Our Boys* – though with Heaney, the allure of the local soon began to make itself felt: 'I . . . knew the whole of Keats's ode "To Autumn" but the only line that was luminous then was "To bend with apples the mossed cottage trees", because my uncle had a small orchard where the old apple trees were sleeved in a soft green moss.'

Heaney has recorded his sense of how the ordinary civilities of everyday life took precedence over atavistic antagonisms – except at times of particular tribal significance. This is borne out by the painstaking research and clearly presented findings of Rosemary Harris, whose *Prejudice and Tolerance in Ulster* (from which I've selected the chapter concerning 'The Social Separation of Catholic and Protestant') tells us a thing or two about the intricacies of protocol, during the middle part of the twentieth century, governing social relations between the two religious groups in an archetypal Ulster country town which is given the name of Ballybeg. The book makes riveting reading; you're agog throughout for the next instance of esoteric social usage which goes some way towards endorsing Louis MacNeice's labelling of the whole province 'darkest Ulster'. Only in darkest Ulster would you find a couple of young men, friends and neighbours, for whom any discussion of political matters was totally out of the question: because one was Protestant and the other Catholic.

5

It seems fitting to follow the Harris extract with the story by Benedict Kiely, 'The Night We Rode With Sarsfield', in which a good-humoured attitude to the icons of the other side – at least when it's a small boy who parades them – is shown in action. (It is true that Kiely is the only Catholic writer in this section – whose heading, 'As native in my thought as any here', implies a Protestant viewpoint – but the story is about Presbyterian tolerance and neighbourliness, as much as anything else.) This is heartening, but for Protestant integrity ('protestant', ideally, with a small 'p') in its most cogent form, you should turn to John Hewitt, who never felt his Planter ancestry excluded him from the deepest affiliation with Northern Ireland or, for that matter, Ireland. 'As native in my thought as any here.' Native as well, if less securely so, are harassed landowners like the narrator's grandfather in Caroline Blackwood's *Great Granny Webster*: inheritors of unmanageable Ulster mansions in terrible states of disrepair, with rain-soaked gorse on view from every window and exceptionally dismal conditions proliferating indoors.

Great Granny Webster gives a deadpan and very funny account of life in a great house between the First and Second World Wars, with the fittings coming down around one's ears and decrepit relatives – inherited with the house – demanding to be ministered to. The Anglo-Irish roof, and the failure to keep it watertight, has been a feature of Irish fiction from Maria Edgeworth on. Northern Ireland, in this particular reading, suggests decay and lunacy on a grand scale. Caroline Blackwood is a thoroughgoing social critic, whether she's writing picturesquely (as in this enthralling piece of fiction), or with the matter-of-fact distaste for the shortcomings of Northern Irish life – boredom, bigotry and the rest of them – that we find in her 'Memories of Ulster', written in 1972 in reaction to the province's sudden notoriety. With the Belfast novels of Brian Moore (starting in 1955 with *Judith Hearne*) comes a good-natured onslaught on the constituents of a peculiar Northern Irish malaise, adumbrated by Caroline Blackwood. Moore's social criticism abounds in energy and intelligence: he's productively exasperated by all that indigenous misery and monotony. However, the extract I've selected from Brian Moore's fiction depicts a city that, just for the moment, has ceased to be the archetypal place where nothing happens: it is 1941, and the central character in *The Emperor of Ice-cream* is experiencing the blitz on Belfast.

Behind both the Blackwood and Moore critiques lies Louis MacNeice's enumeration of a few of Ulster's ills:

> Thousands of men whom nobody will employ
>   Standing at the corners, coughing.
> And the street-children play on the wet
>   Pavement – hopscotch or marbles;
> And each rich family boasts a sagging tennis-net
>   On a spongy lawn beside a dripping shrubbery.
> The smoking chimneys hint
>   At prosperity round the corner
> But they make their Ulster linen from foreign lint
>   And the money that comes in goes out to make more money.
>
> A city built upon mud;
>   A culture built upon profit . . .

With MacNeice, though it was always a case of '*odi atque amo*' – as he put it himself – of being repulsed by the place and drawn to it at the same time. This, indeed, is the rational attitude: Northern Ireland has much to repudiate and much to cherish. In the very evocative chapter from *Zoo* – well titled 'A Personal Digression' – that I have chosen for *The Rattle of the North*, MacNeice revisits Belfast (the time is the late 1930s) and finds it less a hellhole than the city of his imagination. But MacNeice's consequent testimonial to Ulster's assets – the hills around Belfast, swans on the Lagan, the astringent personality of the place – is expressed cautiously, and with reservations. Ambivalence persists: Northern Ireland is all 'mud and puritanism' on the one hand, and 'amethyst and moonstone' on the other.

The last phrase does as well as any to usher in the section of this anthology in which the wonders of the locality are most sympathetically apprehended, and which includes the piece by C.S. Lewis (from *Surprised by Joy*) extolling the view southeastwards from the Holywood Hills. If the splendour of the scenery goes to his head a little, Lewis soon recovers an exactitude of notation: 'You are looking across . . . the Plain of Down, and seeing beyond it the Mourne Mountains.' This section of *The Rattle of the North* is chockful of enthusiasm and expertise – botanical, geological, linguistic and literary. An article on Northern Irish architecture, by Denis O'D. Hanna, brings home to us the shocking extent to which the look of the province has changed for the worse; on the same theme, the first of two pieces by C.E.B. Brett (written in 1985) deplores the dwindling building heritage of Belfast. This author quite often calls to mind the late Alec Clifton-Taylor, who used to go around England pointing the finger at architectural enormities – and quite right too. Here is C.E.B. Brett on the old Lunatic Asylum on the Falls Road: 'It is a pity that a building of so much distinction should have been demolished in 1924 by the lunatics of Belfast.'

A good deal more has gone since then, at the hands of the lunatics. Indeed, with the look and character of Belfast (for example) undergoing continuous disfiguration, it is good to be reminded – as many of the articles and extracts in this anthology should remind us – that some things are ineradicable, such as the feeling for history and local lore. If the appearance of a place no longer evokes anything but the tawdriness of the present, it is still possible to get at its essence through a different medium: poetry, for example, or descriptive prose. So, we have Seamus Heaney revelling in the sense of place, of home ground; 'Robin Bryans' (that is, Robert Harbinson) travelling alertly through the six counties, never missing an item of interest or a pungent detail; Robert Johnstone remembering the glories of burned-out Smithfield; and Ciaran Carson bringing the utmost acuity and originality to bear on blighted Belfast and the vanished streets of the Falls.

Michael McLaverty, whose second novel, *Lost Fields*, was set in these lost streets, evokes a bygone Belfast with all its proletarian paraphernalia, brickfields and mill girls and rickety carts. (Turning his back on the luminousness of his first two novels, *Lost Fields* and *Call My Brother Back* – from which a chapter is reprinted here – McLaverty became a purveyor of Catholic family romances of very small interest.) And from Michael Longley comes a pointed account of the social divisions of the Lisburn Road; autobiographical writing is one of the genres to which we look for valuable sidelights on Ulster's vagaries. It's a genre to which a good many first-rate Northern Irish writers have contributed – we think of Denis Donoghue being dispassionate about tribal exclusiveness ('A Protestant was as alien to me as a Muslim'), Seamus Deane recalling the ghetto aspect of 1950s Derry, and Max Wright disclosing a thing or two about the peculiarities of an evangelical upbringing. As autobiography takes on the guise of fiction, we get John O'Connor summoning up, with the most diverting authenticity, the spirit of Mill Row, County Armagh (very far in feeling from the weak and saccharine Gape Row of Agnes Romilly White). Polly Devlin's early exposure to sectarian baiting makes us 'burn with Catholicism' (in the tribal, if not the religious, sense), though it doesn't take too much to procure an opposing effect: Peadar O'Donnell's mockery of a church mustering all its forces to defeat a lone socialist agitator in County Donegal can do it.

It's true to say that the liberal ethic in Irish writing has always aligned itself with Catholicism – not the religious force, indeed, but the elements in society coming under its heading – since social oppression (roughly speaking) was a prerogative of the other side. 'Avaunt his verses be they ne'er so fine,/Who for the Catholics – refused to sign!' wrote William Drennan in 1811 about a clergyman/poet who declined to add his signature to a petition calling for Catholic emancipation. But it shouldn't be forgotten that Catholic bigotry is just as virulent and exclusive, and in many cases smugger, than its Protestant counterpart; if the latter seems to have more aggression about it, it's probably through being more insistently thrust in our faces. There's an essay by Tom Paulin (included here) on that monument to Ulster Protestant intransigence the Reverend Ian Paisley, which gets to the heart of Paisley's larger-than-life fundamentalism and fearful benightedness. (Interesting to learn of Paisley's applause for A.T.Q. Stewart's *The Narrow Ground* – a source of embarrassment, one imagines, for A.T.Q. Stewart.) You cannot properly get to grips with Northern Ireland without taking account of archaic figures like Paisley.

For the rest, it is satisfying to be told exactly what it was that country people ate around the turn of the century (Florence Mary McDowell), or how damask linen was made before the industrial revolution (John Gamble). It is thought-provoking to read Maurice Leitch's description of an Antrim mill village on its last legs; or Naomi May on how opinions expressed in good faith can make you a target for extremists. (Naomi May's novel *Troubles* has as one of its themes the defeat of liberalism among unionists of the 1960s.)

This is an anthology of mainstream writing, by and large; but one or two oddities have crept in. Like Ian Paisley, the egregious author Amanda

9

McKittrick Ros puts us in touch with one kind of Northern Irish exorbitance – and very entertaining it is too, with its sheer lunatic gusto and wrongheadedness. Amanda Ros had several King Charles's Heads which kept intruding into her preposterous plots, and the episode towards the end of *Helen Huddleson* in which the Reverend John Davis DD, of Third Ballynahinch Presbyterian Church, is repeatedly commended whilst all other clerics get it in the neck, is among the funniest things she wrote.

In assembling this anthology, I have tried to confine myself to those pieces of prose literature, both fiction and non-fiction, which express a peculiar and very vivid Northern Irishness; among the qualities I have looked for are resonance, illumination, high-powered analysis, vigorous recollection or re-creation. My aim, or one of my aims, has been to produce a collection of pieces that interact with one another, so that light is cast on one topic by something read elsewhere in the anthology. I have also arranged the contributions under various headings according to theme, angle of vision or whatever – though I can't claim to have achieved utter consistency in this. Things have gone in where they seemed to fit best, for one reason or another.

I would hope, as well, that an anti-sectarian stance is implicit throughout this anthology, in so far as it posits a good deal of common ground (we have *all* inherited the whole imbroglio – or, to look at it another way, we can *all* lay claim to a colourful past, along with a highly charged present). Northern Ireland, for the purposes of this collection, is to be regarded as a geographical rather than a political entity; it consists of seven counties, not the partitioned six or the historic nine. Donegal seems to me inescapably part of the 'North', whereas Cavan and even Monaghan have a less decided orientation. I cannot, for example, think of Patrick Kavanagh as a Northern writer, any more than I would wish to allocate Peadar O'Donnell to the South. Not everyone will agree with this view. *The Rattle of the North*, indeed, presents a personal selection, and undoubtedly readers will find some surprising inclusions and omissions. Why (for example) Denis Ireland and not George Buchanan? Why Kathleen Fitzpatrick and not Janet McNeill? Where are Cathal O'Byrne and St John Ervine? Well, as far as the last two are concerned – *As I Roved Out* is full of interesting information about old Belfast (among other things), but written in a style unacceptably banal, while St John Ervine seems to me very stodgy and old-fashioned (the same, to be sure, is true of Shan F. Bullock with his 'slow-blooded Loughsiders' and their tiresome goings-on, but Bullock's description of how 'Protestant' and 'Catholic' qualities got imparted to the landscape deserves inclusion, I think, for its sociological bearing).

Some things have been left out with reluctance; for instance, I had hoped to have some passages from Mary McNeill's very good biography of Mary Anne McCracken, but found, on rereading, that the lengthy quotations on nearly every page interfered with the flow of the narrative. Considerations of the same sort made me decide against including literary criticism; while regretting that this cut out such forceful authors as John Wilson Foster and Terence Brown, I felt that, since *The Rattle of the North* is largely a collection of extracts from books, to have extracts from books about books would be bordering on the tautological. However, I have found space for Denis Donoghue's incisive essay 'The Literature of Trouble'. Indeed, with the associations and insights this essay offers, it seems as good a piece of prose as any with which to end the anthology. (A technical point: this essay was originally delivered as a talk, and so is mercifully free of footnotes; where these occur in other contributions, I have simply – perhaps high-handedly – taken them out, since I believe they have no place in an anthology designed, as much as anything, to provide an introduction to Northern Irish writing for the general reader. Readers keen to pursue any of the issues raised will need to trace the article or extract to its source, and follow up references from there.)

Still on the subject of omissions – I have not included some competent storytellers like Brian Friel and Bernard MacLaverty, whose work simply cannot be broken down into sections but needs to be taken whole, as it were, and others whose angle on Northern Irish matters simply isn't compelling enough (as far as I am concerned). Then, having obtained some impressive travel writing from such authors as Robert Lloyd Praeger and Robin Bryans, I feel at liberty to ignore the many books 'in praise of Ulster' (that particular title is Richard Hayward's) that go in for a facile approach or a tourist-board cheeriness. The deplorably facetious Lynn Doyle is left out, along with overwrought Anthony C. West (he of the reputation for sensitivity, and actual fixation on women's busts and bottoms), and Michael J. Murphy (whose work strikes me as being a bit

11

folksy and chimney-cornerish). Going back to the nineteenth century, Lady Ferguson's biography of her husband, *Sir Samuel Ferguson and the Ireland of His Day* (a promising title), proved informative about neither, being all hagiography and dullness. And so on, and so on. What remains will – I hope – alert the reader to the riches of the Northern Irish literary tradition, with all its vitality and distinctiveness.

I should like to acknowledge my indebtedness to the late John Hewitt, who – long before this anthology was thought of – drew my attention to a good deal of the material included. And thanks are due to Jeffrey Morgan, Nora T. Craig, Gerry Keenan and Robert Johnstone; to my agent Araminta Whitley; to John Gray, John Killen and Mary Hughes of the Linen Hall Library, Belfast; and especially to Michael Longley for some helpful suggestions, and encouragement throughout.

PATRICIA CRAIG

LONDON, 1992

1

'For history's a twisted root'

PAUL MULDOON

RETROSPECT

A.T.Q. STEWART

On the morning of 7 December 1688 an advance party of the Earl of Antrim's regiment reached the waterside on the right bank of the Foyle opposite Derry. Two of the officers, a lieutenant and an ensign, crossed the river by the ferry and, presenting warrants directed to the mayor and sheriffs, demanded admittance and quarters for His Majesty's soldiers. For several weeks now the city of Londonderry had been without a garrison, since the withdrawal of Lord Mountjoy's Regiment of Foot. Mountjoy's men had been for the most part Protestants, and in 1688 the Lord Deputy of Ireland, the Earl of Tyrconnell, was engaged in removing all the Protestant officers from the Irish army and replacing them with Catholics. On the instructions of King James II he had also raised a new regiment in each of the four Irish provinces. The regiment in Ulster was commanded by Alexander MacDonnell, the Catholic Earl of Antrim, and was recruited from his Irish followers and Scottish highlanders, all of them Catholic.

The news in the first days of December that this force of 1,200 men, with a large number of women and children, was moving towards Derry to secure the city's allegiance to the King in the coming struggle with William, the Prince of Orange, caused great concern among the Protestants within the walled city. For days, rumours had been circulating. It was said that the Irish in the neighbourhood had been collecting pikes and knives; friars had been preaching sermons alluding to the slaughter of the Amalekites. Anxiety was not allayed when it became known that an anonymous letter found far away in the streets of Comber, County Down, and addressed to a Protestant nobleman, had warned that on 9 December the Irish would fall upon Protestants and planters, and kill them man, wife and child. These hastily raised soldiers of Lord Antrim were kin to the men who had attacked the Protestant settlers in the Rebellion of 1641.

Thus when it was seen that the officers' warrants were not signed, the anxious sheriffs seized on the pretext to play for time. An excited debate was taking place among crowds gathered in the market square. Many of the younger citizens were for keeping the regiment out, and even some of the aldermen, though fearful of the consequences, hoped that this might be done without their having to take the lead. The waiting soldiers on the opposite bank, suspecting some such design, now began to cross the river in considerable numbers and move swiftly towards the city walls. Suddenly, when the first of them were within sixty yards of the Ferry Gate, a group of thirteen apprentices ran to the main guard, seized the keys, and drawing up the bridge, shut and locked the gate. Then they hastened to shut the other three great gates of the city, leaving an armed guard on each. Though the city was not closely invested until the following April, this exclusion of King James's soldiers marked the beginning of the famous siege of Londonderry, which was not raised until August 1689.

On 12 August 1969 the Apprentice Boys of Derry celebrated the lifting of the siege by their annual parade on the city walls. The political atmosphere in Northern Ireland was extremely bad, worse than it had been since 1922, as a consequence of the accelerating Catholic civil rights agitation which had led to clashes with the police in 1968. The Apprentice Boys and the Orange Order had turned down requests from the government to cancel their processions. It was widely forecast that if they took place, there would be serious disorders, and even an uprising of the entire Catholic population. This prophecy proved to be true. As the Orangemen marched through the centre of the walled city, stones began to rain down upon their heads, thrown by crowds of Catholic rioters who had assembled for the purpose. The parade broke up in disorder, and serious rioting developed. When the police, issued with steel helmets and riot shields, tried to drive the mobs back into the Catholic districts beyond the walls, they were repulsed again and again with stones and petrol-bombs.

After forty-eight hours a scene appeared in Derry which no one in Northern Ireland could remember seeing before, though something like it had happened more than once in the nineteenth century. Against a backdrop of blazing buildings, small groups of exhausted policemen huddled in doorways or lay in the streets, their faces streaked with blood and dirt, their tunics torn and even burned, like the weary survivors of some desperate and costly offensive.

16

These images began to flicker round the world. In Belfast, diversionary attacks were made upon the police to prevent reinforcements being sent to Derry. Firing broke out in republican areas of the city. The police replied with sub-machineguns. A child was killed when a bullet came through the wall of his home. The disorders spread all over the province. The Government of Northern Ireland was obliged to ask for the assistance of the army. On every previous occasion the army had acted in aid of the civil power, but this time Westminster acceded to the request only on condition that political control was taken out of the hands of the local government. Thus began the crisis in Ulster.

Everyone knows that these two episodes of Ulster history are connected. But in what way? To people whose history stays flat on the printed page it seems incredible that 'old, far-off, unhappy things, and battles long ago' should exert such influence upon the present. Is it true that the Irish are obsessed by their history? And what is the nature of the influence which the past exerts upon them? Ireland, like Dracula's Transylvania, is much troubled by the undead. King William III, Wolfe Tone and Patrick Pearse sustain an unnatural immortality with the blood of succeeding generations, and when people talk about the inability of the Irish to forget the past, this is usually what they mean. As a matter of fact, the Irish are not only capable of forgetting the past, but quite deliberately expunge from their minds whole areas of it. Like other nations, they have woven for themselves a garment of myth and legend which they call Irish history. Having designed it themselves, they have taken great care to make it as comfortable as possible, eliminating the loose threads and sharp edges, and making it so snug and warm that when they are wearing it they sometimes imagine themselves to be immune to the ordinary dictates of humanity. Moreover, it exports extremely well, and has been sold in every country in the world. The general opinion is that it is a superb article and well worth the price.

The price is high. To the Irish all History is Applied History, and the past is simply a convenient quarry which provides ammunition to use against enemies in the present. They have little interest in it for its own sake. So when we say that the Irish are too much influenced by the past, we really mean that they are too much influenced by Irish history, which is a different matter. That is the history they learn at their mother's knee, in school, in books and plays, on radio and television, in songs and ballads. But they are influenced in another way by the past, as everyone is, and since they are often quite unconscious of this kind of influence, it is rarely discussed. . . .

At an early stage of the Ulster troubles, it became apparent that attitudes, words and actions which were familiar and recognizable to any student of Irish history, but which seemed hardly relevant to politics in the twentieth century, were coming back into fashion. This was not to be explained by the deliberate imitation of the past; it could be accounted for only by some more mysterious form of transmission from generation to generation. In many ways it was a frightening revelation, a nightmarish illustration of the folk-memory of Jungian psychology. Men and women who had grown to maturity in a Northern Ireland at peace now saw for the first time the monsters which inhabited the depths of the community's unconscious mind. It was as if a storm at sea had brought to the surface creatures thought to have been long extinct.

The metaphor is appropriate. For most of our lives we see only the surface of our society, as a man strolling on a marine promenade sees only a calm and uniform expanse of water. But in certain lights he will discern the meandering streams which traverse the sea as they do the land. He does not know from whence they come, or what determines their course. He cannot see the foul ground, the towering mountains and drowned valleys, the dark currents scouring the headlands, or the intricate ebb and flow in the sound where the tides meet.

The historian likes to think of himself as an oceanographer rather than a stroller on the promenade. He prepares his charts of the past from precise data, the most accurate he can obtain. But he labours under many disadvantages. Not only does his discipline usually concern itself with limited and carefully defined questions; it requires him to use only one kind of evidence in finding the answers. It may be that written evidence does not contain the answer, and even that the determinant factors had already operated before any records were kept.

Nevertheless, there are times when he can read between the lines of his written record, and try to provide his own response to Prospero's question, 'What see'st thou else in the dark backward and abysm of Time?'

18

Like the aerial archaeologist, or the Lough Neagh fisherman of Ulster legend, he may glimpse the distinctive patterns of the past below the surface.

from *The Narrow Ground*, 1977

Truths, Half-Truths and Mythology

Eamonn McCann

It is often said that Irish people pay too much attention to history. This is not true. Irish people pay very little attention to history.

Some Irish people do pay attention to a mixture of half-truths and folk mythology about the past. At meetings in Free Derry Republican speakers would quite unselfconsciously reel off the names and speak with natural emotion of those who had gone before in the fight against oppression and of the fate which had befallen them. Each name triggered remembrance of that particular phase of the struggle and excited the tingling realization that what we were about was yet another episode – perhaps, hopefully, the last – in the long chronicle of our nation's distressed indomitability. 'If you really love me,' wrote Sean Heuston to his sister in 1916 just before the British shot him, 'teach the children the history of their own land and teach them the cause of Caitlin ni hUllachain never dies' (*Capuchin Annual*, 1966). Sean can rest content that we were well enough taught.

There is a large body of opinion in Catholic Ireland which holds that that is half the trouble: that since 1922 successive Southern Irish governments, aided by the media, have bombarded the people with propaganda about the evils done to Ireland and about the continuing evil of partition; that the Catholic schools, including those in the North, have pumped children full of history, and a history distorted so as to idealize the gun. Thus, the theory goes, young men in places like the Bogside turn easily to the waging of unnecessary war.

It is an easy point of view to argue. The traditional Catholic view of Irish history does contain a great deal of myth which it is not difficult to debunk. A Catholic child in the Bogside, for example, would gather at an early age that Wolfe Tone, who led the United Irishmen's rising in 1798, was a Protestant who came over to our side. One would not gather that Tone, the 'Father of Irish Republicanism', took his inspiration from the French Revolution, was as bitterly opposed to the Catholic church as any

Orangeman and, if he had had his way, would have sponged the church from the face of the Republic he hoped to build. One gathered too that in every subsequent generation the Irish people – or at least the majority, Catholic section of it – rose against the English oppressor, sometimes in arms, sometimes in constitutional movements, and that there were direct links between each stage of the struggle. This is not true either. The Irish people as a whole never rose. Whole peoples rarely do. And there was little organizational or political continuity between the movements which did arise. The Catholic emancipation movement which was led by Daniel O'Connell in the 1820s, for example, owed nothing to Tone's ideas. It was conservative, constitutional and anti-republican. The radical and thoroughly unconstitutional Fenian movement of the 1860s had nothing in common with O'Connell. And so on.

But underlying all the mythology there is a deep stratum of truth. The Irish people, particularly the Catholic Irish people, *were* exploited and oppressed for hundreds of years by Britain. The overwhelming majority of them were born in misery and reared in squalor. They lived from day to day, fighting to tear some dignity from life, most of them finally to die amid the ugliness in which they first saw the light of day. And knowing that one of the reasons for their condition was that the country was ruled by Britain.

If the movements they threw up lacked any continuity neat enough to please the detached historians' sense of order, they did not lack in the desperation of their adherents' search for a remedy. Irish history is hair-raising. In that it is not dissimilar from the history of many other countries. History almost everywhere is terrible. The main reason why Republican rhetoric about the past continues to evoke a gut response from many people in Ireland is that most of it is true. That it is encrusted with myth alters nothing essential. Some people need myths, need them to glorify their history in order to push away the grim reality of the way they have to live now. If the traditional Republican account of Irish history has been most fervently believed in the Catholic ghettoes of the North, in the Bogside and Creggan, Ardoyne and Ballymurphy, it is because the people who live there, ground down by oppression and with no apparent possibility of escape, have needed an ennobled history, have needed to postulate a line of continuity between the glorious struggles of the past

21

and a liberation yet to come. When a man lives in a world of bookies' slips, varnished counters and Guinness spits he will readily accept an account of the past which tends to invest his living with dignity. Observers such as C. Cruise O'Brien, such circumstances of life being beyond their range of experience, may find it difficult fully to understand this.

Protestants, too, have had a mythology, and it has supplied source material for an equally rich fund of educated sneers. It too is now being derided, by a growing section of 'enlightened' Protestant opinion. Protestants have believed that for almost four hundred years their community has been besieged by rapacious Catholic hordes intent on the destruction of the civil and religious liberty won by the Reformation, and that it was the Orange Order which provided the organizational framework for the successful prosecution of their struggle; that every movement against the link with Britain, or against partition, has been motivated, however hiddenly, by a desire to extend the hegemony of Rome over them and that the retention of the link with Britain guaranteed against this. Rome Rule meant return to the dark ages, envelopment in black superstition, the loss of civil and religious liberty, the loss of the right of a sturdy people to think for itself won, at terrible cost, when the Reformation shattered medieval papal power. Some of this is true. Moreover, the organizations embodying the Orange mythology – the Orange Order and its associate institutions – offered the people of crumbling areas like the Shankill in Belfast and the Fountain in Derry a sense of vigour and a colourful life-style in sharp contrast to the workaday drudgery which was their normal lot.

The difference between the two traditions is most sharply evident in accounts of the founding of the Northern state. There is a Catholic folk-myth which holds that in the early part of this century the Protestants, blackmailed and befuddled by sectarian loyalist propaganda, chose, against their own interests as Irish people, to retain the link with Britain; that had it not been for the agitational activities of Carson and Craigavon, supported by the British Tories, the Protestant masses might well have seen that their real interests lay in joining with their fellow Irishmen in the South to create an independent republic. As against that, there is a Protestant legend telling that in order to prevent their economic ruin and their ideological domination by totalitarian Catholicism the Protestant people rose and, by setting up the Northern Irish state, won freedom for their community.

Before partition the Protestant myth was promoted by a powerful section of the British establishment. This did not happen because the British establishment believed it to be true or that endorsement of it would lead to equitable political arrangements in Ireland. They endorsed it because its practical implications met the requirements of the overall British interest in Ireland. When Randolph Churchill decided in 1886 to 'play the Orange card' he did so because his class, then in its imperial heyday, was best served by meeting the central Unionist demand – that Ireland remain within the Empire. When, in the changed circumstances of 1912–20, the Unionists gave up hope of holding all Ireland within British rule and campaigned instead for partition, they were, again, and for precisely the same reason, supported by the British Conservative Party and their cause was trumpeted by *The Times*.

The fact was, and is, that the Republican tradition, for all the distortions of history contained within it, stemmed from a genuine, if episodic, anti-imperialistic struggle; the Orange tradition was, objectively, pro-imperialist.

After partition the two traditions provided the official ideologies of the new states. The North became a 'Protestant state for a Protestant people' and the Protestantism of the state was demonstrated by the destruction of local government democracy in areas where Catholic representatives were in power, the systematic exclusion of Catholics from the civil service and from sectors of private industry, and the use of state forces and of the law to discourage Catholics from attempting to change this situation. The ideology was most stridently expressed when sizeable sections of the Protestant people broke, or attempted to break, from the Unionist Party. When that happened the Unionists' unique political apparatus, the Orange machine, went into action, drowning dissident voices with bible-and-thunder rhetoric, herding the masses back into Orangeism and isolating those who refused to return. For a long time it was very successful. Although the Unionist Party and the system over which it presided was never able to supply the Protestant working class with the means for a decent life – despite discrimination – it managed on the whole to retain mass Protestant support.

One of the reasons why it was so successful was that in the South of Ireland the counter ideology was being promulgated with equal vigour. All the main parties in the South have until very recently described themselves as 'Republican' and insisted that the main purpose of their activity was to bring about a united Ireland. Much of the argument between them, particularly during election campaigns, has been about which of them was best equipped to do this.

What lent plausibility to Unionist propaganda were not actual attempts by Southern governments to assimilate Northern Ireland but their ceaseless, strident declarations that Northern Ireland *ought* to be assimilated into the South. Which is a very different thing. This rhetoric was accompanied by the gradual institutionalization of Catholic teaching in Southern law so that the state into which Southern leaders said the North ought to be incorporated became, more and more clearly, a Catholic state. The more Catholic it became the more repulsive to the Northern Protestants did united-Ireland rhetoric sound.

Any ideology which is propounded or accepted by a large group of people is based on the economic interest of a class. Protestant Unionism was based on the interests of the owners of land and industry in the North of Ireland. Nationalism was based on the interests of the owners and potential owners of industry in the South.

The owners of land and industry in the North of Ireland needed, for commercial reasons, to retain the link with Britain. Potential capitalists in the South, if they were going to have an industrial infrastructure at all, needed protection from British competition. In 1922 the two classes agreed to part. By that time the essential characteristics of the movements they led and the ideologies of those movements had already been decided.

For almost four decades they went their separate ways. In the South, through successive changes of government and variations in economic strategy, the attempt to build up native Irish industry proceeded. It involved a short-lived 'economic war' with Britain, 'Buy Irish' campaigns, opposition to – and sometimes destruction of – foreign goods being offered for sale. The fierce anti-British, 'Ireland-for-the-Irish' propaganda which constituted the official ideology of the state was a reflection of all this. In ideological terms it expressed the economic needs of the establishment. It served, too, to divert the attention of those elements –

workers and small farmers – discontented with their lot under the new order, away from the rising Dublin bourgeoisie towards putative and more distant culprits. The Catholic church was used, and was more than willing to be used, to isolate and politically to destroy anyone who threatened seriously to disrupt the set-up.

In the North the constant reiteration that 'Ulster-is-Protestant-and-British' was, equally, an ideological refraction of the economic needs of property. Here, unlike the South, there was no need after partition to create anything new, rather a need to retain access to British markets and sources of raw material already enjoyed. The 'threat' from expansionist, Southern Catholic Nationalism without which no speech from a Unionist leader was complete encouraged the preservation and intensification of a creed, as opposed to a class, consciousness; encouraged the Protestant community, all classes within it, to act and react as a whole, under the leadership of the established political bosses. That is, under the leadership of those making the speeches.

North and South, it was a neat arrangement. Each ideology fed on the other. But it could not last.

By the nineteen-fifties things had changed. In the South the industries created behind a protective tariff-wall had reached the limits of their growth. Further development could not be sustained by the small home market. The economy ground to a halt, almost went into reverse. It became necessary to discard economic isolationism and to seek reintegration into wider, commercial empires. That meant, in effect, reintegration into the British market.

Something similar happened in the North. The industries which had given the Northern economy its original dynamic – linen, shipbuilding, heavy engineering – were in decline in the years after the Second World War. The nature of the economy changed as the slack created by this decline was gradually taken up by new enterprise. The new enterprise was financed from outside, mainly from the British mainland.

By the end of the fifties the economic basis of partition was being eroded. The interests of the dominant classes, North and South, converged. And, by the same token, the British interest in Ireland changed.

While British economic interests in Ireland were concentrated in the North, successive British governments, Liberal, Tory and Labour, were content to allow the Unionist Party to get on with the job of ruling in whatever way it saw fit and using whatever means it claimed were necessary. On occasion this meant allowing the armed supporters of the Unionist Party to massacre Catholics. But once the South tore down the tariff-walls and the barriers to outside investment crumbled, things changed. The British interest now lay, not in giving uncritical support to an Orange government in the North, but in balancing between the Orange and the Green, between North and South, between Protestant and Catholic capitalism in Ireland. That was to become very significant in August 1969.

At the beginning of the sixties it did not occur to the economic planners who were guiding Northern and Southern Ireland closer to one another, and guiding them, together, towards a closer economic relationship with Britain, that the gutters of Belfast and Derry might run red as a result. But the gutters in the Falls and the New Lodge Road, the Shankill, Ballymacarrett and Bogside did, and the reason why they did was that ideologies and the political institutions which embody ideologies do not necessarily exist in a constant state of adaptation to the changing needs of the class in whose interest they were originally built. They can resist change. They can have a life of their own and in certain circumstances they fight for their life.

As the more far-seeing sections of the Belfast and Dublin establishments moved hesitantly towards one another they were, in effect, betraying the beliefs which, for decades, they had claimed to cherish and which they had *demanded* that their people, under pain of national apostasy, accept as eternal truths. The anti-British, united-Ireland propaganda which had blared forth from Dublin for decades had to be stilled. The anti-Catholic, pro-partition hysteria which had been the stock-in-trade of Belfast governments for just as long had now to be calmed. It was inevitable that there were those who would shout 'traitor'. In other circumstances that might not have mattered. In other circumstances it might have been possible to dismiss the objectors as 'backwoodsmen', gradually to isolate them and to move forward into a new era – rather as the British Conservative Party dealt with those who objected in principle to postwar welfare legislation.

That could not happen in Northern Ireland. The main political representatives of Northern capitalism, the Unionist Party, had not just proclaimed their ideology from election platforms – which is all their more fortunate Southern counterparts had ever found it necessary to do. The Northerners had had to put their ideology into practice. They had had to create a vast and intricate apparatus which, day in, day out, ensured that political decisions and public life in every part of the state conformed to a predetermined pattern. The apparatus was the Orange machine, as remarkable a piece of political equipment as has existed anywhere. It involved tens of thousands of people, each of whom had an interest in the machine retaining its central position in the power structure – indeed in its retaining its position *as* the power structure. And that interest did not forever coincide with the overall needs of the Northern Ireland economy. By the sixties it was in sharp conflict with it.

The Unionists had had to create such a machine. Discrimination was necessary in Northern Ireland. It was necessary in order politically to disarm the Catholics. It was necessary, too, if the Unionist Party was going to retain the vital allegiance of its 'own', the Protestant community. Because, contrary to the image of Northern Protestants commonly projected backwards into history, all classes within that community did not automatically act and react together. What emerges most starkly from a study of the Orange machine is not the ease with which it was able to contain the mass of Protestants, but the continual difficulty it experienced; not its efficiency but its fragility. There has not been a decade since the foundation of the Unionist Party in which it has not been challenged from within for the leadership of the Protestant community. Thus the machine needed constantly to be tended, needed to be fuelled and refuelled with the spoils of discrimination – jobs, houses and social prestige – which could be paid out to the faithful to endow them with a sense of privilege. The threat from without had constantly to be inflated and 'dealt with' in order to discourage and buy off the threat from within, if for no other reason.

The new economic pattern in Ireland in the sixties made the Orange machine redundant. Northern-Protestant and Southern-Catholic capitalism could not come together as economic common sense demanded while the main political expression of Northern Protestantism continued to brow-beat the Catholics within its territory.

Hence 'liberal-Unionism'. And thus the heightened expectation of Catholics that they were about to get their 'rights'. And, in reaction, the habituated response of the Orange machine. And thus 5 October and August 1969, the British army. The British army enmeshed in the machine, internment and Bloody Sunday. Direct rule: Northern Ireland up for grabs, chunks of political masonry falling from the monolith; the Provos blazing, going for bust, now at last to destroy it for ever. Furtive Protestant guerrillas in twos and threes with small-arms at night in the back streets of fringe areas of Belfast, waiting. British cabinet ministers wringing their hands in horror on the telly and talking on about 'gunmen'. 'The psychopaths have taken over,' chirruped Mr Roy Hattersley, former Secretary of State for the Army.

The psychopaths have not taken over. There is a war in Ireland because capitalism, to establish and preserve itself, created conditions which made war inevitable. Essentially, there is no other reason. There rarely is for war.

from *War and an Irish Town*, 1974

The Londonderry Plantation

JAMES STEVENS CURL

It is one of the ironies of history that Ulster, the most Gaelic of all the old Provinces, now contains the largest proportion of Protestants, partly as a result of the Plantation, and partly because of immigration from Scotland in subsequent years.

It must be remembered that the Protestant population of Ulster is partly descended from persons who were granted lands *on condition* that they upheld English law, were loyal to the British Crown, and conformed to the Protestant religion: the Plantation of Ulster was a result of Crown policy to replace a Gaelic, Irish, disaffected, Roman Catholic population with a British, English-speaking, loyal, Protestant people. Those Protestant settlers, who could lose their privileges and holdings if they failed to honour their obligations, were later joined by Moravians from Central Europe, by Huguenots from France, and by other minority Protestant groups who had been persecuted by Roman Catholics. It is one of the more absurd views of present received opinion in certain quarters that the descendants of those Protestants should somehow abandon the historical positions they were obliged to adopt by the State (including allegiance to the Crown), should suddenly come to terms with the people who resented their presence, and should discard a siege mentality born of a certain knowledge that succour from London was always too little, too late, and given with an ill grace. That siege mentality was born in 1641 and grew from 1689: it has not diminished with the years.

After the Cromwellian and Williamite settlements the Protestants were placed in a dominant position, although they were very much in a minority. Every Irish attempt to retrieve power and land brought further disaster on the native, Roman Catholic, population, and increasingly associated Roman Catholicism with Nationalism, underprivileged majorities, rebellion, disloyalty, and poverty in Protestant minds. These factors ensured that Protestants would always be on guard, would always have to depend

29

on England for protection, and would only maintain their positions by force of law and armed might. The Roman Catholic Irish, on the other hand, had a sense of national identity partially through their religion, their history, and their position as third-class citizens. Official policy only weakened the organisation of the Roman Catholic Church in Ireland and the economic well-being of the native Irish, who veered between bouts of apathy and violent outbreaks in which a seething hatred of the Protestant oppressor was given full expression. With the formation of a 'Protestant State' in six of the nine counties of Ulster, Protestants in the Province did not achieve a sense of nationhood: on the contrary there has always been some confusion about nationality in Northern Ireland, exacerbated by the strong links with Lowland Scotland and an insistence on the Britishness of Ulster combined with ambivalent and often antipathetic feelings for England and the English on the part of both the Protestants and Roman Catholics of Ulster. The problems of Ulster lie embedded in history, and the Irish sense of history, with perhaps inevitable distortions, is burned deeply into national consciousness.

. . . The City of London did not wish to get involved in Ulster: it was placed in a very difficult position by the Crown, and the events of 1625– 41 drove it into supporting Parliament in the great struggle for supremacy that ended with the decapitation of King Charles. The Londonderry Plantation was only a part of the Plantation of Ulster, but it was one of the most important parts: it not only formed a settlement that held part of Ireland for the Protestant cause, but created a symbol for Protestant resistance to Roman Catholic retaliation. The defence of Londonderry and Enniskillen was the beginning of a counter-attack that established the Protestant Ascendancy and the elegance of that society in 18th-century Ireland, yet drove a vast proportion of the Irish population into exile or an inferior status. 'No Surrender', the rallying-cry of the Siege of Londonderry, has become a catch-phrase of Protestant resistance, and has bitten deep into the consciousness of Ulstermen. Yet the events of 1689 and the wars that followed started as an English problem, and England did not rush to help Londonderry: that sense of being abandoned has always remained with Protestant Ulstermen.

The tragedy is that the events that created the Ulster problem have been obscured: now there are hundreds of thousands of innocent descendants caught in the aftermath of a failure (in overall terms) that was, paradoxically, a partial success from the State policy point of view. In other words, the English colonisation of Ireland did not succeed either in the establishment of Protestantism as the main religion of the people or in making Ireland as a whole loyal to the British Crown. After the Plantation of Ulster, however, what had previously been the most Gaelic part of Ireland was colonised, and that colonisation proved to be rather more substantial in terms of population and area. Yet the partial success of the colonisation created a problem for Ireland as a whole: it left several counties of Ulster secured in Plantation terms, and therefore opposed to any attempt to submerge them in a Roman Catholic Irish State. This has placed ordinary people in a curious position created by the wider aspects of historical events: British commentators, for the most part, have failed to understand the inevitability of the effects of those events that are living and real to the people of Ireland, yet are incomprehensible and antediluvian to the pundits. [On the one hand are] the dilemmas of a native Irish–Gaelic culture in its struggle to protect old values and the old faith against the forces of a dynamic nation-state [and on the other] the problems of the English Crown and the appalling difficulties that faced the Protestant settlers in hostile Ulster. . . . It is clear that both communities in present-day Ulster are the victims of history and of policies and struggles that have long been abandoned, have ceased to matter much, or have been forgotten in Europe as a whole.

It is hardly surprising that such a troubled history has not left all that many buildings of antiquity or quality, yet some remaining fabric, including the best of pre-Plantation work and the great legacy erected under the aegis of The Honourable The Irish Society and the individual Livery Companies, is of considerable architectural importance. Throughout Ireland, the colonisation brought architecture and planning of quality, notably in Dublin, Cork, and other cities. In Ulster the contribution of the Planters created a distinctive pattern of villages and towns, often with central squares (or Diamonds), regularly planned streets, and pretty, modest churches. In the County of Londonderry buildings from two distinct periods can be found: those erected before the Flight of the Earls in 1607, and those put up afterwards. Not much survives from the earlier time, but what does is impressive. Banagher old church, for example, is one of the most important (albeit ruined) medieval churches in the whole of Ulster, and appears to date from the tenth century. . . .

There are some raths in the County, and a pedestal and shaft of a cross associated with St Comgal at Camus dating probably from around 1000. Of medieval churches there are several ruins: Maghera old church has the nave, chancel, and western tower more or less intact, but much of the fabric is post-Plantation. The great glory of the church is the western doorway (masked by the Planters' tower) that has a Crucifixion on the lintel and spiral patterns on the jambs. Part of the lintel carvings suggest a very early date of perhaps the 8th century, but a comparison with Banagher may point to a later period, possibly 11th century. A fragment of a pre-Christian fertility symbol is built into the north side of the tower some five metres up from the ground.

The Augustinian Priory of St Mary at Dungiven has fragments of earlier 11th-century masonry, and contains the magnificent O'Cahan tomb with its effigy, galloglass-weepers, and extraordinary *Flamboyant* tracery that must date from the second half of the 15th century. The north-eastern corner of the nave has odd dressings that are reminiscent of timber-framed construction, and must be very early, possibly even *c.* 980. It is unlikely to date from the time of the arrival of the Augustinians in the 12th century. As has been described, the O'Cahan tower-house, later adapted as a Plantation house, was attached to the church. Of the Cistercian monastery at Macosquin, some of the masonry of the church of St Mary is medieval, and fragments of carving survive in the churchyard.

Some remains of other medieval churches survive, but they are almost without exception just that. Near Portstewart are the ruins of Agherton old church and of Ballywillan old church. The latter was a big structure of basalt and limestone dressings, and preserves several features including lancets of the 13th century, an aumbry of the same period, and some other details. Until 1842 this building was the only pre-Reformation Irish medieval church still being used for worship in the County of London-derry: the authorities of the Church of Ireland have a lot to answer for when the destruction of the early architectural heritage of Ulster is considered: a bijou building in Portrush replaced this noble edifice that now lies ruined in its bleak churchyard. Tamlaghtard church ruins, Magilligan, appear to date from the 13th century. In the churchyard is a fragment of a mortuary or skull-house that must have been similar to those at Banagher and Bovevagh: it is supposed to be the tomb of St Aidan, Bishop of Lindisfarne, who spent his last years in an Irish monastery.

. . . Seventeenth-century ecclesiastical architecture is gloriously represented by the Cathedral of St Columb in Londonderry, but there are some surviving fragments of detail at Walworth old church, Dungiven Priory, Eglinton, Kilrea, and elsewhere. Company castles are represented by Salterstown and Brackfield, while bawns and flankers are best envisaged by a study of Walworth, Salterstown, Bellaghy, Brackfield, and Movanagher. Sites of castles and bawns read best at Macosquin, Agivey, Walworth, and Bellaghy. Virtually no early 17th-century domestic architecture of the Planters survives, except for what has been excavated in Londonderry and Coleraine. Some late 17th-century buildings have remained for study at New Row, Coleraine, and among the rich heritage of vernacular buildings that dot the countryside, notably in the Parish of Dunboe and in the lush countryside of Magilligan. . . .

Street-patterns of the 17th century survive at Londonderry and Coleraine, and elements of the village plans can be seen at Moneymore, Bellaghy, Limavady, Macosquin (virtually intact and quite clear when compared with the Raven maps of 1622), and Ballykelly. Most of the fabric of the towns and villages built by the Londoners dates from the 19th century, and most of that from the 1810s, '20s, '30s, '40s, and '50s. The most distinguished architecture is Suter's at Ballykelly and Banagher, Gibson's and Booth's at Moneymore and Draperstown, the work of the Mercers' Architects at Kilrea, that of the Grocers at Eglinton, that of the Clothworkers at Coleraine-Waterside and Castlerock, and that of the Salters at Magherafelt.

Among the churches may be singled out those associated with the Earl-Bishop of Derry (Tamlaghtfinlagan at Ballykelly, Banagher, Ballyscullion at Bellaghy, and others), but most of the Church of Ireland structures were the new churches and rebuildings erected under Government-sponsored schemes, and these are generally small, Georgian-Gothic erections with simple towers at the west end. A good example of this type can be found at Aghanloo. The most ambitious Gothic churches of the 19th century are St Patrick's at Coleraine, Magherafelt Parish church, the Roman Catholic church also at Magherafelt, and the great Roman Catholic Cathedral at Londonderry by the 'Irish Pugin', J.J. McCarthy. . . . Other Roman

33

Catholic churches tend to be modest, although there are some architecturally significant buildings at Swatragh, Drumgarner, Limavady, The Loup, Dungiven, and elsewhere. It is regrettable that many Roman Catholic churches have been unsympathetically altered inside in recent years, with considerable loss of period detail. The finest 19th-century Gothic Revival interior to survive is that of the Roman Catholic church at Magherafelt. In more recent times the extraordinary church of St Malachy at Coleraine (an assured essay in somewhat austere Romanesque by Padraig Gregory of 1937) should be mentioned as an example of Roman Catholic ecclesiastical taste of the inter-war years. Places of worship of other denominations are most successful when they are Classical: Farrell's Methodist church at Coleraine, Stewart Gordon's splendid Great James Street Presbyterian church in Londonderry, and Richard Suter's magnificent churches at Ballykelly and Banagher are especially fine. Presbyterian Gothic is rarely successful, except in a whimsical Georgian Gothick style, while a veil should be drawn over some edifices put up by other recent dissenting sects.

Of the public buildings the Court Houses of Londonderry, Coleraine, Moneymore, Draperstown, Eglinton, and Magherafelt deserve mention, while the Town Hall at Coleraine does not lack distinction. Among the banks, Lanyon's Belfast Bank in Londonderry of 1853 is one of the finest, and indeed several banks in the County deserve to be taken seriously as good architecture, including the fine Northern Bank in Kilrea.

The County has several houses of rare quality, although the greatest of them (those built by the Earl-Bishop at Downhill and Ballyscullion) are ruined and vanished respectively. Drenagh, near Limavady, Bellarena, Ballyscullion House, Lizard Manor, the Manor House at Kilrea, Roe Park (Daisy Hill), Ardnargle, and Culmore House are admirable, while there is a host of Rectories and minor houses that delight the eye. Probably the most perfect building in the County is the Mussenden Temple at Downhill, designed by Michael Shanahan, and built 1783–5: it is a domed rotunda perched on the top of the cliffs overlooking the wide waters and Inishowen. The frieze is embellished with a quotation from Lucretius.

Among monuments, the collection in St Columb's Cathedral in Londonderry is the best and most wide-ranging in period and style, and those in St Patrick's, Coleraine, are interesting. In Tamlaghtfinlagan Parish church is the best early 18th-century monument in the County, while the mausolea at Limavady, Walworth, Eglinton, Downhill, and Dunboe old church deserve a visit. One of the largest of the mausolea in the County can be found in the churchyard of St Cadan at Tamlaghtard (the Gage mausoleum). Throughout the County are tombstones dating from the 18th, 19th, and 20th centuries, many of them extremely good examples of monumental design, but some of the later products have added new terrors to death.

A Martello tower can be found at Magilligan, guarding the approaches to Lough Foyle. The setting is not improved by the hideous prison that disfigures the beautiful landscape near by. There is an obelisk at Ballyquin, and two extraordinary follies (one near Ballykelly that serves as a memorial to Arthur Sampson, and an 18th-century Gothick piece of frippery at Bellarena).

There are plenty of good, decently reticent, and civilly designed terrace houses in places like Limavady, Moneymore, Londonderry, and Kilrea, but the advent of poorly proportioned modern windows and doors is wreaking havoc on the appearance of far too many buildings. Modern bungaloid growth does nothing for the landscape, and it must be said that very little contemporary housing in Ulster towns, villages or countryside is in sympathy with the subtle colours and delectable scenery of one of the loveliest places on earth. Much of the appearance of the County of Londonderry today, however, is the direct result of the Plantation, and the many historic buildings, roads, arrangements of fields, and mature trees are there because of the policies and management established by London-based institutions. It is perhaps unfortunate that the attempts to improve the appearance of buildings and landscapes by aesthetic control made in the era of the great landowners have not continued into modern times.

The Londonderry Plantation was a remarkable event in the history of the British Isles: its story deserves to be better known. . . . An understanding of the history of Ulster is essential in order to grasp something of why contemporary problems are so convoluted: the Plantation was a complicated business, yet it has been subjected to simplistic comment and contemptuous dismissal. The Londonderry Plantation itself has not enjoyed universal understanding in historical terms in Ulster, while in England

and elsewhere the involvement of the City of London is generally unknown, unappreciated and obscure.

It is more than tragic that a country, endowed with beauties second to none; inhabited by people who still understand the rules of hospitality, of civility, and of conversation; and graced by buildings and towns of great quality set in landscapes of a haunting loveliness, still wallows in the problems of the 17th century. To the objective historian it is not surprising that this is so: what is alarming is that so few understand that it is the case, and that so few have grasped the historical predicament of the descendants of the Plantation settlers and of those who resisted them: the legacy left by the Planters is now as much a part of the Irish heritage as are the great monuments of Gaelic antiquity.

from *The Londonderry Plantation 1609–1914*, 1986

UNITED IRISHMEN IN BELFAST

MARIANNE ELLIOTT

I

Belfast in 1791, with its population of 18,320, was small and intimate. Whig Club members, Volunteers and United Irishmen shared the same membership, mixed socially and attended the same Presbyterian meeting houses. This was the middle-class capital of Ireland, and like many other towns in Ulster, Belfast had a very Protestant aspect,.which made English travellers feel at home. It was, according to Arthur Young, 'a very well-built town of brick, the streets are broad and strait . . . lively and busy'. The town was dominated by its entrepreneurial business class and Tone found its members as animated about the loss of a new power loom to the town as about radical politics. Indeed all too often their enthusiasms were directed by economic issues and their opposition to the American war owed as much to that war's closure of markets as to patriotism.

In 1791 Belfast was thriving. Its mill owners were passionate innovators, particularly in the field of new technology. The auction of John Haslett's Waring Street cotton factory in 1798 listed carding machines, spinning jennies and 'a horizontal wheel for turning the machinery' among its contents. In 1791 there were 695 looms operating in the town and by 1800, 11 factories gave employment to 27,000 people within a ten-mile radius. Although cotton still dominated Belfast's economy, the damp climate and abundant streams tumbling from the Antrim plateau made it perfect for linen production and its hills were dotted with bleaching greens.

Tone was fascinated by what he saw. 'Rode out with P.P. [Russell] and Sinclair to see his bleach-green', he wrote in his journal for 24 October. 'A noble concern; extensive machinery'. Sinclair, he noted, had been the first to introduce American potash, and he applauded the extensive use of machinery in the interests of progress, despite the massive loss of employment and resistance from the work force. 'Great command of water, which is omnipotent in the linen, etc. Three falls of 21 feet each in 10 acres, and ten more in the glen if necessary. A most romantic and beautiful country.'

By the 1790s Belfast had replaced Dublin as the main centre for Irish linen exports, with maritime developments to match. Much of the surrounding countryside served the needs of the town's industrial growth and was extensively populated by weavers occupying tiny farms. Business revolved round the old Brown Linen Hall in Donegall Street and a new White Linen Hall. Built through public subscription in the 1780s, it stood on the site of the present-day City Hall and dominated the up-and-coming fashionable Linenhall Street (Donegall Place). The list of subscribers in 1782–3 is revealing. Of the future United Irish leaders, Thomas McCabe and Gilbert McIlveen donated £100 each, the apothecary John Campbell £200. Neilson, the Hasletts, the Simmses and Russell's particular friends, the McCracken and Templeton families, also contributed. This was a tightly knit, often intermarried business world, its centre within yards of High Street, the main thoroughfare.

Like the White Linen Hall, the poorhouse and infirmary to the north-west of the town (still standing in Clifton Street) was also something of a monument to the Presbyterian mercantile community which dominated the town's civic life. It was another project paid for by public subscription, organised by those same men who had been involved in the White Linen Hall. Designed by Robert Joy, Henry's brother, it was one of those exercises in pragmatic philanthropy which marked much of late eighteenth-century thinking. The problems of poverty were answered by the philosophy of work and Joy, McCabe and John McCracken rounded off their enterprise by introducing cotton spinning as employment for the young inmates.

However rapid its industrialisation, Belfast was still very much a market town. In 1791 it was congested and dirty, with dunghills a constant nuisance in the streets and pigs wandering at will. The streets were unpaved and unlit and peopled by a complete cross-section of society. A famous painting of High Street in 1786 shows the masts of ships docked at the end of the street, and in the left foreground the Donegall Arms, where Tone and Russell often dined and socialised. Rebuilt in 1786 by Thomas Sheridan, its distinctive roofline was one of Belfast's landmarks until it finally succumbed to urban planners in the 1960s.

Bridge Street, which linked High Street to Waring Street, opened on to the elegant new Exchange Building and Assembly Rooms (today the Northern Bank), built in 1769 and designed by the distinguished Palladian architect Sir Robert Taylor. It stood at the juncture of Bridge, Rosemary, North and Waring Streets, the so-called 'Four Corners', a large open public space, where the main open-air public meetings took place and where publishers advertised the latest books and pamphlets. This central network of streets was linked by innumerable entries and lanes lined with small shops and inns, and peopled by ships' chandlers, rope-makers and carpenters. It was in one of these, Sugarhouse Entry – destroyed in the blitz of 1941 – that the United Irish Society was founded.

Belfast was a closed borough. Its members were returned by the sovereign and twelve burgesses, many of whom were absentees. Lacking a parliament – indeed lacking even a sizeable political class, since none of these rich Belfast merchants could vote for their MPs – Belfast had few ostentatious town houses like those of the southern aristocrats. Linenhall Street, running between the White Linen Hall and High Street, was beginning to be laid out as a fashionable area for the rich. There the Marquis of Donegall – sovereign of Belfast – and a number of its magistrates were investing in handsome terraces. It was Belfast's only really fashionable area, but by the end of the 1790s it was setting new standards of cleanliness, which were beginning to radiate out to the rest of the town.

It was an introspective town. Drennan, a native son, found it stifling, though it was much to the taste of Tone who revelled in intimate friendship. The other side of Belfast's internationalist thinking and industrialising economy was a provincialism which isolated it from the rest of the country and bred in its citizens an instinctive distrust and very often an intellectual disdain for their fellow countrymen. Certainly Tone and Russell found a remarkable ignorance of Catholicism among these northerners. It bred extremes of unrealistic fear and – when countered – equally unrealistic optimism about the nature of popery and the ease with which obstacles to religious co-operation might be overcome. The town was physically cut off from the rest of the country. A daily postal service with Dublin had only been established in 1789. Transport was erratic and rudimentary. There was still no means of transport to the west of Ireland, and even within the province communications were difficult.

The town was predominantly Presbyterian, as were the neighbouring counties of Antrim and Down. There were five Presbyterian meeting houses, three in Rosemary Lane alone (and two or them of the New Light persuasion). The number of Catholics was insignificant, if on the increase. Only 7 were recorded in 1708, 556 by 1779, and Belfast acquired its first mass house in 1784. By the 1790s rapid industrialisation was bringing more and more Catholics into the town, and suburbs of mud cabins sprang up to the north and west to accommodate them. Even then, they accounted for only 8 per cent of the population. With such insignificant numbers, active sectarianism was negligible. But growing industrialisation brought in rural outworkers and with them that sectarian strife already rampant in neighbouring counties. The bitter sectarian rioting that had gone on in Armagh since the 1780s between Catholic Defenders and Protestant Peep-of-Day Boys was already sweeping through other counties by the early '90s.

II

But Belfast had yet to experience it, and in 1791 Tone found 'blend[ing] of the sects' fashionable – one hairdresser even boasting of having his two children christened by a priest, though he himself was a Dissenter. Among those of the so-called 'secret committee' of Volunteers responsible for inviting him to Belfast, Tone likewise found a general willingness to co-operate with and learn more about the Catholics. Russell assumed the role of spokesman for the Catholics. He had communicated with members of the Catholic Committee that summer and gave the Belfast committee a full history of its proceedings.

With the Northern Whig Club, however, it was quite another matter, and Tone recounts 'a furious battle' on the Catholic issue, just after he had taken up his membership, paid his fees and signed their declaration. Bruce assumed the leadership of the anti-papists, presenting an emotional case one day at the McTiers' house in Cunningham Row, which took the reformers nearly two hours to disentangle. 'His ideas,' Tone noted, 'are, 1st. Danger to true religion, inasmuch as the Roman Catholics would, if emancipated, establish an *inquisition*. 2nd. Danger to property by reviving the Court of Claims, and admitting any evidence to substantiate Catholic titles. 3rd. Danger, generally, of throwing the power into their hands, which would make this a Catholic government, incapable of enjoying or extending liberty.' These were the same arguments which had been used against Catholic reform for much of the century. But Tone still found the majority of the Northern Whig Club, apart from himself, Russell, McTier and the timber merchant and Volunteer, Robert Getty, supporting them, while at the same time protesting their liberality and good will towards Catholics generally.

Tone was angry and depressed by such initial opposition and tried to brush it aside by dismissing it as wine talk. But he did recognise the need to tread carefully in Belfast. The ground would first have to be prepared by a writing campaign. Indeed the heady optimism of much of Tone's journal may present a rather different image of the man than that perceived by contemporaries. He met and liked Haliday and the respect was mutual, despite Tone's rabid emancipationism. 'The gentleman himself,' Haliday wrote to Charlemont on 5 November, 'passed a good many days among us lately, and proselyted [sic] not a few. I thought myself so unlucky in seeing so little of him; professional and other engagements deprived me of the pleasure of meeting him except for one day, when his good sense and modest unassuming courage were truly engaging. I believe it was under his auspices that the society of "United Irishmen" at Belfast was formed.'

This had been the main reason for Tone's journey north, and correspondence over the previous few months reveals a rather different lead-in to the formation of the famous movement than is commonly presented. It was not entirely a Belfast initiative. Rather members of Tone's old political club at Trinity, Catholics such as McCormick, the Dublin printer John Chambers, seasoned radicals like Tandy and Rowan, and Belfast men like McTier, Sinclair and McCabe had been in frequent communication over the summer. The name of the society and its prospectus had already been decided. Tone's July resolutions were to be remodelled – which he did on his first day in Belfast – printed and widely distributed, and a special United Irish Society edition of his *Argument* was already being printed by Chambers before Tone and Russell set off for Belfast. Its appearance was to coincide with the inauguration of the new society, and Tone wrote impatiently on 13 October urging Chambers to make haste. Chambers was also printing the prospectus for the *National*

Journal, and Tone and Russell returned to their inn on the night of the 16th to find 2,000 of these sent instead of the pamphlet. Tone was beside himself with frustration, and writes of storming and cursing while Russell teased him by quoting Seneca and Boethius' *De Consolatione.* The commissioned re-edition of the *Argument* did finally arrive during his stay in Belfast – the first batch of a printing of 10,000 ordered by the United Irish Society – and was advertised in the *News Letter* at threepence on 25 October.

There was another reason for Tone's frustration. Preparations for the launching of the new society were proceeding far too leisurely. 'We journalize everything here,' he complained to Chambers two days after his arrival, 'but nothing more than eating and drinking has yet gone forward.' On the previous day, the 12th, he, Russell, McTier and McCabe had made arrangements for a dinner at which his resolutions would be discussed. Tone marvelled at the changed opinion in Belfast which had rejected them as 'too hazardous' in July, but now required him to remodel them as 'too tame'. It was not till Friday, 14 October, that a full meeting of the 'street committee' was convened and the Society of United Irishmen established. The committee was composed of Sinclair, McTier, Neilson, McCleery, McCabe, the Simmses, Henry Haslett, John Campbell, McIlveen and William Tennent. The thirty-two-year-old Tennent was the eldest son of a Presbyterian minister and one of the most progressive of the Belfast merchants. He went on to found Belfast's first bank, was considered by the government 'a person of the first abilities' and one of the more dangerous United Irish leaders. Tone and Russell were sworn in as members and the United Irish Society held its inaugural meeting on Tuesday, 18 October. . . .

III

Tone's visit to Belfast marked the start of his regular journals. It is through them that Tone has become one of the most popular of Irish historical figures. Their tenor is fast, perceptive and amusing, though their flippancy has given rise to serious misunderstandings about Tone's character. The idea originated in his special friendship with Russell, and much of the tongue-in-cheek posturing is directed at his friend. 'I did not tell you my news,' he wrote to Matilda from Belfast on 20 October, 'as I journalize everything, and promise myself great pleasure from reading over my papers with you. I have christened Russell by the name of P.P. Clerk of this Parish, and he makes a very conspicuous figure in my memoirs.' . . . Russell was the constant object of Tone's teasing. On his first Sunday in Belfast, Tone accompanied Russell to church and listened to 'a vile sermon' denouncing smuggling as disloyal. Tone thought it nonsense, but Russell took it to heart and was greatly distressed by it. After church they joined the Belfast Sunday strollers on the Mall, which ran along the Blackstaff River south of Belfast, from the White Linen Hall to Joy's Paper Mill. Russell's sense of guilt at his own moral failings intensified as Tone remarked on how all the women were flirting with him.

In Belfast at that time a large number of card clubs, dances, balls and coteries were held and the two friends were on the receiving end of some lavish private hospitality. At his home in Bridge Street Dr James McDonnell, one of the town's outstanding intellectual figures at the time, though unusual in his Gaelic-Irish background, was one of their more frequent hosts. 'I find the people here extremely civil,' Tone wrote to Matilda, 'I have dined out every day since I came here, and have now more engagements than I can possibly fulfil.' He disliked the card clubs, accompanied Russell twice to coteries at the Donegall Arms, but did not enjoy them. He found the women ugly, disapproved of their heavy make-up and had a dispute with Russell about the teeth of one unfortunate young lady. These were a particular obsession with him and suggest worries about his own. On the second occasion, when much against his better inclinations Tone had agreed to accompany his friend, Russell lost his nerve in the lobby and they returned home. There Russell again changed his mind and wanted to return. It was after midnight and Tone was angry with him.

It was just the kind of indecision in Russell which Tone mocked when in good humour, but criticised when not. Every journal entry carries references to Russell's hang-ups: 'in the blue devils – thinks he is losing his faculties' and 'P.P. at home in the horrors; thinks himself sick generally.' Tone blamed these rather on Russell's drinking, smoking and late nights and constantly nagged him about his bad habits. 15 October: 'I had been lecturing P.P. on the state of his nerves, and the necessity of early hours; to which he agreed, and as the first fruits of my advice and his reformation, sat up with Digges until three o'clock in the morning, being four

43

hours after I had gone to bed.' Tone looked upon his friend as something of a wayward 'youth' and frequently assumed an elder-brother role. Russell wore his mental anguish openly and tended to invite such chiding from his friends.

Russell took the criticism in good part, and seems to have been rather more tolerant of Tone's failings than Tone of his. On Sunday the 23rd Alexander Stewart had them to dinner 'with a parcel of squires of County Down'. The conversation was dominated by 'Fox hunting, hare hunting, buck hunting' and the superiority of the northern potatoes. They then went on to the Washington Club, where in Tone's opinion another silly argument was in progress. It had been a tiring day which ended with Tone getting drunk in the Donegall Arms. The next morning he was sick and felt guilty about his rudeness to Russell, who took it all with patience.

No stay in a new town would have been complete without a visit to the theatre and Tone and Russell took in the *Carmelite*, playing in Rosemary Lane. It was not, however, one of the theatre's better seasons. It had been neglected by actor-manager Atkins because of his plans to build a second theatre in Belfast and another in Derry. A promising season with the celebrated Thomas Ryder was cut short by illness on 10 October and Tone and Russell were not impressed by the remaining actors. Instead they spent their time searching the audience for a pretty face. Russell fell asleep and they left early.

from *Wolfe Tone: prophet of Irish independence*, 1989

A GENERAL SURVEY

T.W. MOODY

The public life of Ulster in 1800, as of Ireland as a whole, was dominated by protestants. But unlike the ascendant element elsewhere Ulster protestants were very numerous, and contained a strong middle class, largely presbyterian, which had constituted the driving force behind the liberal–national movement of the preceding twenty-five years. It was a movement for a self-governing Ireland, under protestant leadership and a reformed parliament, in which civil and religious rights would be extended to catholics and the animosities of the past would be healed. Thwarted by the hard core of protestant ascendancy and inspired by the French revolution, the more resolute and radical liberals moved rapidly to the left until, organized in the Society of United Irishmen (founded at Belfast in 1791), they finally staked all on rebellion – and lost. The rebellion of 1798 led directly to the extinction of Ireland's separate parliament and the incorporation of Ireland in the United Kingdom by the union of 1800.

1798 was a turning point for Ulster liberalism. Defeat, dismay, and disillusionment at the contrast between United Irish ideals and the crude realities of the rebellion combined to produce a liberal recoil against nationalism. The sons and grandsons of the United Irishmen were generally liberals, but, though they might revere the memory of Henry Joy McCracken and Henry Munro, they abjured the ideal of national independence for Ireland. During much of the nineteenth century, Ulster liberals resembled liberals in Britain, and they returned a small but significant number of MPs to Westminster. But though Ulster liberals long remained vigorous and influential, especially in the intellectual life of Belfast, the conditions of Ulster politics were increasingly unfavourable to liberalism and increasingly favourable to that militant protestantism which had taken shape in the Orange Society, founded in County Armagh in 1795 as a counterblast to the United Irishmen.

Liberals were courageous advocates of catholic emancipation, the first great popular issue in post-union Ireland Under the tremendous leadership of O'Connell, the catholic masses were awakened to a sense of their collective strength, and a reform that liberal protestants had failed to achieve was conceded before a tidal wave of catholic agitation. This caused protestants to draw together in defence not merely of vested interests, but of liberties that they felt to be threatened by the rising power of the Catholic Church. Presbyterians hitherto generally liberal both in politics and theology tended to make common cause with conservative anglicans. While liberal politics came to be specially associated with the non-subscribing presbyterians, or unitarians, political conservatism was reinforced by the tendency of Ulster protestantism in all its forms to assume an evangelical character. The removal of the remaining religious grievances of presbyterians, and the disestablishment of the episcopal church in 1869 eliminated much of the traditional bad-feeling between the two main protestant bodies.

The dilemma of Ulster liberalism is clearly exemplified in the field of education. Liberals were the pioneers of mixed education, that is the combined secular, and separate religious, education of protestants and catholics. The Belfast Academical Institution was largely their creation. But the catholics they had helped to emancipate became implacable opponents of mixed education, with the result that Queen's College, Belfast, founded by the crown in 1845 to take over the work of the Institution on university level, was condemned by the catholic hierarchy and shunned by the catholic laity. On the other hand, presbyterians and anglicans were won over to mixed education as conducted in Queen's College, so that, in a sense, the liberals had their reward.

The predicament of the liberals was brought to a head by the rise of the home rule movement and the conversion of Gladstone, as leader of the liberal party, to the home rule cause in 1885. Ulster liberals had given Gladstone unwavering support even when his reform acts of 1884–5 had undermined their electoral position by extending the vote to agricultural labourers, who were either home rulers or Orangemen. Exposed to both these hostile fires, the liberals had lost all their nine seats in the general election of 1885. The Home Rule Bill of 1886 revolted them no less than the conservatives, and in bitter indignation they turned away from Gladstone. From that point they ceased to be an independent force in Ulster politics; liberalism had become irrelevant in a situation where one great issue dominated everything else. The entire parliamentary representation of Ireland was now divided into the two essential categories, unionists and nationalists.

Liberalism, with its roots in the tolerance, the optimism, and the rationalism of the eighteenth century, had occupied a middle position between militant catholicism and militant protestantism. Liberals had been influential out of all proportion to their numbers. Through the *Northern Whig* they had for sixty years brought a stream of independent and often pungent criticism to bear on public affairs. But after 1886 the *Northern Whig* ceased to justify its name and became indistinguishable in its political outlook from its conservative rival the *News-Letter*. All this helps to explain why no effective middle party was to arise in Northern Ireland after 1920. The Ulster liberal tradition did not entirely disappear, but in general it assumed a non-political character.

. . . Had the British parliament after 1800 set itself to remedy Ireland's ailments, the union might well have become acceptable to Irish opinion. But in fact, in the experience of most Irishmen, the union regime was soon identified with a cynical denial of civil rights to catholics and with callous indifference to the needs of a poor and backward country chained to one of the strongest and richest states of the world. From the thirties onwards the central theme of Irish politics was the demand of the majority, roused to political self-consciousness by the emancipation struggle, for social reform and national independence (or home rule). To gain these objectives by constitutional means two conditions were necessary: (1) the Irish representatives in parliament (about 100 out of 670) must be spokesmen of the popular will, and (2) the support of one of the two British parties must be obtained. Neither condition was present so long as the landed interest and the upper middle class dominated the electorate. The situation was altered when the Reform Act of 1867 enfranchised large sections of the urban population in Britain, and the introduction of the secret ballot, in 1872, deprived landlords in both countries of their power to intimidate voters. A new era in Anglo-Irish relations opened when Gladstone, to whom the new electorate in Britain had given its confidence, embarked on his great crusade to do justice to Ireland. Under his spell the liberal party committed itself to a policy of far-reaching reform, beginning with the Disestablishment Act of 1869 and the Land Act of 1870.

The nucleus of an Irish home rule party appeared in parliament in 1874, which, under the leadership of Parnell and with the powerful backing of the Land League, was fashioned into a constitutional fighting force, prepared to treat with either British party while remaining independent of both. Electoral reforms in 1884–85 extended the process of democratizing parliament, and brought the Irish electorate into line with the British. In the first general election, that of 1885, to be held under the new conditions, the liberals were returned in Britain with a large majority over the conservatives, and in Ireland pledge-bound home rulers were returned for 85 out of 103 constituencies. Ireland had thus given an overwhelming popular verdict for self-government, and this was reaffirmed at every subsequent general election. It was in this situation that Gladstone took the fateful step of adopting the home rule cause.

Gladstone's first home rule effort, in 1886, was defeated in the House of Commons through a split in the liberal party. But even had it passed the commons the Home Rule Bill would have been thrown out in the lords. This was the fate of Gladstone's second attempt made in 1893 with a small combined majority of liberals and home-rulers. When the liberals tabled their third and final Home Rule Bill, in 1912, British democracy had made two important gains: first, there was now a distinct labour party in parliament, allied with the liberals on the home rule issue; secondly, the veto power of the House of Lords was severely restricted by the Parliament Act of 1911. In consequence the bill of 1912 passed into law in 1914. But this parliamentary victory had been nullified in advance by events that had taken place in Ulster.

Hostility was shown by protestant Ulster to every phase of the independence movement from O'Connell's time onwards, but the conflict became clearly defined only in 1886. In the general election of 1885, 17 of the 33 Ulster seats went to nationalists and 16 to unionists, which roughly agreed with the ratio between catholics and protestants. The minority opposed to self-government was concentrated within the area that is now Northern Ireland. This pattern of representation, the inevitable outcome of democratic conditions, remained unchanged as long as the union lasted.

Protestant and unionist were not synonymous terms but broadly speaking protestants in Ulster represented the descendants of a colony that had proved the most successful ever planted by England on Irish soil. The oldest tradition of that colony, unyielding resistance to all attempts of the dispossessed to retrieve their losses, was not invoked against home rule. Home rule was condemned on three main grounds: (1) it would banish Ulster protestants from the British community with which they had their closest ties and subject them to a people from whom they had always been culturally distinct; (2) it would imperil their prosperity, since an Irish parliament would be bound to adopt tariff policies fatal to Ulster's industries; (3) above all it would threaten their most vital liberties to be ruled by a parliament dominated by catholics. Behind this third contention there lay not only an age-long inheritance of religious conflict but an alarming sense of the great and growing power of the Roman Catholic clergy in nineteenth-century Ireland. That 'Home Rule would mean Rome Rule' was for most Ulster protestants an unanswerable indictment.

Against the overwhelming weight of numbers in Ireland itself Ulster protestants appealed to British public opinion to maintain the union, while contemplating forcible resistance to any attempt to bring their area under the authority of an Irish parliament. A great revival and expansion of the Orange order provided the framework of a resistance movement, and this organization was brought to perfection in the Ulster Unionist Council (formed in 1905). In 1886 and in 1893 home rule was defeated in parliament itself. But in 1912 the last parliamentary obstacle to the passage of a home rule bill had been removed, and Ulster unionists therefore prepared in deadly earnest for rebellion. The threat of rebellion, however, sufficed, because on the one hand they had the wholehearted – though far from disinterested – support of the British conservative party, and because on the other the liberal government under Asquith was not, in the last resort, prepared to coerce them. The imminence of European war also worked to their advantage.

So in the end Ulster unionists frustrated the Gladstonian plan of home rule for Ireland. But the final outcome was not what they, or the unionists of the south, or their British supporters, had aimed at. A scheme that had been mooted in 1886 but not seriously considered till 1913, the exclusion of the north-eastern counties from the jurisdiction of Dublin, was eventually made the basis of settlement. The six counties selected comprised the two (Antrim and Down) in which the strength of protestantism and of industrialism lay, two (Armagh and Londonderry) that had a protestant majority, and two (Tyrone and Fermanagh) in which, though catholics slightly preponderated, the protestant colonial element was strongly rooted. The three excluded counties, Donegal, Cavan, and Monaghan, were those in which the seventeenth-century colony had succeeded least. This arrangement involved the partition both of Ulster and of Ireland, which neither unionists nor nationalists had contemplated, and within the area of Northern Ireland it left one-third of the population irreconcilably nationalist. As for the rest of Ireland, the success of the Ulster resistance fatally discredited the parliamentary nationalists and opened the way for the revolutionary nationalists. So while the six counties were endowed with a home rule system of their own which they had never sought, the twenty-six counties acquired through rebellion an independence that far exceeded the limits of the home rule denied to them in 1914. Both Northern Ireland and the Irish Free State thus owed their origin not to the force of argument, on which the national movement from O'Connell to Redmond had relied, but to the argument of force, and their history bears the marks of that tragic but inescapable fact.

from *Ulster Since 1800*, 1954

A Catholic in the Civil Service

PATRICK SHEA

Northern Ireland came into being in 1921 in an atmosphere of political turmoil which, particularly in Belfast, took the form of a religious war between Catholics and Protestants. By the time I came to Belfast the violence had come to an end but the signs of it – burned buildings and bullet-scarred gable walls – were there to be seen and feeling was still high in the most densely populated parts of the city. The Catholics, large numbers of them crowded into the streets along the Falls Road, were cowed and dispirited; they had seen riots and death, the burning of homes and business premises, the violent expulsion of their men from the ship-yards and factories and building sites. They had stories of murder and cruelty, of the wild exploits of the Special Constabulary, the bigoted out-bursts of political leaders. The Protestants had something to say about the involvement of the IRA in the city's troubles but the Catholics discounted any allegations that blame lay on their side. They feared their Protestant neighbours with the anger of people who had been subdued by force and left without any means of retaliating against their persecutors.

Catholics in the Northern Ireland Civil Service in those days were very few. Because of the hard times through which many had lived and from which they had emerged as losers the Northern Catholics were not dis-posed to claim anything from what they regarded as a hostile government; in any case, they believed that worthwhile employment under the Unionist administration was available only to Unionists and friends of Unionists. It was my experience that some Catholics, and especially those in Belfast where, I had been told, the Bishop had advised them against seeking Government employment, looked with suspicion on Catholic civil serv-ants. We had joined the enemy; we were lost souls. When we were seen to practise our religion it might be hinted that we were secretly Freemasons. It was not easy to establish kinship with one's co-religionists in Belfast.

Within the Civil Service I saw the other side of the coin. To many of my colleagues Catholics were strange animals of which they had astonishingly little knowledge. When we talked about religion, which was not very often, I learned of their beliefs about the power of the Pope and his clergy and no words could persuade them that I was not subject to malevolent direction by black-robed priests to whom Rome had entrusted its master plan for world domination. I was astonished to meet youths of my own age who had never met a Catholic until I appeared in the office, who believed, as one of them told me, that in the event of their coming under a Nationalist government the Pope would require his obedient Irish flock to banish the Protestants from the land.

Although I had many experiences of the prejudices and the lack of understanding between the two communities – to each of which I was a cuckoo in the nest – the native kindness of the people compensated for moments of embarrassment. I had grown up in a family which was free of strong political loyalties and had joined the Civil Service without any feeling of having done something unconventional or unworthy. Many people were, as I was, anxious to live normal lives after troubled years. The competition for jobs was fierce and my attitude was simply pragmatic. I was, for better or worse, a citizen of the new state of Northern Ireland and I was claiming my piece of it.

My first reaction to the Civil Service had been that it was something to get out of as quickly as possible but my attempts to escape came to nothing. As time went on work became more interesting and as my non-official pursuits began increasingly to brighten my leisure hours the desire to change my occupation lost its urgency.

I had taken up rugby with enthusiasm and through it had made many friends. I had become a regular theatre-goer. In the Ministry we had a debating society and in evening debates we got some pleasure taking the mickey out of our elders and betters. My brother Tim had enrolled at Queen's University in 1927 and during his years there we shared digs. We went to debates in the Students' Union and occasionally, if the University soccer team in which he played was a man short, I filled the vacancy. We went to house-parties and dances, played bridge and pontoon and poker, frequented fish-and-chip shops and pubs, tried our hands at billiards and snooker, visited our friends in their digs to talk about sport and religion and politics and Sir Crawford McCullough who it seemed would be Lord Mayor of Belfast for evermore. We took girls to the pictures or to dances or, if we were out of funds, walking along the Malone Road.

In the office I had got to know more about my colleagues. Many of the ex-servicemen had been in the Ulster Volunteer Force and on the declaration of war in 1914 had joined the Ulster Division (which they referred to as the YCVs, the Young Citizen Volunteers). Some of them had been wounded and when one heard of their experiences in the trenches their shortcomings as officials, for some of them were very poor material, were overlooked. A later generation would have shown less forbearance than they towards a government which had done so little to fulfil the extravagant promises which had been made to those who volunteered for war service. But they were the lucky ones; they had come through alive, albeit many with serious disabilities, and they had jobs. Towards me they were friendly and helpful. Bob Stewart, a big, easy-going man who took a fatherly interest in my welfare, told me about the Battle of the Somme. In his quiet Ulster voice he described his experiences on 1 July 1916 when the Ulster Division advanced into the German lines, a day in which many of the friends of his youth died. His account of what he experienced made a lasting impression on me and since then I have stopped at many a village war memorial and looked down the list of names which still bear witness to that day.

In 1931 all Government departments except the Ministry of Commerce were gathered into the new Parliament Buildings at Stormont and the change brought the migration to the eastern suburbs of Government officials of every rank and class. I moved with three kindred spirits into a trim, detached house at Belmont where we were attended to by a kind and patient landlady.

The change to Stormont widened still further my circle of acquaintances in the Civil Service and my knowledge of what was happening in other departments.

We were a young service, not overworked, and carefree. Young women were coming into the service in numbers and their presence brightened the scene. During the lunch hour on a summer's day the spacious grounds of Stormont had something of the atmosphere of a leisurely university campus. We talked about sport and the cinema, criticised our betters, explored the estate and watched, without enthusiasm, the coming and going of members of the Houses of Parliament.

from *Voices and the Sound of Drums*, 1981

Sermons in Stones

A.T.Q. STEWART

No one who has been caught in a Belfast riot against his will is likely to regard it as one of the higher forms of human activity, which is one reason why most of the population of Belfast prefer to watch riots on television. It can only be assumed that feelings of intense hatred, combined with the excitement of participation, somehow anaesthetize the individual rioter to its horror and its dangers, often with fatal consequences. But it is a naïve and fundamental error to regard rioting as a 'mindless' and irrational mode of human behaviour. Stone-throwing, for example, is a military art of considerable sophistication and great antiquity. Even in the twentieth century, well-organized stone-throwing can inflict very serious casualties on armed and disciplined troops who are forbidden to shoot the stone-throwers. That simple fact has determined the image of Ulster most frequently presented to the world – that of well-armed soldiers and police cowering behind armoured cars and street corners under a hail of bricks and stones. These soldiers might as well be Roman legionaries, for all the good their modern weapons are; their only protection is a shield, a steel helmet and a visor. Schoolboys can dance right up to the armoured vehicles and launch a brick or a nail-bomb with deadly accuracy, but woe to the soldier who fires a single round, with or without orders; not the least of the rioters' advantages is in the field of propaganda. The stone-throwers may be barbarians, savages, Neanderthal men, but from a military point of view, they know what they are doing. Their art has been perfected in the streets of Belfast and Derry, Lurgan and Portadown, for a century and a half at least.

A proper appreciation of this caused the paving of Belfast in the early nineteenth century to be a matter of great concern to the city fathers. Many of the city's streets and squares were originally paved with cobble stones, which were found in quantities along the coasts of Antrim and Down. These, from their shape, were known locally as 'kidney stones', and were a highly prized and readily available source of ammunition.

When macadamized surfaces of broken granite and basalt were introduced, they proved even more useful to rioters. The scene which Frankfort Moore witnessed as a child was enacted in the streets round the Custom House, in the Belfast dockland. This building, or, more accurately, the flight of steps in front of it, was traditionally Belfast's equivalent of Speakers' Corner, and on Sunday afternoons it frequently became a pulpit, from which 'highly-seasoned Protestant doctrines' were preached. This open-air preaching was sometimes, as in 1857, the actual cause of the riots; and since the square where Victoria Street, High Street and Corporation Street met had a loose macadam surface, the whole neighbourhood would, after 'a warm interchange of opinion on the basis of basalt', assume the appearance of a battlefield, and 'the strain upon the resources of the surgical staff of the hospital' would reach breaking point.

The corporation therefore decided to substitute 'a more prehensile system of paving in all the argumentative localities of the town'. Heavy granite squares, called 'setts', were put down instead. They did not bring peace, but, as Moore observes, 'there was a marked difference in the range at which the discussion began'. Further experiments were made, and ultimately all new streets were paved with flagstones, though this placed a heavy burden on the ratepayers. Even this did not stop the habit, for the flagstones were pulled up by rioters and broken into smaller pieces.

The stoning was not carried out in a haphazard way. Moore describes how he learned 'the proper way to conduct a street riot' in Portadown in 1869. 'Every boy and girl in the crowd understood the art thoroughly. When the police charged in military fashion, they hurried to one side or the other, refraining from obstructing them in the least, but returning immediately afterward to the place they had occupied before the "charge".' The reminiscences of the architect Robert Young, a distinguished Belfast citizen who died in 1917, make the same point:

'This was my first experience of rioting. I mean I was so near the stonethrowers that I saw the women gathering stones in their aprons and supplying their male friends with this ammunition . . .

'In the shameful riots lately that culminated in the loss of two or probably more lives these kidney pavers played a leading part. Judging by the accounts of the police and military they were prepared beforehand in a systematic plan for the assault of the military *in the ordinary way* [my italics] and also by flinging pavers over the spaces between the narrow streets jutting from the Falls Road where it was expected their enemies must pass. Stores of these pavers were prepared in the upper rooms of the workers' houses, and when the riotous mob was being driven through one of these streets up came the windows and an avalanche of paving stones descended on the heads of the ill-fated Tommies. It was the outcome of a most carefully planned and almost accomplished scheme for massacring the English soldiers that had been brought to the city on account of the incipient mutiny of the constabulary. Law and order were vindicated, but not till many wounded had been carried to the hospitals.'

In the very serious riots of 1886 Moore observed all these tactics in use again. He had in the meantime seen nasty riots elsewhere in the world, but in his opinion none of the principals in these actions knew anything of strategy when 'compared with those who engineered the sacking of York Street on a dark night in August 1886'.

'The lamps had nearly all been extinguished – perhaps they had not been lighted at all – but when I came to the mouth of the road, scarcely a light was to be seen; still I had no difficulty in making out the movements of the dense crowds surging in every direction, and shot after shot I heard above the shouts that suggested something very like Pandemonium. Once or twice I was carried along in the rush of people before a police charge, and I was taught in the most practical way how to avoid a casualty; for I was simply hurried through the street and into the nearest by-lane, where I was forced to stand with the rest of the fugitives until the projectile, in the form of a squad of police or soldiers, had charged past. Then I was allowed a leisurely return to the field of battle . . . I felt I had learned something of the impotence of every arm except artillery in the case of street fighting.'

Gradually it becomes clear that these periodical outbursts of violence follow a complex internal logic of their own, which is unaltered by the current political circumstances, the ululation of politicians and clergy, or the military strength used to suppress it. The 'troubles' (to use the Irish term which is more comprehensive than rioting) go through well-defined stages. The first is usually confined to provocation of the opposite party, intense and often prolonged over weeks and months. This provocation, which is not the cause of the ultimate outbreak, but appears to be a ritual part of it, may take the form of marching, jeering, waving flags and singing party songs. Where a main road divides Catholic streets from Protestant the displaying of flags and hurling of insults may go on all through the summer, slowly building up to the inevitable clashes and bloodshed. The first stage is followed by physical violence, fisticuffs, stone-throwing, forays into enemy territory by men armed with clubs, the smashing of windows and the starting of fires. This automatically introduces the police who must take the routine steps to preserve the peace, apprehend troublemakers and, if possible, separate the two mobs. The violence is then re-directed by one side or the other towards the police, who are accused either of partiality or over-reaction. It is not unusual for both sides to attack the police, or for one side to cease hostilities in order to enjoy the spectacle of the other fighting it out with the police.

The police begin to sustain casualties; reinforcements are called in, and the conflict is aggravated. If really serious disorders develop, the police will lose control of the situation and be obliged to call for military aid. At some point before this stage is reached, the whole character of this ritual dance of provocation and aggression will have been changed by the use of firearms. The firing of weapons at night, from a quarter which is predominantly of one religion, may often be simply a signal to the other side that the inhabitants mean business; but it usually begins unexpectedly and dramatically when someone emerges from a jeering crowd and deliberately fires a weapon into the opposing crowd. The reaction is total shock, and bitter recrimination, conducted on the basis that no one in the long history of Ireland has ever seen a gun, let alone used one, and that the other side have broken the rules, in the most treacherous manner, which is all one can expect from them.

The first use of firearms is always by the other side, and there is invariably a sensation of shock and anger at the elevation of the conflict to a more lethal plane. This creates a momentary pause, followed by indiscriminate retaliation. Death and injury initiate the vendetta, and if it has been caused by police or troops, then they are fired on also. Actual contests between Protestant and Catholic mobs do not last long. Some of the worst, like the 'Battle of the Brickfields' in 1872, have been over in twenty minutes, but sporadic rioting, cowardly assassination and attacks on the police and troops may continue for days or weeks. A 'flashpoint' usually

57

cools in three or four days. The rioters seem to tire of the activity, no doubt because of extreme physical exhaustion, and the rioting may be transferred to another locality, where the able-bodied men are fresh for combat. Riots die away for no apparent reason, or for reasons which seem illogical; for example the prolonged fighting of 1886 ended because of three days of continuous rain. That is to say, the rioters were more demoralized by rain than by rifle fire.

Moore shrewdly noticed an aspect of rioting which is just as apparent today as it was a century ago. The army is almost totally ineffective as a means of restoring order. It would of course be extremely effective if it were allowed to operate *as an army*, but this is what it must never do. The addition of armed troops to the situation in the streets aggravates the disorders, and for the last one hundred and fifty years has been a required element in the scenario. If 'the military' did not take part, some essential ingredient in the street fighting would be felt to be absent. On the ineffectiveness of the army in 1886, Moore makes this significant comment. 'I have seen how little value troops are to put down a disturbance in a few streets of a large city even when every respectable inhabitant is hostile to the disturbers of the peace, and I have, I trust, sufficient imagination to know what would happen when every respectable person has gone over to the other side.'

The Belfast riots of 1857, 1864 and 1886, and the Londonderry riots of 1869 and 1883, were the subject of commissions of inquiry. The evidence which they collected, and the reports which they finally presented, provide the historian with a vast amount of information on the peculiarities of this kind of urban warfare. After each riot the commissioners did their best to isolate what they believed to be the immediate and long-term causes, so that their labours might help to avert such events in the future. The subsequent explosions clearly proved that they had not succeeded, and it may be assumed that the same is true of those commissions which have sat in recent years. With depressing frequency, the nineteenth-century commissions laid the blame squarely on two main factors – the partiality and inefficiency of the police, and the provocative nature of the Orange celebrations.

In 1857 the commissioners found that the town police of Belfast, a local force established by Act of Parliament in 1845 and separate from the Irish

Constabulary, consisted of one hundred and sixty men, unarmed except for light walking sticks. Of these all but six or seven were Protestants 'and many were Orangemen'. They were considered sympathetic to the Sandy Row mob and enemies to the Catholic Pound; consequently they could appear safely in Sandy Row but not in the Pound. The police were attacked and had to be defended by the Constabulary. 'All these matters lead us to believe,' the commissioners reported, 'that in the constitution of the present police force there are serious errors, calling for immediate remedy; and to recommend that a total change should be made in the mode of appointment and the management of the local police of Belfast.' . . .

The formula of tinkering with the police was tried after each successive outbreak, and always without the slightest effect. The Irish Constabulary, the Royal Irish Constabulary and the Royal Ulster Constabulary were each in turn criticized for allowing riots to develop, and failing to contain them when they did develop. If they were unarmed, it was recommended that they should be armed; if they used their arms, it was recommended that they be disarmed. When Lord Hunt recommended in 1969 that the RUC be instantly disarmed, he was, whether he knew it or not, following a well-established precedent. Again the move did not have the desired effects. On the contrary, it loosed a deluge of violence which led to the deaths of many policemen and soldiers, and hundreds of civilians. The police were quickly re-armed, but the damage had already been done – less from the disarming than from the general doubt cast upon the effectiveness and impartiality of the RUC. It was an old story, as the nineteenth-century riot reports show, and it had little to do with the IRA.

The commissioners found little difficulty in isolating what they believed to be the chief cause of riots in Belfast. They blamed the Orange lodges for the provocative displays which inflamed the atmosphere in Belfast during the weeks leading up to the Orange festival on 12 July. 'The celebration of that festival,' declared the commissioners on the riot of 1857, 'is plainly and unmistakably the originating cause of these riots.' It was used 'to remind one party of the triumph of their ancestors over those of the other, and to inculcate the feelings of Protestant superiority over their Roman Catholic neighbours'. This view has been accepted uncritically by many writers, and is heartily endorsed in the south of Ireland, while opinion outside Ireland often seeks no further explanation. In its crudest form it is used to explain the mechanism by which religious rancour is carried 'like a hereditary disease' from generation to generation.

Such an explanation is probably too simple. A quarrel of this vitality cannot be sustained through the ages by provocations from one side only, and the strength of Orangeism depends upon opposite and equal forces of anti-Protestant feeling, often more subtly displayed. Again, the antithesis between the liberality of Belfast in the last decade of the eighteenth century and the intolerance of the years after 1830 is a false one, based on a misreading of the earlier period, and ignoring (among many other factors) the alteration in the balance of population caused by industrialization, which both sharpened the hostility and shaped the forms which it assumed.

One historian has calculated that Orange processions were 'a precipitating factor' in at least six out of fifteen major riots in Belfast between 1813 and 1914; that is to say, they cannot be proved to be the cause of more than six out of the fifteen riots. Such a finding is not surprising, for there is a good deal more to the process of causing a riot than is apparent on the surface. The fact that an Orange procession is not the immediate cause of a riot does not exculpate the Orangemen from responsibility in helping to bring it about. To understand why requires some familiarity with the curious patterns of Belfast rioting. Orangemen, when engaged in their rituals, do not physically attack anyone, unless they are provoked beyond discipline. The provocation alleged by Catholics may arise simply from the fact that Orangeism is a symbol of something intensely hated; or from the display of party colours and playing of party tunes; or from that most menacing of sounds, even to Protestant ears, the thunder of Orange drums; or – the classic and strongest cause – from the routing of a procession through territory traditionally considered to be Catholic. Belfast riots have rarely, if ever, been begun by Orangemen marching in their regalia. The archetypal situation is for an Orange procession to be attacked by Catholics, so initiating full-scale retaliation at a time when 'Orange blood is up'.

The actual cause of an outbreak of rioting is not in any event the matter of first importance; it may be almost anything if the political atmosphere is ripe – the waving of a flag, a ranting sermon, a funeral, a Sunday school procession. 'To such an extent does the inflammability of the populace seem to extend,' reported the 1886 commission, 'that even the excursion through the town of school children . . . if accompanied by a band, appears effectually to lead to an attack by the excursionists or the mobs who collect on hearing a band.' The Orange summer revels would appear to be the most visible and colourful part of a much more complex, and largely concealed, structure of ritual social behaviour which has not yet been satisfactorily explained.

Terrorism in the advancement of a political cause is at once part of, and a new pattern imposed upon, the tapestry of civil disorder. It first appeared in its familiar modern form during the troubles of 1919–23, but it is probably a mistake to distinguish too sharply between traditional violence and that motivated by contemporary politics. The distinction lies in the use of more deadly weapons; the bomb and machine-gun have been added to the pistol and the pike. The troubles in Ireland after 1918 reflected both the technology and the horror of the First World War, and in turn set a pattern for nationalist terrorism throughout the world. In the north, the worst outrages followed the setting up of the State of Northern Ireland in 1920. Between June 1920 and June 1922 the total casualties were 428 killed and 1,766 wounded, a staggering increase on the remarkably low figures for persons killed in all the Belfast riots of the nineteenth century. The total deaths between 1813 and 1907 numbered 68, and of these almost half occurred in 1886. At the time of writing the casualty figures for Northern Ireland since 1969 are approaching a total of 1,700 dead.

In both the earlier and the present campaigns, the original attacks by the IRA provoked severe reprisals on the Catholic population. Once this mechanism is operated, it cannot be halted or reversed, except perhaps by resolute action by a popularly based administration which has the confidence of the Protestant majority. Thus a ceasefire declared by the IRA has little effect on continuing sectarian violence. The whole process of muted insurrection, so familiar in Irish history, is an elaborately structured and ever-changing development which obeys no laws except those intrinsic to it. Once the civil rights movement assumed a militant, and to all intents and purposes a sectarian, form in 1969, the entire escalation of the conflict was easily predictable. This process has little to do with the merits of the civil rights issue as such.

The Ulster war has shown yet again that, irrespective of the political aims of those who resort to violence, the conflict has developed along lines determined by the cumulative experience of earlier clashes. When we turn to the nineteenth-century riot reports we find some of the familiar features of today: the setting up of barricades in Protestant areas of Belfast, the extinction of street lighting, the manufacture of home-made pistols and ammunition, the accusation that the police joined the Protestant rioters, the use of 'snatch squads' by the army to drag ringleaders from the mob, police complaints at meeting 'a wall of silence'. In 1865 and 1872 Catholic gun clubs were formed, and a Protestant Defence Association came into being. In 1872 the army was caught in the middle while trying to establish a peace line between the Falls and the Shankill; there was widespread burning, looting and intimidation in the streets between the two roads, which was precisely re-enacted in 1969 in the very same streets. In 1886 what are now called 'no-go areas' appeared after the police had been driven from the Shankill Road; after nearly two months, during which there was little ordinary crime, and the men of the area did their own vigilante policing, authority cautiously returned in the form of joint army–police patrols.

from *The Narrow Ground*, 1977

2

'Flax-pullings, dances, summer crossroads chat
. . . And always, Orange drums
And neighbours on the roads at night with guns'

SEAMUS HEANEY

SIGHTSEEING BY CHAISE

MARY DELANY

Mrs Delany to Mrs Dewes.
Mount Panther, 8th August, 1758.

Mr and Lady Anne Annesley, their son, daughter, and two or three friends live in *ten houses* laid into one, situated on the summit of a high mountain, and surrounded by several very high and very melancholy ones, *I think*, but if he goes on with his wonderful improvements he may make them beautiful; for the land surrounding his present dwelling (which is part of a town he is building), was the last time of my being in this country a mere bog, and as unpromising as any land I ever beheld, and now hay is making, corn is growing, trees planted and cattle feeding; and above an hundred and twenty labourers, constantly employed, and fifteen hundred pounds a-year expended on the improvements. . . .

Sunday we went to Downpatrick; D.D. [Dean Delaney] preached as well as ever I heard him. We had a dinner, as usual, for as many as filled a table for twelve people. Our dinner was a boiled leg of mutton, a sirloin of roast beef, six boiled chickens, bacon and greens; apple-pies, a dish of potatoes – all set on at once; time between church and church does not allow for two courses; tea after we came home, and talking over our company was refreshing to us. We brought a *young cat home* with us, *but she was so cross* we sent her home again this morning, and I, alas! am catless! Our church and congregation at Down very decent, and there were a great many at the Sacrament. . . .

Mrs Delany to Mrs Dewes.
Mount Panther, 28th Aug., 1758.

On Wednesday we dined at Killalee, 12 measured Irish miles from hence, at Mr Hall's, a clergyman of a very singular character, not very worthy; but we wanted to see the place, which we had heard much commended: Mr Bayly's family were of the party which made it more agreeable.

The situation is on the side of a hill with a most extensive view of the sea. In one place they tell you is *Portaferry*, in another *Lady Anne Ward's Temple*, in another *Strangford*, but it requires such very clear eyes and weather to distinguish these objects, that I confess they gave me no more pleasure than only reading of them that they were there would do. The wind was high, we walked up a high hill to a castle, our *negligées* fluttered like the streamers of a ship, and when we came to the castle where we were to see wonders of prospect, no admittance, the gates locked, and we staggered back again with much difficulty, facing the wind, but we had a good dinner and good company. Mr Bayly went in the coach with us; the scene was new, the road excellent, and part of it very pleasant, – so on the whole it was an agreeable day, but we were most heartily tired. . . .

Sally and I grumble a little at the weather, which prevents our going about among the *herbs and flowers* to find out some that may be rare to you. There grows a little pale purple aster, with a yellow thrum (very like the *asterattims*), in all the borders near the lakes and sea: it grows in great clusters, and in some places near two feet high, and we have great plenty of thrift grows wild between this and Belville. As to the common plants they seem much the same as in the high ways, rather more luxuriant; the tawdry rag-weed in vast abundance, but mollified by the bloom and hue of the scabius and rest harrow. *Matfellon* and *figwort* flourish here remarkably, and the purple vetch and eyebright soften the golden furs, and glowing heath. A poetical pen might have done their beauties justice.

Mrs Delany to Mrs Dewes.
Mount Panther, 2nd Sept. 1758.

According to the country phrase, yesterday Sally and I '*fetched* a charming walk' – at least six miles! We set out at a quarter after ten with bags and baskets to store our curiosities in. John, like a pedlar, with our cloaks buckled to his back by a belt – or rather a pilgrim, with his hat slouched and a long staff in his hand, Fitz Simmons, our harper, who knows all the paths and walks of this place, with our store-basket. We left the Dean with his workmen, about *ten such invalids* as are fitter for an hospital than a spade; but with good clothing and gentle work they *come on finely,* and gather strength!

If I tell you where we walked, you would not know whereabouts we were; the castle of Dundrum is a ruin on a very steep rude shapen hill, a vast extent of the sea, on which were several vessels, chiefly fishing-boats; and the vast mountains of Moran, which are so near us that we can perceive the rivers which run down the side of them. The highest mountain, they say, is a mile and half perpendicular, and on the top of it is a well of fine water; there is a ridge of these mountains – they are indeed tremendous, but make a fine background to our picture. In our way to Dundrum, which was the point we aimed at, we walked over a hill covered with bushes, intermixed with rocks, the verdure fine and soft as velvet; sheep, goats, and cows, with little ragged shepherds attending them.

We examined every blade of grass for new plants, but found only a purple flower, four-leaved like a star; it shuts up in the middle of the day, it is of a violet colour. I wanted to know what species it is of? but fear before it reaches you, it will be too much withered for you to find out its family? I will watch for the seed and save it. A little yellow and white flower we found, like linaria, but grows thinner.

Thursday spent the day at Castle Wellan, Mr Annesley's, and walked two or three miles before dinner, saw all his farming affairs, which are indeed very fine. Three large courts: round the first, which is arched round a kind of piazza, are houses for all his carriages, and over them his granaries; the next court are stables and cow-houses, and over them hay-lofts; the third court two such barns as I never saw, *floored with oak*, and finished in the most convenient manner for all the purposes of winnowing, &c., and in that court are the stands for hay and corn. I am sure Mr Dewes would be pleased with the whole apparatus; it is so neat, strong, and clever. . . .

Mrs Delany to Mrs Dewes.
Mount Panther, Sept. 9th, 1758.

My dearest sister's most entertaining letter with the account of Warwick races made me happy last (post) Thursday.

We cannot possibly pretend to vie with you in splendid appearance, *nobility*, and *jewels*, nor can I say much for the beauty and elegance of *our room* at Downpatrick on Thursday last, where I carried our Sally, but

I had much more diverting company than you can boast of, I am sure, with all your lords and ladies! though *we had one earl as well as you* – Lord Hillsborough, a very sensible agreeable man. . . . We went to the *assembly at seven.* Three sets of dancers, not more than ten in a set; they *draw* for partners (except the strangers), and then *choose first;* Sally chose Mr Cole, Mrs Price's nephew – a vast estate, and a very good sort of a young man; he seems (and I hope is) much enamoured with Miss Bayly. After four dances they sat down, and Sally was chosen in the second set by a strange man indeed, but to her credit – I can't say comfort – he fell to Miss Bayly's lot afterwards. Such a figure, such a *no-dancer,* a *mopstick* with a brown, dirty *mophead!* and his sense (if he had any), seemed as stupid as his figure and his heels, all but in the choice of his partners.

Lord Hillsborough hath engaged us to take Hillsborough in our way to the Giant's Causeway, which I believe we shall do. . . . We have fixed our time for leaving this place, please God, on the 26th of this month.

Mrs Delany to Mrs Dewes.
Belvoir, 1st Oct. 1758.

We left Mount Panther on Tuesday, the 26th, at nine o'clock; a train of two chaises and two cars with us, Mr Bayly and Mr Mathews, one of D.D.'s curates, on horseback, and our sumpter-car. From Mount Panther to Ballanehinch (7 miles) is the rudest country I ever saw – rough hills, mountains, and bogs, but some of them covered with furze in blossom, heath, and thyme.

We got to Hillsborough about half an hour after one, which is fifteen miles from Mount Panther, and the scene was then much mended with the view of a very fine cultivated country, little inferior to some parts of Gloucestershire. The house is not extraordinary, but prettily fitted up and furnished; the dining-room, not long added to the house, is a fine room, 33 f. by 26. Lord Hillsborough is very well bred, sensible, and entertaining, and nothing could be more polite than he was to all his company. . . .

Mrs Delany to Mrs Dewes.
Bally Logh, 5th Oct., 1758.

It is too dark, I can hardly see. I know my dearest sister will want to know how we get out of the Giant's claws, and I must tell her we are just returned from seeing the most wonderful sight that, perhaps, is to be seen in the world, but have not time for description, only to tell you that we are well after four hours' walking, wondering, and puddling – no accident.

Mrs Delany to Mrs Dewes.
Hazlebrook, 8th Oct. 1758.

I am now quite at a loss to give you any idea of it; it is so different from anything I ever saw, and so far beyond all description. The prints you have represent some part of it very exactly, with the *sort of pillars* and the remarkable stones that compose them of different angles, but there is an infinite variety of rocks and grassy mountain *not at all* described in the prints, nor is it possible for a poet or a painter, with all their art, to do justice to the awful grandeur of the whole scene. When we got out of our coach, Mr Leslie and his brother took the charge of me and Miss Chapone, and Mr Mathews of the Dean. We walked along a path on the side of a hill that formed an amphitheatre, of a great height above us, and sloped down a vast way below us to the sea from the path we walked on. The grass very fine and green, and a variety of field-flowers of the season, though none of a peculiar kind from those in your own fields. At the bottom, the sea foaming and dashing among the rude rocks; on the side of the hill, sheep feeding undismayed at the roaring of the sea and terror of its waves, and shepherds tending their flocks. Our next scene was a second amphitheatre, diversified with amazing rocks, and the pillars and loose stones which are peculiar to this place, the entrance guarded on one side by a range of rocky mountains, and on the other two pyramidal mountains of a singular form. From that point we walked round the semicircle that forms the second amphitheatre on a precipice that was very formidable indeed, persuaded by our guides that the lower way was not practicable; but D.D. was not so ambitious, and kept the low way on the rocky strand, and had the advantage of us, as our path led us a great way about, and was so frightful that we could not look about us. However, we got safely to the part that is called 'the Causeway', which forms a point into the sea, and begins the third amphitheatre; this contains the greatest quantity of the pillars, some so very exact and smooth that you would imagine they were all chiselled with the greatest care. After gazing, wondering, and I may say *adoring* the wondrous Hand that formed this amazing work, we began to find ourselves fatigued. Our gentlemen found out a well-sheltered place, where we sat very commodiously by a well (called the Giant's Well) of as fine sweet water as any at Calwich, and cold mutton and tongue refreshed us extremely after three hours' walking, climbing, and stumbling among the rocks.

I took an imperfect sketch of the place, which if I can make anything of you shall have a copy. Mrs Drury, who took the draughts (of which you have the prints), lived three months near the place, and went almost every day. I can do nothing so exact and finished; in the last amphitheatre facing the entrance, about half-way up the side of the rocky mountain, the pillars are placed in such a form as to resemble an organ: you will see it in one of Mrs Drury's prints.

What is called the Causeway is a most wonderful composition of pillars, which in some part form a mosaic pavement, in others appear like the basement of pillars; but when you are on the strand below, then you see they are all pillars closely fitted to each other, though the angles vary; they chiefly consist of hexagons. The sun shone part of the time and shewed the place to great perfection, but we had a sprinkling shower or two that made us wrap up in my brother's good lambswool cloaks, and shelter ourselves under some of the rocks.

Whilst we were at our repast our attendants were differently grouped, at some distance on the left hand the servants, a little below us women and children that gathered sea-weed and shells for us, about twelve in number; with very little light drapery; on the right hand men that were our guides, of different ages, seated on the points of the rocks, whose figures were very droll, and I believe we ourselves were no less so: eagerly devouring our morsel, and every now and then a violent exclamation of wonder at some new observation. We sat just facing a most aspiring pyramidal hill, and whilst we were there a shepherd drove his flock to the summit of it, and they looked like so many little white specks; the shepherd stood for some minutes on the highest point of the rock. I don't know how to give you a clear idea of this place, such as it appeared to me, and shall only make what I have said already, confused should I say more.

from *The Autobiography and Correspondence of Mary Granville, Mrs Delany*

THE BENEVOLENT MR SKELTON

THE REVEREND SAMUEL BURDY

The strict attention that Mr Skelton paid to the duties of his profession prevented his being engaged in the softer concerns of human life. I question if he ever was really in love, though it is allowed he had a variety of sweethearts. He seems indeed to have been proof against the fascinating charms of the fair, whose gentle weapons have conquered the greatest heroes and philosophers and made them submit to their yoke. Monaghan was the scene of his loves, and possibly a short account of these may not be unentertaining to my readers.

He was once courting a young lady, and when they were just on the point of being married, she said to him one day, 'my dear, as you are but a poor curate, how will you provide for our children?' 'Why my love,' he answered, 'suppose we have three sons, I'll make one of them a weaver, another a taylor, and the third a shoemaker, very honest trades my jewel, and thus they may earn their bread by their industry.' 'Oh!' she replied, 'never will I bring forth children for such mean occupations.' 'Well then,' said he, 'I have no other expectations, and of consequence you and I will not be joined together, for between your pride and his poverty poor Phil. Skelton will never be racked.' Thus the match was broke off. . . .

He seemed indeed once to have had an ardent passion for a Miss Richardson, for in his eagerness to see her, he rode across the lake of Coothill in the great frost, without perceiving he was riding on ice. However, we may suppose his fondness soon began to cool. His being a curate, I should think, made him cautious of plunging too deep into love. He knew that marriage must have confined him still more in his charities, which were always nearest to his heart; unless he could get a good fortune by it, a boon seldom conferred on one of his station. He therefore strove to keep down his passions by abstinence, and lived for two years at Monaghan entirely on vegetables. . . .

In 1741, he published the *Necessity of Tillage and Granaries in a Letter to a Member of Parliament*. . . . In this letter he shows by the strongest

71

arguments the excellence of agriculture over pasturage, advising the gentleman of fortune, from motives of private interest, to encourage the one in preference to the other. As a consequence of the neglect of tillage, and the want of public granaries, he takes notice of a horrible famine that prevailed in this country for the two years before he published his letter. 'It was computed, that as many people died of want, or of disorders occasioned by it, during that time, as fell by the sword in the massacre and rebellion of forty one. Whole parishes in some places were almost desolate; the dead were eaten in the fields by dogs for want of people to bury them.' A shocking picture of national calamity. . . .

In the same year he published, in the transactions of the Royal Society, a piece entitled a *Curious Production of Nature*. It gives an account of the great number of caterpillars, that crawled (in 1737) on some trees in the county of Monaghan, leaving behind them a fine silken web on the bark of the trees. Some of these continued for two years, but were mostly all destroyed by the frost in the terrible winter of forty. Many distempers, he imagined, are owing to invisible insects. . . .

In Pettigo the greater number of the inhabitants were poor catholics living in wretched hovels among barren rocks and heath; of whom there were many real objects of charity, that required the assistance of the humane. In such a place the benevolent disposition of Mr Skelton found full room for exercise; and I may safely say, that no human breast ever had more genuine charity than his. His wonderful acts of goodness will be remembered for ages in that remote corner of the North, and be transmitted from father to son for successive generations. . . .

The want of rational company seemed to add to the natural gloominess of the place. Pettigo he called Siberia, and said he was banished to it from all civilised society. I heard him often declare, he was forced to ride seven miles before he could meet with a person of common sense to converse with. He found it necessary, in his own defence, to take frequent excursions to hear some rational conversation, and to get rid for a while of the illiterate people of Pettigo, whose lingo was constantly dinned in his ears. Sir James Caldwell, Dr Scott, Rev. Dr Mc.Donnel, Rev. Mr Wallace, and some other clergy of the diocess of Clogher, were the persons he used generally to visit.

Plunket, with whom he lodged, could give him but one room with an earthen floor where he slept and studied; in which he had a screen or curtain so fixed that he could let it down upon occasions to conceal his bed. Here Sir James Caldwell, and other gentlemen of the country, have dined with him; for he was always fond of polished society. His chief meal at that time was his dinner, as he ate but little breakfast, and no supper; a sort of abstinence he found requisite to keep his passions in due order. He was for the same reason equally abstemious in sleep as in food; for he took but four hours sleep, and passed the rest of the night in prayer and meditation. Being at that time unhappily afflicted with religious melancholy, to which many good men are liable, he was seized with doubts about his salvation, and in the middle of the night often fell a crying, imagining he should be damned, he was so sinful a creature. While he was in these gloomy fits, he used to raise the man of the house out of his bed, and beg of him to waken the rest of the family, that he and they might pray with him, as he stood in need of all good christians' prayers, his case was so desperate. . . . He was also at that time . . . more liable to the hips, imagining often that he was just on the point of death. One day he told his servant that his hour was approaching, and his thread of life spent, and desired him to get the horses ready, that he might go to Dr Scott's and die there. The servant obeyed; but when he got a short way on the road, he began to whistle and sing, and said he was happy. The ride, it is to be supposed, helped to raise his spirits, an effect which it is often able to produce. . . .

Another time, while these plaguey hips were on him, and he was telling the people about him, that he was just going to die, one Robert Johnston of Pettigo who was present said to him, 'make a day, Sir, and keep it, and don't be always disappointing us thus.' This made him laugh, and shook off his disorder. It may be remarked, that all this tends to degrade the person whose life I write; but in my opinion it only shows, that he had his own peculiarities, to which great characters are in general more subject than ordinary men.

The private stills in the parish of Pettigo being at that time innumerable, made the whiskey cheap and plenty, which caused the people to be addicted to drunkenness, a vice among others prevalent there. The catholics, who were most numerous, were chiefly remarkable for this;

though the protestants, as they called themselves, were but little better. At burials in particular, to which they flocked from all quarters, they drank most shamefully. It was the custom then with them, as soon as the corpse was buried, to meet all in a field adjacent to the churchyard, and pour whiskey, like cold water, down their throats. . . . In 1757, a remarkable dearth prevailed in Ireland; the effects of which were felt most severely in the rough and barren lands of Pettigo. Mr Skelton went out into the country to discover the real state of his poor, and travelled from cottage to cottage over mountains, rocks, and heath. . . . One day, when he was travelling in this manner through the country, he came to a lonely cottage in the mountains, where he found a poor woman lying in child bed with a number of children about her. All she had, in her weak helpless condition, to keep herself alive and her children, was blood and sorrel boiled up together. The blood, her husband, who was a herd, took from the cattle of others under his care, for he had none of his own. This was a usual sort of food in that country, in times of scarcity; for they bled the cows for that purpose, and thus the same cow often afforded both milk and blood. Mr Skelton tasted the odd mixture, the only cordial the poor woman had to strengthen her in her feeble state. His tender heart being touched at the sight, he went home immediately, and sent her a hundred of meal, a pound of brown sugar, and a bottle of brandy. He then visited her every second day in her cot among the mountains, bestowing on her such comforts as seemed requisite, until she recovered.

At that time, he and Jonas Good, the strong man, regulated Pettigo market on a Monday, standing among the meal-sacks, each of them with a huge club in his hand, and covered over with meal. They were obliged then, when the carriers were bringing the meal to Pettigo, to guard it with their clubs, as the people of the adjacent parishes strove to take it by force, and eat it themselves; in which they sometimes succeeded; for hunger makes people desperate.

from *The Life of the Late Reverend Philip Skelton*, 1792

A Rebel Parrot

652. MRS M. MCTIER to DR WM. DRENNAN at Dublin.

[1797] Mar. 17 [Belfast]. – 'Murders and assassinations are dreadful subjects, but common here, and the natural consequence of what I often witness – men torn from their friends and country, put on board a tender without trial, or anyone here at least knowing for what. The higher officers are well liked, and do not seem to relish the searching business. . . . The country people treat the officers well, ask them to breakfast, etc., and give them old, rusty guns. . . . They shall never get Sam McTier's gun. . . .

Whatever you may think of Belfast in Dublin, people are flocking to it from the country, and even Government country squires, where can they go without money? Londonderry, it is said, is going to sneak into Newtown[ards] after being guarded by soldiers all the winter at Mount Stewart. His father seldom bolted his windows. Not a penny of rent is paid him. The Bank is no more, and Hamilton out of the yeomen. Smith, his son, fled from Pine Hill, which is in the possession of Lisburn yeomen, otherwise Orangemen, who are destroying the property of its very loyal master. He, therefore, soon leaves his corps. . . .

Vance has been twice applied to to become a Un[ited] I[rishman], but declined. He has now, I know, sought for it, and several days have passed without an answer to his request. He told me he would soon take his ground, the rather, perhaps, that Bruce treated him ill, in agreeing not to pledge themselves, and the very next day took the Yeoman's Oath without informing him. See, then, how these brotherly characters now stand. Do not, however, mention this, though becoming a United Irishman is now little concealed. . . .

Men are brought in daily to be put on board the tender. One was taken from his house yesterday, where Mr Magee was getting some work done. The only reason, a piece of an ash tree in his loft. On the quay a decent man who was seeing others shipped off was asked, "What has that man now going done?" "Nothing," replied the other, "but lived in peace and union with his neighbour. I have the honour of being his father." A day of dreadful retribution is at hand. There were great fears for Patrick's night. The justices met, and Barber came from Dublin in time to come on service the generals certainly do not relish. . . . The Marquis of Downshire was at a ball at Purdysburn the other night, where he looked like the Devil, and I heard it said he owed his life to a mistake in the hour of leaving it. . . . He leads a dreadful life, and here without any domestic comfort.' 12 *pp*.

653. THE SAME to THE SAME at Dublin.

[1797] Mar. 29 [Belfast]. – 'One would think the power of the proclamation sufficient for any purpose in a town where I can walk from one end to the other without a servant at 9 o'clock; yet I have reason to believe other strong measures are hatching and will be enforced whenever the town is got out of the peace. At present Lake (a good man) is responsible. Next week it is thought any officer may command to any service, and the *Star* Office, I suspect, will be a third time stormed. The officers, I believe, in general behave well and hate their present degrading service. Indeed, a stranger entering the town would be struck by the sounds of innocence, for the children are eternally crying "ba-ee ma-ee" – after every yeoman, while the mothers run after them crying if they do not behave themselves they will be put on board the Fleet.

Lord Templeton is come over. . . . This young man declares he is come here to learn the true state of the country, that neither soldiers or yeomen shall be on his estate, and that he will stand or fall with the people.' 3½ *pp*.

658. THE SAME to THE SAME at Dublin.

[1797, about Mar., Belfast]. – Marriage settlement discussed. Perjury and acquittals at Armagh. 'God grant Antrim may do as well, for, in despite of all parties, this is no time for executions. I am told there has not one taken place for years among the soldiers. Mr Skeffington has received an anonymous letter, written, as he says, by no vulgar hand, approving of his conduct and impartiality hitherto, and desiring him to continue it, for, if he dared to pack a jury, his blood should answer it. The Marquis is gone away, as it is said, to take possession of an estate left him in England of

5,000 a year. In his absence Castlereagh doubles his diligence and men crowd the tender.

Lady H. Skeffington has a favourite parrot, on whose education the servants having bestowed some pains, and General Lake noticing him, he squalled out, "*Are you up*," on which Her Ladyship, sorrowing, remarked that the people had made him an UI man while he was at her country house.' . . . 5 *pp.*

661. THE SAME to THE SAME at Dublin.

1797, May [19] [postmark 22] Belfast. – 'A party of the Monaghan M[ilitia] attacked the [*Northern*] *Star* Office this morning, gutted it, threw out the money from the windows, destroyed all the books, types, papers, etc., by which a property of many thousands may be lost. No magistrate, no officer, the offence, refusing to print the part of their advertisement reflecting on the town, with risk of their lives. Some of the men belonging to the office stayed in it long enough to identify the actors. . . .

The Committee make up now for the insipidity of their former sitting, and I look forward to the destruction of the town and sudden flight to the fields. I have bespoke a chaise for my mother and Miss Young, and thank my God I can foot it. . . .

I am of no other society except the Lying-In H[ospital], nor know of no other female one in this town.

The papers found here are wonderful, and I am told the U[nited] I[rishmen] say since papers were to be found, they are sorry they were not the last returns, which have added much to their number by being that of two months instead of one. You will see the *public* meeting of the County Down is given up by a bullying conversation of the Lord C[astlereagh] with Ward, his brother-in-law. He then declared he would break every mag[istra]t[e] in the county and then let them see if they would call a rabble into the fields of a proclaimed county. Ward wrote then to Dr Haliday, and the squires resigned. . . . Could one get to Switzerland?' 2½ *pp.*

662. DR WM. DRENNAN to MRS M. MCTIER at Belfast.

[1797, about May] Friday [Dublin]. – 'You seem unreasonably terrified at the riot of the Militia. Their passions might have been as easily moved in some opposite direction. I should have wished you had given me some account of the procession to the camp. It must certainly have made deep impression on the spectators. I hear the Highlanders refused to be employed and said "Let Irish kill Irish." This was bitter, and might be versified –

> When bid to take aim at the Irishman's heart,
> The stout Caledonian recoiled with a start –
> "The first o' my country, the first o' my clan,
> E'er order'd to fire on a blindfolded man.
> You'll find fitter tools to perform sic a deed;
> And by Irish hands, let the Irish bleed.
> In the spirit of Cain, let them murder each ither
> And the United fall by his United brither."
> So spoke the indignant and high-minded Scot.
> As a soldier he'd serve, as a hangman would not.
> But the Irish went first, and the Irish went last,
> And, guarded by Irish, the prisoners passed,
> On their coffins knelt down, took a silent farewell.
> The United then fired, and the United fell.

Mum!

They are taking the lower kind of people up by dozens, selecting some for the tender and letting the rest escape, and I suppose this kind of man-hunting will soon come upon the higher ranks, if they be assembled at dinner or supper in any unusual number. The yeomanry mount a real guard of duty every night, and the Lord Lieutenant visited them the night before last at 12 o'clock as a compliment, I suppose, for though his looks be sufficiently military, I question much whether his mind be so, and if Lord Cornwallis is to come over, as is confidently reported, the military half of the lieutenancy will, it is likely, supersede the civil. . . . You could more readily get to B[otany] Bay than Switzerland. It is the very centre and kernel of Europe, with the hard, stony Alps enveloping it, and my mother and Mrs [*sic*] Young could scarcely go over these mountains in a chaise or you afoot. . . .' 2 *pp.*

665. THE SAME to THE SAME at Belfast.

1797, June 10, Dublin. – 'Several aristocrats have been mentioning your name as being a very busy woman in Belfast at present, and that you should take care of yourself, as you were supposed to write for the *Northern Star* while in existence. . . .

We are all gaping here for news from the Fleet. I should wish liberty to come from any quarter, rather than mutiny or desertion of duty, either among sailors or soldiers, and I think Sheridan's conduct magnanimous, though it endangers his popularity among democrats.' 1½ *pp*.

666. MRS M. MCTIER to DR WM. DRENNAN at Dublin.

1797, June 16, Belfast. – 'Except an advertisement for the Union School, and one paper on *its* cause, . . . I never penned a single line for a newspaper in my life. . . .

I know of no Society of United I[rish] women.' 3½ *pp*.

668. THE SAME to THE SAME at Dublin.

[1797] July 7 [Belfast]. – 'We escaped the 1st of July. The 12th is now held out as a night of terror, for which great preparations are making, and the body of Orangemen to be reviewed by General Lake are so great that it is said part only appear in this town in the morning and he meets the rest, 1,500, at Lurgan. *A review of Orangemen!* . . .

The people left to *choose this time* whether to illuminate or not.' Uneasiness at naming of military without much respect in letters meant to be private. 'I heard that Lake asked Barber the other day what news. "Very bad, by G–d" was the reply, "three spies and not a sixpence to pay them." Some way or other, the system must fall.' . . . 3½ *pp*.

from *The Drennan Letters*

79

ORANGE LILIES AND BLEACH GREENS

JOHN GAMBLE

Banbridge.

I walked to Loughbrickland, a distance of eight miles, yesterday, before breakfast. The morning was beautiful – the hedges were blooming with the flower of the hawthorn – the air was loaded with fragrance – I could have fancied myself in Elysium, had I not met numbers of yeomen in every direction. They were in general good looking men; and were well and uniformly dressed. They all wore orange lilies. I now recollected that it was the 12th of July; (the 30th of June, old style,) and of consequence the anniversary of the battle of the Boyne.

I entered into conversation with a little group, who were travelling my road. They were very desirous to have my opinion of the Catholic Bill, as they called it, that is expected to be brought forward next Session of Parliament.

'Never mind acts of parliament, my lads,' said I, 'but live peaceably with your neighbours. I warrant you your fields will look as green, and your hedges smell as sweet this time next year, whether the bill passes or not.'

'May be so,' said one of them; 'and may be we wouldn't be long here to smell or look at them.'

I made little reply to this, for I could not expect that any thing I should urge would weaken even the rooted prejudices of their lives. What I did reply they heard with respect, though not with conviction.

'Ah, reverend Sir,' said a middle-aged man, 'you speak like a good man and a great scholar; but, Lord love ye, books won't make us know life.'

'Tell me,' said I, 'why you take me for a clergyman; is it because I wear a black coat?'

'No,' returned he, 'but because you have a moderate face.'

The lower class of people in Ireland are great physiognomists – good ones, I am bound to suppose, for my face has often received the above moderate compliment. It speaks favourably, however, of the manner of

80

the Irish Protestant clergy, that a man of mild demeanour is almost always taken for one of them.

Loughbrickland consists of one broad street. It takes its name from a lake standing near it, called Loughbrickland, or the lake of speckled trouts, with which it formerly abounded, till the spawn of pikes finding a passage into the lake, multiplied so exceedingly, that they have almost destroyed the whole breed.

That body of English forces which were quartered in this part of the north, in the year 1690, had their first rendezvous here under King William, who encamped within a mile of the town.

Nearly at the same distance from it I turned off the great road to go to Tanderagee. I passed a number of gentlemen's seats. I was struck with their uncommon neatness. I asked a countryman if he could tell me the reason. He knew no reason, he said, except that the owners were not *born* gentlemen.

Much of the landed property of this part of the country has passed from the extravagant children of idleness, to the sons of the thrifty merchants of Newry and Belfast. I find, in general, they are good landlords.

I passed likewise through several villages, and a sweet little town called Acton. It was built by a Mr Stewart, who calculated on making it a great market, which would benefit the neighbourhood, and enrich himself. Projectors in general are bad logicians, and Robinson Crusoe's boat is a kind of foolscap that will fit most of them. The neighbourhood was not benefited, but he was ruined.

I came in sight of Tanderagee about two o'clock. As it is situated on a hill, I saw it at a considerable distance. The planting of the late General Sparrow's extensive demesne, which seemed to overshadow it, gave it a gay and picturesque appearance. Nor was the spectacle of the interior less riant. Only that the bright green of nature was displaced by the deep orange of party. Tanderagee was a perfect orange grove. The doors and windows were decorated with garlands of the orange lily. The bosoms and heads of the women, and hats and breasts of the men, were equally adorned with this venerated flower. There were likewise a number of orange banners and colours, more remarkable for loyalty than taste or variety, for King William on horseback, as grim as a Saracen on a sign post, was painted or wrought on all of them.

There was much of fancy, however, in the decoration of a lofty arch, which was thrown across the entire street. The orange was gracefully blended with oak leaves, laurels, and roses. Bits of gilded paper, suited to the solemnity, were interwoven with the flowers. I passed, as well as I could, through the crowd assembled under this glittering rainbow, and proceeded to the house of an acquaintance at the upper end of the street. I had purposed spending a day with him, but he was from home. I, therefore, sat half an hour with his lady, and after having taken some refreshment, descended the hill. The people were now dancing. The music was not indifferent. The tune, however, would better have suited a minuet than a country dance. It was the (once in England) popular tune of Lillybullero, better known, in this country, by the affectionate and cheering name, of the Protestant boys.

I stopped an instant, a man came up and presented me a nosegay of orange lilies and roses, bound together – I held it in my hand, but did not put it in my hat, as he expected.

'I am no party man,' I said, 'nor do I ever wear party colours.'

Nor did the crowd, who heard both the speech and reply, appear to take the slightest offence. This was the more wonderful as I stood before them rather under inauspicious circumstances. It seems, though I was then ignorant of it, the gentleman out of whose house they had seen me come, was highly obnoxious to them. He is minister of the Presbyterian congregation – a few months ago, with more liberality than prudence, considering what an untractable flock he is the shepherd of, he signed his name to the Protestant petition, in favour of the Catholics. The following Sunday he found his meeting-house closed against him, nor is it yet opened, and probably never will be.

The county of Armagh Presbyterians are the very Spadassins of Protestantism. Their unhappy disputes a few years ago with the Catholics are well known. It is, therefore unnecessary, (and I rejoice at it,) for me to touch on them here.

On quitting Tanderagee, I walked a little way on the road which I came. I then seated myself on the top of a little hill, to meditate on my future route. The world was all before me where to choose – and a most delightful world I had to choose from. Armagh is as much beautified by the industry, as it has been disfigured by the passions of men. . . .

I hardly know a more beautiful object than a bleach-green on a fine day. Mr C——'s is situated on the declivity of a hill, interspersed with trees, and watered by a pretty brook. The whiteness of the cloth presents a bright contrast to the greenness of the grass, while the murmuring stream excites the ideas of pastoral retirement rather than of the habitations of art. The manufacture of linen, may, indeed, be truly said to be a pastoral one. It is one of the most ancient, as it is one of the most beautiful. . . .

Woollen is the manufacture of art, and of commerce; linen, of nature, and of agriculture. In this country it still partakes of its origin; the weavers are likewise cultivators of the earth, and the great bleachers all reside in the country, and occupy considerable tracts of land. The weavers in consequence, are a hardy, vigorous, and virtuous race of men. The English manufacturers, I am concerned to remark, are generally the reverse in all these particulars. The fair face of nature is a volume, addressed by the Almighty to the heart of man; and when, by the nature of his occupation, he is debarred access to it, his affections become deadened; and his heart becomes corrupt.

The linen manufacture has been carried to the greatest extent it ever arrived at, in this province. Those who have been accustomed to stigmatise the Irish as indolent and lazy, will think it strange to be told that by indefatigable industry they have made their manufacture the second greatest in the world – for only to the woollen manufacture of England, is it second. It has been supposed that the linen manufacture is not a beneficial one, because Ireland is a poor country – but the conclusion does not follow, even granting it to be a fact that Ireland is so. The wealth of Mexico did not make Spain rich, because her out-goings were equal to her in-comings – that manufacture must, surely, be a beneficial one, which, confined to a single province, enables Ireland to pay England such an immense sum in taxes, pensions, and, above all, in the entire income nearly of all the great landlords which is spent in England.

This trade is said to be of great antiquity in Ireland. The Phœnicians, about twelve hundred years before the Christian Æra, planted colonies at Carthage and Cadiz, whence, according to the Irish historians, they passed into Ireland, and brought with them, among other useful inventions, the spindle and loom. However that may be, acts of Parliament, passed in the reign of Henry the Eighth, prove that linen was a very considerable article of commerce, at that time in Ireland. In the reign of Charles the First, Lord Stafford adopted the most effectual measures for the encouragement of the linen manufacture, and in 1673, Sir William Temple asserts, that if the spinning of flax were encouraged, the Irish would soon beat both the French and Dutch out of the English market. In that year England imported linen from France to the amount of half a million. At the revolution, however, the importation of French linen was declared a common nuisance in the Parliaments of the three kingdoms, and finally suppressed. In 1698, the woollen manufacture had taken such deep root in Ireland, as to excite the jealousy of the English to such a degree, that both houses of Parliament addressed King William on the subject, beseeching him to take effectual measures to discourage the woollen manufacture in Ireland, and promising, in this case, every encouragement to the manufacture of linen. This stipulation was announced to the Irish Parliament by the Lords Justices in their speech from the throne. The two houses acquiesced, and this transaction has ever since been considered by the Irish, as a solemn compact between the two nations. The protection England has since afforded the linen manufacture, they regard, therefore, as a payment, not an obligation; a very inadequate payment they consider it for what they relinquished, for it is the nature of men to undervalue what they receive, as it is likewise to overrate what they give. . . .

Irish linen is made from the prepared stalk of a small round reddish coloured seed. The Irish do not rear their own flax-seed – formerly they imported it from Riga, the Low Countries, and America – of late years they could only have it from America. Where it is to come from the ensuing year, is here at present a subject of sorrowful consideration. The quantity annually consumed is about forty thousand hogsheads. Flax-seed is generally sown in April, and the flax pulled in August. Of the various operations it undergoes, watering flax is the most difficult, and the most disagreeable. It is a process of fermentation which requires the greatest attention – the proper period for stopping it, depends upon the temperature of the water, the substances with which it may be impregnated, and the degree of ripeness of the flax. The last operation flax undergoes is called dressing, after which it is delivered into the hands of the spinner.

The art of spinning was practised in the early ages with very simple instruments, the distaff and spindle – the distaff resembles a common walking stick, to one end of which a strike of flax is tied, the other end is fastened in the girdle of the spinner. The spindle is a small, round, wooden instrument, about sixteen inches long, thick at the middle, and small at each end, resembling the spindle of a large wheel for spinning wool. The operator begins by twisting a thread by hand, from the flax on the distaff, fastening it to the spindle, and giving it a rotatory motion with the fingers, which twists the thread. The motion thus given did not long overcome the resistance of the air, and of the thread. The wheel, therefore, was added to the spindle – which operated by causing the motion to continue longer, and more regularly, as a fly-wheel does in more complicated machinery.

Some wheels were of wood, but they were generally of stone, very well turned; from the great number of them found in the ground of this country, it is concluded this method of spinning was commonly in use in it; it is even now practised by some old women here, and in the Western Isles. The rim of the Irish spinning wheel (as it is mostly used at present) is of oak perfectly turned, twenty inches' diameter. The spokes are of the same, or of some other heavy wood, which causes it to act both as a fly and a wheel; one end of the axis is formed as a crank, which the spinner moves with the foot. The right hand is left free, and at liberty occasionally to assist the left, in letting down the thread. As the distaff and spindle were the first utensils used in spinning, and the motion was given to the spindle, and to the ancient wheels with the right hand, the left became the spinning hand universally. Many attempts have been made within these few years, to teach girls to spin with both hands at the same time, but as far as I have learned, without success.

Spinning flax has been brought to such perfection in Ulster, that many girls spin so fine, that twenty hanks, and sometimes thirty, weigh only one pound. A young woman in Comber, in the county of Down, a descendant of the ancient family of M'Quillin, in the county of Antrim, spins so fine, that sixty-four hanks weigh only one pound; each thread round the reel is two and a half yards long, one hundred and twenty threads in each cut, twelve cuts in each hank. A specimen of her spinning was sent to the linen board, for which she received a small premium; she spins this fine yarn only in summer. She fixes, I understand, a black cloth behind the thread, and often divides the fibres of the flax with a needle.

The looms mostly in use, resemble a bedstead upon a large scale, with six posts. The posts, which correspond to the head-posts of a bed, connect the whole frame, support the seat of the workman, and the breast-board over which the wrought cloth is strained as it passes to the cloth beam. Looms on an improved plan are made with two long head-posts only, and four short posts, which support that part of the frame on which the ends of the yard-beam rest; – on this part of the frame two wooden slides are placed, on which the workman lays the ends of the yarn-beam, and slides it on these to a proper distance for one dressing.

Cambrics, lawns, and diapers, or damask, as they are more frequently called, are likewise manufactured from flax. The damask invented at Damascus, was silk cloth ornamented with flowers in their natural colours, thrown up in it by the workmen in the loom. The damask of Ulster is fine linen, with flowers or other figures woven in it, all of the same colour as the rest of the piece – it does not shew the figures by the colours being different from the ground, but by reflecting the rays of light more perfectly.

Damask looms are on the same plan as those generally used, but much larger and stronger. Some of them are furnished with five thousand sets of pullies, which support as many threads, on each of which a loop resembling a heddle is formed – to the lower end of each a lead weight, like thick wire, is suspended. The threads of the warp intended to form the pattern, are drawn through the loops – when one of these is pulled up, it draws up the weight, and the thread of the warp in its loop, out of the shade formed by the common heddles, so that it cannot be drawn by them to the lower part of the common shade.

The method of drawing up the threads of the warp, so as to correspond perfectly with any painted flower or figure, is very curious. The figure is first drawn with a transparent colour, upon paper, divided by engraved lines into squares, each side of which is about half an inch – these sides are sub-divided by finer lines, into ten parts – thus, each of the larger squares is divided into a hundred smaller. This figure-paper is laid upon a desk – and opposite to it, on the other side of the desk, is a frame of cords, which pass through a reed, like warp in a loom – these cords or threads correspond with the lines on the design, or pattern paper. A man sits on each side of the desk – he who sits on the same side with the pattern-paper, tells off the squares as he sees them covered with the colour. The person who sits at the side of the desk on which the frame of cords is fixed, has a very long coarse needle threaded, which he passes in a horizontal direction, through the threads or cords in the reed, raising some of them, and depressing others, as he may be directed by the person at the opposite side of the desk, who tells off the squares as he sees them covered with the colour of the pattern. This is done as often as there are ranges of squares in the depth of the design-paper. The threads thus darned into the cords passed through the reed, are allowed to continue as lay-bands. When all the squares in the pattern are thus told off, the cords with the lay-bands between them, are taken out of the reed, and attached to the small cords, which have loops in them like heddles, with lead weights suspended to them, and which are passed over pullies, fixed above the loom. The other ends of the pattern-cords are fixed to the still of the loom. When a thread of the warp designed to form a part of the figure, is passed through a loop of one of the perpendicular cords, and the cord drawn, this thread is raised above the general shade of the web. Five threads are drawn through each of these loops which take up as much space in the web as is between each of the small lines.

When the weaver or weavers have wrought to the part of the web where the pattern is to begin, a boy standing at the pattern-cords, passes a staff between them, as the cross threads, or lay-bands, were passed with the needle, and pulling it out fixes it to rests attached to the loom. The heddle-cords are thus pulled up, and the threads of the warp which have been passed through their loops are drawn out of that part of the warp which forms the common shade. Eight leaves of heddles next the workmen are attached to each loom, which are so contrived, that the weaver by treading one of the treddles attached to one of the heddles, depresses one eighth part of the threads from the body of the warp, raised by the draw-boy as he is called – and raises at the same time one eighth from that part of the warp which forms the lower side of the shade, and thus the figure is produced on both sides of the piece. When the boy takes away the staff, the lead weights draw down the cords and loops, and allow the warp which they raised to fall into the common shade. The boy, after a certain number of shots, passes the staff along another lay-band, and raises another part of the figure, in the same manner as at first.

The twill, which is formed on the ground and pattern, is of such texture, that the damask is stronger than any other description of linen. Although the warp and woof are of the same colour; yet, because the figure and the ground are differently woven, they reflect the rays of light differently – the figure resembling satin, generally reflects most rays; and, therefore, appears whiter than the ground. The patterns are as various and extensive, as the productions of the pencil in the hand of the painter. Rich centre-pieces, coats of arms, crests, and mottoes, are accurately delineated. The table-cloths are made from one yard and a half wide, to three yards and a quarter, sometimes twenty yards long, and of various degrees of fineness. The napkins are from five-eighths to a yard wide – the patterns wrought in them, correspond to the patterns of the cloths – if arms are wrought in these, the napkins are wrought with a correspondent crest or cypher in each. This elegant branch of the linen manufacture was introduced into Ireland about fifty years ago, by a person of the name of Coulson, and is now carried on at Lisburn by his sons, on the most improved and extensive scale.

Linen is purchased in its brown state by the bleachers. They have men employed for this purpose, who attend at fairs and markets. They have in general a salary of one hundred a year each, and a small allowance for keeping a horse. The fatigue these men undergo is extraordinary – some of them ride upwards of four thousand miles in the course of a year, which, considering the storm and severity of an Irish winter, is equivalent to six thousand in many other countries. In their robust frames and florid countenances, we perceive the favourable and benign influence of the open air on man, and how infinitely the advantage of almost constant exposure to it, counterbalances the slight inconveniences of cold and rain. A habit of riding in all weathers, is, I am persuaded, the most effectual means of strengthening the frame, and I should recommend every delicate person, whose avocations will permit it, (to make use of the words of Doctor Fuller,) to learn like a Tartar to live on horseback, by which means he will acquire in time the constitution of a Tartar. I have known several instances of young men, who appeared to have the strongest predisposition to consumption, and who, had they been put to sedentary employments, would, in all human probability, have lived a very short time, by the healthful fatigue of even severe riding, and long journies, become stout and vigorous men.

from *A View of Society and Manners in the North of Ireland*, 1813

RIBBONMEN AND ORANGEMEN

WILLIAM CARLETON

Of course it must not be supposed that I neglected to visit my mother and family during this period of absence. So far from that, I went home, I think, at least once a month, if not oftener. These visits sometimes lasted three or four days, and I not infrequently went to Clogher market on these occasions – feeling naturally anxious to see and meet many of my young friends, who were also anxious to see me. I may add here for once that there never was in that part of the country a young fellow more popular or better beloved by persons of all creeds and classes – by the Protestants as well as by the Catholics. On such occasions, however, my associates were generally of my own religion. During those reunions I was struck with one fact, for which I could not by any means account. These young fellows, and others, frequently looked with a very mysterious kind of inquiry into my face, and occasionally asked me what age I was. I generally replied, 'I'm in my nineteenth year,' upon which the expression of their faces became lengthened and indicative of disappointment. This puzzled me very much: I could not by any train of reasoning understand it. I now return to a particular visit I made to see my mother and other relations at Springtown. The day was Saturday, and the month either June or July, when, having started for home from Glasslough, a distance of at least sixteen miles across the country, which to me was nothing, I had arrived at the townland next to Springtown, named Caragh, immediately above which was a very pretty smooth eminence ending in a flat greensward. On this table-land I found there was a dance, in which was engaged a number of young men and women, with nearly every one of whom I was acquainted. It was not, I soon found, an ordinary dance, but what they call in the north an *infare*, or the haling home of a newly-married bride to the house of her husband, of which she is to be the future mistress. At these *infares*, there was generally such a dance as I found on the table on Cargah Hill, animated to a greater sense of enjoyment by plenty of excellent poteen whisky. Here I danced with the bride,

90

whom I looked upon for the first time, and several other girls with whom I was intimately acquainted. Even at this time I was celebrated as a dancer. After my last dance was concluded, I stood to observe the progress of the general amusement, when I observed the young fellows getting together into knots and looking at me as if I had been the subject of their conversation. Before this period the bridegroom had forced me to take two glasses of the poteen, which, as I was not in the habit of drinking anything in the shape of spirits, had got a very little into my head. They offered me a third glass, which I refused, lest my mother might observe the signs of drink upon me. After some time, about half a dozen of them were led behind a dry green ditch by a red-haired fellow named Hugh Roe McCahy, who lived in the townland of Cloghleim, not half a mile distant. He was one of those important individuals who make themselves active and prominent among their fellows, attend dances and wakes, are seldom absent in fair or market from a fight, and, I may add, lose no opportunity of giving rise to one when everything else fails them.

'William,' said he, 'aren't you ashamed to be ignorant of what is going on about you over the whole country?' He had a prayer-book, or what is called a *manual* , a book of Roman Catholic devotion, in his hand as he spoke – a fact which greatly puzzled me, as I was perfectly aware that he could not read. I had once before this, while book-hunting throughout the neighbourhood, called upon him and found in his house an odd volume of Catholic theology in Latin. The fellow was rapid in his language as well as in his personal motions.

'Why,' said I, 'what is going on in the country?'

'I will tell you,' he replied; 'but first take this *manual* in your hand, and repeat after me what I will say.'

He then went over the oath of Ribbonism, which he had got by heart, until he concluded it; after this he made me kiss the book.

'Now,' said he, 'you're *up* – you're a Ribbonman; all you want is the words and signs – and here they are.'

He then communicated them to me, and, although but a schoolboy, I went home a Ribbonman.

Here was a new view of life opened to me, and that with such dexterous rapidity, that I found myself made a member of a secret and illegal society by this adroit scoundrel, before I had time to pause or reflect upon the consequences. In like manner were hundreds, nay thousands, of unreflecting youths seduced into this senseless but most mischievous system.

I now discovered that the whole Catholic population, with the exception of the aged heads of families, was affiliated to Ribbonism. In fact it was not only almost impossible, but dangerous, to avoid being involved in the system. If a young man happened to possess the sense and spirit to resist the Ribbonmen's importunities to join them, he would probably be waylaid and beaten by persons of whom he knew nothing.

The following is the Ribbon oath, a curiosity in its way:

'I, A.B., with the sign of the Cross do declare and promise, in the name and through the assistance of the Blessed Trinity, that I will keep inviolate all secrets of this Fraternal Society from all but those whom I know to be regular members of the same, and bound by the same solemn oath and fraternal ties:

'1st. I declare and profess, without any compulsion, allegiance to his present Majesty, George the Third, King of Great Britain and Ireland.

'2nd. That I will be true to the principles of this Society, dedicated to St Patrick, the Holy Patron of Ireland, in all things lawful and not otherwise.

'3rd. That I will duly and regularly attend on the shortest possible notice, at any hour, whether by night or by day, to perform, *without fail or inquiry*, such commands as my superior or superiors may lay upon me, under whatever penalty he or they may inflict for neglecting the same.

'4th. I will not deliberately or willingly provoke, challenge or strike any of my brothers, knowing him to be such. If he or they should be ill spoken of, ill-used, or otherwise treated unjustly, I will, according to circumstances and the best of my judgment, espouse his cause, give him the earliest information, and aid him with my friendship when in distress as a Ribbonman.

'5th. I also declare and promise, that I will not admit or propose a Protestant or heretic of any description as a member of our Fraternal Society, knowing him to be such.

'6th. That, whether in fair or market, in town or country, I will always give the preference in dealing to those who are attached to our national cause, and that I will not deal with a Protestant or heretic – but above all with an Orangeman – so long as I can deal with one of my own faith upon equal terms.

92

'7th. That I will not withdraw myself from this Society without stating my reasons for the same, and giving due notice to my superior or superiors; and that I will not without permission join any other society of different principles or denominations, under penalty of God's judgment, and whatever penalty may be inflicted on me – not including in these the Masonic Institution, Trade Societies, or the profession of soldier or sailor.

'8th. That I will always aid a brother in distress or danger by my person, purse, and counsel so far as in me lies; and I will not refuse to subscribe money, according to my means, for the general or particular purposes of this our Fraternal Society.

'9th. That I will not, under the penalty inflicted by my superiors, give evidence in any Court of Law or Justice against a brother, when prosecuted by an Orangeman or heretic; and that I will aid him in his defence by any means in my power.

'10th. That when forced to take refuge from the law in the house of a brother or of any person friendly to our national cause, I will not have any improper intercourse or foul freedom with his sister, daughter, wife or cousin, and thus give cause of scandal to our Society.

'Having made the above solemn declaration and promise of my own free will and accord, I swear true and real allegiance to the cause of Ireland only, and no longer to be true as a subject nor to bear allegiance to George the Third, King of Great Britain and Ireland; and I now pray that God may assist me in my endeavours to fulfil the same; that He may protect me and prosper our Society, and grant us to live and die in a state of grace! – Amen.'

I may as well give what were then the 'Words' and the 'Grip', as I am on this subject. The words were as follows: *'What age are we in?'* Answer. *'The end of the fifth.' 'What's the hour?'* Answer. *'Very near the right one.' 'Isn't it come yet?'* Answer. *'The hour is come, but not the man.' 'When will he come?'* Answer. *'He is within sight.'*

The grip was, when shaking hands, to press the point of the thumb on the second joint of the forefinger, and if the person with whom you shook hands was a brother, he was to press upon the middle joint of your little finger. Such were the words and grip of Ribbonism about the year 1814.

The reader will observe that there was a vagueness and a want of object in this ridiculous oath which gave conclusive evidence that it must have proceeded from a very ignorant source. I subsequently made inquiries into its origin, but could never ascertain the name of any man possessed of the slightest claim to respectability in connection with it. It originated with, and was confined to, the very lowest dregs of the people. That some scheming vagabonds must have been at the head of it, or the bottom of it, is evident enough. Money was subscribed for fictitious objects, but where it went to no one could tell. In the county Louth it was set going by an Orangeman called Gubby (evidently an assumed name), and I think it was afterwards discovered that he was a native of Middleton, in that part of the county Tyrone which projects into the county of Armagh. This discovery, however, was made too late – for he had left the country.

I am not a friend to any of these secret societies, because they were nothing but curses to the country. The Orange system is a curse to the country, and will be so as long as it exists. It is now comparatively harmless, but at the period of which I write it was in the very height of its ascendancy, and seemed to live only as if its great object were to trample upon 'Popery'. The truth, however, is, if there can be an apology for Ribbonism, that it was nothing more nor less than a reactive principle against Orangeism, of whose outrages it was the result. In my works I have depicted both systems to the marrow, without either favour or affection, as the phrase has it. I never entertained any ill feeling against the people on either side; it is their accursed systems which I detest. . . .

Having shown how I was made a Ribbonman, and stated that it was actually impossible to live safely in the country without joining the society, I must add a few words more upon the subject before I dismiss it for the present. I have said that the evening on which I had the honour of being admitted as a member of the society was that of Saturday, and as I made my visit home, on this occasion but a short one, I resolved to be present in my class on the following Monday morning. I accordingly made my appearance there at the proper hour. On that day I made a discovery which surprised me not a little. Frank McGough and John McNally – both have been dead for more than half a century – and myself were walking in the chapel yard. . . . I don't recollect what the topic of our discourse was, but I remember that McGough, looking me severely in the face, said –

'William, are you a good historian?'

'The worst in the world,' I replied, 'I never read a line of history in my life.'

'You don't know, then, what age we are in?'

'Oh, yes, I do,' I returned, 'in the end of the fifth.'

'Well, as to time – what's the hour?'

'Very near the right one.'

'Isn't it come yet?'

'The hour is come, but not the man.'

'When will he come?'

'He is within sight.'

We then shook hands and gave the grip, and McNally, who was also a member, joined us. The reader may thus judge of the hold which Ribbonism had upon the lower classes of society, when it wrought its way into the schools. This, however, he will not wonder at, when he is told that there was scarcely a Lodge schoolmaster in Ireland who did not 'hold articles', or in other words, who was not master of a Ribbon Lodge. . . .

Now that I am on this subject, I cannot forbear to mention an event connected with, and resulting from, the combined influence of these two accursed systems – Orangeism and Ribbonism. In point of time, it occurred at least four or five years previous to the occasion on which I was seduced into Ribbonism. There is in my 'Traits and Stories of the Irish Peasantry', a full and historical detail of it under the name of 'The Party Fight and Funeral'. In other words, it was the greatest battle that ever took place in the North of Ireland between the two parties. The reader need not expect me to describe it here, because I have done it at full length elsewhere. It occurred in the Lammas fair of Clogher, and never since that terrible day was the town of Clogher crowded with such vast numbers of people.

Such a fight, or I should rather say battle – for so in fact it was – did not take place in a state of civil society – if I can say so – within the last century in this country. The preparations for it were being made secretly for two or three months previous to its occurrence, and however it came to light, it so happened that each party became cognizant of the designs of the other. This conflict, of which I was an eye-witness – on my way home from school, being then about fourteen years of age – was such as never had a parallel. The reader may form an idea of the bitterness and ferocity with which it was fought on both sides, when he is informed that the Orangemen on the one side, and the Ribbonmen on the other, had called in aid from the surrounding counties of Monaghan, Cavan, Fermanagh and Derry, and if I mistake not, also from Louth. In numbers the belligerents could not have been less than from three to four thousand men. The fair day on which it occurred is known simply as 'The Day of the Great Fight'.

There was a man named 'Jerry Boccagh', or 'Hop and Go Constant', for he was frequently called both, who fell the first victim to this violent feeling of party spirit. He had got arms on seeing his friends, the Orangemen, likely to be defeated, and had the hardihood to follow with charged bayonet a few Ribbonmen, whom he attempted to intercept as they fled from a large number of their enemies, who had got them separated from their comrades. Boccagh ran across a field adjoining the town in order to get before them on the road, and was in the act of climbing a ditch, when one of them, who carried a spade shaft, struck him a blow on the head which put an end to his existence.

The person who killed this man escaped to America, where he got himself naturalized, and when the British Government claimed him, he pleaded his privilege as an American citizen, and was not given up. Boccagh was a very violent Orangeman and a most offensive one.

On the part of the Ribbonmen, a man named Hacket or McGaughy, who lived not half a mile from our house, performed a very extraordinary exploit on that remarkable day. He got his skull broken by a blow inflicted with the butt of a gun, and yet he walked home afterwards, a distance of two miles – but the next morning I saw him in bed as insensible as a log. Sir William Richardson and other magistrates were at his house, accompanied by a Surgeon Shone, who trepanned his head with very equivocal success, for although he recovered so far as to be able to walk about, he never got beyond idiocy, and died in about three months afterwards. He sat for the picture of Dennis Kelly in 'The Party Fight and Funeral'.

In those days there were such things as Ribbon funerals and Orange funerals. For instance, it sometimes happened that when a Ribbonman was murdered – Hacket's case was considered a murder – the Ribbonmen attended his funeral in a body, every man wearing a red silk ribbon indicative of the murder that had been committed. This, however, occurred only occasionally, and in cases where party spirit ran high and bitter. I do not think there has been an instance in my native parish within the last thirty-five or forty years.

from *Autobiography of William Carleton*, 1896

THE TROUBLED LAND

BENEDICT KIELY

The people existed precariously on the land, an almost completely agrarian community. They were at the mercy of the owners of the land who in most cases cared nothing about the people, nothing about the country in which they lived, except in so far as their rack-rented tenants provided them with money to spend in London or in pleasure places on the continent. The people were mostly Catholic in religion but the tithe-demands of a Protestant state-established Church pushed them down still deeper into the dirty swamp of poverty and misery and ignorance. Their hunger left them little protection against rabid proselytisers ready to buy a very literal lipservice to Protestantism with offers of hot soup and good potatoes. They were at the mercy of the armed forces of the bitter and bigoted thing that called itself Orangeism, and Orangeism, except in periods of special enlightenment, had the approval and encouragement of men in high places. The poor man on the land could go out from this through the door beginning to open into American places, or he could seek relief through reprisals: murder or robbery or destruction of property. The remedy was worse than the disease. It meant that the government of Ireland was one act of repression and coercion after another, and those who suffered from repression and coercion were logically enough those who had had no official approval in the committing of outrage.

That was the social and political and economic background to the lives of Carleton's people. It was the gallows under which they danced with the wild irresponsibility of men daring death and the devil to do their worst. It was the great cloud that overhung their merriment and their sorrow, their singing and love-making, and going on pilgrimage. The religious hates of the sixteenth century, the imperialism that came to life in the eighteenth, the cant of law and landed property and economic necessity that draped like a heavy cloak over the sins of the nineteenth, came together and festered on one small island on the fringe of Europe. Witnessing the unholy meeting, waiting and watching for every favourable moment were the black shadow of hunger, the red shadows of murder and sudden death.

The English visitor who came to Ireland with a really observant eye and a belief in the necessity of justice could find out extraordinarily illuminating things. Phil McClutchy, the worthy son of Val the Vulture, drawing three yellow fingers across his chin in a secret sign of Orangeism, pointed out to Evory Easel, the visitor, that being a member of the Church of England or the Church of Ireland was scarcely sufficient unto salvation. 'The great principle here,' he said, 'is to hate and keep down the Papists, and you can't do that properly unless you're an Orangeman. Hate and keep down the Papists, that's the true religion.' Evory Easel, with the great gift of an enquiring mind, investigated both the theory and the practice of the Orangeism of Castle Cumber and Val McClutchy, which was also the Orangeism of the nineteenth century and, with the addition of a great deal of respectability, the Orangeism of the present day. In the qualifications laid down by rule as essential for the good Orangeman he saw that it would be 'almost impossible, to find in any organised society, whether open or secret, a more admirable code of qualifications'. But these excellent abstract moral and religious principles had absolutely no influence on the practical working of the society. Its sole purpose seemed to be to 'inflame the passions of the lower classes of Protestants', stimulating them 'too frequently, to violence, and outrage, and persecution itself, under a conviction that they are only discharging their duties by a faithful adherence to obligations'.

It was more natural for the novelist, more entertaining for his readers than the English visitor's dry comment on Orange rules and Orange practice, to follow McClutchy's yeomanry when they plundered houses in an alleged search for arms or met together in blunt and plain-spoken council. Solomon McSlime in all his glory attended the Castle Cumber lodge-meetings less as an active participant than as a pious and edifying influence, drinking whisky punch with them to counteract any tendency to pride, rewarded after the humility of the third cup by 'an easy uprising of the spiritual man', by a greater sense of inward freedom, and an elevation of soul. Solomon McSlime was the conventional hypocrite or a caricature of the conventional hypocrite, praying prayers over the poor that he robbed, psalm-singing over the servant-maids he seduced. But the conventional hypocrite and the Irish Orangeman had, and have, a common possession in a *naïveté* about which it is very easy to be obviously funny. Bob Clendinning, the typical ordinary Orangeman, reacted violently against the suggestion that his rule of life would ever allow him to cheat a Papist. 'No,' Bob bellowed from the bottom of his honest Orange soul, 'I'd chate no man; no, no – a'm not that bad aither. A'd fight a Papish, a'd lick a Papish, an' a hope a'll help to drive them out of the country yet. No sir; my name's Bob Clendinning, but a'd chate no man. A know my duty better.'

When McClutchy's yeomanry had completed a ransacking of the house of a Catholic who had the misfortune to be a personal enemy of the great Valentine, one armed man asked for something to drink as a reward for the unusual civility with which they had treated their victim. They hadn't broken his doors and furniture, or stabbed bayonets into his beds or bedclothes. But another raider roared that he'd drink no Papish whisky, because it was – as every well-instructed Orangeman knew – specially blessed and christened at the hands of the priest. The grounds on which one man claimed the whisky and those on which another rejected it may seem fantastic even in a fantastically unsettled period. But William Carleton remembered the night his sister had cried in pain, stabbed in bed by an Orange bayonet; and, in twentieth-century Belfast, a high Orange official prohibited under severe penalties the members of Orange lodges from slaking their thirst in public houses owned by Catholics.

from *Poor Scholar*, 1947

AN ULSTER PROSPECT

SHAN F. BULLOCK

If you climb Rhamus Hill, mount the castle wall and set your face towards the setting sun, on your right will be Emo and the long glitter of Lough Erne, behind will lie Thrasna river and the wilderness of Bilboa; on your left Lackan lough will gleam darkly among the hills, Armoy and its boglands stretch away towards my Lord the mountain, and the pastures of Gorteen spread out below your feet even unto the distant whiteness of the Ferry road and the rude borders of Drumhill townland.

Should the day be cloudy and in summertime, the wind south-west and moist, the sky high and grey, your eyes will have happy sight of a characteristic Ulster prospect. The scene will be fair, wide-spreading and varied, at once heartsome and subdued: mountains blue and misty, valleys long and shallow, hills low, rounded, and cut fantastically by ditch and hedgerow into little fields, the great tracts of bogland lying flat and sullen beneath the sun. Trees will abound, white cottages peep forth here and there, roads and lanes crawl in and out. You will have the flash of water, the gloom of heather, the quick vividness of lush meadow-land and widespreading pasture. There will be cattle upon the hills, men and women in the valleys, a fisher lonely upon the lake, a clanking cart upon the road. Shadows will flit along the mountain and trip across the hedges. Bilboa will be clothed in the sombreness of rush and whin. Far back the roofs of Bunn will gleam and darken. By Thrasna river the valley will be one medley of trees, hedges, haycocks, green cropland and brown heatherpatches, a hand's-width of river and a gleam of whitewash. Out below the horizon my Lord will drowse in the dimness and the Lake wind lazily for the sea. A great peace will fill the land, a softness as of sleep; you will dream and brood and admire; at last find the hedges running together, the hills crowding their crests, and the scene come narrowing in, till of all the broad countryside but the land of Gorteen, lying there before you, has room in your eyes.

Now Bilboa, Armoy, and Drumhill are big and bare, and these regions are Catholic; but Gorteen is small and fruitful, and this is Protestant. In many ways, Gorteen – that land of wisdom – differs wholly from its neighbours, and with them has no sympathy. Enter its confines, by way of these, where and when you will, and at once you have signs of change. You seem to have stepped into a new country. Hedges become trim, lanes and fields orderly, houses neat, offices clean, crops flourishing. You have gardens and lawns, flowers in the windows and curtains behind them, knockers upon the painted doors and steps before them. In the fields are ploughs and harrows, mowing-machines upon the meadows, flocks and herds amid the pastures. Orchards stand everywhere, with beehives ranged in the shade and linen bleaching in the sun. You meet fewer stragglers and no beggar-men. Pigs keep their styes; goats and donkeys are missed from the wayside. The carts are painted, the cars clean and jaunty. An air of prosperity is abroad, of industry and rude comfort, of independence also and a more rigid rule of life. The country seems blessed of God, slavery and terror banished from its confines. Even the hills look free; you stand and gaze within the borders of a new country; nor can you fail to see that you are in the midst of a new race. Altogether different are these good folk – these men you meet, these women you see – from the unfortunates who dwell without. They are better clothed and better fed, bolder of eye and hearing; bigger, harder, coarser, tighter of lip, stronger in hand and body; more prosaic also, narrower in mind, and less variously gifted. The men are sturdy, stern and broad of feature; the women big in the bone, and not renowned for comeliness. Ordinarily they wear tweeds and leggings, linsey bodices and quilted petticoats; on Sundays you find them stepping to church or preaching in stuffs and broadcloths. They eat plentifully of eggs and bacon, tea and stirabout, potatoes, butter and white bread. Among them drunkenness is uncommon, immorality ill-known. As hagglers in fair or market, poachers and litigants, their fame is great. They speak a slow and oily dialect, part Irish and part Scotch; have some gifts of humour and a talent for religion and politics. Sons of freedom, they call themselves, stern upholders of Protestantism and sworn foes of Pope and Popery. In every garden Orange lilies flourish; a Bible lies on every parlour table. For Queen and Country, Self and pelf, God and the Church: these are watchwords in Gorteen. Also they are hospitable there, kind and warm-hearted: and a more strenuous race does not cumber the earth.

Descendants they are, and not far removed, of Puritan and Covenanter: a hardy, dogmatic, prideful stock.

If you enter Gorteen by way of the Bunn road, you come soon to Lackan bridge and, just beyond it, strike a narrow roadway which runs obliquely uphill away from Armoy. Following this you pass the old Chapel gates (the Chapel itself is gone now, thatch and all), have sight as you go of a few homesteads, and a glimpse across the bog of the wilds of Drumhill; then dip into a hollow, bend sharply round past a wayside drinking-pool, and find yourself, all suddenly, looking down a slope straight into the heart of Gorteen. And just at your elbow, on the right as you stand, a gap in the hedge makes room for the gateposts and avenue of Hillside House.

The gateposts are battered now, the gate rotted and gone. Weeds infest the avenue, the hedges stand gaunt and wild, only stumps remain of the stately firs that once moaned in the winds; the fields on either hand are rush-grown, the garden a tangle, the orchard a wilderness. The offices are dilapidated, thistles flourish in the haggard, grass covers the yard. In the stable where once stood Martin's hunter pigs wallow and grow fat, fowls roost in the empty barn; and now in all the rooms and passages of Hillside – once so cleanly and garnished, in the days whilst Martin's mother ruled there – tattered barbarians do riot. The windows are broken, doors battered, walls and roof cracked and moss-grown; the steps by the hall door are gone, the flower-beds before it and the creeper on the walls and the painted fence that bordered the lawn, all are vanished with the years. Ruin and desolation have made Hillside their own, and of its former glory remains now but traditions and memories. So do men wither from the earth and their fair works decay, leaving ruin and tombstones to mark their place.

from *The Squireen*, 1903

103

Better Times Remembered

AMANDA MCKITTRICK ROS

Helen, who stood stricken with delight at the friendly reception received from Lily Lentil, could not help indulging in a happy moment of silent meditation when compared with the horrible and trying hours that were hers on the last day she had spent in her native land by the stratagem of what should have been a nobleman, not a trait of which dwelt within him and whose wretched vices characterised largely some, in fact many, of our present-day passion-hunters.

Wringing her hands, she laid them upon her uncle's breast and wept woefully, refusing to be pacified, crying out:

'I am wondering what my beloved parents will think of me not returning to Crow Cottage ere setting sail for Sydney to meet Maurice Munro? If they, perchance, find out the wicked treachery forced on me by Lord Rasberry I feel they will both lie down and die with grief. I must write to my dear friend, Mabel Moag.'

Rising abruptly she stood before her uncle, placing her tiny hands upon his hot forehead already beaded with brilliants of grief because of her sorrow.

Lily Lentil then entered, announcing something savoury might be welcomed by one and all and which she felt anxious to distribute. Henry Huddleson led Helen to partake of the many varied dishes of edibles, which they all appreciated immensely, as prepared by Lily Lentil, having proved herself a first class cook.

Henry Huddleson, being of a remarkable kindly nature, never made the slightest comment regarding what hour his inmates went to bed, he being delighted to have his beautiful niece under his roof of calm, free from the vicious vortex she had stemmed and which he was now resolved to hold in abeyance while she remained in custody.

As he prepared to adopt his nightly custom reading a chapter from the book of books, a happy air reigned throughout, Helen and Henry Jn., with Lily Lentil having marked the roll as present. This trio of affection, surveying keenly the wonderful magnet of modishness, absolutely devoid of the man make-ups that tend to despise the forms of so many female features, thought Helen Huddleson the most perfect figure of attractive attributes the world has ever held within its vast circumference.

On looking at her a shade of graveness swept across Henry Huddleson's wrinkled visage and, moving to her he embraced her, leading her to a seat without uttering a word, Henry Jn and Lily Lentil being also silent members. Raising his drooped head, tears dripping slowly from his globes of glare, he glared at her in a foreign manner, which affected her amazingly.

'Oh, Helen,' he spake, 'I ask you not to leave me during my term of existence. I feel it is not far off, besides it would be detrimental to me were I to linger on without you, my dove, that could easily blank the snowy whiteness of Noah's messenger history hints was adorned with all those gorgeous colours flung against the clouded face of the blue sky. I ask you – do not leave me!'

'But uncle,' Helen pleaded, plaintively looking north and using all her cornices of conception, 'I must go to Australia to join Maurice Munro who is waiting for me.'

'All parts of this earth to-day,' continued Henry Sn., 'are equally vile. This I attribute to the exhaustless batches of clerics who swarm in our midst like bees in a hive.'

The drops of sweat resting on his forehead he allowed to sink into the furrows age had streaked across it.

'Yes, yes, my darling niece,' he went on, 'in my youthful days it was the sweetest treat I wished for always while in our dear little Crow Cottage, going to the house of prayer on the Sabbath day where that great divine (pointing to a picture on the wall) expounded the holy scriptures in a manner that the youngest child within its sanctified precincts could repeat and understand.'

'Oh, Uncle,' cried Helen, her eyes flooded with dew and joy, 'that was the Reverend John Davis, DD, of Third Ballynahinch Presbyterian Church.'

'Precisely,' exclaimed Henry Sn., his human spectacles laded with tears he anon wiped off. 'I have travelled for years in three continents and never missed one Sunday morning at my church and strange, yet true, I found more room within my inner cells for salvation in the many carefully-studied sermons delivered with a zeal and earnestness by this Ballynahinch divine than I did from all other ministering money-bags.'

'Dear me! Dear me!' exclaimed Helen.

'I often grew sleepy,' her uncle continued, 'under what I considered the sloppy spueings of other divines, who try to thrust upon their congregations of mixed-seekers a rigmarole of what they consider theological spoutings, but I never benefited one iota by their twenty-minute impartings under the nom-de-plume of sermons. How appalling were all those compared with the ninety-minutes deliveries by that great divine from Ballynahinch.'

'He didn't place his gold watch on the pulpit cushion,' expostulated Henry Huddleson, 'in order to be seen and act as a stay when twenty minutes were heralded by its little hands. Oh, No! He prepared his sermons thoroughly, never curtailing them by one second, even to the last, preceding his retirement. How sad, my dear Helen, how few of the dog-collar tribe have followed in his footsteps. He differed in countless ways from the so-called clerics of to-day who, during the last five decades, seem more to be an amalgamated body of holy-stockbrokers than disciples of Jesus Christ.'

After a moment, Henry Sn. continued:

'Ah, yes! There is a great laxity to-day prevailing among the majority of our present day apostles who instead of looking minutely after the youths of their respective flocks of worshippers are often spending the greater part of their time playing golf or cards, rearing pups for exhibitions at dog-shows and last but not least transferring their calling to that of egg-merchants rumaging through the country to find out (not by any means the number of Christians in each house) but who kept the best breed of Rhode Island Reds and Leghorns, etc., being most particular to what breed laid the largest eggs.

'Ah, my dear Helen, I feel heart sick of the frivolous, frittering fraternity of fragiles flitting about and around Earth's great plane wearing their mourning livery of religion as a cloak of design tainted with the milk of mockery,' wiping his moistened brow with a crimson handkerchief while Helen acquiesced, Henry Jn. and Lily Lentil remaining silent.

from *Helen Huddleson*, 1969

Why Mrs McRea Returned to the Faith of Her Fathers

KATHLEEN FITZPATRICK

One soaking wet day in September Patsy was sitting by the kitchen fire eating bread and sugar for want of better amusement when he was cheered by the sight of a tall figure in a green plaid shawl hurrying past the window in the driving rain. He got up from his creepie stool to go to the other children who were playing in the schoolroom when Lull, sprinkling clothes at the kitchen table, exclaimed – 'Bad luck to it, here's that ould runner again.'

Patsy quietly moved his stool back into the shadow of the chimney corner. In that mood Lull, if she saw him, would chase him from the kitchen when the news began, and clearly Teressa was bringing news worth hearing. As far back as Patsy or any of the children could remember Teressa had brought the village gossip to Rowallan. One thing only – a dog in her path – had power to turn her aside. The quietest dog sent her running like a hare, and the most obviously imitated bark made her cry.

She came in shaking the rain from her shawl.

'Woman dear, but that's the saft day. I'm dreepin' to the marrow bone.'

'What call had ye to come out?' said Lull shortly.

Teressa sank into a chair and wiped her wet face with the corner of her apron.

'Deed, ye may well ast me. My grandson was for stoppin' me, but says I to myself, says I, the Mistress be to hear this before night.'

'She'll hear no word of it then,' said Lull; 'she's sleepin' sound and I'd cut my hand off afore I'd wake her for any auld clash.'

Teressa paid no heed.

'Such carrying on, Lull, I niver seen the like. Mrs McRea, the woman, she beats Banagher Fair. She's drunk as much whiskey these two days as would destroy a rigiment, an' now she has the whole village up with her talk.'

'Andy was tellin' me she was at it again,' said Lull.

'Och, I wisht ye'd seen her,' said Teressa, 'she was neither to bind nor to hould. And the tongue of her! Callin' us a lot of papishes and fenians.

Sure she was sittin' on Father Ryan's doorstep till past twelve o'clock wavin' an orange scarf and singing "Clitter clatter, Holy Watter".'

'Dear help us!' said Lull.

''Deed I'm sayin' it. An' when his riverence come out to her it was a hape of abuse an' "to hell with the Pope" that she give him.'

'That's forty shillings and costs if the police heard her,' said Patsy, forgetting he was in hiding.

'Lord love ye, did ye ever heard the like of that? It's a wee auld man the child is.'

But Patsy wanted to hear more.

'What did Father Ryan say to her, Teressa?' he asked.

'Troth, he tould her she'd be in hell herself before the Pope, for all her curses,' said Teressa.

'And will she?' asked Patsy.

'As sure as an egg's meat,' said Teressa. 'If she doesn't give over drinkin' the ould gentleman's comin' for her one of these fine nights to take her away with him.'

'Does she know when he's coming?' Patsy asked.

'Not her, the black-mouthed Protestant divil,' said Teressa.

'Whisht,' said Lull, 'that's no talk before the child.'

'And a fine child he is,' said Teressa, 'and a fine man he be makin' one of these days.'

But Patsy had heard enough, and was off to tell the others. They were playing in the schoolroom when he brought the news. Mrs McRea was drunk again and had cursed the Pope on Father Ryan's doorstep, and the divil was coming to take her away if she did not stop drinking.

It was bitter news, for Mrs McRea kept the one sweetie shop in the village.

'I'll go and see her,' said Jane.

'What good will that do?' said Mick.

'I'll tell her the divil's coming.'

'She won't heed you,' said Mick.

'I know,' said Fly, who had said nothing so far but had been thinking seriously, 'let's send her a message from the divil to tell her to give over or he'll come for her.'

This plan commended itself to the others as a brilliant solution of a difficulty. Mrs McRea had been known to see devils and rats when she was drunk – she would be prepared for another visit, and a devil with a warning would have to be taken seriously. It was well worth trying, for Mrs McRea in spite of her drunken habits and the fact that she was a turncoat – had been born a Roman Catholic and had married into the other camp – was a great favourite with the children. She had often given them sweets when they had not a farthing between them to buy.

As the idea was hers, Fly was to go with the message.

Mick raked down a handful of soot from the chimney, and rubbed her face and hands till they were black; then dressed her in a pair of old bathing drawers and a black fur cape. Patsy got the pitchfork from the stables for her to carry in her hand.

Fly started off for the village. The others waited patiently for her to come back. She was gone nearly an hour and came back wet to the skin, and frightened by the success of her mission.

'Go on, tell us right from the start,' said Jane.

'Well, when I got outside the gate who should I see but Teressa going home. So I just dodged down behind her and barked, and she took to her heels and ran the whole way. And when we came to the village I hid behind a tree and then dodged round to Mrs McRea's. The door was shut, so I knocked with the pitchfork. Says she, "Who's there?" Says I, "Come out of that, Mrs McRea." Says she, "What would I be doin' that for?" "Because," says I, "it's the divil himself come to see you, Mrs McRea."'

'But you weren't to be the devil,' Jane interrupted, 'you were only one of his wee devils.'

'I clean forgot,' said Fly, 'indeed, indeed I clean forgot. And oh! Jane, I wished you'd seen her. She opened the door and when she saw me she gave a screech, and went down on her knees, and began praying like mad. I danced round and poked her with the pitchfork. "I'll learn you not to curse the Pope, Mrs McRea, you black-mouthed old Protestant. Look here, my girl," said I, "I'm coming for you at twelve o'clock this night – so see and be ready." And with that she ran in and shut the door and I could hear her praying. Oh Jane, I've scared the life out of her.' Fly began to cry.

'You have just spoilt all,' said Jane, 'the devil wasn't going to come to her only if she wouldn't give over drinking.'

Fly shivered and sobbed.

'Yes, you jackass, and how can we take her away at twelve?'

But Fly only shivered and sobbed the more.

'Look here,' said Jane, 'she'll be sick if we don't dry her.'

So they all went upstairs, and Fly was bathed and dressed in her own clothes and sent down to sit by the kitchen fire, having first sworn to cut her throat if she let out one word to Lull. Then the four went back to the schoolroom to think the matter over.

'We can't have Mrs McRea going about saying the devil told her a lie,' said Jane.

'And we can't have her sittin' there all night scared to death,' said Mick.

'We'll have to send her another message,' said Jane.

'Another devil?' asked Patsy.

'No,' said Jane, 'it must be a person from heaven this time to tell her that if she'll quit drinking the devil won't be let come.'

They agreed that this was the only plan. But who was it to be?

'I'll be the Blessed Virgin,' said Jane, 'there's mother's blue muslin dress in the nursery cupboard, and I can have wax flowers out of the glass shade in my hair.'

'But Mrs McRea's a Protestant,' Mick objected, 'and what would she care for the Blessed Virgin?'

'Let's send the ghost of Mister McRea,' said Patsy.

But here again there was a difficulty, for Mr McRea could only have come from Purgatory, and who would let him out?

'Is there never a Protestant saint?' asked Mick.

'Not a one but King William,' said Jane.

'And he's the very old boy,' Mick shouted.

Upstairs they ran to search for suitable clothes. Jane begged to be King William, but by the time she was dressed it was dark night and she was afraid to go alone, so Mick and Patsy went with her.

Honeybird was sent downstairs to the kitchen to wait with Fly till they came back, and if Lull asked where they were she was not to tell.

When they dropped out of the dressing-room window into the garden the rain was over. The wind now chased the clouds across the sky and piled them up to hide the moon.

The children crept along the road terrified that they might meet Sandy McGlander, the ghost with the wooden leg, or see Raw Head and Bloody Bones ride by on his black horse.

When they reached Mrs McRea's cottage all was in darkness, but they could hear through the door the crying that had frightened Fly.

'Hide quick, you two, I'm going to knock,' said Jane.

There was a yell of terror from inside.

'It's all right, Mrs McRea,' said Jane, 'Come out, I want to speak to you.'

'Who are you?' said Mrs McRea.

'Sure, I'm King William of glorious, pious and immortal memory, come to save you from the devil.'

They heard Mrs McRea fumbling with the latch, and then the door opened. Jane stood up straight, and as luck would have it the clouds parted and the moon shone bright on King William in an old hunting coat stuffed out with pillows, a pair of white frilled drawers, and a top hat with a peacock feather in it.

'God help us, but the quare things do happen,' said Mrs McRea.

'Aye, and queerer things will happen if you don't give over drinking, Mrs McRea,' said King William. 'Fine going-ons these are when decent people can't rest in Heaven for the likes of you and your vagaries.'

'It's Himself,' said Mrs McRea, and went down on her knees.

'If it hadn't been for me meeting the devil this evening you would have been in hell by this time, but said I to him said I, "Give her another chance," said I.'

'God save us!' sobbed Mrs McRea.

'And said he to me, "No! the black-mouthed Protestant, she cursed the Pope and waved an orange scarf on Father Ryan's doorstep."'

'Whisht!' said a warning voice round the corner, 'King William's a Protestant.'

'What do I care about Protestants,' shouted King William, getting excited; 'if I didn't know you for a decent woman I'd let the devil have you. But says I to myself, says I, where would the children be without their sweetie shop?'

Jane was losing her head. The whispers round the corner began again. King William took no notice but went on again.

'And he'll let you off this once, but you are to go down to Father Ryan first thing in the morning, and take the pledge.'

'Did your honour say Father Ryan?' gasped Mrs McRea.

''Deed I did; and who else would I be saying?'

'But I'm a Protestant, your honour.'

'So you are. But I'm telling you, Mrs McRea, you'll be sorry for it. Sure, there is never a Protestant in heaven but myself, and I only got in by the skin of my teeth. There's nothing but rows and rows of Popes there. Sure, many's the time I'd be sorry for you down here singing "Clitter, clatter, holy water", and wearing orange scarves when I know where you'll go to through it.'

'Och-a-nee, and me knew no better!' said Mrs McRea.

'You did know better once and you know better again now. Go down to Father Ryan in the morning and take the pledge, and let me hear no more about it, or it will not be telling you, for divil a foot I'll stir out of heaven again for you or anybody else.'

The clouds once more hid the moon and in the darkness Mick and Patsy seized King William and hurried her away.

'You very near spoilt it all,' said Mick.

'But I didn't,' said Jane; 'let's hide and see what she'll do.'

Mrs McRea got up from her knees, went into the cottage, and shut the door.

It was late when they got home. Jane crept upstairs and changed her clothes before she went into the kitchen for supper.

Next morning Teressa came with the strange news that Mrs McRea had been converted, and had been to Father Ryan to take the pledge.

'Small wonder! for the divil himself come to see her,' said Teressa, 'and sure enough I seen himself with my own two eyes. As I was going home last night who would come after me but a black baste wid the ugliest face on him I ever seen. And it wasn't long after that that the neighbours heard her yellin' "Murder!" She sez herself that he come to her as bold as brass like a wee auld black man and poked holes in her with a fiery fork. And by strake of dawn she was down at Father Ryan's house, tellin' him she was converted, and not a drop of drink on her. The whole parish is colloguing with her now. And she houlds to it that King William is a saint in glory!'

from *The Weans at Rowallan*, 1905

The Orange Idealist

ROBERT LYND

There was once a woman – I knew her well, for she helped to nurse me – who believed in her heart that God was an Orangeman. She also believed that a strong family likeness existed between Satan and the Pope of Rome. She was a mild woman, thin and worn about the cheeks, and inestimably patient under a child's buffetings. She had the gentlest of eyes behind her black-rimmed spectacles. Her face was saintlily sad under a bonnet rich in a widow's bugles. Yet, much as she looked the part, she was no self-torturing ascetic. She had a dear regard for snuff, a little nasty-smelling parcel of which always lay on the nursery chimney-piece. She indulged, too, in the luxury of ideals. She dreamed from morning till night of an Ireland out of which all the Catholics had been driven, and in which Protestants would be able to live without the fear that at any hour evil-eyed people might sweep down upon them and cut their throats. So far as I could gather, Catholics – or Papishes, as she preferred to call them – had no definite object in life but to cut the throats of Protestants. Being a Protestant, I naturally went about the streets in a state of considerable trepidation. Every one whom I met and who had at all a doubtful cast of face, I put down at once as a Papist and hurried past, with a horrified, dry feeling at the back of my mouth. One day , at a time when the town was in a flutter of riotous excitement, I was going to school with my sister, when we found ourselves in the middle of a great crowd, shouting and rushing hither and thither. I had no doubt in the world that the campaign of throat-cutting had begun. 'The Papishes have risen!' I cried to my sister, and, hoping that she would follow me, made helter-skelter for home. My sister, being of a less bigoted and fearful turn of mind, went on to school; and she was right, for the crowd was only running to a fire. She was less intimately instructed than I, however, in the wicked designs of the Catholics, for my nurse had no mind to waste the stores of her wisdom on a mere girl.

There is a book which has afforded entertainment to many broad-minded grown-up people. The name of it is 'Forty Coming Wonders', and the author a Mr Baxter, who does not like Catholics or socialists, and who has a habit of prophesying the date of the end of the world. This book my nurse reverenced next to the Bible. There were pictures in it representing lions or tigers or some such beasts, each of them provided with seven or more heads. She spent hour after hour gazing at these and puzzling out to herself the points of resemblance between the many-headed beasts and the Church of Rome. She loved, too, to sit in a rocking-chair beside the fire, with its tall wire screen, and read out the most horrible details of the massacres of St Bartholomew's Day. Every tale, of course, found its local habitation in my mind, and the world became to me a place which only a kind Protestant English government prevented from becoming a shambles. This gentle woman was herself full of butcherous thoughts enough. She loved no song so well as 'The Protestant Boys', and the version she sang of it – a version very common in the North of Ireland – portended a sufficiently drastic doom for the Catholics. Her thin face lit up with a sort of delight as, with her arms wrapped round me, she shrilled out the chorus. It ran like this:

> Slitter, slaughter,
> Holy Water!
> Sprinkle the Papishes every one!
> And that's what we'll do,
> And we'll cut them in two,
> And the Protestant Boys'll carry the drum!

I was trained up in this song, an infant Hannibal, pledged to eternal enmity towards Rome. Every opportunity was taken to strengthen me in this vehement faith. Our favourite recreation soon came to be a walk down Sandy Row, a territory, as I recall it, of low-built, white-walled Orange dwellings, where my nurse had many friends. She took us to a house in the neighbourhood with a regularity we loved, and set us down in front of the fire with cakes of potato bread in our hands. Over the fireplace, a coloured delph image of William the Third stood – a necessary idol in every true Orange household. I learned to worship that image, as I am afraid I did not worship God. I looked reverently upon King

William, sitting there on his delph horse with the air of a man leading an army to victory, as an heroic person who had somehow or other saved my family and myself from being foully murdered.

Every year in the North of Ireland a day is set apart for the worship of King William. On the Twelfth of July, the Orangemen remember how years and years ago Protestant William chased Papist James from the banks of the Boyne, and can scarcely contain themselves with delight in consequence. As the great day approaches, the town becomes dazed at night with the thud of drums here, drums there, drums everywhere. Over the Orange streets broad arches are hung, rich in tags of orange and blue paper and in garlands of orange lilies, and containing pictures of King William and instructive scenes from Irish history. Mottoes are set in them, eloquent about 'civil and religious liberty', and calling upon true Protestants to remember sundry things for which 'our fathers fought and died'. My nurse was not a person to allow me to forget. On the eve of 'the Twelfth', as it is called, she led me into the noisy country of the arches, and, taking me into a dark little shop, bought me a paper orange sash for a penny. In some years, when money was abundant, she provided me with a shilling drum as well: she never let a year pass without seeing that I had, at least, a tin whistle. She was an infectious propagandist. She was, for the time being, a saint admitted to the splendours of Paradise, or – a better simile – a war-horse smelling the battle not too far off. As for me, she led me into every extravagance of enthusiasm. She had often taken me by the hand and pointed out the huge drums in the Orange procession, showing me with a thrill of pride in her voice the drumheads bespattered with blood from the wrists of the maddened drummers. Every drummer, as he flogs his instrument in a kind of Bacchanalian frenzy, feels himself in duty bound to gash and cut his wrists on the wooden rim, and if the drumhead be not red with blood by the end of the day, he looks askance at himself as one who has not offered due sacrifice to King William's pious, glorious, and immortal memory. Naturally, it was the earliest ambition of my childhood to be an Orange drummer. I could achieve no bloody feats, however, on my fragile shilling instrument. Consequently, I had to go elsewhere to obtain the required training for my future profession. I found a hard enough substance in the kitchen table. Night after night, I stood before it, hammering my tiny wrists upon its square corners, until the skin was red and bruised and aching, and uplifting what lusty voice I had in a rapturous singing of 'The Protestant Boys', or 'The Boyne Water'. I do not know if I ever actually succeeded in making the blood flow. I hurt myself sufficiently, however, to feel mighty proud and Protestant for several days afterwards.

The Twelfth of July I loved more than Christmas Day. On the Twelfth thousands and tens of thousands – nay, hundreds of thousands – of Orangemen marched forth, with banners rioting in the wind and drums roaring. Every man in the gaudy and haphazard army wore a tasselled sash, curiously coloured, about his shoulders. Here and there a fellow carried a wooden Bible on a wooden pole. Others walked along the sides of the procession with a sort of spear in their hands, and woe to any man who tried to cross from one side of the road to the other until the procession had gone completely by. At a few yards' distance from each other, fife band and brass band flung different tunes into the air, horrible as the warring of creeds. Cromwell and King William, in all sorts of odd shapes and attitudes and colours, looked down from countless banners, and other flags showed Queen Victoria presenting a Bible to a humble heathen king, with 'The Secret of England's Greatness' as a motto at the foot of the picture. Flute-players, drunk with their own music, walked backwards in an odd kind of dancing step before the drums, grotesque Orpheuses in their Sabbath clothes. Everywhere was loud din and colour – the din and dust and colour of war, and the curiously angry brows of men with haunted imaginations. Beautiful in my strip of orange paper, terrible with my shilling drum, a dangerous flute peeping from my pockets, I was led out by the hand to watch the passing of these mighty Joseph's-coated warriors. If I had not yet ridden the goat, as they say of those who have been initiated into the Orange order, I was an Orangeman at least in my beating pulses and along my quivering spine. When the carnival had gone by, I was trotted back to the nursery, and coached in the story of a few more massacres. I learned how the Orangemen had beaten the Catholics into the waters of the Lough, and I praised them for it. I heard of innocent girls shot, and of little boys cut down in open daylight as they were running messages for their parents. The police I was taught to distrust as men who were Fenians at heart, and I admired an Orange assault upon a police-barracks more than the storming of

116

Sebastopol. Like nearly all Protestant children brought up in an Ulster town, I came to look on Catholics as a kind of wild beasts to be avoided, if not exterminated. There was a very mild old Catholic gentleman, who lived two doors away from our house. I often burst into tears when he stopped and spoke to me in the street.

'The Orange Idealist', from *Irish and English*, 1908

THE DARK WALK TO THE MILL

FLORENCE MARY MCDOWELL

Near the crossroads at Cogry at the turn of the nineteenth century stood McFerran's corn mill, and the spinning and weaving of linen was still to a great extent a cottage industry. But the influence of the Huguenots and of the Industrial Revolution was working inexorably towards even this secluded spot and in 1845 the buildings of the old corn mill became the nucleus for the great linen-spinning concern to be known as Cogry Mills. To the new mill Granpa James came, aged 21, to learn the business and to become manager of the mills, which were owned first by Mr Moon and then by Mr Broadbent; and to remain here, loved and respected by all in spite of the harsh nature of nineteenth-century industry, until his retirement in 1879. By the time he retired the mill had become a concern of international repute and provided hundreds of local people with employment.

The children, awaking suddenly in the dark cold of a winter's morning, would hear the tramp of the workers' feet as they went by on the road to begin work in the mill at 6 a.m., to work their twelve hours and then to walk home again. Some of them would come distances of up to five or six miles and could have had time for little but walking and working and sleeping. There were some whose feet could not be heard as their shawled figures passed in the darkness, for they were barefoot. Many a mill worker had no boots until he or she earned them, and Mary knew of little girls of eleven who were carried to work by their fathers because they had no boots to keep out the cruel frost on the road. But one child's earnings of a shilling or two could make all the difference to a family's eating. Then the central interest in life was to stay living, and to do that one needed food. It made life uncomplicated.

from *Other Days Around Me*, 1966

3

'As native in my thought as any here'

JOHN HEWITT

No Rootless Colonist

JOHN HEWITT

In my experience, people of Planter stock often suffer from some crisis of identity, of not knowing where they belong. Among us you will find some who call themselves British, some Irish, some Ulstermen, usually with a degree of hesitation or mental fumbling. Living as I do in the English Midlands, when I hear an Irish voice in a public place, I frequently salute the speaker. If he or she comes, as is most often, from the Republic, the response and acceptance of identification is instantaneous. If, however, the person challenged is, to my ear, from the Six Counties, the response is usually subdued, reluctant or truculent. Frequently, from the place or circumstances of the encounter, I can be fairly sure that the person I address is not a Roman Catholic; then the reluctance is very marked.

This has to do with the exile's relationship to his church. The Catholic Church obviously is a focus for the Catholic Irish; socially, for he will likely be among kinsfolk or folk from the same district; ideologically or emotionally, since, just as in Poland, because of its baffled history of occupation and partition, the Catholic Church has come to stand for the Polish nation among the peasants and working class, so, as the only continuing institution not overtly associated with the settlers, the Catholic Church in Ireland has been bound closely to the idea of nationality in Ireland. William Allingham the poet, himself of Planter breed and a man who suffered most sharply from this crisis, once declared: 'I love Ireland: were she only not Catholic: but would she be Ireland otherwise?'

Although born in and deeply involved with County Donegal, Allingham never to my knowledge described himself as an Ulsterman. The horns of his dilemma were Ireland and England. His friend, Alfred Tennyson, once remarked to him: 'You don't care a pin about the grand Empire of England. You ought to be proud surely to be part of it. There you are with an English name, English in every way, but you happened to be born in Ireland, therefore you are for it.'

Allingham left Ireland to live and work in England in 1863; and, there-after, once, when his father was ill, and a second time, for his father's funeral, two brief visits in a quarter of a century were his only footings on Irish ground.

For in England he readily found the companionship of literary people and a congenial atmosphere of liberal concern with the arts. Yet, late in life, he could write to Samuel Ferguson 'the thought is dear to me of distinctly connecting my name as a poet with that of the old country'; and A.P. Graves, who met him first at that period, noted his 'soft Donegal accent'.

But while he lived in Ireland, he could identify neither with the older Catholic population nor the strict Protestantism of his own people. As he wrote in 1851, 'I know of but three persons in Ireland besides myself who are distinctly separated from the creeds.' Indeed, with Allingham, I am often reminded of Shakespeare's one Irishman, Captain Macmorris in *King Henry V*, with his outburst – 'Of my nation! What ish my nation?'

Much of the temper and tone of the Catholic Church in England has a distinctive Irish quality. The old Catholics tend only to emerge at corona-tions or in the older universities. The bulk of the clergy bear Irish sur-names, and, if not Irish born, have Irish antecedents. The congregations have been built up by successive waves of immigration. So, for the Catho-lic exile, the faces in the crowds at Mass look familiar, the accents sound neighbourly. But the immigrant Protestant will find no church so exactly matches that which he left behind. The Church of England is too high, too richly vestmented and ritualistic, too ecumenical, for comfort. And, in England, nonconformist meeting-houses are known as chapels, an omi-nous name. The Baptist tabernacle will likely be surmounted by a large cross; the Wesleyans will have a smaller one on the communion table. And, in all of these, the clergymen will speak with the tongues of stran-gers. Perhaps only among the evangelical sects will the average Northern Protestant feel himself on firm ground.

I can appreciate Allingham's uncertain stance; with an English surname myself, of Protestant stock planted in County Armagh, I too have moved beyond the creeds. And recognising the level and extent of communal violence, not to mention the general feebleness of toleration for opposing views, in a country which has the highest church-attendance figures in

Western Europe, and an area with the highest percentage of believers in the most orthodox doctrines in the British Isles, my lack of enthusiasm for any creed is not surprising. But then, the 'Bible Belt', where fundamentalism flourishes in the southern states of America, is precisely where feeling against black fellow-Americans is at its most acute.

My mother tongue is English, instrument and tool of my thought and expression; John Ball, the Diggers, the Levellers, the Chartists, Paine, Cobbett, Morris, a strong thread in the fabric of my philosophy, I learned about in English history. There are many others, but these epitomise for me the British democratic tradition. I also draw upon an English literary tradition which includes Marvell, Crabbe, Wordsworth, Clare, as well as the American tradition in English of Emerson, Thoreau, Whitman, Frost. *Sir Gawaine and the Green Knight* means no less to me than the *Táin Bó Cuailnge*, besides, I think Cuchulainn was a very dirty fighter.

In varying degrees these circumstances set me apart from the majority of people in my native country. Yet when I first came to live in England I found that it was automatically assumed by my new colleagues or acquaintances that, since I had come from Ireland, I must be a Catholic, and among those who heard me speak that I was Scots, or in rarer instances, from Devon or the West Country.

Growing up in Ireland of the thirty-two counties, until I first set foot outside I never consciously thought of myself as Irish or of any nationality at all. As a boy of seven or eight I was fascinated by a book I received as a Christmas present, *Deeds That Won The Empire*, and proud when Michael O'Leary won the Victoria Cross. Both were firmly part of my personal myth. I accepted Sir Edward Carson and his twin, John Redmond, as men from the same country as myself, who had diverging ideas about the governing of it. There were unionists and nationalists, just as there were people with red hair and people with fair or black. There were Protestants and Catholics and Jews, and we played together in Gaw's Field.

Easter Week 1916, without the immediacy of television or radio, seemed some distance away and unrelated to my circumstance. Hence it evoked no clear or deep reaction in a boy of eight-and-a-half. The Armistice of November 1918 was more real, with the barefoot newsboys shouting their special editions, with the singing people in the streets and men in uniform carried shoulder-high. I saw King George when he drove through

Belfast to open the new Parliament in the City Hall in 1921, and the strife which came with Partition was shockingly close: 'curfew in the town, armoured trucks covered with wire mesh passing along the street, a sniper at the corner, burnt-out public houses from the Crumlin Road to the Shankill. But again no political attitude was required of me. I pitied the victims, the hysterical woman, the young man shot in the entry; and from that period I developed the belief that physical violence is self-defeating, and, as I should now phrase it, *anti-man*.

Then, by the mid-1920s, with the new ministries in gear and the nonentities trooping to the Westminster back benches, it seemed evident that the Unionists were a right-wing offshoot of the British Tory Party, who at home fought every election on the border, and that the Nationalists, the representatives of the Catholic minority, were merely obsolete clansmen with old slogans, moving in an irrelevant dream, utterly without the smallest fig-leaf of a social policy. So my concern went to the Labour Party – I was branch delegate at one annual conference – the party of Sam Kyle and Billy McMullen, who had a policy about 'the ownership of the means of production, distribution and exchange'.

At the same time, with my friends at the [Queen's] University and outside, our linking interest in literature, English and American, introduced us to the best writers of our period, Yeats, Joyce, Shaw, and to younger men of the Irish literary revival, O'Flaherty, O'Donnell, Stephens, as well as Theodore Dreiser, H.L. Mencken, Robert Frost, Upton Sinclair. We began to appreciate that Dublin was our literary capital. Three of us were very proud to have poems in the *Irish Statesman* and to have those badly typed letters from the editor, AE, a man from our North – my 'Christmas Eve' being in the style of Vachel Lindsay, the American. AE warned me to avoid his influence and study Yeats.

Out of this attachment-at-a-distance and our eager reading developed a vague sense of a romantic Irish nationalism, with Oisin and Connolly, Maeve and Maud Gonne, bright in the sky. Yet our politics looked beyond to the world. Sacco and Vanzetti were, for us, far more significant than any of the celebrated 'felons of our land'.

After I went to work in the Belfast Museum and Art Gallery late in 1930, part of my duty looking after portraits and relics of notable men of Planter stock which had been gathered into the collection, the American

Presidents of Ulster descent, the explorers, the empire builders and those in less easily labelled categories, I found myself almost unconsciously selecting those I favoured from the rest.

Fourteen Presidents were claimed. A little study of the references in time reduced the number to a more acceptable six or eight, and in the years which followed my consistent scepticism has done something to bring the inflated claim down to more verifiable proportions. The sad, long-jawed painting of James Hope and the faded daguerrotype of Mary Ann McCracken proved themselves icons of greater charismatic power. I was led by the likenesses back to the records. The marble bust of Dr James McDonnell lured me into a study of the circumstances which had compelled Wolfe Tone to nickname him 'The Hypocrite'. So, unintentionally, I was becoming equipped with a local imaginative mythology.

Very shortly, by what route I cannot now recall, I became involved in a local political issue. The National Council of Civil Liberties planned an investigation of the Special Powers Act, that very idiosyncratic piece of Stormont legislation. My interest was that this was a reactionary repressive weapon, to be criticised in any context where democratic values were respected. So my wife – I was just married – and I, with R.M. Henry and Alexander McBeath, professors of the [Queen's] University, engaged ourselves in preliminary investigation to pilot the Council's examination. This was my first acquaintance with the nature of state authority and its techniques of the opened letter and the tapped telephone.

In my literary reading I had discovered the verse-plays of the English poet Gordon Bottomley, and stirred by his use of historico-legendary themes as the core of these, I thought to try my hand at the same form. So I wrote *The Bloody Brae* in 1936 or 1937, a one-act dramatisation of the confrontation of folk who had been caught up in the massacre at the Gobbins, Islandmagee, in 1641. The story which I invented turned into a plea for forgiveness for the wrongs of our past and tolerance between the communities. But, having been written, it lay among my papers till, nearly twenty years later, it was tidied up for a broadcast production from the North of Ireland Region, and several years after that put on at the Lyric Theatre and printed in *Threshold* in 1957.

In the late 1930s we belonged to the Left Book Club, and some of us were active in the Belfast-based Peace League. With regard to the latter, I recall being wedged in a cruel paradox: working for international peace, for sanctions against Italy because of her aggression against Abyssinia, at the same time in my native city, Catholics were burnt out of the York Street area and fled to the new houses of the Glenard Estate. As I wrote in a longish poem 'The Return' (1935):

> in the city of our dreadful night
> men fought with men because of a threadbare flag
> or history distorted in temper. In the streets
> crowds brandished the blunt slogans of their hate,
> drove from their midst the strangers of a creed
> and set the lithe flame leaping up the curtain.
> . . . All authority impotent
> before the frantic chalkmarks on the wall . . .

I printed this poem in a pamphlet, nine years later, for it was too long for the usual journals to consider.

My work at the Stranmillis Art Gallery, while enriching my knowledge of the local historical past, involved me in the study of and care for the visual arts. And my leisure was taken up with writing verse and engagement in leftwing politics. To the visual arts I soon realised that the contribution of these islands had been meagre, that masterpieces had come more readily from the sensibilities and hands of Italians, Frenchmen, Spaniards, Dutchmen. In politics I could be no less an internationalist. Injustice, the exploitation of man by man, the paramountcy of the profit motive applied to the coolie in the paddy-field, the Welsh miner at the coal-face and the riveter at the Belfast shipyard. It was a dead German Jew who gave me my guidelines. It was an English poet who, for me, most movingly evoked the quality of the Good Society in his *News from Nowhere*.

The Spanish Civil War and the mounting of fascism on the continent kept my gaze fixed away from local political affairs. But, with the Second World War, we were cut off from the larger island to the east and from the Europe which, by travel, we had grown to enjoy and accept as also part of our inheritance. Consequently, we were forced to take our holidays in Donegal or elsewhere in the province of Ulster. It was then that our long acquaintance with the middle Glens of Antrim began. Even dutiful exercises like lecturing in army camps broadened my experience of

126

the six partitioned counties of the North. And walking in the Rosses I felt myself no stranger.

Yet, when, in the spring of 1943, I was writing *Conacre* – the very title shewed the direction of my intuition, for conacre has to do with the renting of land under certain conditions, not with its ownership – I could be no more definite than:

> This is my home and country. Later on
> perhaps I'll find this nation is my own.

During this period my thought, stimulated by the ideas of Le Play and Patrick Geddes, mediated through the successive books of Lewis Mumford, found itself directed towards, and settled upon, the concept of regionalism. This proposed that since the world about is so vast and complex, strangled by bureaucratic centralisation – 'apoplexy at the centre, paralysis at the extremities' – we must seek for some grouping smaller than the nation, larger than the family, with which we could effectively identify, with which we could come to terms of sympathetic comprehension, within which our faculties and human potentialities could find due nurture and proper fulfilment. In a word, the region, an area of a size and significance that we could hold in our hearts.

It seemed obvious to me that the province of Ulster was indeed such a region; so I set about deepening my knowledge of its physical components, its history, its arts, its literature, its folklore, its mythology scrupulously examined and assessed, its weaknesses confronted, its values recognised. It seemed also to hold the hope and promise that in this concept might be found a meeting place for the two separated communities which dwelt within its limits, where the older and the less old peoples might discover a basis for amity and co-operative progress.

I was far from alone. In writing, the novel, the short story, the poem shewed a surprising vitality. Three enterprising young men started a literary annual, *Lagan* – in this I had a long regionalist essay and a long poem 'Freehold' – the local Group Theatre staged plays about our present and, once or twice, our past, the visual arts were energetic, local scholarship in the university bore fruit. It is clear that this was all part of the same general movement, attention turning inward of necessity, and deepening. It was also occurring in other parts of the United Kingdom, with the

Lallans Makars in Scotland, among the Welsh, in the West Country. But at home nobody went so far as I did in analysis, definition, assertion. Indeed I met with strong criticism from fellow writers, had my encounters with the vice-chancellor of the university and the then Minister of Education who held that 'Northern Ireland was as much a part of the United Kingdom as Yorkshire'.

I wrote articles, letters to the editor, reviews, poems, lectured, talked, broadcast, when I could find an audience. Even after the war's ending, the momentum continued for four or five years. *Lagan* was wound up. A new magazine, largely of verse, *Rann*, was started by a fellow poet, Roy McFadden, my most consistent critic, who even got a couple of fine satirical poems out of my shortcomings. But by 1951 this, too, came to a halt, though in the last issue I was able to quote John Mitchel – 'a deep enough root those planters have struck into the soil of Ulster, and it would now be ill striving to unplant them' – a forthright challenge even more pertinent in 1972.

That phase of local concentrated creativity ended. The doors to the rest of the world were now open, though I did not then imagine that before long I myself should have left the country, to observe new phases of greater promise, particularly among the young poets, from across the Irish Sea.

Towards the end of the phase – I can be precise about the dates – while at our cottage near Cushendall after Christmas 1949, I was caught in a strange gust of verse-making, and discovered myself to be working on three new poems in the space of less than a week, switching, as the spirit seized me, from one to the other and back again. The best of the three, perhaps, 'The Colony' allegorised the regional circumstance as that of a Roman colony at the Empire's waning, and in what terms the colonists viewed the situation and the future.

For me, this is the definitive statement of my realisation that I am an Ulsterman. I had already, in another poem, 'Once Alien Here', established the claim that I was . . .

> . . . because of all the buried men
> in Ulster clay, because of rock and glen
> and mist and cloud and quality of air
> as native in my thought as any here . . .

But that was in some way a physical identification with the earth, with the climate; it was little more than locating my place on the map, mine by a respectably long tenure.

Among 'The Colony''s 140 lines of decasyllabic blank verse occurs the phrase 'the curfewed ghetto', perhaps the first recorded use of the term in relation to areas where the Catholic minorities are gathered in Northern Ireland: certainly in the many political speeches I had heard I cannot recollect that word 'ghetto' being uttered.

There is, too, the passage:

> . . . sure that Caesar's word
> is Caesar's bond for legions in our need

which, twenty years ago, seemed pompous rhetoric. Those legions have now suffered their casualties and inflicted them.

After a description of how the colony came into being, every statement backed by historical fact, the narrator goes on to record the colonists' behaviour to the natives, and follows this with a very harsh appraisal of how these natives had become conditioned by the long years of servitude and deprivation. He concludes with his rather grudging plea . . .

> admit our load of guilt . . .
> . . . and would make amends
> by fraternising, by small friendly gestures,
> hoping by patient words I may convince
> my people and this people we are changed
> from the raw levies which usurped the land,
> if not to kin, to co-inhabitants,
> as goat and ox may graze in the same field
> and each gain something from proximity;
> for we have rights drawn from the soil and sky;
> the use, the pace, the patient years of labour,
> the rain against the lips, the changing light,
> the heavy clay-sucked stride, have altered us;
> we would be strangers in the Capitol;
> this is our country also, no-where else;
> and we shall not be outcast on the world.

'The Colony' appeared in the *Bell* in 1963, but no one seems to have paid much heed. When, however, in the winter of 1970 the Arts Council of

Northern Ireland organised a tour of poetry readings by John Montague and myself, the accompanying booklet, *The Planter and the Gael*, carried it among our texts. And this time it secured some attention, and since then the lines I have quoted above have been used in a speech by Mr [Jack] Lynch on St Patrick's Day in Philadelphia and in a leading article of the *Irish Times*. This would suggest my statement has some representative validity. I should be glad if the Prime Minister of Northern Ireland were to quote them, having first read the whole poem.

I have so far no more than outlined the chart of a highly personal journey to a point of self-realisation. I have not offered a routing for another's setting out, for I do not know of anyone to whom it may now be relevant. I have not loaded the margins with references to the places and people that are the necessary stuff of my allegiance and regard.

I have not attempted to predicate by what means we may isolate the moment when a colony set among an older population ceases simply to be simply a colony and becomes something else, although I have not hesitated to take that 'something else' to be a valid *region* with the inalienable right to choose its place within a smaller or larger federation. Nor have I discussed the matter of the Two Nations which should have required an examination of the concept of nationality, and a consideration of when the people of Ireland became the Irish Nation, whether in 1641, when the indigenous population made its most sustained effort to expel the Planters, or in 1848, when the myth of nationality was given its symbolism by the Young Irelanders. I have proposed no immediate tactics or strategies which might resolve the tragic confusion of this heart-breaking present.

My cast of mind is such that I am moved by intuitions, intimations, imaginative realisations, epiphanies, which, after all, may not be the worst way to face life and its future in our bitter, hate-riven island.

We have had enough of the rigid clichés of stubborn politicians, the profit-focused intensity of men of business, the dogmatic arrogance of the churches, the intolerance of sectarians, the lack of human sympathy of doctrinaire ideologues, of all those whose ready instinct is for violence in word and act.

I have experienced a deep enduring sense of our human past before the Lion-Gate of Mycenae and among the Rolright Stones of the

Oxfordshire border, but it is in the north-eastern corner of Ireland where I was born and lived until my fiftieth year, where the only ancestors I can name are buried:

> Grain of my timber, how I grew,
> my syntax, cadence, rhetoric,
> grammar of my dialect.

'No Rootless Colonist', *Aquarius*, 1972

Another Oliver Cromwell

George A. Birmingham

I find by consulting my diary that it was on the 30th of June that I went to Dublin. I am not often in Dublin, though I do not share the contempt for that city which is felt by most Ulstermen. Cahoon, for instance, will not recognize it as the capital of the country in which he lives, and always speaks of Dublin people as impractical, given over to barren political discussion and utterly unable to make useful things such as ships and linen. He also says that Dublin is dirty, that the rates are exorbitantly high, and that the houses have not got bath-rooms in them. I put it to him that there are two first-rate libraries in Dublin.

'If I want a book,' he said, 'I buy it. We pay for what we use in Belfast. We are business men.'

'But,' I explained, 'there are some books, old ones, which you cannot buy. You can only consult them in libraries.'

'Why don't you go to London, then?' said Cahoon.

The conversation took place in the club. I lunched there on my way through Belfast, going on to Dublin by an afternoon train. I was, in fact, going to Dublin to consult some books in the College Library. Marion and I had been brought up short in our labours on my history for want of some quotations from the diary of a seventeenth-century divine, and even if I had been willing to buy the book I should have had to wait months while a second-hand bookseller advertised for it.

Trinity College, when I entered the quadrangle next day, seemed singularly deserted. The long vacation had begun a week before. Fellows, professors and students had fled from the scene of their labours. Halfway across the square, however, I met McNeice. He seemed quite glad to see me and invited me to luncheon in his rooms. I accepted the invitation and was fed on cold ham, stale bread and bottled stout.

Thackeray once hinted that fellows of Trinity College gave their guests beer to drink. Many hard words have been said of him ever since by members of Dublin University. I have no wish to have hard things said about me; so I explain myself carefully. McNeice's luncheon was an eccentricity. It is not on cold ham solely, it is not on stale bread ever, that guests in the Common Room are fed. If, like Prince Hal, they remember amid their feasting 'that good creature, small beer', they do not drink it without being offered nobler beverages. When the University, in recognition of my labours on the Life of St Patrick, made me a doctor of both kinds of law, I fared sumptuously in the dining hall and afterwards sipped port rich with the glory of suns which shone many many years ago on the banks of the upper Douro.

After luncheon, while I was still heavy with the spume of the stout, McNeice asked me if I had seen the new paper which was being published to express, I imagine also to exacerbate, the opinions of the Ulster Unionists. He produced a copy as he spoke. It was called *The Loyalist*.

'We wanted something with a bite in it,' he said. 'We're dead sick of the pap the daily papers give us in their leading articles.'

Pap is, I think, a soft innocuous food, slightly sugary in flavour, suitable for infants. I should never have dreamed of describing the articles in *The Belfast Newsletter* as pap. An infant nourished on them would either suffer badly from the form of indigestion called flatulence or would grow up to be an exceedingly ferocious man. I felt, however, that if McNeice had anything to do with the editing of *The Loyalist* its articles would be of such a kind that those of the *Newsletter* would seem, by comparison, papescent.

'We're running it as a weekly,' said McNeice, 'and what we want is to get it into the home of every Protestant farmer, and every workingman in Belfast. We are circulating the first six numbers free. After that we shall charge a penny.'

I looked at *The Loyalist*. It was very well printed, on good paper. It looked something like *The Spectator*, but had none of the pleasant advertisements of schools and books, and much fewer pages of correspondence than the English weekly has.

'Surely,' I said, 'you can't expect it to pay at that price.'

'We don't,' said McNeice. 'We've plenty of money behind us. Conroy – you know Conroy, don't you?'

'Oh,' I said, 'then Lady Moyne got a subscription out of him after all. I knew she intended to.'

'Lady Moyne isn't in this at all,' said McNeice. 'We're out for business with *The Loyalist*. Lady Moyne's – well, I don't quite see Lady Moyne running *The Loyalist*.'

'She's a tremendously keen Unionist,' I said. 'She gave an address to the working-women of Belfast the week before last, one of the most moving –'

'All frills,' said McNeice, 'silk frills. Your friend Crossan is acting as one of our agents, distributing the paper for us. That'll give you an idea of the lines we're going on.'

Crossan, I admit, is the last man I should suspect of being interested in frills. The mention of his name gave me an idea.

'Was it copies of *The Loyalist*,' I asked, 'which were in the packing-cases which you and Power landed that night from the *Finola*?'

McNeice laughed.

'Come along round with me,' he said, 'and see the editor. He'll interest you. He's a first-rate journalist, used to edit a rebel paper and advocate the use of physical force for throwing off the English rule. But he's changed his tune now. Just wait for me one moment while I get together an article which I promised to bring him. It's all scattered about the floor of the next room in loose sheets.'

I read *The Loyalist* while I waited. The editor was unquestionably a first-rate journalist. His English was of a naked, muscular kind, which reminded me of Swift and occasionally of John Mitchel. But I could not agree with McNeice that he had changed his tune. He still seemed to be editing a rebel paper and still advocated the use of physical force for resisting the will of the King, Lords and Commons of our constitution. It is the merest commonplace to say that Ireland is a country of unblushing self-contradictions; but I do not think that the truth of this ever came home to me quite so forcibly as when I read *The Loyalist* that it would be better, if necessary, to imitate the Boers and shoot down regiments of British soldiers than to be false to the Empire of which 'it is our proudest boast that we are citizens'. The editor – such was the conclusion I arrived at – must be a humorist of a high order.

His name was Diarmid O'Donovan and he always wrote it in Irish characters, which used to puzzle me at first when I got into correspondence with him. We found him in a small room at the top of a house in a side street of a singularly depressing kind.

McNeice explained to me that *The Loyalist* did not court notoriety, and preferred to have an office which was, as far as possible, out of sight. He said that O'Donovan was particularly anxious to be unobtrusive. He had, before he became connected with *The Loyalist*, been editor of two papers which had been suppressed by the Government for advocating what the Litany calls 'sedition and privy conspiracy'. He held, very naturally, that a paper would get on better in the world if it had no office at all. If that was impossible, the office should be an attic in an inaccessible slum.

O'Donovan, when we entered, was seated at a table writing vigorously. I do not know how he managed to write at all. His table was covered with stacks of newspapers, very dusty. He had cleared a small, a very small space in the middle of them, and his ink-bottle occupied a kind of cave hollowed out at the base of one of the stacks. It must have been extremely difficult to put a pen into it. The chairs – there were only two of them besides the editorial stool – were also covered with papers. But even if they had been free I should not have cared to sit down on them. They were exceedingly dirty and did not look safe.

McNeice introduced me and then produced his own article. O'Donovan, very politely, offered me his stool.

'McNeice tells me,' he said, 'that you are writing a history of Irish Rebellions. I suppose you have said that Nationalism ceased to exist about the year 1900?'

'I hadn't thought of saying that,' I said. 'In fact – in view of the Home Rule Bill, you know – I should have said that Irish Nationalism was just beginning to come to its own.'·

O'Donovan snorted.

'There's no such thing as Irish Nationalism left,' he said. 'The country is hypnotized. We've accepted a Bill which deprives us of the most elementary rights of freemen. We've licked the boots of English Liberals. We've said "thank you" for any gnawed bones they like to fling to us. We've –'

It struck me that O'Donovan was becoming rhetorical. I interrupted him.

'Idealism in politics,' I said, 'is one of the most futile things there is. What the Nationalist Party –'

'Don't call them that,' said O'Donovan. 'I tell you they're not Nationalists.'

'I'll call them anything you like,' I said, 'but until you invent some other name for them I can't well talk about them without calling them Nationalists.'

'They –' said O'Donovan.

'Very well,' I said. '*They*. So long as you know who I mean, the pronoun will satisfy me. They had to consider not what men like you wanted, but what the Liberal Party could be induced to give. I don't say they made the best bargain possible, but –'

'Anyhow,' said McNeice, 'we're not going to be governed by those fellows. That's the essential point.'

I think it is. The Unionist is not really passionately attached to the Union. He has no insuperable antipathy to Home Rule. Indeed, I think most Unionists would welcome any change in our existing system of government if it were not that they have the most profound and deeply rooted objection to the men whom McNeice describes as 'those fellows', and O'Donovan indicates briefly as 'they'.

'And so,' I said, turning to O'Donovan, 'in mere despair of nationality you have gone over to the side of the Unionists.'

'I've gone over,' said O'Donovan, 'to the side of the only people in Ireland who mean to fight.'

Supposing that Ulster really did mean to fight, O'Donovan's position was quite reasonable. But Babberly says it will never come to fighting. He is quite confident of his ability to bluff the conscientious Liberal into dropping the Home Rule Bill for fear of civil war. O'Donovan, and possibly McNeice, will be left out in the cold if Babberly is right. The matter is rather a tangled one. With Babberly is Lady Moyne, working at her ingenious policy of dragging a red herring across the path along which democracy goes towards socialism. On the other hand there is McNeice with fiery intelligence, and O'Donovan, a coldly consistent rebel against English rule in any shape and form. They have their little paper with money enough behind it, with people like Crossan circulating it for them. It is quite possible that they may count for something. Then there is Malcolmson, a man of almost incredible stupidity, but with a knowledge, hammered into him no doubt with extra difficulty, of how to handle guns.

O'Donovan and McNeice were bending over some proof sheets and talking in low whispers; there was a knock at the office door, and a moment later Malcolmson entered. He looked bristlier than ever, and was plainly in a state of joyous excitement. He held a copy of the first number of *The Loyalist* in his hand. He caught sight of me at once.

136

'I'm damned,' he said, 'if I expected to see you here, Kilmore. You're the last man in Ireland –'

'I'm only here by accident,' I said, 'and I'm going away almost at once. Let me introduce you to Mr McNeice and Mr O'Donovan.'

Malcolmson shook hands with the two men vigorously. I never shake hands with Malcolmson if I can possibly help it, because he always hurts me. I expect he hurt both McNeice and O'Donovan. They did not cry out, but they looked a good deal surprised.

'I happened to be in Dublin,' said Malcolmson, 'and I called round here to congratulate the editor of this paper. I only came across it the day before yesterday, and –'

'You couldn't have come across it any sooner,' I said, 'for it's only just published.'

'And to put down my name as a subscriber for twenty copies. If you want money –'

'They don't,' I said, 'Conroy is financing them.'

'Conroy has some sound ideas,' said Malcolmson.

'You approve of the paper, then?' said McNeice.

'I like straight talk,' said Malcolmson.

'We aim at that,' said O'Donovan.

'I'm dead sick of politics and speech making,' said Malcolmson. 'What I want is to have a slap at the damned rebels.'

'Mr O'Donovan's point of view,' I said, 'is almost the same as yours. What he wants –'

'I'm glad to hear it,' said Malcolmson, 'and I need only say that when the time comes, gentlemen, and it won't be long now if things go on as they are going – you'll find me ready. What Ireland wants –'

Malcolmson paused. I waited expectantly. It is always interesting to hear what Ireland wants. Many people have theories on the subject, and hardly any one agrees with any one else.

'What Ireland wants,' said Malcolmson dramatically, 'is another Oliver Cromwell.'

He drew himself up and puffed out his chest as he spoke. He must, I think, have rather fancied himself in the part of a twentieth-century Puritan horse soldier. I looked round at O'Donovan to see how he was taking the suggestion. Oliver Cromwell I supposed, could not possibly be one of his favourite heroes. But I had misjudged O'Donovan. His sympathy with rebels of all nations was evidently stronger than his dislike of the typical Englishman. After all, Cromwell, however objectionable his religious views may have been, did kill a king. O'Donovan smiled quite pleasantly at Malcolmson. I dare say that even the idea of a new massacre of Drogheda was agreeable enough to him, provided the inhabitants of the town were the people to whom he denied the title of Nationalists and Malcolmson wanted to have a slap at because they were rebels.

Then McNeice got us all back to practical business in a way that would have delighted Cahoon. McNeice, though he does live in Dublin, has good Belfast blood in his veins. He likes his heroics to be put on a business basis. The immediate and most pressing problem, he reminded us, was to secure as large a circulation as possible for *The Loyalist*.

'You get the paper into the people's hands,' he said to Malcolmson, 'and we'll get the ideas into their heads.'

Malcolmson, who is certainly prepared to make sacrifices in a good cause, offered to hire a man with a motorcycle to distribute the paper from house to house over a wide district.

'I know the exact man we want,' he said. 'He knows every house in County Antrim, and the people like him. He's been distributing Bibles and selling illuminated texts among the farmers and labourers for years. He's what's called a colporteur. That,' he turned to O'Donovan with his explanation, 'is a kind of Scripture reader, you know.'

If any one in the world except Malcolmson had suggested the employment of a Scripture reader for the distribution of *The Loyalist*, I should have applauded a remarkable piece of cynicism. But Malcolmson was in simple earnest.

'Will you be able to get him?' I said. 'The society which employs him may perhaps –'

'Oh, that will be all right,' said Malcolmson. 'There can't be any objection. But if there is – I happen to be a member of the committee of the society. I'm one' – he sunk his voice modestly – 'of the largest subscribers.'

I am inclined to forget sometimes that Malcolmson takes a leading part in Church affairs. At the last meeting of the General Synod of the Church of Ireland he said that the distribution of the Bible among the people of

Ireland was the surest means of quenching the desire for Home Rule. Free copies of *The Loyalist* for the people who already have Bibles and a force of artillery are, so to speak, his reserves.

from *The Red Hand of Ulster*, 1912

SAVING SOULS IN BANGOR AND BELFAST

MAX WRIGHT

When I was nine years old my father was killed. On the night of 15 April 1941 there was a heavy air raid on Belfast. We lived twelve miles away in Bangor, then a middling-sized seaside resort. One bomber, lightening his load for the long haul home, dropped his last bomb in our front garden. And so as I fled the house where my mother lay, or so it has always seemed to me in what must surely be a nightmare quasi-memory, at some distance from one of her legs, I saw my father for the last time, dying at the turn of the stairs.

My memories of my father are jejune, suggesting to me that I must have suppressed a good deal, perhaps out of an early reluctance to be drawn into a sentimental communion with my grieving mother. 'Do you remember when your father . . . ?' she must often have asked, and I imagine that my response was frequently ungracious and negative. I do remember that he bought me a secondhand bicycle and had the good sense to push me vigorously down the incline which led from Broadway into Hazeldene Gardens, so that after only two tumbles I was up and away, as free as Marie in the mountains. He bought a secondhand baby Austin which even then looked out of date, and then delighted me by buying another which, though still secondhand, was the very latest edition. One dark night at the beginning of the Second World War, between Newtownards and Conlig, we ran out of petrol. My father went to the nearest farmhouse and returned with a can of what he claimed was airforce petrol which, strictly speaking, he said, we should not be using. For the remaining miles I entertained the liveliest expectation that we would take off, if only a foot or so above the tarmacadam.

The few memories I have of my father are for the most part centred on the brethren and their gospel hall in Central Avenue, Bangor, which were such a large part of his life and therefore, perforce, of mine. Of this assembly he was, though comparatively young, an elder, or in our jargon one of the overseeing brethren, or, for short, one of the oversight. I was proud of him as in this capacity he led the open-air meetings on blustery summer evenings before the war in the extravagantly named Marine Gardens under the McKee Clock.

Then let our songs abound
And every tear be dry.
We're marching through Immanuel's ground
To fairer worlds on high.
We're marching to Zion,
Beautiful, beautiful Zion,
We're marching upward to Zion,
The beautiful city of God.

The world strolled past sucking icecream sliders (wafers) and pokes (as cones or cornets were innocently styled by our cold maids) totally indifferent to the beautiful city of God. This was only to be expected for as the world would shortly learn, perhaps from my father, wide is the gate, and broad is the way that leadeth to destruction, and *many* there be which go in thereat, while strait is the gate and narrow is the way which leadeth unto life, and *few* there be that find it (Matthew 7:13–14). Certainly the summer crowds appeared to confirm Matthew in his pessimistic estimates, and in memory our group seems pathetically small, perhaps surprisingly so when you remember that this was the evangelical, Protestant northeast of Ireland in the unpermissive 1930s.

One curious memory is of my father's frequent ministry to the assembled saints at the Lord's Day morning meeting. On these occasions he was often moved to read from the Book of Psalms and invariably that odd little word 'Selah' would be pronounced by him not once but several times. As, for example, 'Hear my prayer, O God; give ear to the words of my mouth. For strangers are risen up against me, and oppressors seek after my soul: they have not set God before them. Selah' (Psalm 54:3). Or, a firm favourite: 'When I kept silence, my bones waxed old through my roaring all the day long. For day and night thy hand was heavy upon me: my moisture is turned into the drought of summer. Selah' (Psalm 32:3–4). I was always very impressed by the authority, not to say the insouciance, with which my father delivered himself of this mysterious vocable, just as if he knew what it meant. Did he know what it meant? Did I ever ask him? If so, I have forgotten.

On one occasion I found myself covered with reflected glory through the visit of my father's first cousin, who was to stay with us while conducting a week of special meetings in the gospel hall. This cousin was a celebrated missionary, and was known throughout our little community, in the style of famous evangelical missionaries of the past like Fred Stanley Arnot of Africa and Hudson Taylor of China, as Bobbie Wright of Japan. He was home on his first leave, or 'furlough', as the missionaries would refer to it, savouring the military nuance. On his first Sunday he 'took' the Sunday school and we heard from the horse's mouth about the rather dim prospects of those unfortunate children who had been foolish enough to be born in heathen darkness and about whom it was our custom to sing on most Sunday afternoons.

> When mothers of Salem their children brought to Jesus,
> The stern disciples drove them back and bade them depart. ·
> But Jesus saw them ere they fled
> And sweetly looked and kindly said,
> 'Suffer the children to come unto Me.'
>
> How kind was the Saviour to bid those children welcome,
> But there are many thousands who have never heard His Name.
> The Bible they have never read,
> They know not that the Saviour said,
> 'Suffer the children to come unto Me.'

Then Bobbie taught us to sing 'Jesus Loves Me' in Japanese ('Wah Gah Shoo Yessu' or phonemes roughly to that effect). But this was kid's stuff. At the evening meetings, which I was given a special, late-to-bed dispensation to attend, the grown-ups were encouraged to sing, to the splendid rollicking tune of 'Bringing in the Sheaves':

> Bringing Japanese, bringing Japanese,
> We shall come rejoicing, bringing Japanese.

Six years old, I blushed with embarrassed pleasure, anticipating that golden harvest evening when we would carry in from the fields great yellow stooks of saved Japanese sinners to lay at the Saviour's feet.

Within the year, Bobbie had returned to Japan where he was caught by the war and languished in Japanese internment camps. He survived to return (like General MacArthur) for a post-bellum tour of duty. In later life he would describe, affectingly (I suppose), his joy at being met on the quay at Yokohama by eight Japanese brethren who had kept the faith, through trials and tribulations both psychological and physical that had forced others into apostasy. Doubtless it is only the world, with its miscalculated priorities, that would think the cost of bringing the good news from Tyrone to Tokyo a bit excessive. At the time, of course, I found it entirely natural that Bobbie should have obeyed the injunction to go into all the world and preach the gospel to every creature (Mark 16:15), devoting his life to bringing a handful of Japanese ('where two or three are gathered together in my name, there am I in the midst of them' – Matthew 18:20) into little assemblies of born-again Christians just like those in which he himself had grown up in Omagh and Letterkenny and Fintona and Castlederg, in his home town of Strabane, and five miles down the road at Sion Mills, locus of the story of the doubtless apocryphal brethren death notice, the encomium of which was transmitted to the newspaper as 'For forty years a watcher on Sion's hills' only to appear as 'For forty years a watchman at Sion Mills'. . . .

For years after I had become to the best of my belief a convinced atheist, with not the slightest residual doubt, still less any fear that there might be at least some grain of truth in the brethren's crazy *Weltanschauung*, I continued to bow in the House of Rimmon, attending conferences and meetings (my mother leaning on my arm), actually praying in prayer meetings and preaching the gospel both in the open air and in the gospel halls.

Why? I would have said at the time, and I still think the answer is fairly near the truth, that I was extremely conscious of my mother's plight. She never missed an opportunity to make me aware of it, but to be fair, her condition did surely make her a legitimate object of concern, none better placed to feel sorry for her, none more obliged to pity her than myself.

I was the only child, worse, the only son of a widowed mother who had lost one leg and had little use of the other and whose whole ambition, she would have said, was only to see me go on in the ways of the Lord, following in the footsteps of my sainted, tragically dead father. She would tell me, not only once, and always as if she was doing me a great, unselfish favour, that like Hannah with the infant Samuel, she had lent me to the Lord (1 Samuel 1:28). When the brethren sang

> Can a mother's tender care
> Cease towards the child she bare?
> Yes, she may forgetful be,
> Yet will I remember Thee,

my mother kept her silence thereby indicating, I suppose, that such a response on her part would be absurd since for her the question could be only rhetorical. The silliest things made her grieve. For example, she wept when, aged fifteen, I gave up physics and chemistry in favour of French and Spanish, thus cutting off my path to a medical degree and a mission in the Copperbelt. How could I do such a thing to myself (and to her)? No triumphal furlough addresses, enthralling the Easter crowds at Glengall Street, could now be anticipated – no heart-rending stories of how M'Gombo had been delivered, appendix and soul, from the machinations of the witch doctor.

In this matter I compared most unfavourably with a young acquaintance in the Knightsbridge assembly, Fred Stanley Arnot Stevenson, son of Gibson Stevenson, the man from the Pru who raised the hymns and prayed somewhat aggressively. Fred was already well on his way to medical school, and if his ambitions were not directed towards the Copperbelt it was only because he had conceived a rather special, indeed a unique exercise towards a neglected sector, the very rich. He had already confided to me and to his special mentor, Moses Bartholomew's son, Aaron, his hope that in the pursuit of this end he would be able to specialise in psychological medicine, eventually becoming a psychoanalyst. That a young fundamentalist Christian (*circa* 1947) should have entertained any ambitions in that direction may seem odd, but his motives were of the very purest.

There were some exceedingly well-off people, he explained to me, who would actually go to a psychoanalyst complaining of feelings of incapacitating guilt, sometimes accompanied by a fear of hell and damnation. The analyst would explain to his clients that these feelings of guilt were irrational and would disappear only when in dialogue with a skilful therapist their origins came to be properly understood. What an opportunity, thought Fred, to speak a word in season to some who might otherwise never hear the gospel, a parish of rich women whose eternal prospects were as uncertain as those of the average camel attempting to negotiate the eye of a needle. Fred would tell the rich patients who came to his consulting rooms the truth, that, far from being irrational, their feelings of guilt were well founded, being the proper response to their desperate situation. They were indeed guilty sinners, estranged from a righteous God and on their way to hell, and the only remedy was recognition of their guilt, repentance from their sins and faith in the atoning work of Jesus Christ. He did not tell me if he thought a hundred guineas would be an appropriate fee for such uniquely excellent advice. Quite unfitted to follow Fred, how then could I deny my mother a merely cosmetic submission to the ways of the brethren, which meant so much to her, when she had already suffered so much?

I considered my own situation, not I fear without some adolescent self-pity and a good deal of *mauvaise foi* in the excuses I made to myself for continuing therein. It seemed to me about as bad as it could be. If only there had been a brother or a sister with whom to spread the burden then surely, I told myself, I would have gone my own way. Or if I had been my mother's daughter, then without what I convinced myself was an additional Oedipean complexity, I would have outfaced her, woman to woman, calling her emotional bluff. More plausibly, if it had been my father rather than my mother who had survived to be my tormentor with his other-worldly, professedly disinterested ambitions for me, surely I would have been able to cope; to tell him straight out that while he might be march-ing to Zion, the beautiful city of God, most assuredly I was not, even though such defiance would certainly have turned his moisture into the drought of summer, Selah. Gosse, escaped to London, although consumed with despair at his own feebleness and want of will (my feelings exactly), together with pity for his father's obvious distress, managed to cope with Philip Gosse's 'postal inquisition'. 'When your sainted Mother died, she not only tenderly committed you to God, but left you also as a solemn charge to me, to bring you up in the nurture and admonition of the Lord. That responsibility I have kept constantly before me. ... Before your childhood was past, there seemed God's manifest blessing on our care; for you seemed truly converted to Him; you confessed in solemn baptism that you had died and been raised with Christ; and you were received with joy into the bosom of the Church of God, as one alive from the dead' and so on and so on and so on.

Substitute a sainted father for a sainted mother and I could well imagine my mother's tearful litany, subsequent on any overt apostasy of mine, at once more incoherent than Gosse's and because of that so much harder to deal with: tender commitment, solemn charge, responsibility, conversion, baptism, reception into the bosom of the Church of God. 'How can I go up to my Father (to say nothing of *your father*) in heaven and the lad be not with me?' Only a very heartless lad would have been impervious to such a plea.

I also recognised that the greatest handicap of all was my mother's physical condition. From very early days, while still at preparatory school, still a believer, trusting Jesus most of the time (doubting days always excepted), I was resentful of and deeply ashamed of my mother's broken frame – and full of guilt that I should feel such resentment and shame against and for a state for which she was blameless. Her frequent references to her condition filled me with unease. When she left hospital and went to live on the Stranmillis Road, the rector of St Bartholomew's Church of Ireland church visited her, wondering if she might be a new parishioner. My mother told him her sad story. She then explained that as a simple, born-again Christian, saved when she was a little girl aged only ten, who had learned the biblical truth about believers' baptism and assembly fellowship according to New Testament principles, she had no need for the rituals of the so-called churches. Did Dr Lindsay, she wondered, know and love the Lord Jesus Christ as his own and personal saviour? Nettled, the rector took his leave, asking her if she expected in heaven to be reunited with her errant limb as well as with my father. The story was told over and over again, as the saints exclaimed at the shocking behaviour of a minister of Christ (so-called), but I fear I was less appalled by the rector's rudeness than by my mother's unashamed reference in mixed company to her missing leg. Why did she have to be so explicit? Why did she have to talk about it at all? When she confided in me, as she frequently did, that she had a bad pain in her stump today, I was disgusted, and dismayed that I should be disgusted. Stump! What a word! The only stumps I wanted to know about had bails on them. Thus

146

to my lasting shame were my teeth set on edge, like the teeth of those children in the Book of Jeremiah whose fathers had eaten a sour grape.

On a hot July day just after the end of the Second World War she came to school for the Father's Day cricket match to watch me play. Cars and petrol were still in short supply but all the parents at Cabin Hill seemed to have been able to lay their hands on at least a taxi. My mother would have said she could not afford one, and so taking two trams she toiled across Belfast, finally limping up the half-mile of the school drive with her heavy stick and her artificial leg, shod in ugly black boots. She watched the game uncomprehending, and at teatime was fussed over by a non-playing prefect, more gracious than I. (Easy for him, I thought, she's not his mother.) When my friend Spender (whose father Captain Spender, on leave from a good war in Whitehall had just made 33 not out) later remarked, ingenuously or disingenuously, that he had seen me with my granny, I did not dispute the description. The match over, I had to give her my arm and walk her back to the main road while private cars and taxis, Austin Twelves and Standard Tens, Humbers and Rileys, an Alvis, an Armstrong-Siddeley rolled down the hill past us. As she limped off and hoisted herself onto the tram I recognised that it would be wicked in anyone, and beyond belief in me, a sinner saved by grace, to wish that she had stayed at home. But I did, fervently. For a father dropping catches and coming in at the ninth wicket, for two parents with four legs evenly distributed in a Sunbeam Talbot I would have dealt with Mephistopheles.

So, four years later, how was I to say to her that the beliefs of the brethren were unmitigated nonsense? That at death the dome of many-coloured glass is trampled to fragments, the million-petalled flower of being here disintegrates, the insubstantial pageant fades, leaving not a rack behind. No heaven, no hell, no salvation, no damnation, no lake burning with fire and brimstone, no glad reunion with my father, no great advantage to be gained from keeping out of picture houses. When, further years on, I did eventually stammer some of these things in a half-hearted way, her reaction was what I had suspected all along that it would be: not alarm at my eternal damnation but dismay at what relatives and fellow saints in the assembly would say and think. Her exact words were what I felt I had always known they would be: 'How can you do this thing to me when I have already suffered so much?' What she dreaded was the false pity, the Schadenfreude of the closed community ('Of course she should never have sent him to that school'), the clammy prayers of visiting elders for the backslider.

Therefore I procrastinated. . . . drawn more and more into practices which both embarrassed and shamed me. After the march round the houses to advertise the Sunday evening gospel meeting, the brethren would retire, to have a prayer meeting, to the small room at the back of the gospel hall where I had so recently been dried off. Here, in almost identical words, those simple men would pray, turn and turn about, for the success of the gospel meeting about to begin. Almighty God, our Heavenly Father, they would invariably begin. Then they would boldly approach the throne of grace (Hebrews 4:16) that they might obtain mercy and find grace to help in time of need. The speaker, Thy servant, our brother, would be brought before the Lord, that his arms might be strengthened and the fear of man (Proverbs 29:25) removed, as he sought faithfully to bear witness yet again to the saving power of the finished work at Calvary. As the hymn writer had put it so beautifully, it is finished yes indeed, finished every jot, sinner this is all you need, tell me is it not? Might our brother be granted the power of the Spirit to speak a word in season which would fall into good ground bringing forth fruit, thirtyfold, sixtyfold, even a hundredfold to the glory of God (Matthew 13:8). As the hymn writer had written, Mercy drops round us were falling but what we pleaded for was showers of blessing. Almighty God was reminded that it was not His will that any should perish but that all should come to repentance (2 Peter 3:9), that His hand was not shortened that it could not save nor was His ear heavy that it could not hear (Isaiah 59:1). Optimistic mention would be made of those friends who might come in off the street, perhaps to hear the gospel for the first time, and, more realistically, of named individuals, the children of believers, who would certainly be present, that young Malcolm Bleaney for example, that child of many prayers, might this very evening close with God's offer of salvation, accepting that Christ had died in his guilty room and stead (never 'instead of him' but always 'in his room and stead'). Finally, support would be invoked for the gospel wherever it was preached this evening, to earth's remotest bounds, that wherever Christ was lifted up to the gaze of the perishing, men would be drawn to Him (John 12:32). All this would be asked in the Name of, and for the sake of Thy Son, our Saviour, the Lord Jesus Christ.

There were not many of us, and I would keep a furtive eye on my watch hoping that the half-hour of prayer would be filled and to spare by senior suppliants. All too often, however, by ten minutes to seven all the saints in the little room except me would have prayed. There would be a long silence when sighs short and frequent were exhaled, interspersed with the odd pious groan, indicative of some private wrestling. Then one of the elders would get to his feet signalling that we might all rise, dusting off the knees of our trousers. Reproachful looks, so it seemed to me, were directed at the non-participant.

And so, not too many Sunday evenings after I was baptised, I was dismayed to hear myself boldly approaching the throne of grace to find help in time of need for Thy servant our brother that he might be granted a word in season and enabled to lift up Christ to the gaze of the perishing, since it was not God's will that any should perish but that all should come to repentance – that the gospel to earth's remotest bounds might prosper and wherever Christ was lifted to the gaze of the perishing, men might be drawn to Him – all these requests being understood to have been made in the Name of, and for the sake of Thy Son, our Saviour the Lord Jesus Christ. This performance was amen-ed much more enthusiastically than any of the regular contributions, both during the prayer and after, when all the brethren loudly said 'Amen!', two of them twice. They were not, of course, moved to such a fulsome endorsement by my eloquence, but were in their artless way saying, 'Well done!' I curled my toes until I thought they would go into cramp.

As the years went by, further participations were exacted. I avoided the commitment to take a Sunday school class on the grounds that my attendances while I was at boarding school would be too irregular to permit such an undertaking. But on the Sundays when I was in attendance I went to the so-called Bible Class, which was devoted to scriptural exposition for saved young people, and which was held in a corner of the hall at the same time as the Sunday school. So if, as often happened, some brother or sister who was a regular Sunday school teacher was absent, I would be asked to supply the need and could hardly refuse. On these occasions much of the time could be spent in hearing the children's verses.

149

They would be required to learn a chapter by heart, say John chapter 3, or Romans chapter 5, a verse at a time. So if I was in luck they might have progressed as far as John 3 and 36, which involved a lot of time-consuming recitation, all the way from 'There was a man of the Pharisees, named Nicodemus' to 'he that believeth not the Son shall not see the life; but the wrath of God abideth on him'. The children of the brethren would be well drilled and even if the lesser breeds were totally unprepared, I was ready to prompt them at every other word through the thirty-six verses, so putting in half an hour. Those who were waiting to recite or who had already performed became bored and fought with one another. But since such confusion was general all over the hall it was not something for which I felt I need hold myself responsible. If they had just started their chapter, I filled the time by telling them Bible stories, David and Goliath, Moses in Egypt, Joseph in Egypt, Jacob and Esau, Joshua and Jericho, Daniel in the den of lions. Aged fifteen, I found the duty of telling ten-year-olds that they needed to be born again quite beyond me, so at no time did I urge God's plan of salvation on those whom the elderly super-intendent quaintly referred to as the 'scholars'.

On Wednesday evenings during the summer months, the younger breth-ren would assemble at the gospel hall for a short prayer meeting prepara-tory to an excursion with the gospel message into darkest Edenderry or Lambeg or Dundonald or Newtownbreda or Holywood or Mossley. This exercise was known as the Village Work and seems to have been a tradi-tion in most of the working-class assemblies in Belfast, going back to the early years of the century when these places really were villages and not dormitory towns or suburbs in the Belfast conurbation. Great missionary brethren grown famous in Angola or the Belgian Congo would tell at conference time how during the First World War they had on such a foray spoken their first stumbling words in the gospel. (And hadn't they come on!) Clearly it was an environment that might have been made for the tyro, a hunting party of young males, far from the inhibiting presence of elders and women and mothers. So I was frequently egged on to have a go, that is to say, encouraged to witness for my Lord. As, eventually, I did, on a cold, windy evening in August, shouting the gospel message into a terrace of two-up two-down houses, the doors of which were all tightly shut against it. 'Hebrews chapter nine and verse twenty-seven,' I screamed.

'It is appointed unto men once to die, but after death the judgment. Hebrews nine and twenty-two: Without shedding of blood is no remission. The Gospel According to John chapter three and verse seven,' I yelled, 'Marvel not that I say unto thee, Ye must be born again.' All this was heard only by the amen-ing brethren and a small boy with his dog, my Nicodemus, who, far from marvelling, did not so much as blink at the obstetric absurdity. 'Is it nothing to you, all ye that pass by?' I bleated, but there were no passers-by, only rain in the wind, and soon it began to spit. So big Jim Sheridan gave the last short word, briefly advised everyone 'within the sound of my voice' to remember Lot's wife ('Luke seventeen and thirty-two'), shouted a prayer that God would in his rich mercy save some listener, and we went home.

from *Told in Gath*, 1990

THE SOCIAL SEPARATION OF CATHOLIC AND PROTESTANT

ROSEMARY HARRIS

Despite the fact that Catholics and Protestants lived side by side throughout the area studied, and despite the fact that their relationships with each other were in many contexts both close and friendly, it must also be emphasised that there were a great many contexts also in which their social spheres remained quite distinct. Often this was due not so much to the fact that they sought to exclude each other from their activities, but because each group tended to share in relationships from which the members of the other group excluded themselves.

In the first place it is obvious that the majority of the people were involved in religious and political organisations in which members of 'the other side' had, by definition, no wish to participate.

Roman Catholics almost invariably attended Mass once each Sunday. In Ballybeg this did not mean that all the Catholics in the area met together each week, for there was not only the main Catholic church in Ballybeg itself, but a chapel had been built nearer the hill area to which most of the people from that district went. Moreover, even those who attended the same church did not necessarily meet since there were usually two and sometimes three Masses performed in each place each Sunday. Nevertheless, the opportunities for Catholics to meet other Catholics regularly were obviously great; and they were increased by the holding of special services on saints' days that the more devout attended. . . .

By comparison, Protestants were brought somewhat less into contact with each other by their church attendance. This was partly because Protestant men were rather less regular church attenders (although very active church-goers by English standards) and partly because amongst Protestants there were denominational divisions that reduced the chances of common participation in a church service. Nevertheless, even amongst Protestants, at least one adult member of a household normally attended church each week. Moreover, and this was extremely important for the formation of social relationships amongst the young, the Protestant community expected children until well into their teens to attend their church Sunday School each week. Since a family was very strongly criticised if the children were not sent, most children had very good records of Sunday School attendance. . . .

Women had their most important non-kin ties with other members of their churches with whom they were brought into contact through actual church services. Men were commonly also brought into contact with their fellow co-religionists through politically oriented groups.

Protestant men whatever their denominational allegiance had for the most part close ties with the local Orange Lodge and/or the Free Masons. . . .It is important to note that this was not only based on antagonism to Catholics, but on their sense of local pride *vis-à-vis* other Protestants. This competitive spirit of the lodges in relation to one another was displayed in the preparations each lodge made for its participation in the annual large Orange demonstrations, especially that of the Twelfth of July. Members, and to some extent their wives, spent much time beforehand in activities designed to enable 'their' lodge to put on a good display. Each lodge had its band, which practised for months for its public performance. But even those not involved as players were active. The strong inter-lodge competitive element focused on the acquisition of good instruments and fine uniforms for the band, and the purchase of the huge painted banners that led each band on the most important public occasions. Alongside the convivial lodge meetings, therefore, a lot of effort was put into the collection of money that could often be ill-afforded. All this inevitably involved joint activity.

Some of the Catholic men belonged to the Ancient Order of Hibernians, a moderate Nationalist organisation that in appearance was very similar to the Orange Order. In this organisation, too, there was a stress on bands and banners and traditional demonstrations and attendance at lodge meetings . . . however, the Hibernian Order was less significant for the Catholics than the Orange Order was for the Protestants, and its reputation for political moderation had perhaps lost it some local support. At any rate, it did not appear that membership of the Hibernian Order was particularly high, nor was the attachment to fellow Lodge members particularly intense. There were, however, other activities that did serve to unite Catholic men. Many of the younger ones were brought together through their interest in the Pioneers, the Catholic temperance movement. Many of these, as well as others, were united through their interest in sport.

It was, and is, a feature of Northern Ireland that Protestant and Catholic children seldom learn to play the same games. Non-team games such as badminton and table-tennis were usually associated with Protestant youth clubs and were played mostly by the sophisticated. . . . In rural Ulster, in general, it was in fact only golf and, to a lesser extent, tennis (games that demand considerable expense in laying out their playing areas) that ever drew people from both religious groups. Golf courses and tennis courts were, however, not a feature of the Ballybeg countryside; they were found only some miles away in the bigger towns and it was only the very unusual Ballybeg resident, whether Catholic or Protestant, who went there to play.

The Catholic/Protestant division was even more marked in relation to team games. It would have been quite impossible to have had a 'Ballybeg' football team representing the district as a whole. The games Protestants learnt were soccer, rugby and hockey, whilst Catholic children learnt Gaelic football, hurley and camogie – this was the result of sectarian schooling and the association of Nationalism with the 'Gaelic revival'. Protestant boys were, in fact, not much involved with team games of any kind. The local Protestant school had no sports field and most of the parents would have considered time spent in playing football a waste. Only those boys and girls who went on to grammar schools elsewhere ever became really keen on such games. It seemed indeed evidence of the Protestant lack of involvement in sports generally that a Protestant committee, planning children's sports as part of the Coronation fête, expressed fears that Catholic children would come along and infuriatingly scoop up all the prizes (to which only Protestants had contributed) because with the much greater emphasis on games at their school they would be in much better practice for athletics.

There was, conversely, considerable enthusiasm amongst Catholic young men for Gaelic football. This was partly because of its association with Irish Nationalism; and it was in part because of this association that they were encouraged and actively supported by the rest of the Catholic community, both men and young women. Many attended the Sunday matches when the Ballybeg team was playing at home, and some even went by coach when the team was playing away. Some local Protestants would

154

ask interestedly after the results, and were obviously quite pleased if the local team won. Nevertheless, the connection of the game with Nationalism meant that not only did Protestants not play as members of the team, but that it was rare for them even to watch a match. This was partly because the matches were always played on Sundays, which Protestants considered unsuitable; more important, however, was the fact that the whole activity was suspect to the Protestants just because of its symbolic significance. Sometimes they suggested that the matches might well provide occasions for the rallying of IRA members from different districts. More common, however, was the feeling simply that the Protestant, even if he wanted to watch, would be regarded as an interloper and be made to feel self-conscious and uncomfortable. For all these reasons attendance at Gaelic football matches held regularly throughout the winter months was almost as much a purely Catholic activity as was attendance at Mass.

Just as teams and fans were recruited on a religious basis, so were the audiences at the local film shows; and partly for the same reasons. There was no cinema in the normal commercial sense in Ballybeg, a fact of some importance at this time since there was only one television set in the place. Film shows were, however, given regularly once a week, but only on Sunday nights and only in the Parochial Hall of the Catholic Church. The only Protestants who attended these shows were a few lads in their late teens and early twenties. These young men were severely criticised by other Protestants. Their basic fear was that they would become involved with Catholic girls, but the criticism openly voiced was that to break the Sabbath so blatantly and in such company showed they had 'no self-respect' – 'they can't think much of themselves to do a thing like that.' Clearly such film shows could not form a common meeting ground for the community as a whole.

Dances too were invariably held in halls which had such close religious or political connection with one side or the other that these too were patronised predominantly or wholly by either Catholics or Protestants, seldom both. The exceptions were to be found only at the level of expensive formal dances in the County Town. There at the Hospital dance and the Golf Club dance Catholics and Protestants were to be found together – but of course since people came as firmly paired couples, or in organised little parties to such affairs, there was not the same opportunity for mixing as at the local hops. These took place either in the Catholic Parochial Hall or in the Church of Ireland Hall (not in the Presbyterian Hall since a clique in this church disapproved of dancing under any conditions), or in one or other of the Orange Halls – and again the Catholic dances often took place on a Sunday. The 'riff-raff' on either side might not be too particular about the place and time of the dances, but this involved only a tiny minority, for most youngsters were 'respectable' enough to keep to the rules about where and when they might dance. I think it will be obvious from all that has been said that most parents hoped devoutly that their children would restrict any thought of marriage to those of their 'own side', and since dances were specifically designed to bring about friendships with those of the opposite sex, parents sought by every means in their power to restrict their children's attendance to dances run by the 'right' religious group.

Even bazaars and sales of work that so often in the rest of the British Isles bring the whole of the community into contact with each other, failed to do so in Ballybeg. Fund-raising was never undertaken for charities of a non-sectarian and non-political character. The only annual collection which might have been expected to have been an exception was Earl Haig's Poppy Day appeal – but although it was well recognised that there were large numbers of Catholic as well as Protestant ex-servicemen even in Northern Ireland, the association of the armed forces with Britain as a political unit meant that the organising of the appeal and donations to it were an entirely Protestant affair. For the rest, most of the appeals concerned local sectarian issues – fund-raising for the respective churches and for the various political organisations; for the bands and banners of Orange Lodges, for example. It was both interesting and significant of attitudes between the Catholics and Protestants that individuals could and did collect money and offerings for bazaars from neighbours of 'the other side' if the object were purely religious, but no one could do this for a political purpose – it was good for all people to be supporters of religious causes, and neighbours, whatever their own faith, could worthily support each other here ... To think of attending any bazaar, however, even though it was held for a religious cause, was quite a different matter. Occasionally someone might take a neighbour 'from the other side' to visit some particular stall for a brief period, but basically attendances at

156

these functions were almost entirely confined to members of one side or the other.

It was, however, in the matter of schooling that sectarian influences exerted some of their strongest pressures on the pattern of social relationships. It was, in fact, only the children from the hill districts who came to know children of 'the other side' at school. Almost all schooling was sectarian, but in the days before school buses were thought of it was felt unreasonable for the Protestant children of the hill area to be expected to attend the Protestant school in Ballybeg since this would have entailed a walk of over four miles each way. These children therefore did attend the local Catholic primary school. It would be idle to pretend that the ensuing contacts between Catholic and Protestant children spread only sweetness and light – boys everywhere gang up and what more natural than that at this school the gangs should be recruited on a sectarian basis. Fred Richards talking about Catholics said to me, 'I know what they're taught – I went to a Catholic school. Not that the teachers weren't more than nice to us, but we boys used to fight and then they used to call us, well, illegitimate . . . because our parents hadn't been properly married because they hadn't married in a Catholic Church.' Nevertheless, years in the same class and general school contacts undoubtedly gave the Protestant children involved an ease of relationship with the Catholics of their district, and sometimes long-standing friendships that were especially important in the case of girls, who as women would have so few occasions for coming into contact with each other. Yet it must be emphasised that it was only a very small proportion of children who came into close contact with any other than their co-religionists at school. Only the hill Protestant children went to the Catholic school. Children who lived nearer went, for the most part by foot, to the Protestant school in Ballybeg itself, even as in the case of the little 'infield' Jamisons, if this meant a walk of over six miles a day. With the increasing use of cars it was obvious that the tendency to separate schooling was going to increase rather than decrease.

In the great majority of cases, therefore, Catholic children went to Catholic schools and Protestant children went to Protestant schools, and out of school they had hardly any activities in common.

from *Prejudice and Tolerance in Ulster*, 1972

The Night We Rode
With Sarsfield

BENEDICT KIELY

That was the house where I put the gooseberries back on the bushes by
sticking them on the thorns. It wasn't one house but two houses
under one roof, a thatched roof. Before I remember being there, I was
there.

We came from the small village of Dromore to the big town of Omagh,
the county town of Tyrone, in the spring of 1920, bad times in Ireland
(Violence upon the roads/Violence of horses) particularly bad times in
the north-east corner of Ulster. There have been any God's amount of
bad times in the north-east corner of Ulster. There were no houses going
in the big town and the nearest my father could find to his work was
three miles away in the townland of Drumragh and under the one roof
with Willy and Jinny Norris, a Presbyterian couple, brother and sister.
They were small farmers.

That was the place then where I put the gooseberries back on the
bushes by impaling them on the thorns. But not just yet because I wasn't
twelve months old, a good age for a man and one of the best he's ever
liable afterwards to experience: more care is taken of him, especially by
women. No, the impaling of the gooseberries took place seven to eight
years later. For, although we were only there six or so months until my
father got a place in the town – in the last house in a laneway overlooking
the green flowery banks of the serpentine Strule – we went on visiting
Willy and Jinny until they died, and my father walked at their funeral and
entered their church and knelt with the congregation: a thing that Roman
Catholics were not by no means then supposed to do. Not knelt exactly
but rested the hips on the seat and inclined the head: Ulster Presbyterians
don't kneel, not even to God above.

It was a good lasting friendship with Willy and Jinny. There's an Irish
proverb: *Nil aitheantas go haontigheas*. Or: You don't know anybody
until you've lived in the one house with them.

Not one house, though, in this case but two houses under one roof which may be the next best thing.

Willy and Jinny had the one funeral because one night the house burned down – by accident. Nowadays when you say that a house or a shop or a pub or a factory burned down, it seems necessary to add – by accident. Although the neighbours, living next door in our house, did their best to rescue them and to save the whole structure with buckets of water from the spring-well which was down there surrounded by gooseberry bushes, they died, Willy from suffocation, Jinny from shock, the shock of the whole happening, the shock of loneliness at knowing that Willy was dead and that the long quiet evenings were over. However sadly and roughly they left the world, they went, I know, to a heaven of carefully-kept harvest fields, and Orange lilies in bloom on the lawn before the farmhouse, and trees heavy with fruit, and those long evenings spent spelling-out, by the combined light of oil-lamp and hearth fire, the contents of *The Christian Herald*. My three sisters who were all older than me said that that was the only literature, apart from the Bible, they had ever seen in the house but, at that time, that didn't mean much to me.

The place they lived in must have been the quietest place in the world. This was the way to get there.

The Cannonhill road went up from the town in three steps but those steps could only be taken by Titans. Halfways up the second step or steep hill there was on the right-hand side a tarred timber barn behind which such of the young as fancied, and some as didn't, used to box. My elder brother, there, chopped one of the town's bullies, who was a head-fighter, on the soft section of the crown of his head as he came charging like a bull, and that cured him of head-fighting for a long time. Every boy has an elder brother who can box.

The barn belonged to a farmer who would leave a team of horses standing in the field and go follow a brass band for the length of a day. Since the town had two brass bands, one military, one civilian, his sowing was always dilatory and his harvests very close to Christmas. He owned a butcher shop in the town but he had the word, Butcher, painted out and replaced by the word, Flesher, which some joker had told him was more modern and polite but which a lot of people thought wasn't exactly decent.

If you looked back from Cannonhill the prospect was really something: the whole town, spires and all, you could even see clear down into some of the streets; the winding river or rivers, the red brick of the county hospital on a hill across the valley, and beyond all that the mountains, Glenhordial where the water came from, Gortin Gap and Mullagharn and the high Sperrins. Sometime in the past, nobody knew when, there must have been a gun-emplacement on Cannonhill so as to give the place its name. Some of the local learned men talked vaguely about Oliver Cromwell but he was never next or near the place. There were, though, guns there in 1941 when a visit from the Germans seemed imminent and, indeed, they came near enough to bomb Belfast and Pennyburn in Derry City and were heard in the darkness over our town, and the whole population of Gallowshill, where I came from, took off for refuge up the three titanic steps of the Cannonhill road. It was a lovely June night, though, and everybody enjoyed themselves.

If any of those merry refugees had raced on beyond the ridge of Cannonhill they would have found themselves, Germans or no Germans, in the heart of quietness. The road goes down in easy curves through good farmland to the Drumragh River and the old graveyard where the gateway was closed with concrete and stone long before my time, and the dead sealed off forever. There's a sort of stile made out of protruding stones in the high wall and within – desolation, a fragment of a church wall that might be medieval, waist-high stagnant grass, table tombstones made anonymous by moss and lichen, a sinister hollow like a huge shellhole in the centre of the place where the dead, also anonymous, of the great famine of the 1840s were thrown coffinless, one on top of the other. A man who went to school with me used to call that hollow the navel of nothing and to explain in gruesome detail why and how the earth that once had been mounded had sunk into a hollow.

That same man ran away from home in 1938 to join the British navy. He survived the sinking of three destroyers on which he was a crew member: once, off the Faroes; once, for a change of temperature, in the Red Sea; and a third time at the Battle of Crete. It may be possible that the crew of the fourth destroyer he joined looked at him with some misgiving.

160

A fellow townsman who had the misfortune to be in Crete as a groundsman with the RAF when the Germans were coming in low and dropping all sorts of unpleasant things to the great danger of life and limb, found a hole in the ground where he could rest unseen, and doing no harm to anybody, until he caught the next boat to Alexandria.

When he crawled into the hole who should be there but the thrice-torpedoed sailor reading *The Ulster Herald*. He said hello and went on reading. He was a cool one, and what I remember most about him is the infinite patience with which he helped me when, impelled by a passion for history, I decided to clean all the table tombstones in old Drumragh and recall from namelessness and oblivion the decent people who were buried there. It was a big project. Not surprisingly it was never completed, never even properly commenced, but it brought us one discovery: that one of the four people, all priests, buried under a stone that was flat to the ground and circled by giant yews, was a MacCathmhaoil (you could English it as Campbell or McCarvill) who had in history been known as the Sagart Costarnocht because he went about without boots or socks, and who in the penal days of proscribed Catholicism had said Mass in the open air at the Mass rock on Corra Duine mountain.

For that discovery our own parish priest praised us from the pulpit. He was a stern Irish Republican who had been to the Irish college in Rome, had met D'Annunzio and approved of him and who always spoke of the Six Counties of north-east Ulster as *Hibernia Irredenta*. He was also, as became his calling, a stern Roman Catholic, and an antiquarian, and in honour of the past and the shadow of the proscribed, barefooted priest, he had read the Mass one Sunday at the rock on Corra Duine and watched, in glory on the summit like the Lord himself, as the congregation trooped in over the mountain from the seven separate parishes.

This ground is littered with things, cluttered with memories and multiple associations. It turns out to be a long three miles from Gallowshill to the house of Willy and Jinny Norris. With my mother and my elder sisters I walked it so often, and later on with friends and long after Willy and Jinny were gone and the house a blackened ruin, the lawn a wilderness, the gooseberry bushes gone to seed, the Orange lilies extinguished – miniature suns that would never rise again in that place no more than life

161

would ever come back to the empty mansion of Johnny Pet Wilson. That was just to the left before you turned into the Norris laneway, red-sanded, like a tunnel with high hawthorn hedges and sycamores and ash trees shining white and naked. My father had known Johnny Pet and afterwards had woven mythologies about him: a big Presbyterian farmer, the meanest and oddest man that had ever lived in those parts. When his hired men, mostly Gaelic speakers from West Donegal, once asked him for jam or treacle or syrup or, God help us, butter itself, to moisten their dry bread, he said: Do you say your prayers?

—Yes, boss.

They were puzzled.

—Do you say the Lord's prayer?

—Yes, boss.

—Well, in the Lord's prayer it says: Give us this day our daily bread. Damn the word about jam or treacle or syrup or butter.

When he bought provisions in a shop in the town he specified: So much of labouring man's bacon and so much of the good bacon.

For the hired men, the imported long-bottom American bacon. For himself, the Limerick ham.

He rose between four and five in the morning and expected his men to be already out and about. He went around with an old potato sack on his shoulders like a shawl, and followed always by a giant of a gentleman goat, stepping like a king's warhorse. The goat would attack you if you angered Johnny Pet, and when Johnny died the goat lay down and died on the same day. Their ghosts walked, it was well known, in the abandoned orchard where the apples had become half-crabs, through gaps in hedges and broken fences, and in the roofless rooms of the ruined house. Nobody had ever wanted to live there after the goat and Johnny Pet died. There were no relatives even to claim the hoarded fortune.

—If the goat had lived, my father said, he might have had the money and the place.

—The poor Donegals, my mother would say as she walked past Johnny Pet's ghost, and the ghost of the goat, on the way to see Willy and Jinny. Oh, the poor Donegals.

It was a phrase her mother had used when, from the doorstep of the farmhouse in which my mother was reared, the old lady would look west

162

on a clear day and see the tip of the white cone of Mount Errigal, the Cock o' the North, sixty or more miles away, standing up and shining with shale over Gweedore and the Rosses of Donegal and by the edge of the open Atlantic. From that hard coast, a treeless place of diminutive fields fenced by drystone walls, of rocks, mountains, small lakes, empty moors and ocean winds the young Donegal people (both sexes) used to walk eastwards, sometimes barefoot, to hire out in the rich farms along the valley of the Strule, the Mourne and the Foyle – three fine names for different stages of the same river.

Or the young people, some of them hardly into their teens, might travel as far even as the potato fields of Fifeshire or Ayrshire. They'd stand in the streets at the hiring fairs to be eyed by the farmers, even by God to have their biceps tested to see what work was in them. The last of the hiring fairs I saw in Omagh in the early 1930s but by that time everybody was well dressed and wore boots and the institution, God be praised, was doomed. There was a big war on the way and the promise of work for all. But my mother, remembering the old days and thinking perhaps more of her own mother than of the plight of the migratory labourers, would say: The poor Donegals. Ah, the poor Donegals.

Then up the sheltered red-sanded boreen or laneway – the Gaelic word would never at that time have been used by Ulster Presbyterians – to the glory of the Orange lilies and the trim land and, in the season, the trees heavy with fruit. Those gooseberries I particularly remember because one day when I raided the bushes more than somewhat, to the fearful extent of a black-paper fourteen-pound sugar-bag full, my sisters (elder) reproved me. In a fit of remorse I began to stick the berries back on the thorns. Later in life I found out that plucked fruit is plucked forever and that berries do not grow on thorns.

Then another day the three sisters, two of them home on holidays from Dublin, said: Sing a song for Jinny and Willy.

Some children suffer a lot when adults ask them to sing or recite. There's never really much asking about it. It's more a matter of get up and show your paces and how clever you are, like a dancing dog in a circus, or know the lash or the joys of going to bed supperless. Or sometimes it's bribery: Sing up and you'll get this or that.

Once I remember – can I ever forget it? – the reverend mother of a convent in Dublin gave me a box of chocolates because in the presence of my mother and my cousin, who was a nun, and half the community I brazenly sang:

Paddy Doyle lived in Killarney
And he loved a maid named Bessy Toole,
Her tongue I know was tipped with blarney,
But it seemed to him the golden rule.

But that was one of the exceptionally lucky days. I often wondered, too, where the reverend mother got the box of chocolates. You didn't expect to find boxes of chocolates lying around convents in those austere days. She dived the depth of her right arm for them into a sort of trousers-pocket in her habit, and the memory of them and of the way I won them ever after braced me in vigour (as the poet said) when asked to give a public performance.

—Up with you and sing, said the eldest sister.

Outside the sun shone. The lilies nodded and flashed like bronze. You could hear them. On a tailor's dummy, that Jinny had bought at an auction, Willy's bowler hat and sash were out airing for the Orange walk on the twelfth day in honour of King William and the battle of the Boyne. The sash was a lovely blue, a true blue, and the Orangemen who wore blue sashes were supposed to be teetotallers. Summer and all as it was the pyramid of peat was bright on the hearth and the kettle above it singing and swinging on the black crane, and Jinny's fresh scones were in three piles, one brown, one white, one spotted with currants and raisins, on the table and close to the coolness of the doorway.

—Sing up, said the second sister. Give us a bar.

—Nothing can stop him, said the third sister who was a cynic.

She was right. Or almost. Up I was and at it, with a song learned from another cousin, the nun's brother, who had been in 1920 in the IRA camp in the Sperrin mountains:

We're off to Dublin in the green and the blue,
Our helmets glitter in the sun,
Our bayonets flash like lightning
To the rattle of the Thompson gun.

164

It's the dear old flag of Ireland, boys,
That proudly waves on high,
And the password of our order is:
We'll conquer or we'll die.

The kettle sputtered and spat and boiled over. Jinny dived for it before the water could hit the ashes and raise a stink, or scald the backs of my legs where I stood shouting treason at Willy and the dummy in the bowler and the teetotaller's blue sash. It may have been a loyal Orange kettle. Willy was weeping with laughter and wiping the back of his left hand sideways across his eyes and his red moustache. In the confusion, the eldest sister, purple in the face with embarrassment, said: If you recited instead of singing. He's much better at reciting.

So I was – and proud of it. Off I went into a thundering galloping poem learned by heart from the *Our Boys*, a magazine that was nothing if not patriotic and was produced in Dublin by the Irish Christian Brothers.

The night we rode with Sarsfield out from Limerick to meet
The waggon-train that William hoped would help in our defeat.
How clearly I remember it though now my hair is white
That clustered black and curly 'neath my trooper's cap that night.

This time there was no stopping me. Anyway Willy wouldn't let them. He was enjoying himself. With the effrontery of one of those diabolical little children who have freak memories, even when they don't know what the words mean, I let them have the whole works, eight verses of eight lines each, right up to the big bang at Ballyneety on a Munster hillside at the high rock that is still called Sarsfield's Rock.

It is after the siege of Derry and the battle of the Boyne and the Jacobite disaster at the slope of Aughrim on the Galway road. The victorious Williamite armies gather round the remnants of the Jacobites locked up behind the walls of Limerick. The ammunition train, guns, and wagons of ball and powder, that will end the siege rumble on across the country. Then Sarsfield with the pick of his hard-riding men, and led by the Rapparee, Galloping Hogan, who knows every track and hillock and hollow and marsh and bush on the mountains of Silver Mine and Keeper and Slieve Felim, rides north by night and along the western bank of the big river:

'Twas silently we left the town and silently we rode,
While o'er our heads the silent stars in silver beauty glowed.
And silently and stealthily well led by one who knew,
We crossed the shining Shannon at the ford of Killaloe.

On and on from one spur of the mountains to the next, then silently swooping down on the place where, within a day's drag from the city's battered walls, the well-guarded wagons rest for the night. For the joke of it the Williamite watchword is Sarsfield:

The sleepy sentry on his rounds perhaps was musing o'er
His happy days of childhood on the pleasant English shore,
Perhaps was thinking of his home and wishing he were there
When springtime makes the English land so wonderfully fair.
At last our horses' hoofbeats and our jingling arms he heard.
'Halt, who goes there?' the sentry cried. 'Advance and give the word.'
'The word is Sarsfield,' cried our chief, 'and stop us he who can,
'For Sarsfield is the word tonight and Sarsfield is the man.'

Willy had stopped laughing, not with hostility but with excitement. This was a good story, well told. The wild riders ride with the horses' shoes back to front so that if a hostile scouting party should come on their tracks, the pursuit will be led the wrong way. The camp is captured. Below the rock a great hole is dug in the ground, the gun-powder sunk in it, the guns piled on the powder, the torch applied:

We make a pile of captured guns and powder bags and stores,
Then skyward in one flaming blast the great explosion roars.

All this is long ago – even for the narrator in the poem. The hair is now grey that once clustered black and curly beneath his trooper's cap. Sarsfield, gallant Earl of Lucan, great captain of horsemen, is long dead on the plain of Landen or Neerwinden. Willy is silent, mourning all the past. Jinny by the table waits patiently to pour the tea:

For I was one of Sarsfield's men though yet a boy in years
I rode as one of Sarsfield's men and men were my compeers
They're dead the most of them, afar, yet they were Ireland's sons
Who saved the walls of Limerick from the might of William's guns.

No more than the sleepy sentry, my sisters never recovered from the shock. They still talk about it. As for myself, on my way home past the

166

ghosts of Johnny Pet and the gentleman goat, I had a vague feeling that the reason why the poor girls were fussing so much was because the William that Sarsfield rode to defeat must have been Willy Norris himself. That was why the poem shouldn't be recited in his house, and fair play to him. But then why had Willy laughed so much? It was all very puzzling. Happy Ulster man that I then was I knew as little about politics and the ancient war of Orange and Green as I knew about the way gooseberries grew.

It wasn't until after my recital that they found out about the black-paper fourteen-pounder of a sugar-sack stuffed full of fruit. The manufacturers don't do sacks like that any more in this country. Not even paper like that any more. It was called crib-paper, because it was used, crumpled-up and worked-over and indented here and bulged out there to simulate the rock walls of the cave of Bethlehem in Christmas cribs.

For parcelling books I was looking for some of it in Dublin the other day, to be told that the only place I'd come up with it was some unlikely manufacturing town in Lancashire.

'The Night We Rode With Sarsfield', from *The State of Ireland*, 1980

New Help at Rathard

SAM HANNA BELL

The farm of Rathard sat crescent-shaped on a low green hill screened by
beech trees from the misty winds that rose from the lough in winter. On
summer evenings the cream-washed homestead, eyed by the setting sun,
blushed warmly under the dark foliage. Swelling gently from the shores
of Strangford Lough, the hill had borne habitation for centuries. Behind
the dwelling-house lay an ancient rath from whence an earlier people
had looked down on the sinuous waters of the lough. Now nothing more
martial was heard than the cry of a cock, or the low piping of bees from
the seven hives which sat in the curve of the bowed earth walls. The
house faced inland; to its right, towards the lough, were the barns and
byres. To its left, the stackyard, bounded by a delicate file of rowan trees
which ended where the rutted loanen, climbing from the road, emptied
into the close.

When Margaret Echlin turned her face from her husband and sons,
from dung-crusted beasts and hungry fowl and clashing pails, only then
did her husband Andrew realise what part she had filled in Rathard. It
was as if the whole framework of the farm's daily life had been withdrawn. Hardly a task about the kitchen or the fields but now lacked some
essential part. Urgently, Andrew set about finding someone to tend to
himself and his sons.

His task was not an easy one, for Rathard was surrounded by prosperous cottiers, the farms of which absorbed all the labour that each family
could expend. But in the neighbouring townland of Banyil was a group
of labourers' cottages in which lived the old residenters or their children,
tenants of a vanished demesne. In one of these cottages lived Charlie
Gomartin, a thatcher, with his wife and daughter Sarah, now a woman of
thirty years. Charlie had travelled the countryside to ply his trade; but as
time passed and Sarah grew up, his circuits became wider and his appearances at home more and more infrequent, until at last he disappeared entirely, and a rumour drifted to Banyil that he had died on a Sligo
road among tinker people.

168

Martha Gomartin and her daughter earned their money working in the houses and fields of neighbouring farmers, more often that of Mr Bourke, owner of the cottages. Martha was held in regard for her labour, frugality and honesty. Sarah, like herself, was a fine worker, better in the kitchen than her mother. Some said that she was as simple as a mouse, others that she was a sly lady. But she went her road quietly and didn't meddle with the boys.

Andrew Echlin sent word to Mrs Gomartin that he would have her come up to Rathard at her convenience. Accordingly, the next evening, Martha and her daughter entered the close before the Echlins' farmhouse. A collie rose dustily from a corner of the close and stretching out his neck, barked at the two women. They heard the screech of a chair pushed back on the tiled floor of the kitchen, and Andrew appeared on the threshold, twisting his fingers in his beard. 'Come in, Martha,' he said smiling at his neighbour and her daughter.

The Echlins had worked late at some distance from the farmhouse and were now seated at their evening meal. When Martha had spoken to the two sons, who ducked their heads in answer, she and Sarah took seats along the wall close to the door. Andrew reached down cups and saucers from the dresser and filled them with dark pungent tea. When he added milk the tea turned to a bright unappetising brown. Only the faintest thread of vapour rose from the cups. He watched Martha take one sip and then set her cup aside on the shelf of the sewing-machine. Her daughter held her cup cradled in her lap.

The old man laughed apologetically. 'Ye can see, Martha. There's hands wanted here.'

Mrs Gomartin was cautious. She studied the roughly set table and the choked hearth. 'Things might be redd up a wee-thing, Andra,' she agreed.

'Well, there ye are now,' said Andrew slapping his leg softly.

The young men and the young woman studied each other discreetly in passing glances. The seated men were framed in the long black oak dresser on the shelves of which rested row on row of cottage-blue and willow-pattern plates. The women itched to be at the soot that masked their bright faces. The mother saw them sparkling; the daughter saw them sparkling and ranked in symmetry of size and shape. But not a sign was made. Martha, her hands resting lightly on the arms of her chair listening patiently to the patriarch Andrew speaking for himself and his sons; Sarah listening dutifully to the talk of her elders and only seeming to rest when she glanced casually at the young men. Frank, the younger brother, had stopped eating when the visitors arrived and now pushed crumbs around his plate with the end of his cigarette. He lounged carelessly in his chair, slim and brown, glancing thoughtfully at the girl from below his tumbled fair hair. Hamilton, seated in his father's shadow, had politely suspended his meal until the women had tea. Now he pushed his plate away after mopping up the last of the *mealy-creeshy* which had been their evening dish. He spooned honey into the heart of a farl and as the sweet slowly uncoiled from his knife he amused himself with the thought that the hair of Martha's daughter was the same colour, but he turned his dark face stolidly to his father's talk. She's a cold pale one, thought Frank, with no sport in her. Then he caught her calm ever-moving glance, and felt uncertain again.

'Well, Martha, there's room beyont for both of ye,' said Andrew, inclining his head towards the lower part of the house. 'Ye may come as soon as you're free o' the Bourkes. Ye'd be needed here at the harvest, and in the winter it would be a great convenience to have the house tended to.' The old man leaned forward with a smile wrinkling his eyes. 'We dinna often hear a step in the close, but ye can aye go down the road when you're lonely.'

Mrs Gomartin carefully folded her square, work-thickened fingers in her lap. 'It makes no great odds, Andra,' she replied with a quick upward lift of her head. 'A widow's seat is aye a lonely seat.'

'Aye, God knows that's true enough,' answered Andrew, staring sombrely at the wall.

Three days later Mrs Gomartin closed her cottage and came with her daughter to live in the Echlins' house. The women were given the two lower rooms of the house, one as a bedroom and one as a living room. The effect of the Gomartins moving in became quickly evident. In the house, meals were more punctual and a greater variety of dishes appeared on the table. Beds were no longer confused heaps of malodorous clothes. Outside, in the work around the farm, Martha and Sarah took their share of the harvesting. Sarah had an amazing capacity for hard work. She was deft and quick in her movements, and brought her strength to the point where it would have greatest effect. She would have been considered a graceful girl, but she neutralised that by her cold and detached expression.

The Echlins and the Gomartins were members of the same Presbyterian congregation, and on Sundays the five members of the two families drove in the trap to the meeting-house. It had been the custom of the two young men, when the horse was stabled and the trap put away, to join the young men and women in the churchyard where they spent the few minutes before the service began in talking and flirting with each other. On the second Sabbath after they had driven to the church with the Gomartins, Frank was surprised to see his brother hasten into the church with only a nod to his old companions. He sat on a flat gravestone, gazing thoughtfully at the doorway through which Hamilton had disappeared, and quite unmindful of the talk of the young men around him.

The rain and winds which had beaten the corn until it lay tangled like the hair of a sleeping man, gave way to serene weather and the harvesters eked out each hour of light in the mellow August evening. Andrew opened the fields with his scythe, Hamilton or Frank rode the reaper, while Martha, Sarah and Petie Sampson, a labouring man, gathered and tied. Behind them Andrew stooked the sheaves. Frank's satisfaction at Sarah's indifference to his brother was tempered by the knowledge that it extended to himself. It gave way to chagrin when he saw the growing affection between his father and the young woman. From the first, Sarah had felt drawn towards Andrew, inspired by his kindness, humour and prophetic appearance. She was also impelled by a trait in herself, not uncommon in those who have tasted poverty, which made her prefer the father to the son, the master rather than the steward. But Sarah was a woman incapable of coquetry and none of her attentions to the old man was spoiled by lack of innocence.

from *December Bride*, 1951

DUNMARTIN HALL

CAROLINE BLACKWOOD

I asked Tommy Redcliffe if he had known my grandmother Dunmartin. Child of Great Granny Webster, mother of my father and Aunt Lavinia, this faceless woman who had attacked my infant brother at his formal christening still remained a menacing blank in my imagination.

Tommy Redcliffe had often gone over to Ulster to shoot at Dunmartin Hall while he was an undergraduate, and had got to know her then. He always found her very frightening, long before she was officially considered insane. He described her as a woman who seemed to have no centre. She went tossing through life like a leaf blown by every wind of her caprice. If you found her laughing you couldn't tell what amused her; if you saw her crying you couldn't quite tell what distressed her. None of her reactions seemed to be determined by external events. At that time he had also felt quite sorry for her – a pretty Englishwoman who had lost her youth living in a rainy province in an immense grey isolated house that was so cold you had to put on an overcoat to walk through its halls.

Tommy Redcliffe had enjoyed the pheasant-shooting at Dunmartin Hall, but otherwise he did not have very enthusiastic memories of the house where I had lived until my father was killed. Whereas I remembered Dunmartin Hall with affection and nostalgia, he had not seen anything especially attractive in the fact that its smells of damp-infested libraries had mingled with those of cow-dung, potato cakes and paraffin.

He had found the house architecturally very displeasing with its vast and sprawling ivy-coated wings, which at certain periods had been added to, at others pulled down at immense cost in the interests of economy and manageability. He had been depressed by the way it seemed like a gigantic monument to more prosperous and eternally lost times, dominating the countryside in its stately dilapidation.

Although he could admit that its tall and formal windows had very beautiful views – of gorse-dotted mountain, slate-grey lake, and copses of copper beech, he had not felt that they compensated for Dunmartin Hall's

172

many discomforts. He hated the way the food at meals was always stone-cold because it had to be carried by the butler from a dungeon kitchen which was in a different wing from the dining-room. Dunmartin Hall had something wrong with its plumbing, and he had been astonished that in a house of such pretension there was very rarely hot water and it was considered a luxury if anyone managed to get a peat-brown trickle of a bath.

Tommy Redcliffe suffered from rheumatism and he was convinced that the first fatal seeds of it had been sown when he stayed in that Northern Irish house before the war and his sheets were invariably wringing wet. Years later his voice still trembled with astonished complaint as he remembered nights when there had always seemed to be a bat trapped in his bedroom, nights when the cold had been such that he often found it easier to get to sleep lying fully clothed on the floor-boards under a couple of dusty carpets than in his unaired bed.

When he tried to describe my unknown grandmother, his whole description of her was coloured by sympathy for what he felt she must have suffered when her marriage doomed her to spend years and years of her life in the stultifying isolation and relentless biting damp of that ancestral Ulster house. . . .

As I remembered it from having lived there as a child, Dunmartin Hall had always had an aura of impermanence. The house had both the melancholy and the magic of something inherently doomed by the height of its own ancient colonial aspirations. It was like a grey and decaying palace fortress beleaguered by invasions of hostile native forces. Fierce armies of stinging nettles were seizing its once imposing elm-arched driveway; weeds carpeted its tennis court; in its rose garden the roses had reverted to seed and grown wild because no one ever pruned them. All the flower-beds had become blotted out by grass, and only the brilliant blue of hydrangeas gave colour to Dunmartin's nonexistent gardens, because they liked a lot of rain and needed no attention.

In the past, Dunmartin Hall had been intended to rival any English Stately Home in the scale of its magnificence and luxury – but whereas in England many equivalently large and over-ambitious houses could remain solvent by existing like the capital of a country, feeding on a constant flow of produce and income from the riches of the lands and the smaller houses that surrounded it, the system had not worked in Northern Ireland. Very little came into Dunmartin Hall from all its rocky barren acres, and as a result nothing was agriculturally reinvested. Although the estate had many tenant farmers who lived on potatoes and bacon fat, in tiny grey stone cottages, they were in no sense an asset to the 'Great House'. Producing very little except despairing demands for repairs to their abysmally wretched dwellings, they were incapable of paying their rents, and the traditional Anglo-Irish threat of eviction was no terror to them, since they were quite aware that they would never be forced out of their homes, for there was no one in the least anxious to take possession of these derelict little buildings and therefore it was in no way financially advantageous to their landlord in Dunmartin Hall to have his farmhouses left standing empty until time and the corrosive dampness of the Northern Irish climate reduced them to little ruins of rubbled grey stones.

Having tried to exist by aping an English feudal system most unsuccessfully, it was only the scale of the diminishment of this enormous Ulster house that remained impressive in its period of retribution and impoverishment. Its vast stone-carved swimming pool, surrounded by marble busts of Roman emperors, still remained somehow imposing, though it rotted in a scum of dead leaves and insects. The same was true of Dunmartin Hall's once valuable libraries, though many of the pages of their books had become glued together and blue with mildew.

The Irish roof has been the perennial arch-enemy of those who have lived under it. The roof has always had an almost mystical importance in Ireland because of the incessant rain. Throughout the ages a quite inordinate amount of unsuccessful Irish time and energy has been spent trying to do something about the roof. More and more roof specialists have been called in to take a look at it. They potter about among the chimneys for many weeks and almost invariably put their foot through its comparatively sound patches before they declare it hopeless.

Describing Dunmartin Hall in my grandmother's time, Tommy Redcliffe sounded appalled by the way it seemed to have been so generally and passively accepted that the roof was incurable and could only be kept at bay by pieces of dangling string which helped direct the massive flow of uncountable leaks to the various pots and pans and jam jars in which it suited my family that they should land. Then, just as a ship is bailed out, all these motley receptacles were emptied daily before they started to overflow.

Tommy Redcliffe was an orderly and practical Englishman, and the discouraging sight of all those soggy strings hanging down from the lofty, peeling ceilings of winding state-rooms had made an indelible impression on him. He said it had always amazed him that my father never appeared in the least disturbed by them, that apparently he saw them as normal. Tommy Redcliffe also remembered with horror that dangling alongside them there had been long sweet sticky brown papers for catching flies and wasps.

In describing his pre-war visits to Ulster, the terrible state of neglect and the undefeatable damp of Dunmartin Hall had obviously chilled him so much that when he tried to tell me what my grandmother had been like I often thought he felt the house itself might well have been responsible for driving her insane.

In the period in which he had gone over to stay there, Dunmartin Hall appears to have been going through a moment of exceptional crisis. My grandmother was becoming stranger and stranger. For years and years she had made not a single effort to run the house. As it deteriorated and became increasingly derelict and uncared for, she seemed totally unaware of it. She gave the impression that she no longer inhabited the house except in a technical sense, that she lived elsewhere in some troubled world of her own warring fantasies.

My grandfather Dunmartin was in total despair. He had no talent as a housekeeper and he found it impossible to give Dunmartin Hall his full attention when he was already overburdened and preoccupied by all the debts and problems of his failing estate. He had hired an English butler and two English footmen and kept selling fields to pay their salaries, but he was too modest and diffident to instruct them. They did very little work, for they were nearly always drunk, since my grandfather was frightened he might insult them if he hid the Dunmartin cellar key.

Having been professionally trained and having worked hitherto in aristocratic and impeccably run houses in England, these men were horrified by the rudderless and pig-sty conditions that prevailed at Dunmartin Hall. They therefore adapted themselves to the point of caricature. All day long they insisted on wearing heavy rubber farm-boots inside the house, and when my grandfather feebly begged them to remove them they refused. If they were expected to wade through the puddles that were always collecting in the corridors of this house they felt it was their right to be sensibly dressed so that they ran no risk of pneumonia.

Visitors from England were totally scandalised by the sight of these three men in the formal dining-room clumping round the table as they handed out the dishes of food with an unsteady gait that was made more noticeable by the fact that the black trousers of their liveries were tucked inside their mud-splashed wellingtons.

My grandfather had two of his unmarried great-aunts living with him. He had inherited them with the house as if they were heirlooms, and for years they had continued to live on in one of the remote damp wings of Dunmartin Hall, not out of choice but because no one could think of anywhere else for them to go.

These two old ladies were in very bad health. One had a cataract and the other grave trouble with her knees. They were much too irritable and decrepit to be of the slightest help to him in managing the house. All they wanted was to be waited on like little children, and they complained incessantly when they had to have their meals in the dining-room, for they would have liked them served in their rooms.

They were both much too engrossed in their own dissatisfactions to take in that there was anything wrong with my grandmother. My grandfather thought it better not to tell them that his wife had a nervous condition which often made her appear deranged. They realised only one thing. The lady of the house was not very easily available and when they cunningly managed to trap her she was curiously unresponsive to their innumerable complaints. Finding little satisfaction from their hostess, all their bitterness directed itself against my careworn grandfather, and they kept descending on him like two old pecking rooks in their black dresses. Everything was falling apart in their wing . . . the frame of their lavatory door was so warped it was impossible to shut it . . . they were ladies . . . they hadn't been brought up like that . . . it was a disgrace . . . it wasn't decent to use the lavatory in front of the servants . . . Three weeks ago one of the gun dogs had made a mess in their sitting-room. They would like to be given a good reason why no one had yet removed it . . . The carpet had humped away from the floor in one of their corridors and it was only a question of time before someone broke a leg . . . Like the rain that was always pouring down outside the windows, their moans kept splashing down on Grandfather Dunmartin's worried head.

As my grandmother's behaviour became increasingly weird and unbalanced and his great-aunts became increasingly difficult and dissatisfied, my grandfather recklessly staffed the house with more and more cooks, maids and kitchen-maids from the local village. It was as if he were trying to reassure himself that the sheer number of servants could prove that there was still something solid at the centre of his disintegrating home.

The act of employing so many people appeared to fatigue Grandfather Dunmartin to a point at which he had no further energy for explaining what he expected their duties to be. Never knowing what they were meant to do, they stayed in a demoralised huddle round the fire in the servants' hall, where they gossiped and ate soda bread and drank many cups of tea.

In a remote and sleepy country house like Dunmartin Hall, where neither the residents nor the guests found it easy to think of ways to occupy their time, meals had a special importance. They were events which were greedily looked forward to, and everyone who sat down at Dunmartin's gleaming mahogany inlaid table always yearned to be served some long and delicious meal, for they needed to find pleasant and self-indulgent ways of breaking up the tedium of the dragging hours of the day. Unfortunately, the food served at Dunmartin Hall in my grandfather's time was always cruelly disappointing, and his aunts would do their best to make him suffer for it by grumbling relentlessly in their high-pitched querulous tones as they bemoaned the fact that the disgusting food that kept appearing in the dining-room was ruining their delicate elderly digestions.

When these irascible old figures started to make their habitual peevish fuss about the disgraceful quality of the food, Tommy Redcliffe often felt a secret sympathy with them, for he too grew to dread both the sight and the taste of the frizzled unappetising pheasants that were served day after day for both lunch and dinner. No knife ever seemed sharp enough to cut them. Invariably they had been so grossly overcooked that their dehydrated flesh had the texture of plywood. . . .

At the time Tommy Redcliffe had stayed at Dunmartin Hall as a guest, my grandmother could still sometimes seem quite pleasant and normal. 'Her tragedy was – she could never keep it up . . .'

She lived to a quite different time-schedule from anyone else in the house. Often she stayed in her room for a large part of the day and only came out to roam restlessly around the house at night. Sometimes she would suddenly appear in the dining-room when everyone was in the middle of a meal, greeting her husband and her son and her guests very vaguely, as if she barely recognised them and yet was glad to find some company. She would sit down at the table and make general conversation. For a while she would be quite lucid, and an infectious feeling of hope would surge through everyone present. Perhaps she was better . . . But then she would get on to the subject of elves and fairies.

My grandmother had developed an obsessional interest in what she called 'the little people'. When she first claimed she could see them, her family thought she was joking. They imagined that, as an Englishwoman who had taken up residence in Northern Ireland, she must in some silly, whimsical way, be trying to adapt herself to Irish superstitions.

Soon it became clear that her belief in the forces of the supernatural had become a genuine fixation, for she tried to convert everyone to her beliefs and became snarling and hostile if she felt her audience was patronising her. She claimed that she could understand the language of the fairies, that they were continually sending her messages, that it was important only to listen to the instructions of the good ones for they could help you avert the terrible spells that might be put on you by demons. Tommy Redcliffe found her intolerably exhausting and boring when she went on talking like this.

When my grandmother spent most of the day shut up in her bedroom, she sat cross-legged on the floor and cut out coloured pictures of elves and fairies from her enormous collection of children's books. What everyone found blood-curdling was that she herself had started to look very like the model fairies that you see on the top of Christmas trees. She had the same frozen blank expression, the agelessness that made her seem neither child nor woman. Her face was china white, and her curls were still very blonde and arranged in a way that made her appear to be wearing a golden wig. When she entered a room she never walked, she always flitted. Often she kept a fixed smile on her face, and when she talked through this smile in a tense and impassioned manner about spells and curses, potions and magic, it was as if she were incapable of relaxing

178

it because it had been painted on her face in order to radiate her own inner notion of fairylike goodwill.

My grandmother's eyes had unnerved Tommy Redcliffe. He had found them much too bright and artificial, and they had given him the disquieting impression that the poor woman had lost her real ones and had had them replaced be two rounds of glass.

My grandmother liked to wear white diaphanous dresses and she covered her shoulders with a silver-lace shawl. As she darted noiselessly round Dunmartin Hall in her curiously rapid and tiptoe manner, the ends of her silvery shawl would stream out behind her, almost as though she had grown fairy wings. Even in winter she went about barefoot. This always astonished any visitors who came to the house, for they found it impossible to understand why she was so unperturbed by the perishing cold.

I asked Tommy Redcliffe how my father used to behave with his eccentric mother. Apparently he always became very white and withdrawn whenever she came into the room but brightened the moment she left it. Whenever my grandmother was present he would pick up a book and become so immersed in the text that he appeared to be trying to get to the other side of its print so that the words could shield him like a barbed-wire fence. He never wanted to discuss my grandmother with his friend, but regarded her condition much as he regarded the state of his father's house, accepting it as a distressing fact which insofar as was possible, he hoped could be ignored.

My father went over to Northern Ireland only at Christmas and Easter and for one month in the summer. Tommy Redcliffe was convinced that he dreaded his visits and only made them for the sake of my grandfather Dunmartin, for whom he felt both pity and affection.

Aunt Lavinia was apparently much more ruthless. She was adamant in her refusal to visit her parents in their Ulster home. The impecunious and uncomfortable grandeur in which this unhappy and embattled couple lived not only depressed her but struck her as ludicrous. She loved comfort, luxury and amusement. In Ulster there were no night-clubs; there was no theatre; there were very few parties given there that Aunt Lavinia considered entertaining. To her, Northern Ireland was a deadly and provincial No Man's Land, and the secluded and supposedly aristocratic demesne of Dunmartin Hall existed for her as one of its most unappealing features.

179

The beautiful woods of Dunmartin that my grandmother had managed to people with the magical spirits of her hectic imagination were damp monotonous tracts of trees to the pleasure-loving Aunt Lavinia. They were a place where you could take a dull walk in the rain because no one offered you anything better to do. She dreaded being asked to sit up half the night with my anxious grandfather while he showed her all the accounts and the books of his farm and his estate. Aunt Lavinia had no gift for mathematics, and she suspected that his grasp of the figures he liked to show her was almost as weak as her own. All she ever gathered was that the Dunmartin accounts were disastrous. To her, money was an abstraction. If you were gay and well-dressed, it was something that arrived from admiring men. She could see no magical way of making it arrive to salvage my grandfather's rocky and gorse-infested acres. Aunt Lavinia stubbornly kept away from Northern Ireland, because condoling with my grandfather on the horror of his financial accounts and being under the same leaking roof as my unhinged fairy-loving grandmother was not an experience she could see as 'fun'.

from *Great Granny Webster*, 1977

4

'Amethyst and Moonstone'

LOUIS MACNEICE

THE ANTRIM COAST

ROBERT LLOYD PRAEGER

Now we come to one of the most delightful playgrounds in Ireland, one that I have known and loved since childhood – the Antrim coast. . . . It is quite true that, like all other places of whatever kind, its delights are not for all. If you want to motor a couple of hundred miles a day, Antrim's possibilities will be exhausted in no time. If you want to bathe among crowds of people and of rubber porpoises don't go to Cushendall or Cushendun – nor if you yearn to spend the fine afternoons in playing bridge in crowded smoke-rooms. But if you love rocks and cliffs, deep glens, sparkling sea, air like champagne, great stretches of brown moorland, with a sufficiency of tennis and golf and sailing and fishing – then the Antrim coast is the place for you. Best of all are the surprising colour-contrasts supplied by its cliffs and scarps – black basalt, white Chalk, red Trias – and the changing views of the Scottish headlands and islands across the North Channel, from Ayrshire up to Islay, and the grand run of tide which twice daily sweeps down the narrows between Kintyre and Fair Head, and around Rathlin, and twice back again. And what cold water it is! – the coldest to be found on all the coasts of Ireland. Why? for one thing, you are here well beyond Malin Head, which marks the end of the warm drift that comes up along the west coast; for another, there is very deep water close by – 135 fathoms at Rathlin to the north, and 150 fathoms off Belfast Lough to the south. I well remember a cold wet July at Glenarm in my student days, and courageous headers off a rock with James and Eoin MacNeill, and the scramble to get out of the icy water as quickly as arms and legs could accomplish it.

I got to know the Antrim coast intimately in early youth. During three summers especially, every cliff and glen and moor was explored, from Larne to Portrush, and I could have taken a much better degree in local topography, geology and botany that I eventually did in engineering after three years at 'Queen's'. Is there any place in western Europe where there is so great a variety of rocks as in Antrim, or where the rocks take so prominent a part in the production of varied landscape? Over much of the north of Ireland the newer rocks have all been stripped off, exposing the very ancient schist and gneiss which give us the scenery of Donegal and western Derry; but things are different in Antrim. From Cushendall to Cushendun Old Red Sandstone forms a rocky coast; from Murlough Bay to Ballycastle are Carboniferous sandstones and shales, with bands of coal, and fossil trunks of the strange trees of that period. All round the coast the Secondary rocks form a broken ribbon – Trias, Lias, Chalk – red, blue-grey, white – and capping them all the solid beds of black volcanic rock which we know so well. Then comes the Boulder-clay, generally bright red, and finally the black peat of the mountains and the northern inland parts, and along the coast raised beaches full of the flints that Neolithic man worked into weapons and domestic implements. What a twelve-course feast for a hungry geologist!

For the botanist also there are attractions – a large and varied flora (Antrim can claim as large a flora as any county in Ireland) which, as one might expect from the narrowness of the North Channel, has a special Scottish flavour about it in the occurrence here, and in Ireland only on this basaltic plateau, of some plants characteristic of North Britain, such as the Wood Crane's-bill, the Wood Cow-wheat, the Tea-leaved Willow, and the Few-flowered Sedge. But it is the glorious abundance on the coast and in the glens of commoner wild-flowers, rather than the presence of these and other rarities, that make Antrim a garden, especially in spring.

To the ancient peoples, much the most important natural local production was the nodules of flint that are found in the white Chalk, where the contained silica has segregated out from its calcareous matrix. Being insoluble, and much harder than the Chalk, it has remained when the latter was destroyed, and the ice of the Glacial Period has scattered it all over the country as a common ingredient of the Boulder-clay which the ice left behind. Round the coast, the Boulder-clay itself has been in turn attacked, especially by the sea during the low land-level that occurred in Neolithic times. Then the stony materials in the Boulder-clay were sorted into gravel-beds, the clayey part being carried out into deeper water: and these gravel-beds, subsequently raised above tide-level, bequeathed to the early people abundance of flint to fashion into implements – for flint, from its very hard glassy nature, gave especially sharp cutting edges to the skilled worker, and all over the world was highly valued by Stone Age peoples. So it comes about that the raised beaches are full of worked flints, the debris of the implement-makers' trade, mixed with scrapers, knives, axes, spears and what-not, which were imperfect, or which got lost. The most extensive of these raised beaches is that which forms the Curran at Larne – a sickle-shaped spit a mile in length, composed of twenty feet of stratified gravel, full of marine shells to attest its origin.

The main ice-sheet, coming down channel from Scotland, has scattered Antrim flint everywhere to the southward – across Belfast Lough into Down, and away on to Dublin and Wexford. When we were children at Holywood, a great event was the arrival of a load of shore gravel and its spreading on the avenue. We were inveterate collectors – to the great inconvenience of our mother – and the gravel was in a few minutes cleared of its worked flints. We got to know well the different types of implements, and more than one well-formed axe or arrow-head was with pride placed in the box which served as a museum. That and pieces of the riebeckite-granophyre of Ailsa Craig – a granite-like rock with blue crystals in it, brought south by the ice – were the principal spoils yielded by the local gravel.

Years afterwards a vexed question agitated the Belfast Naturalists' Field Club as to whether the worked flints were found at all depths in the Larne gravels – which would show that their manufacture was as old as or older than even the lowest layer – or only at or near the surface, implying a later date. We – a committee of the Club – made two excavations in consecutive years to elucidate this point, and found that the implements occur at all depths, though they are most plentiful near the surface – an important fact that has been confirmed by subsequent investigations.

Good wine needs no bush, and I need not exhaust the reader's patience – and my own – by going into a detailed itinerary of the Antrim coast. From Portrush all the way to Ballycastle bold cliffs prevail, with outlying stacks – of which Carrick-a-rede with its precarious bridge and salmon fishery is the most picturesque – and occasional sandy stretches as at Bushfoot and Whitepark Bay. The finest cliffs are those about Bengore Head (*Beann gabhar*, peak of the goats), just east of the Giant's Causeway. Unlike the cliffs to the east and west, these are of basalt from top to bottom, and display to perfection the sequence of the successive lava-flows, with the red band in the middle that marks a long pause in volcanic activity, and the formation of fertile plains and shallow lakes: above, the black rock supervenes, bed upon bed, showing the resumption of the reign of terror and the local extirpation of fauna and flora alike. At Whitepark Bay, on the other hand, the Chalk stands much higher, and it, not basalt, forms the cliffs which enclose this lovely spot: but out at sea, at *lower* levels, stacks of black rock rise from the water, showing how the Earth's surface has cracked and portions have been dropped down hundreds of feet as a result of deep-seated disturbance.

Here and there along this north coast are ruined castles perched on the edge of the cliff, mostly on isolated projections where they had natural defences in the form of precipices which almost encircled them. Here MacNeills and MacQuillans and O'Cahans fought and wrestled for spoil in old days, and raided each other's cow-pens. And the names of these strongholds – Dunluce (*Dún lios* or *Dur lios*, strong fort), Dunseverick (*Dún Sobairche*, Sobairche's fort), Dunanynie – suggest that they were in occupation long before the days of castles, and formed the 'promontory forts' of older peoples, the neck which joined the headland with the mainland being fortified by a deep fosse, such as is found on other parts of the coast. The sandy stretch between the sea and the encircling cliff at Whitepark Bay was a populous settlement in Neolithic and Bronze Age times, as is shown by the abundance of bones, charcoal, and implements which occur there, especially in the 'black layers' which mark old surfaces. The most interesting of the animal remains are bones of the Great Auk which are found mixed with those of Red Deer and domestic creatures, showing that this extinct bird was in those days an article of food. The Giant's Causeway itself has so often been described and its peculiar columns explained that it seems superfluous here to do that again.

Rathlin Island or Raghery (*Rachra*, genitive *Rachran*: *Rikina* of Ptolemy) lying a few miles off Ballycastle, continues the Chalk and basalt area out to sea. The intervening gap, which now forms a deep and turbulent strait, probably arose from a collapse of the surface during the many and extensive earth-movements resulting from the disturbances which led to the great volcanic outpourings. The island, shaped like a letter L, is mostly cliff-bound, but low at the part which is nearest to Fair Head; the surface is heathy, with cultivation on shallow soil and lakelets or marshes in the hollows. There is now no fuel, which has to be brought from Ballycastle. At the west end the cliffs, which the White-tailed Sea-Eagle used to haunt, run up to over 400 feet, with high outlying stacks, and here there are vast colonies of breeding sea-birds, which include Manx Shearwaters and Fulmar Petrels. The whole island is a delightful open breezy place, inspiring and invigorating. . . .

One of the finest promontories on the Irish coast is Benmore (*Beann mór*, great headland) or Fair Head, which looks across to Rathlin and to Kintyre a few miles east of Ballycastle. Others are loftier, but none has a more imposing or clean-cut profile – a tip-tilted promontory of 636 feet falling in a straight vertical line to a talus of huge blocks sloping to deep water. Here again, as in so many places in Antrim, the geological structure will excite the interest even of one who does not know – nor cares to know – the difference between granite and slate. . . .

Immediately behind the pleasant watering-place of Ballycastle, Knocklayd (*Cnoc leithid*, the broad hill) rises to 1695 feet, a massive dome-shaped outlier of the Antrim plateau. The upper part is basalt, below which the white Chalk peeps out, resting on an ancient floor of schist. . . . south of Fair Head is Murlough Bay (*Murbholg*, a sea-inlet), a place of singular charm. An 800-foot slope descends steeply to the sea, clothed with wood to the water's edge. Once again, it is the great variety of rocks which the bay contains that forms its most remarkable feature. To the north is Fair Head, with its gigantic columns resting on Carboniferous sandstone, shale and beds of coal. In the centre there are elevated cliffs of white Chalk, overlying bright red Triassic sandstone. And the southern horn of the bay is formed of ancient mica-schists, an outlying fragment of the rocks of Donegal. The wet surface of the red sandstone is the home of the Yellow Mountain Saxifrage, which makes here a brave show in July, descending to the level of the sea. In spring the extraordinary profusion of Primroses and Wild Hyacinths, Red Campion and ferns, under the fresh leaves of the sloping woods, with the open sea immediately below, provides a delightful picture, but now trees cut and trampling cattle have wrought havoc. . . .

Next we have Torr Head (*Tor*, a tower, hence tall rock), a few miles to the south, a knob of ancient slaty rocks, in a kind of amphitheatre of high green slopes, where the bright grassy covering betrays the presence of the Chalk. The roads here are metalled with the 'white limestone' and form winding lines of dead white against the hills, where Primroses, Wild Hyacinths and Early Purple Orchis linger almost till July. After an interval comes Cushendun (*Cois abhann Duine*, mouth of the river Dun), with its sheltered bay and curious series of caves cut in the 'pudding-stones' of the Old Red Sandstone; south of that again Cushendall (*Cois abhann Dhalla*, mouth of the river Dall) nestles among its trees – an excellent and popular centre: and beyond Red Bay and the flat that forms the end of the cliff-walled Glenariff, Garron Point (*Garrán*, a shrubbery) stands boldly out, a high and massive promontory. Its remarkable outline is due to a series of extensive landslides. The treacherous slippery clays of the Lias underlie solid beds of Chalk and basalt, which cover them to a depth of close on a thousand feet, and these beds have slid forward and downward, producing a series of gigantic steps descending to the sea, with rocky faces of white or black, and grassy sheltered tops sloping inwards: on one of these steps Garron Tower Hotel stands.

Above the cliffs and land-slips the top of the headland, about 1000 feet above the sea, forms the most unfrequented and remote portion of the basaltic plateau. For ten miles in a south-westerly direction, and a breadth of several miles, this elevated tableland extends, roadless, houseless, covered with deep soaking bog with little lakes here and there, and tenanted only by gulls and moorland birds and hares. Its wild flowers, too, are interesting. Here grow two sedges, *Carex pauciflora* and *C. magellanica*, unknown elsewhere in Ireland, and also the rare Yellow Marsh Saxifrage. Thence you descend east to Carnlough (*Carn locha*, the carn of the lough) and its pretty bay, and you pass on to Straidkilly, where the Lias clays are flowing slowly down after the manner of a glacier, bearing on their surface the wreck of the Chalk and basalt, as well as a village, and for ever striving to overwhelm the Coast Road or to carry it with them into the sea. Beyond the little village of Glenarm we pass below lofty cliffs of Chalk, and a dozen miles more takes us to Larne and the railway, and thence by Larne Lough and Carrickfergus to Belfast.

The whole coast is so full of beauty and interest that, knowing it so well as I do, I find it hard to select, as I have tried to do, a few spots for special mention; I feel that I have by no means done justice to Cushendun and Cushendall, two places of high attraction. One generalization may be ventured – the scenery and varied interest increase northward. You begin at Larne (*Inver an Latharna*, river-mouth of Lathair, son of Hugony the Great) with primrose-starred slopes dropping to the raised beach on which the Coast Road runs: and thence the ground gets more broken and more beautiful all the way to Fair Head, which, with Murlough Bay, must stand as the special jewel in the Antrim crown: along the northern shore other jewels, such as Whitepark Bay and the cliffs of Bengore, are not far behind it in lustre. Weather is an important factor here: to see the coast at its best you should have a keen clear north wind, bringing in a sparkling sea that edges the rocks with snowy foam, and makes the high line of the Scottish coast – Islay, and the Paps of Jura, and the frowning promontory of Kintyre – seem scarcely more than a stone's-throw away.

I have said little about the Antrim glens, that cut deep into the high scarp that fronts the North Channel; but it is they, rather than the narrow coastal fringe, that maintain the prosperous farming population, and make 'The Glens of Antrim', or simply 'The Glynns', a well-known geographical expression, like the Kyles of Bute. For the basalt weathers into a heavy rich soil, and the narrow sheltered valley-bottoms have much good agricultural land, though on the slopes it soon gives way to Gorse and then to Heather. The most picturesque of the nine glens (as they are mostly counted) is Glenariff (*Gleann garbh*, rough glen), cliff-walled, flat-bottomed in its lower part where it debouches to the sea in half a mile of sandy shore; narrowing above into branching wooded gorges, full of ferns and wild-flowers. Glendun (Glen of the Dun [river]) is likewise wide below, from Cushendun up to the viaduct which carries the main road on its way northward towards Ballycastle: above that it forms a fine V-shaped valley, running up into wide moorlands. Glenshesk (*Gleann seisg*, glen of the coarse grass?), behind Ballycastle, contains a more divided river-system, receiving tributary streams from right and left – a broad beautiful valley, with Knocklayd towering over it on the west. All the glens contain good roads, highways by which the coastal region is connected with the interior of Antrim behind the lofty basaltic fringe, so that despite the prevalence of elevated moorland one can walk or drive across at frequent intervals, or on foot strike north or south over the heather from glen to glen. The glensmen, too, are well worth meeting – a fine hardy hearty race, closely akin in descent and in language to their Scottish neighbours, shrewd, friendly and hospitable. . . .

When in the course of our peregrination we pass Black Head, we come within the sphere of influence of Belfast – that great busy place, not quite a *mushroom* city – there is nothing fungoid about it – but one of growth so fast and vigorous that the more deliberate higher races of plants supply no suitable parallel. How far the rapid extension of Belfast (*Béal feirste*, the ford of the sand-bank) is due to natural advantages, and how far to the vigorous blend in the blood of its inhabitants, I am not qualified to enquire: but if we glance at local geological history we unearth some facts which, if they afford no clue to this riddle, at least explain some of the natural aids and also difficulties which have accompanied its development. Belfast Lough, a fine harbour of refuge, twelve miles long and three to four wide, at the head of which the city stands, represents the long-sunken termination of the valley of the Lagan. It is also a marked geological boundary, for the elevated basaltic area ceases abruptly on its northern shore, though the underlying red sandstones of the Trias edge the lough on both sides, giving way on the County Down coast almost at once to the much older Ordovician and Silurian slaty rocks which cover most of the latter county. Belfast Lough and the Lagan valley above it have in fact been excavated in the Triassic sandstones. During the Ice Age these soft rocks suffered severely, and the bright colour of the Boulder-clay about here shows how the red material of the marls and sandstones has been ground up and scattered. When the ice was in process of withdrawal, the Lagan valley was left clear, while the adjoining lough and the sea outside were still choked. This ice formed a dam, behind which, over and around the site of Belfast, a great lake was produced. Into this lake turbid streams brought much sediment, which settled as red sand or fine red clay. Thus are derived the sands of Malone and Knock, which form a dry and excellent foundation in those suburbs, and also the brick-clays out of which most of Belfast is built.

In later times, when Neolithic man roamed the country, the land around Belfast stood lower than at present; the sea lay over the site of the future city, and the tide flowed far up the valley. In the calm waters, sediments accumulated. Deep excavations in Belfast Harbour give us glimpses of this post-Glacial history. Overlying the red sands before-mentioned is a bed of peat, now no less than twenty-seven feet below high-water mark, pointing to a much higher land-level than at present, and a surface on which woods of Scotch Fir, Oak, Alder, Willow and Hazel grew, and in these woods Red Deer, Wild Boar and other large animals roamed at will, while insects crawled among the herbage or flitted among the trees. The forerunner of the Belfast-man was no doubt present in those days, but his traces have not as yet been found in this deposit, and it seems very doubtful if that grand forerunner of the peat fauna, the Irish 'Elk', whose remains are found immediately below the vegetable deposit, actually survived into the peat period. Then the land began to sink, and this subsidence continued till the old land-surface was buried fifty or sixty feet under the sea, which covered the site of the future city and flowed up the valley as far as Balmoral. While Neolithic man was busy with his flint-implement factories at Larne and Kilroot, deposits of fine grey mud, full of marine shells, accumulated in Belfast Lough and elsewhere, burying deeply the old peat-bed. Then at last the land rose again, leaving a flat plain of soft clay from which the sea had retreated, and around it the scarps that told of the old land-edge on which the waves had beaten, and which still stand out boldly, as in the steep bluff at Tillysburn and the sudden little hill at the back of York Street and Royal Avenue in Belfast. Old Belfast, as around High Street, arose a couple of centuries ago on this former sea-bottom, and it was only as the town spread that buildings began to be erected on the firmer foundations furnished by the red Glacial clays and sands – the deltas and sediments of 'Lake Belfast'. Below, on the flat, light buildings were possible; but when taller structures were planned, a firm foundation was necessary, which could only be obtained by piling – by hammering long balks of timber down through the soft silts to the red sands or hard clays far below. So the Belfast of today is essentially a city on stilts. . . .

Belfast has always been a centre of biological research, and even in its younger days, when it was a smaller place than Cork, Galway or Limerick, Belfast men were working actively at local natural history. In this field, which alone I can touch on here, three names stand out pre-eminently – Templeton (1766–1825), Thompson (1805–52) and Stewart (1826–1910). John Templeton was a gentleman of leisure, living at Cranmore near the 'Bog Meadows'. From boyhood he was interested in zoology and botany, especially the latter, and throughout his life this interest retained the form of investigations of a purely local character. Wicklow and Scotland appear to be the farthest points afield that he reached during an active life, and there is no record even of a visit to London, though he was in touch with botanical and zoological leaders resident there. But the flora and fauna of the Belfast region, till then almost unknown, he investigated thoroughly. He was the first to find (on the Cave Hill) the Red Broom-rape, which Sir J.E. Smith described as new from specimens which Templeton sent him; and his critical faculty was shown by his recognition as something novel of *Rosa hibernica*, then looked on as a new species, afterwards shown to be a hybrid hitherto unknown. His main work, his *Hibernian Flora*, remained unfinished and unpublished, but the manuscripts which he left may fairly be said to form the foundation on which our present knowledge of the flora of north-east Ireland has been built.

William Thompson was the son of a Belfast linen merchant, and in his younger days showed no inclination towards natural history. When he was an apprentice to a firm engaged in the linen industry, he came again in contact with an old school friend, William Sinclaire, who was interested in ornithology; that proved the beginning of a lifelong devotion to zoology, for in 1831, when he was twenty-six years of age, he gave up business and thenceforth spent his time in investigation of the local fauna (especially birds) and to a lesser extent of the flora. He soon amassed a large body of notes relating to both terrestrial and aquatic species, from mammals down to rotifers, and the idea of a work on the Irish fauna began to take shape. Much local assistance was forthcoming from energetic zoological friends such as Robert Patterson and G.C. Hyndman; correspondence was maintained with naturalists in other parts of Ireland regarding local animals and with the leading British zoologists of the day: and in 1850, when Thompson was forty-five years old, the first volume of his *Natural History of Ireland* appeared. A second and a third were published in the two years succeeding. These three volumes dealt with and completed the Irish birds, and give an idea of the elaborate scale on which his plans were made. But Thompson's work was destined to go no further. He was seized with illness while on a brief visit to London, and died within two days, at the age of forty-seven years.

. . . Thompson believed he had found in the North of Ireland a new species of rat, which he described as *Mus hibernicus*. This creature seemed most nearly allied to the old Black Rat, which occupied the British Isles before it was driven out by the Norway Rat, the brown species which is so common nowadays. The 'Irish Rat' (which is now known to be widely spread, and not confined to Ireland) differs from the Black Rat by having a triangular white spot on the breast and shorter tail and ears, and it seemed distinct; but later it was shown to be a melanic or dark-coloured form of the Norway Rat: indeed a case is recorded of typical Norway Rats and Irish Rats being produced in the same litter. This phenomenon of melanism is found in many creatures, and is especially well known among some of the insects, such as moths; it is in Great Britain and Ireland associated with the western coasts; but no definite connection appears to have been established between it and the climatic factors which probably affect it, such as high rainfall or limited insolation.

Samuel Alexander Stewart was a man of type quite different from Templeton and Thompson. He began life by working for a Belfast distillery on a wage of two shillings a week. Later he joined his father, who was a trunk-maker, and as a maker of trunks he passed most of his life, in his shop in North Street. Eventually, in 1891, he became curator of the Museum of the Belfast Natural History and Philosophical Society at a salary of £65. So it will be seen that few worldly advantages came his way. But let us consider what he did. As a youth his evenings were spent at a night school, and later he progressed so well in self-education that he became a court of appeal among scientific friends on many subjects – even on points of English grammar and composition. Always inclined towards nature study, his opportunity came when the Science and Art Department established lecture courses in Belfast in 1860. Under J. Beete Jukes and Ralph Tate he eagerly drank in the principles of geology and botany, and was quick to apply to local phenomena all that he learned. Already in 1863, when Tate published his *Flora Belfastiensis*, localities for a number of the rarer plants were supplied by Stewart, and many further notes were contributed to *Cybele Hibernica*, 1866.

He steadily pursued local botanical exploration, and despite strict limitations of both time and means, accomplished this so thoroughly that when in 1888 the Belfast Naturalists' Field Club published his *Flora of the*

North-east of Ireland, the completeness of the account given of the distribution of the Flowering Plants, Mosses and Liverworts was largely the
result of his own unaided work. The Field Club referred to had been
established in 1863 by Tate and his pupils as a direct result of the lectures
aforesaid. From the beginning, Stewart was a leading member, and as his
studies spread from botany into geology and zoology, he became a referee in all these subjects both within and without the Club. In Quaternary
geology he did especially valuable work. He was the first to show that the
clays underlying Belfast and other local estuaries furnish evidence of a
depression and subsequent re-elevation of the land of a considerable
amount – the 'Neolithic depression' so familiar to present-day geologists;
and in a valuable paper he listed all the known fossils of the northern
Boulder-clay. Nor was his work confined to the Belfast region. A.G. More
was not slow to see in Stewart a valuable ally in the working-up of the
Irish flora for the second edition of *Cybele Hibernica*. His museum appointment having made occasional absences possible, he explored,
under grants from the Royal Irish Academy, western Fermanagh, Rathlin
Island, the Lough Allen and Slieveanieran area, and the Shannon estuary;
and I joined him in 1889–90 in a thorough examination of the Mourne
Mountains.

But it was Stewart's successful fight against heavy odds all through life,
and his sterling character, that especially deserve recognition. Of the former
enough has been hinted. His intuitive thoroughness and accuracy, his
clearness of vision and caution in scientific questions, his modesty and
his courage, made him respected and loved. Of 'the strife for triumph
more than truth' he was incapable; and the only thing towards which he
showed intolerance in scientific matters was slipshod work or self-praise.
As to his own considerable achievements he was depreciative, and the
award of the Honorary Fellowship of the Botanical Society of Edinburgh,
the Associateship of the Linnean Society, and eventually a pension from
the Civil List, were to him more than ample recognition of his work.

I am proud to pay this brief tribute to the memory of S.A. Stewart, for I
cannot say how much I owe to him. Ever ready to help, he befriended me
when I was still at school, and was tireless in naming specimens and in
imparting all that lore relating to botanical and geological field-work that
is not to be found in any book, but which passes from mouth to mouth

among those who keep the torch of knowledge burning. No young naturalist ever had a better or more patient teacher, or a more delightful friend than I when in after years we tramped the hills of Down together.

'Away, away, from men and towns.' From the modern city of Belfast, with its modern history and modern buildings and modern factories and shipyards, we turn to the beautiful and attractive area which surrounds it. Not that any slight to Belfast is implied. What does the Belfast businessman himself do (and in Belfast almost every man is a business-man) but get away from it as soon as ever his business is done – to Balmoral or Knock or Bangor: and I may claim the same privilege, and leave the guide-book to do justice to Belfast. Dublin is beautifully situated, with mountains rising only a few miles beyond its southern suburbs, and the richly wooded Liffey vale, with bold headlands of Howth and Bray, and the broad sands of Dublin Bay. Cork can make a good bid too: but to my mind Belfast stands pre-eminent in Ireland for the beauty and variety of its environment. To north and west the high scarp of the basalts rises nobly. The City Hall, standing at sea-level, is distant only two and a half miles from the thousand-foot contour-line; and the lofty cliffs of the Cave Hill are a conspicuous feature from Castle Junction, the central point of the city.

On a volcanic vent at Carrickfergus (*Carraig Fhearghusa*, Fergus's rock) ten miles down the lough, the great castle which John de Courcy built in 1177 stands intact, now a local museum, its stirring military days long past. A significant feature near by is the pit-heads of the Duncrue salt-mines – one of the very few of the many Irish mining enterprises that are not now abandoned. Beds of salt up to eighty-eight feet in thickness occur here among the marls of the New Red Sandstone. In mining, half of the bed is left to form a roof, and the other half is cut away except for massive pillars to support the overlying strata. The mineral is often very pure, containing up to 98 per cent of salt. Beyond, where the coast turns northward, are the Chalk and basalt cliffs of White Head and Black Head. South-west of Belfast lies the valley of the Lagan, richly wooded. South-east, the undulating lands of County Down stretch far – fertile and smiling, but supplying less variety than any other part of Belfast's environment. The Down side of Belfast Lough, however, compensates for this, being well-wooded, varied, with a rocky shore. Then a little further off is the long island-studded lough of Strangford, anciently *Loch Cuan*, the *Strang Fiord* of the Norsemen, full of archaeological and natural history interest. Only twelve miles west of Belfast, across the hills, lies Lough Neagh, the largest sheet of water in Ireland and larger also than any in Great Britain; and beyond White Head is Larne Lough. So delightful a combination of land and water within a few miles of a great city is surely unique; and the variety of rocks which occurs also is striking, representing a remarkable span of world history.

from *The Way That I Went*, 1937

A Belfast Boyhood

FORREST REID

My waking world, also, was gradually expanding, though it still remained the very small world of a provincial town – a rather hard, unromantic town too – devoted exclusively to money-making; yet a town, for all that, somehow likeable, and surrounded by as beautiful a country as one could desire. The Belfast of my childhood differed considerably from the Belfast of to-day. It was, I think, spiritually closer to that surrounding country. Then, as now, perhaps, it was not particularly well educated, it possessed no cultured and no leisured class (the sons of even the wealthiest families leaving school at fifteen or sixteen to enter their fathers' offices); but it did not, as I remember it at any rate, bear nearly so marked a resemblance to the larger English manufacturing towns.

The change I seem to see has, of course, brought it closer to its own ideal. For some not very intelligible reason, a hankering after things English – even what is believed to be an English accent – and a distrust of things Irish, have always characterized the more well-to-do citizens of Belfast. But in the days of my childhood this was not so apparent, while the whole town was more homely, more unpretentious. A breath of rusticity still sweetened its air; the few horse trams, their destinations indicated by the colour of their curtains, did little to disturb the quiet of the streets; the Malone Road was still an almost rural walk; Molly Ward's cottage, not a vulcanite factory, guarded the approach to the river; and there were no brick works, no mill chimneys, no King's Bridge to make ugly blots on the green landscape of the Lagan Valley. The town itself, as I have said, was more attractive, with plenty of open spaces, to which the names of certain districts – the Plains, the Bog Meadows – bear witness. Queen's University was not a mere mass of unrelated, shapeless buildings; the Technical Institute did not sprawl in unsightly fashion across half the grounds of my old school. Gone is the Linen Hall, that was once the very heart of the town in its hours of ease. A brand new City Hall, all marble staircases and inlaid floors, garnished with statues and portraits of

197

Lord Mayors and town councillors, and fronted with wooden benches on which rows of our less successful citizens doze and scratch the languid hours away, flaunts its expensive dullness where that old mellow ivy-creepered building once stood, with its low, arched entrance, its line of trees that shut out the town bustle and dust. The Linen Hall Library, transported to another building, still exists, but, as with the city, expansion has robbed it of its individuality. The old Linen Hall Library, with the sparrows flying in and out of the ivy all day long, fluttering and squabbling, was a charming place. It was very like a club. Its membership was comparatively small; its tone was old-fashioned; it belonged to the era of the two- and three-volume novel; it had about it an atmosphere of quiet and leisure.

Does anybody nowadays read the romances of Jessie Fothergill, of Helen Mathers, of Mrs Alexander? These were the books adored by my sisters, the books I saw lying about the house: – *Healey, Probation, Cherry Ripe, Her Dearest Foe, The Wooing O't.* Yet *Dame Durden* I knew was the most beautiful novel ever written. My eldest sister mentioned this casually one day at dinner, and it never occurred to me to question the statement, so I need not question it now.

In the Linen Hall Library, curled up in a low deep window seat, I would sit gazing out between the trees and right up Donegall Place, which on summer afternoons was a fashionable promenade, where one was almost sure to meet everybody one knew. Here, hidden in a box below the counter, Mr Gourley (then Johnnie) kept the latest novels for his favourite subscribers. Here when, at the request of my eldest sister, I asked one day for Miss Florence Warden's *House on the Marsh*, that same Mr Gourley, knowing the library did not possess a copy, utterly abashed me by suggesting with great severity that perhaps it 'was not a nice book'. I blushed, for I was sophisticated enough to associate 'not niceness' with the improper, even while, for the sake of the family, I asserted indignantly that it *was* nice. And here, one summer afternoon, just outside the tall iron gates, I beheld my first celebrity. Not that I knew him to be celebrated, but I could see for myself his appearance was remarkable. I had been taught that it was rude to stare, but on this occasion, though I was with my mother, I could not help staring, and even feeling I was intended to do so. He was, my mother told me, a Mr Oscar Wilde; and she added, by way of explanation I suppose, that he was aesthetic, like Bunthorne, in *Patience*.

It was years before I heard his name again, years before I came upon the short stories dedicated to Margaret, Lady Brooke; to Mrs William H. Grenfell, of Taplow Court; to H.S.H. Alice, Princess of Monaco. At the time I saw him, he was the guest of a Mrs Thompson of College Gardens, whose two bouncing daughters bore a distinct resemblance to my early vision of the nieces at Bootle. Flaxen haired and voluble, with their mother they got into the carriage now, while the aesthete climbed up on to the box seat beside the coachman.

from *Apostate*, 1926

A View from the Holywood Hills

C.S. LEWIS

Though my friendship with Arthur [Greeves] began from an identity of taste on a particular point, we were sufficiently different to help one another. His home-life was almost the opposite of mine. His parents were members of the Plymouth Brothers, and he was the youngest of a large family; his home, nevertheless, was almost as silent as ours was noisy. He was at this time working in the business of one of his brothers, but his health was delicate and after an illness or two he was withdrawn from it. He was a man of more than one talent: a pianist and, in hope, a composer, and also a painter. One of our earliest schemes was that he should make an operatic score for *Loki Bound* – a project which, of course, after an extremely short and happy life, died a painless death. In literature he influenced me more, or more permanently, than I did him. His great defect was that he cared very little for verse. Something I did to mend this, but less than I wished. He, on the other hand, side by side with his love for myth and marvel, which I fully shared, had another taste which I lacked till I met him and with which, to my great good, he infected me for life. This was the taste for what he called 'the good, solid, old books', the classic English novelists. It is astonishing how I had avoided them before I met Arthur. I had been persuaded by my father to read *The Newcomes* when I was rather too young for it and never tried Thackeray again till I was at Oxford. He is still antipathetic to me, not because he preaches but because he preaches badly. Dickens I looked upon with a feeling of horror, engendered by long poring over the illustrations before I had learned to read. I still think them depraved. Here, as in Walt Disney, it is not the ugliness of the ugly figures but the simpering dolls intended for our sympathy which really betray the secret (not that Walt Disney is not far superior to the illustrators of Dickens). Of Scott I knew only a few of the medieval, that is, the weakest, novels. Under Arthur's influence I read at this time all the best Waverleys, all the Brontës, and all the Jane Austens. They provided an admirable complement to my more fantastic reading,

200

and each was the more enjoyed for its contrast to the other. The very qualities which had previously deterred me from such books Arthur taught me to see as their charm. What I would have called their 'stodginess' or 'ordinariness' he called 'Homeliness' – a key word in his imagination. He did not mean merely Domesticity, though that came into it. He meant the rooted quality which attaches them to all our simple experiences, to weather, food, the family, the neighbourhood. He could get endless enjoyment out of the opening sentence of *Jane Eyre*, or that other opening sentence in one of Hans Andersen's stories, 'How it did rain, to be sure.' The mere word 'beck' in the Brontës was a feast to him; and so were the schoolroom and kitchen scenes. This love of the 'Homely' was not confined to literature; he looked for it in out-of-door scenes as well and taught me to do the same.

Hitherto my feelings for nature had been too narrowly romantic. I attended almost entirely to what I thought awe-inspiring, or wild, or eerie, and above all to distance. Hence mountains and clouds were my especial delight; the sky was, and still is, to me one of the principal elements in any landscape, and long before I had seen them all named and sorted out in *Modern Painters* I was very attentive to the different qualities, and different heights, of the cirrus, the cumulus, and the rain-cloud. As for the Earth, the country I grew up in had everything to encourage a romantic bent, had indeed done so ever since I first looked at the unattainable Green Hills through the nursery window. For the reader who knows those parts it will be enough to say that my main haunt was the Holywood Hills – the irregular polygon you would have described if you drew a line from Stormont to Comber, from Comber to Newtownards, from Craigantlet to Holywood, and thence through Knocknagoney back to Stormont. How to suggest it all to a foreigner I hardly know.

First of all, it is by Southern English standards bleak. The woods, for we have a few, are of small trees, rowan and birch and small fir. The fields are small, divided by ditches with ragged sea-nipped hedges on top of them. There is a good deal of gorse and many outcroppings of rock. Small abandoned quarries, filled with cold-looking water, are surprisingly numerous. There is nearly always a wind whistling through the grass. Where you see a man ploughing there will be gulls following him and pecking at the furrow. There are no field-paths or rights of way, but that does not matter for everyone knows you – or if they do not know you, they know your kind and understand that you will shut gates and not walk over crops. Mushrooms are still felt to be common property, like the air. The soil has none of the rich chocolate or ochre you find in parts of England: it is pale – what Dyson calls 'the ancient, bitter earth'. But the grass is soft, rich, and sweet, and the cottages, always whitewashed and single storeyed and roofed with blue slate, light up the whole landscape.

Although these hills are not very high, the expanse seen from them is huge and various. Stand at the north-eastern extremity where the slopes go steeply down to Holywood. Beneath you is the whole expanse of the Lough. The Antrim coast twists sharply to the north and out of sight; green, and humble in comparison, Down curves away southward. Between the two the Lough merges into the sea, and if you look carefully on a good day you can even see Scotland, phantom-like on the horizon. Now come further to the south and west. Take your stand at the isolated cottage which is visible from my father's house and overlooks our whole suburb, and which everyone calls The Shepherd's Hut, though we are not really a shepherd country. You are still looking down on the Lough, but its mouth and the sea are now hidden by the shoulder you have just come from, and it might (for all you see) be a landlocked lake. And here we come to one of those great contrasts which have bitten deeply into my mind – Niflheim and Asgard, Britain and Logres, Handramit and Harandra, air and ether, the low world and the high. Your horizon from here is the Antrim Mountains, probably a uniform mass of greyish blue, though if it is a sunny day you may just trace on the Cave Hill the distinction between the green slopes that climb two-thirds of the way to the summit and the cliff wall that perpendicularly accomplishes the rest. That is one beauty; and here where you stand is another, quite different and even more dearly loved – sunlight and grass and dew, crowing cocks and gaggling ducks. In between them, on the flat floor of the Valley at your feet, a forest of factory chimneys, gantries, and giant cranes rising out of a welter of mist, lies Belfast. Noises come up from it continually, whining and screeching of trams, clatter of horse traffic on uneven sets, and, dominating all else, the continual throb and stammer of the great shipyards. And because we have heard this all our lives it does not, for us, violate the peace of the hill-top; rather, it emphasises it, enriches the contrast, sharpens the dualism. Down in that 'smoke and stir' is the hated office to which Arthur, less fortunate than I, must return tomorrow: for it is only one of his rare holidays that allows us to stand here together on a week-day morning. And down there too are the barefoot old women, the drunken men stumbling in and out of the 'spirit grocers' (Ireland's horrible substi-tute for the kindly English 'pub'), the straining, overdriven horses, the hard-faced rich women – all the world which Alberich created when he cursed love and twisted the gold into a ring.

Now step a little way – only two fields and across a lane and up to the top of the bank on the far side – and you will see, looking south with a little east in it, a different world. And having seen it, blame me if you can for being a romantic. For here is the thing itself, utterly irresistible, the way to the world's end, the land of longing, the breaking and blessing of hearts. You are looking across what may be called, in a certain sense, the plain of Down, and seeing beyond it the Mourne Mountains.

It was K – that is, Cousin Quartus' second daughter, the Valkyrie – who first expounded to me what this plain of Down is really like. Here is the recipe for imagining it. Take a number of medium-sized potatoes and lay them down (one layer of them only) in a flat-bottomed tin basin. Now shake loose earth over them till the potatoes themselves, but not the shape of them, is hidden; and of course the crevices between them will now be depressions of earth. Now magnify the whole thing till those crevices are large enough to conceal each its stream and its huddle of trees. And then, for colouring, change your brown earth into the cheq-uered pattern of fields, always small fields (a couple of acres each), with all their normal variety of crop, grass, and plough. You have now got a picture of the 'plain' of Down, which is a plain only in this sense that if you were a very large giant you would regard it as level but very ill to walk on – like cobbles. And now remember that every cottage is white. The whole expanse laughs with these little white dots; it is like nothing so much as the assembly of white foam-caps when a fresh breeze is on a summer sea. And the roads are white too; there is no tarmac yet. And because the whole country is a turbulent democracy of little hills, these roads shoot in every direction, disappearing and reappearing. But you must not spread over this landscape your hard English sunlight; make it paler, make it softer, blur the edges of the white cumuli, cover it with watery gleams, deepening it, making all unsubstantial. And beyond all this, so remote that they seem fantastically abrupt, at the very limit of your vision, imagine the mountains. They are no stragglers. They seem to have nothing to do with the little hills and cottages that divide you from them. And sometimes they are blue, sometimes violet; but quite often they look transparent – as if huge sheets of gauze had been cut out into mountainous shapes and hung up there, so that you could see through them the light of the invisible sea at their backs.

from *Surprised by Joy*, 1955

A Piece of Fresh-Baked Soda Bread . . .

FLORENCE MARY MCDOWELL

In most homes, especially the homes of the labouring poor, every day was baking day. When the mother had seen her family off to school or mill or farm, she had her few minutes' leisure. Often with a neighbour for company and talk, she now had her morning tea, made by putting the breakfast tea-drawer back on the coals of the fire, with water added to the remains of the family's breakfast brew. When boiled up again it made quite good tea and was often the poor mother's one luxury. In the poorest homes the leaves were used and re-used until there was no 'good' left in them. Even when the 'good' was gone, they were still useful for scattering on the flagged or earthen floor to keep down the dust of sweeping. Then, with the few dishes washed and the hearth swept, the mother would hook the iron griddle on the chain over the open fire and get out her bake-board.

Her implements were simple – a board for kneading; a glazed yellow bowl for mixing; a buttermilk crock with its dipping tin; a knife for mixing the dough, dividing it and finally for scraping the board; and a goose wing for sweeping board and griddle clear of the residue of flour when baking was finished. From such primitive equipment the most delicious breads were produced by the baker's skill – soda bread, wheaten, oat cake, fadge, reusel, apple fadge, treacle soda and currant soda. The last four were special treats not for everyday eating, for plain soda was the really staple bread.

It seems simple to take four gopinfuls of flour with a pinch each of salt and baking soda, mix with buttermilk, knead and pat into a flat round, quarter and bake on a griddle. But only the skill and experience of the housewife could produce the soft-crusted, delicious-smelling, faintly-brown farls that piled up on every kitchen table daily. A treat for the . . . children in any working home was a piece of fresh-baked, hot soda bread, with melting butter dripping on to childish fingers, washed down with half-a-tin of cool, acid buttermilk – a meal fit for kings but, alas, only to be digested by children.

The wheaten bread was made like the soda except that part coarse wheaten meal was substituted for part flour. Fadge and reusel required a further implement in the baking, something for bruising the boiled potatoes which formed the main constituent of both. It might be a ricer, a two-handled, hinged, triangular vessel into which the boiled potatoes were put. The handles were pressed together and the soft potato emerged in vermicelli-like strands from the holes in the ricer. For those who could not afford such an affluent piece of equipment, a wooden pounder called a beetle might be used; or for the poorer still the base of a pint tin would press the soft potatoes quite adequately on the bake-board itself. For reusel a handful of oatmeal would be incorporated in the bruised potatoes and then came the kneading into a circle, quartering into farls, and baking as before on the griddle. Never can there have been such a nourishing, tasty, solid bread as reusel fried in a little bacon fat, and many a working man went out to face the day feeling warm and well fed, for the reusel had great staying power.

For special occasions a chopped Bramley apple with a little sugar would be added to the fadge potato-cake, or treacle mixed with the buttermilk to turn everyday soda bread into party fare, or a little dried fruit and sugar added to the usual mixture to make that currant-soda which the children loved.

Some women also baked in the oven pot. This was a straight-sided, solid iron pot with a lid and three tiny legs. When it was heated in the fire the solid, well-kneaded lump of soda – plain, wheaten, currant and treacle – could be baked as in an oven, and the dough emerged as a delicious bannock, to be cooled and sliced for eating with butter or for frying.

Frying was the most usual method of cooking, and the black iron pan was swung on its hook over the fire in most homes every day, and sometimes twice a day. The Ulster Fry has a long and solid history. Its popularity was probably due to two things – firstly, the housewife usually had only an open fire, so more sophisticated methods of cooking were not hers to command; and secondly, every man, woman or child who could do so tried to rear a pig on scraps and chat potatoes and whatever the free-rooting pig could find on its own hoking expeditions. Often it was a crowl, the runt of a litter, given away by a farmer to anyone who wanted to take the trouble to rear it. After the local pig-killer had done his gory work, there would be bacon and hams to be salted or hung up inside the chimney to smoke. The pork ribs, liver and offal would make tasty eating in the meantime for the family and neighbours, and there would be plenty of lard for the Ulster Fry. Little of the pig was wasted, even the feet being boiled for succulent eating. Pigs' trotters are possibly not everyone's fancy, but they had their following.

As a treat, baker's bread would be bought occasionally from Bob, the OPB vanman. A ticket of loaves (that is, a square of four loaves still joined) cost sixpence, and if a man's wages were ten shillings weekly, it was seldom that such a luxury could be afforded. For the labouring classes, bread, potatoes and oatmeal made up most of the day's eating. The extra tasty bit that provided the savour and interest of a meal – a piece of boiled bacon, a fried rasher to 'taste' the pan or the occasional egg or bit of fish – was called 'kitchen'.

The Bridge children could enjoy their baked bread only when they visited some neighbouring cottage, for Aunt Laetitia didn't bake regularly, although she did make one kind of bread. It was yellow-meal bread, made from a maize-meal called Golden Drop, and it was greatly to the children's fancy. She was, however, a good plain cook who could produce tasty, filling meals, and the occasional dish of her own childhood, like sowans or flummery. Her own favourite meals were kedgeree for breakfast and curried anything for dinner.

Porridge was a common dish in every home from the highest to the socially lowest. But whereas in the homes of the rich it introduced the bacon, eggs, sausages, kidneys, toast, marmalade and kickshaws of the rich man's breakfast, a bowl of oaten porridge constituted the sole breakfast dish for many of the poor. On the farms it was customary to give 'the man' or 'the girl' a bowl of porridge for both the morning and the evening meal. A large pot of potatoes was boiled for the mid-day meal and as often as not the drained potatoes were turned out by the farmer's wife on to the middle of the scrubbed table, where the labourers sat apart from the family. The potatoes, which then seemed to be always large and floury with daintily-cracked skins, were peeled on the table. When five or six had been peeled by each worker and placed on his plate, a large piece of butter would be laid on top, and with coarse salt for relish and skimmed milk or buttermilk to drink, the dinner would be pronounced 'grand stuff'. Sometimes the potatoes would be 'beetled' with milk and scallions to make that prince of Irish dishes, champ.

From time to time the mother or the farm-wife would provide 'kitchen' for the potatoes with a rasher of bacon and fried oatmeal. This last was called mealie-crushie, delicious but a puzzle for the etymologist. Bacon fried with boiled cabbage was another popular dinner, or if times were hard or the family large, cabbage and potatoes fried together in the bacon fat. This was colcannon. And, above all, there was broth.

Broth needed first a tasty stock. This could be provided by boiling water with almost anything animal – a ham-bone, a piece of bacon which would provide another dinner, an old hen past the lay, a piece of beef (seldom), rabbit or hare 'picked up' by the men as they walked the fields and hills on a Sunday, bacon rinds: anything, in fact, that gave flavour. Then into the stock would go any and every vegetable that the mothers could grow or buy cheaply – barley, dried peas, split peas, lentils, leeks, parsley, celery, carrots, cabbage, turnip, parsnips – any or all of them. The broth was thick and nourishing and, with boiled potatoes, was the invariable Sunday dinner. If vegetables were scarce, delicious nettle-broth would be made. It was health-giving and cheap. The people in the mill village of Cogry, who lived in the dingy rows built by the mill owner to house the workers he needed, were the most warm-hearted and gener-ous of mankind. If someone were ill, if someone were poor, if someone were workless, a can was filled from the Sunday broth-pot and carried hot and ready to the home where need was, and if necessary every meal was shared.

from *Other Days Around Me*, 1966

MOURNE COUNTRY

E. ESTYN EVANS

We know from finds made in turf-cutting that it was the practice in former times to bury butter in containers in the bogs. The object appears to have been to preserve it, for it was made without salt, but the large number of deposits which has been found suggests that not all were buried with the intention of their recovery, and that some were placed in the bogs as offerings. In prehistoric times many such offerings, of gold and bronze, were made in bogs and lakes, and the bulk of Ireland's famous collections of prehistoric gold objects has been recovered from such sites.

From the account given by Harris we know that in the eighteenth century the cattle-herders also cut turf during their stay in the mountains. And it is probable that the women folk engaged in spinning wool from the sheep, though this is not mentioned by Harris. The cutting of turf, though by no means given up, has declined for various reasons, including the availability of coal in this sea-girt peninsula and the closing of the bogs in the High Mournes by the Water Commissioners. Several bogs, including the Castle Bog – named after Pierce's Castle – are almost cut out, leaving a waste of granite sand and bleached boulders. We may first describe a method of securing turf which has died out on the Mournes. Mud turf, as it is termed, was formerly made in the valley of the Leitrim River south of Hilltown. The scraw (sod) was first pared off an area about twelve feet long and six wide, and the turf was dug over to the depth of a spit with an ordinary broad-mouthed digging spade, and chopped up fine. Then water was poured in the hole and the turf worked into a sticky paste with a graip (fork). This was thrown out with a long-handled shovel and spread in a thick layer to dry in the sun. The process was repeated to a depth of four or five spits. When partly dry the layer of mud turf was baked (marked out) with the edge of the hand into oblong bricks. Severed with a spade, the turves were spread out to complete the drying, a long process involving much further handling and turning, footing, turn-footing, castling, clamping, and finally, hauling home and stacking.

209

Turf is cut either by breasting or under-footing, that is, by cutting out the turves either horizontally or vertically. Both methods may be seen in the Mournes, but under-footing is the usual mode. The practice may differ from one bog to the next, depending on the nature of the turf and its depth, for breast-cutting is not possible in a shallow bog. Much depends also on the grain of the turf and the degree to which its fibres have decayed. The Castle Bog is perhaps the only place where one may still see breast turf being cut, though the old style winged spade is now replaced by a broad-mouthed spade fitted with a short handle. Under-foot turf is cut in several places, especially in the Black or New Bog in the valley of the Rowan Tree River, and on Finlieve . . . turf spades vary in some degree from one bog to another, and indeed from one owner to another, for they were made to measure by the smith. They also bear the owner's identification mark, cut on the wing. The stout handle usually terminates in a cow's horn to which a high polish has been given by long use. Besides the labour involved in cutting and drying the turf, transport of this bulky fuel is a costly item, though the small farmer, independent of hired labour, does not count the cost. The right to cut turf goes with his grazing rights on the mountains. The poor farmers of Leitrim used to cut more than they needed and sell the surplus at Banbridge, a half a crown the cart-load. This was one of the methods by which poteen made in the hills and contraband goods smuggled from the coast were distributed inland. Those were the days when 'Hilltown kept Downpatrick jail full'. But turf had many uses: large quantities were consumed, for example, for burning lime on the farms.

Interesting types of vehicles are used to convey the turf from the high bogs to the farmsteads. The slide-car, still used for this purpose in the Antrim Glens, is not now known in the Mournes, though I was told by Mick Kane of Clonachullion that his grandmother was taken to her new home on her wedding day on a slide-car. The ass and creels probably put an end to the slide-car; it is generally thought that the ass did not reach Ireland until the beginning of the nineteenth century. But the horse-drawn slipe (sled) is sometimes used for carrying turf, though its more general purpose is for hauling stones. There are still a few block-wheel cars kept for bringing home the turf in the townlands of Tullyframe and Kilfeaghan, and I have seen discarded solid wheels in other townlands, for example, Mullaghmore.

We suggested that the replacement of cattle by sheep was responsible for many minor changes in the vegetation of the hills, and especially for the reduction of trees and bushes, and therefore of bird life. As a rule, only prickly growths can survive the sheep's bite: wild roses, blackthorn, hawthorn, holly, bramble and whins. But sheep must always have played some part in the mountain economy, even if it was subordinate to the role of cattle. In the old days they probably shared the sweet summit pastures with the red deer in summer. The shepherd will tell you how the flocks move uphill on fine summer nights, climbing out of the valley mists until they face the rising sun on northeastern slopes. Stone sheepfolds are numerous on the flanks of the mountains. They are known as 'buchts' and are either circular or square in shape and from five to ten yards across, with one narrow opening. The sheep are collected there for keeling (branding) and splaying. The owner's initials are marked on the horn with a branding-iron or, in the case of a young sheep, with tar on the fleece. There are some old buchts near certain groups of booleys, and disused ones are common. Nowadays the mountain grazing is controlled by committees set up by the farmers on the various estates when the land was bought out. In general, the grazing rights have been jealously guarded and follow the same lines as was customary under the landlords. Groups of from four to seven townlands share adjacent stretches of mountain, several thousand acres in extent. These groups were probably units in Celtic times, and it was suggested that in early times the stock had a free run from the lowlands in winter to the hills in summer. The sheep, at any rate, still seem to make instinctively for the mountains in spring. Although a few farmers own a 'plan' of mountain and have exclusive grazing rights, nearly all the hill-grazings are held in common. Excluding the area owned by various Water Boards there are fifteen commonages. The farmers of the Kingdom of Mourne have suffered most from the encroachment of the Water Boards, and the hill-grazings of the former Kilmorey Estate – mainly in the townland of Mourne Mountains Middle – are overstocked. Mourne Mountains West is less congested.

There were certain Fine Towns, as they were called, enjoying free grazing, among them Lisnacree, Glenloughan and Ballaghanery, but in most cases there was a charge on the rent for the right to graze. Sheep were also brought from some distance for 'the summer's run', a practice which is a modified form of the older transhumance. The charge made was ninepence per head if a herd accompanied the sheep; otherwise one shilling per head. The year-old sheep were sent in March, the ewes and lambs, together with dry heifers, in May. The Slieve Donard pastures, running south to include Spence's Mountain and Seefin, attracted summering stock from as far as Kilkeel in the south and beyond Castlewellan in the north. That this movement from the northern lowlands into the Kingdom of Mourne is of great antiquity is suggested by the name Ballaghanery, which O'Donovan translates 'the shepherds' pass', given to the townland between the mountains and the sea where one enters Mourne. Nowadays young sheep from the Eastern Mournes generally winter around Annalong or Dundrum, but it is recognized that the land immediately along the coast does not suit them: the reason may be that the rarity of frost renders the climate too mild for animals which spend most of their life in the mountains.

Although we have argued that there was an expansion of sheep-rearing in the early nineteenth century, it was nothing like the wholesale invasion of sheep which affected the Scottish Highlands in the preceding half-century. Nor was there any drastic change of breed. It was stated in the 1830s that the sheep 'had undergone little or no change in the vicinity of the mountains: they are a small hardy race, with a long hairy fleece, some of them horned'. Presumably changes made were in the direction of the Welsh mountain black-face. Fine-boned, long-legged sheep are at home in a mountainous environment. They must keep on the move and work hard to gather enough nutriment from the mountain grasses, for bone-forming minerals are scarce on heavily leached soils. The thick fleeces are for warmth, and the long hairs they contain serve as a thatch to lead off the rain. There is a saying in the State of Vermont that the sheeps' noses had to be sharpened specially to enable them to reach the grass among the rocks. Certainly the long legs of the Mourne sheep are an advantage among the boulders and in time of snow, and I know to my sorrow that no ordinary wall will keep them out of gardens, especially in spring and autumn when the wandering instinct is on them. The Mourne Sheep Breeders' Association is developing and perfecting the local breed. One advantage of the black-face is that they will disperse instead of working the ground as a flock. 'Every ewe has her own pasture' says the mountain shepherd, and to it she will return, but she will wander far in search of food and shelter, and the shepherd can tell from the weather where he is likely to find his sheep.

It was the shepherd who knew the hills best, and under all climatic conditions, for whereas other stock was taken to the mountains in summer only, some sheep were there at all seasons, and he was constantly coming and going through the hills. His marks were the great boulders, and scores of them have their names, though the Gaelic forms are almost forgotten. Some of them, which were probably ancient standing stones, were kept whitewashed, for example, the Grey Woman on Crotlieve. Other examples of named stones are the Holly Rock, the Chair, the Grey Lady and Cockley Rock on Leckan More, the Brown Rock, the Dane's Chair and the Giant's Stone on the slopes southeast of Finlieve. Cloghmore, thanks to its proximity to Rostrevor, is the best-known example. These landmarks, natural or man-made, were gathering places at certain times of the year for the folk of the neighbouring townlands. On Easter Monday fires would be lit and eggs rolled, and young people would go sliding down between the rocks on flat slabs of stone. Father B.J. Mooney tells me that the Grey Woman on Crotlieve used to be elaborately dressed up like a woman for the Easter festivities.

There were also gatherings at Midsummer and early in August. On June 23rd, Bonfire Night, fires of whins and turf were lit on the hill-tops, generally on the foothills, as part of an ancient ritual to guard the crops and animals and encourage the declining sun to shine through the months to harvest. Leode Hill near Hilltown was a bonfire hill, and Leitrim Hill in the south. There would be fiddling and dancing, interrupted by the firing of shots to keep away evil things. Elsewhere in County Down, as we have mentioned, on Slieve Croob, young folk gather to dance on the first Sunday of August. This ceremony is connected with the blaeberry harvest, and Blaeberry Sunday is well remembered in Mourne, though now it is no more than an occasion for family picnics. Mr. T.G.F. Paterson tells me that in the adjacent hills of South Armagh he was informed that 'many a lad met his wife for the first time on Blaeberry Sunday'. Every part of the Mournes has its Blaeberry Mountain or Blaeberry Rocks, usually among the screes high in the mountains. Coming midway in the summering season, between May and November, it was in the old days the time when visits would be made from the lowland farms to the booleys, food brought to the herders, and the products of their industry taken home to be stored or sold at the Lammas fairs. The August mountain picnics may originally have been fairs, which were held, in Gaelic tradition, at the times of great gatherings in the hills. It has often happened that fairs which once served many purposes have declined into fun fairs or a token celebration among the young people, just as ritual objects of high antiquity like the bull-roarer have survived as children's toys. At the August picnics little baskets of rushes used to be made to collect blaeberries, and it was the custom to catch butterflies or grasshoppers and imprison them in small cages made of rushes or mountain grass, a practice which can be paralleled far from Ireland in the Gobi desert, in West Africa, in Maine, USA, and no doubt in other parts of the world. It is referred to by ancient Greek writers. Theocritus writes of boys weaving asphodel stalks into locust-traps.

from *Mourne Country*, 1951

The Past in the Present

E. ESTYN EVANS

If the historic tension between Protestant and Catholic is still a living issue in Ulster, splitting the people in education and in other ways, it is but one of many facets of life which bear the imprint of the past. Outside the city suburbs you are in a visibly ancient land, and as you travel towards the west you journey into the past. Already in Belfast you will notice old-fashioned words and turns of speech: you will be given a friendly 'good-evening' as soon as mid-day is past; you must admire the 'delph' – the crockery – if you look into the bright coloured kitchen of a worker's home. You may hear the full flavour of Elizabethan English in the speech of County Tyrone. A visiting Scotsman told me he had not heard since his childhood old Scots dialect words which he found in current use on the coasts of Antrim and Down. But there is also an admixture of words and phrases borrowed or translated from the Gaelic tongue. 'That's a brave (i.e. a fair) day!' is a greeting you cannot fail to hear. Gaelic, by the way, has gone from all parts of Northern Ireland as the language of the people, though in remote corners a lingering few still remember the time when it was spoken. But the names on the land are overwhelmingly Gaelic.

It is characteristic of this land that its best-known industrial product should be based on a crop grown here since prehistoric times. And it was through flax and linen that textile skills have passed to cotton and rayon. Many examples of this persistence of old ways and customs might be cited from the history of art and architecture; the survival of prehistoric Celtic art-motifs in the manuscripts, metal-work and high crosses of the early Christian period; the persistent medieval and Gothic conceptions of Ulster Colonial architecture; the retention of Georgian proportions and modes of building far into the nineteenth century. No doubt material poverty has had something to do with it, and it has certainly acted as a safeguard against vulgar extremes. But there is a deep-grained tendency to retain things that serve their purpose well, whatever changes of fashion may be popular elsewhere.

You will see this in the survival of many old-fashioned farm implements which have become rare or extinct in other parts of the British Isles. The wheel-less slide-car of the Antrim Glens, now mainly used for transporting peats, was until recent years harnessed to the sturdy Cushendall pony with ropes of straw. The Ulster spade, while it has dozens of differing shapes adapted each to its own district, is in general form neither Irish nor English but an ingenious compromise between them. The old Irish one-eared spade is really a push-plough operated with the right foot, whereas the Ulster spade, derived from styles introduced by Protestant planters, is normally used with the left foot. Thus the phrase 'he digs with the wrong foot' became an oblique way of referring to someone of the other religion, Protestant or Catholic. The spade keeps its place on hill farms because it can be used in ground where a plough would be dangerous; the slide-car because no other vehicle could negotiate the soft bogs and steep mountain tracks. From it has been evolved the one-horse cart, gaily painted in red and blue, which is best suited to the small Ulster farm. The large farm waggon is unknown here.

It is not that the Ulsterman lives in the past. (He will mechanize his farm where possible and has taken kindly to the tractor – not merely because Harry Ferguson, the maker of tractors, happens to be a Belfast man.) It is rather that the past lives in him, so that he is not conscious of it. 'Remember 1690' – another of those crisp Ulster wall-slogans – is not the motto of an historical cult (which insists on remembering the battle of the Boyne where the Protestant William of Orange defeated the Catholic King James on July 1, 1690) so much as the reminder of present threats to the Ulsterman's security and independence. To savour to the full this quality of timelessness you must, in the Ulster idiom, 'talk with' a peasant – and I use that word in its most honourable sense – among the hills. For him 'all time is foreshortened into a living present'. He will speak about people and events of centuries ago as though he had known and witnessed them. The 'forths' of a thousand years ago, the days of St Patrick, even the Great Stone Monuments of forty centuries ago come alive as he speaks. I remember an old man telling me that Finn McCoul, the legendary Irish giant, owed his prowess not to his size but to his skill. 'He was a man of average height,' he said, 'between 5 feet 8 and 5 feet 9', and his words carried conviction.

The Great Stone Monuments or Giants' Caves are still part of a land-scape in which man-made relics of many different ages lie together like memories in the mind of the peasant. They were built, not by giants, but by 'men of average height' like ourselves. The learned nonsense about Druids' Altars and Sacrificial Stones invented by romantic antiquarians is best forgotten. In the Lagan valley just outside the city of Belfast, at an old crossing-place of the river, you may see a great ceremonial circle called the Giant's Ring built around a chambered grave of the megalithic (Great Stone) period, and dating somewhere about 1800 BC. It is a place of infinite quiet from which nothing save the drifting clouds is visible, but you have only to climb the rampart to see the gantries and the mill-chimneys. North-west of the city, beyond Ligoniel, are the remains of Hanging Thorn Cairn, and to the east, near Dundonald, is the Kempe Stone at Greengraves. But it is on the fringes of the mountains and on the naked plateau top that the great stones stand out most clearly. If you would sense their beauty and their mystery, see Legananny dolmen fac-ing the long line of the Mournes from the slopes of the Slieve Croob granites.

from *Northern Ireland*, 1951

217

The Architectural Idiom of Ulster

Denis O'D. Hanna

The seed-bed of a nation's architecture is the home. Architecture is born when primitive man, not content with mere shelter, attempts to beautify and embellish his house. In spite of the fact that it is important for the architect to consider a building's function, it may be said with truth that architecture begins at the point where the merely functional approach leaves off.

The different methods and materials used by the various nations in an attempt to house themselves is one of the important components in nationality. A pertinent question then is, on the score of architecture: has Ulster got an idiom? It may be said that, while she is a part of the Irish cultural pattern, she has nevertheless a strong regional character of her own – a cultural pattern which is not identical with those of her neighbours Eire and Scotland, though in many ways similar to both.

Primitive people resemble jackdaws. They like little unusual trinkets and things that shine – sea-shells, a piece of Giant's Causeway basalt, a boat in a bottle. I have even known an appendix preserved in alcohol to be among the ornaments on a cottage mantelpiece, but these bric-à-brac decorations are probably similar all over Europe, and could scarcely be said to lend nationality to the room in which they are found. It is to the time-honoured traditional trades and crafts of the people – the carpenter, blacksmith, weaver, and others – that we must look for our national homescape. Those articles that recur with enough frequency to deserve the term 'national institution' are the dresser, the creepy stool, the crane with wrought-iron oxter piece and pot, the crude maw of the open hearth with the decorated harnen stand.

Before the Roman invasion of Britain building in England and Ireland was doubtless similar. Rome of the Cæsars appears to have changed the character of England, while Ireland and Scotland resisted more or less effectively the order and authority of the Empire; whether or not this was to their advantage may be argued, but that it happened is beyond doubt, and today there are left inside the small compass of these islands five

218

broad groupings – English, Irish, Scottish, Welsh, and Manx, as well as a number of regional developments, of which Northern Ireland may be regarded as one.

There is every reason to believe that up to the Viking invasion of Ireland this country was culturally abreast of the rest of Europe, and probably as advanced architecturally as any territory outside the Roman Empire. We hear, for instance, that Irish innkeepers were recognized as among the best in Europe, and the level of accommodation provided for travellers is not a bad criterion of a country's civilization; but our culture was shaken with the loss of Ireland's High Kings, in 1172, and further heavy blows were dealt by the subsequent centuries of Norman and English invasions, which left Irish art almost inarticulate. Today Ireland is again developing an idiom of her own. Her task is to become a modern European country prepared to recognize that her cultural contribution must include that of native and settler alike, for by now all these ingredients go to make up Ireland.

The country had a Romanesque architecture, small in scale but rich in detail. She had a characteristic Gothic architecture, enhanced by the fact that its remoteness made it less derivative than other Gothic architecture. This style achieved vitality and beauty, but never on the scale of England or France. It remained to the end one of those interesting national variations upon a European theme without which the main movement would be much the poorer.

There are the steep stone-roofed cells of the seventh and eighth centuries in Ulster, long since in a ruined state. Perfect specimens of the Round Tower are to be seen at Antrim and Devenish. A few broken chancels and gables, parts of triple lancet windows, are almost all that remain to us of our abbeys, of which Greyabbey is the most perfect. Armagh has a Gothic cathedral, as has Downpatrick, both in a much restored condition. A number of parish churches, notably that of Carrickfergus, date from the twelfth century, and there are innumerable castles in the Province, the earliest and still the most impressive of these, that of Carrickfergus, having been built between 1180 and 1205, by either John De Courcy or Hugh De Lacy, Anglo-Norman invaders from the Pale.

Kilclief and Audley's Castles are interesting specimens of a type of castle peculiar to County Down, built in the fifteenth century by later invaders from the Pale who could only maintain a foothold on the rim of the land. Dundrum was a round-keep castle, one of the few in the country, and was probably built first during the decade 1230–40. Among the most interesting castle developments in the country is that of Dunluce, for here we see signs of a Scottish character, which was common all through this Province and which may perhaps bear testimony to a development in castle building outside Norman influence which for lack of a better term might be called 'Celtic Baronial'. The tower house in Scotland and Ireland is a phase of this style.

But this survey begins in earnest with the Ulster Plantation, for these phases and surviving fragments of Ulster's past which I have briefly indicated, are impossible to summarize within our limits here, are remote in time and temper, are debatable ground where as yet dogmatism would be inadvisable, and, anyhow, have little obvious relevance to contemporary Ulster which is, after all, the product of three and a half centuries' interplay, within a very special context, of economics, politics, and ideologies. It was during that period that the Province became remarkable for that regional development which today is so strong as all but to deserve the title 'nationality'. Wars had brought Ulster low. Only one of her nobility, Hugh O'Neill, Earl of Tyrone (1550–1616), was a man of European culture and outlook, and with him passed any hope there ever had been of the survival of an independent Gaelic state. Dense forests covered much of the area which is now Northern Ireland. Widely famous centres of learning such as Armagh and Bangor, whence Paris and Oxford brought some of their early scholars, had lapsed into semi-barbarism.

The Normans had never conquered more than the eastern fringe of Antrim and Down. Their culture had been resisted by the clans, only a few of whom had consented to Normanize themselves. The tendency had rather been in the opposite direction, certain Norman families, notably De Burgh, having gone over in sympathy and way of life to the Irish. Into a wellnigh disintegrated country poured the English and Scottish planters in the reigns of Queen Elizabeth and James I. They brought with them into the areas where they settled the ideas of building which they had learnt in their own countries. You can easily trace to this day whether or not you are in an English or Scottish Plantation, and that not merely by reading the names over the shop windows.

There was no shortage of stone in Ulster, and so inevitably masonry became the building material of the Province, though brick was introduced where English influence was strong. Many of the native houses in Ulster before Plantation times were oval and thatched with bracken, having stone walls, the chinks closed with mud, as in the style of the Scottish crofts. Turf-and-mud wall was common. Various forms of rubble masonry were in use, but there was always the tendency to use land stones, which in their smooth state weakened walls and caused buildings to fall into disrepair more easily than in the case of dressed stones. This practice accounts for some of the impermanence in Irish building. Thatch was almost the universal roof covering, both for native Irish and English settlers, but the Scots showed a preference for slates, probably on account of the hardness and dampness of their climate, and because in their own country they possessed a fine slate tradition. Corbie steps on the gable may be taken as a sign of Scottish influence. Mud-walled houses are common in Northern Ireland, and in some English districts the cruck roof may be seen. After the 1641 Rebellion the English rebuilt the settlement towns by more or less Irish methods, for it was in this rebellion that the Province suffered the irreparable loss of all her half-timber English houses, black oak beams, and white panels. These were burned down and pillaged to such an extent that not one example today remains in the whole settlement. This beautiful style of English yeoman building had been established in County Londonderry and in the Lagan Valley, many examples at one time existing in Lurgan, Lisburn, and the Guild towns of Derry.

There are regional developments in architecture, not only in Ireland, but even in Ulster. It is possible to distinguish, as I have said, not only English from Scottish Plantations, but native Irish from either, for these were largely pushed up into land about the 500-feet mark, where conditions were not conducive to carrying on an architectural culture. Still, the ancient Irish conception of building modified the architecture of the Plantation, and today we have towns and villages which, though English in origin, could not be found in that country. There is a region round Lough Neagh basin which is the home of the jamb-wall cottage. Hipped gables do not occur north of Lough Erne. The maritime mode architecture of the coast is easily recognizable, and the red English brick of County Armagh, hiding among its apple-blossom, makes one think of Surrey, and if one considers a nine-county Ulster, including Donegal, you have a region where houses add on pieces as the family grows, till they trail like white caterpillars over the hump of hills. It is a land where the corbie-stepped gable can be found, and where the roofs are held down against the gales of the Atlantic by rope pegged into the eaves.

There is a feeling for strong peasant colour in this country – blue, red, or orange doors against whitewashed walls – and the outside steps leading to a door in the gable is a tradition not only in Donegal but in every Ulster county and, for that matter, in many parts of Ireland. The round gate-pillars with conical tops are a feature of the Province, and if a window tax did nothing else for us it at least left us with the ever-open welcome of the half-door, across which the turf-fire flickers so cheerfully.

There are several types of thatching in Ulster – one where the thatch comes right over the gable, which is common in English districts, and one where the stonework of the gable ends in a coping which occasionally is corbie-stepped, as in Scotland. This latter type of thatching belongs to the Scottish areas as well as to those where native Irish influence is strong.

The Callagh, or bed-niche, is frequently found in Tyrone and mid-Ulster, and the built-in bed has not a little in common with that of Denmark, though it must be admitted that Danish neatness and care of detail are usually lacking in the furnishings of cottages in this country. I have, however, seen domestic furnishings at no great distance from Belfast which are as beautiful as those of any peasantry in the world, and if Ulster lived up to her best in this matter she would be a very fine country.

When the Planters came to northern Ireland they instituted a type of architecture for which there is little counterpart in the British Isles. It was a version of Gothic which has come to be known as Planters' Gothic. The settlement had few, if any, sophisticated architects practising in it, and it is to the mason, the country carpenter, and blacksmith that we must attribute this style. Building was carried out often under conditions of war, and styles were modified by available materials and the infiltration of native Irish ideas. Most important of all, at that time the Province was less touched by Renaissance thought than any part of the British Isles, with the possible exception of Highland Scotland.

Planters' Gothic churches usually consist of a nave and chancel with western tower. Occasionally they blossom into three towers and single spire, as at Hillsborough, or into side aisles, like Londonderry Cathedral, but as a rule are like the sort of building produced when the schoolmistress says, 'Draw me a church, dear.' It is primitive, yet often the more effective for this reason. Planters' Gothic is probably the only Protestant development of the Gothic style in the world. You feel that it is different from monastic-born architecture: no triforium, no abbey buildings, but a neat and naked parish church set in the centre of a planting community, built by a squirearchy. It is an architecture of congregational worship. The pageantry of Corpus Christi processions and mystery and morality plays is foreign to it. Too often on Sunday nights the doors are locked for a week, and frequently can be opened only after a determined search for the sexton. But in Waringstown Parish Church (1691), Moira, and others, the style reaches a high level of beauty and originality, and somehow starts one thinking of Denmark. It has a naïve method of mixing Gothic mullioned windows with little touches of Jacobean and Classical ornament. It lived almost long enough to see Gothic revived again by the Romanticist.

Ulster of the Planters' Gothic period is not as prolific in monumental sculpture as one would expect. Doubtless much of it perished with the Plantation churches in the 1641 Rebellion, for more Planters' Gothic buildings were destroyed at that time than now exist; and it is natural to expect that in a country where the Gothic mode was still alive Jacobean monuments similar to those in England would be rare. Nevertheless, we are fortunate in still possessing a good example of the period in the Chichester Memorial, in Carrickfergus Parish Church. The sculptor is anonymous, but the work is contemporary with, and somewhat similar to, that of Archbishop Jones in St Patrick's Cathedral, Dublin, and it may well be the work of the same hand. There are monuments of somewhat later periods in the north transept of Armagh Cathedral. These still retain all the character of the early Renaissance, as do two tablets on the north aisle of Londonderry Cathedral. There are fragments of wood carving and pulpits of this period which show a taste similar to that prevailing in England.

The eighteenth century was very ruthless with Jacobean ornament and church furniture which it considered barbaric, and it is depressing to think how much work of the early Plantation must have been destroyed to make room for Strawberry Hill Gothic and the mid-Victorian vogue for marble fonts and pulpits.

The domestic version of the Planters' Gothic may be said to be the 'bawns', or defended farms, built by the planting landlords, or 'undertakers' as they were called. These are peculiar to Ulster and look like castles born out of time. It is hard to believe their battlements and corner towers were built for service and were not the folly of someone with a knight errantry complex. These bawns change character according to whether they are in an English or Scottish district. A fragment of the bawn of the Skinners' Company may still be seen at Dungiven, a relic of the days when Londonderry was owned by the London Companies. There is another English bawn at Bellaghy in the country of the Vintners' Company. Scottish bawns may be seen at Ballygally, Galgorm, and Kirkiston Castles, and an interesting example of bawn house is Castle Monea, in County Fermanagh. Castle Balfour possessed many Scottish peculiarities, as did Newtownstewart Castle. Bawns were probably an adjunct of these houses, but little is now left to testify to this. Most of these buildings were erected during the period 1617–25.

The Planters' castles in Ulster retained the appearance of defence long after their counterparts in England had become entirely domestic. The ground floors were small-windowed, mullioned or oriel windows rarely making an appearance till the first floor. These Tudor and Jacobean homes have heavy string courses, curling or battlemented gables, and if they permit themselves a flight of fancy it is round their great Jacobean doors or in the fireplaces in the hall. Unfortunately, one of the best of these, Antrim Castle, was gutted by fire a few years ago, but Glenarm Castle (*c.* 1636), Bangor Castle (now largely revival work), and Castle Upton, as well as Richhill Castle (*c.* 1660), are examples of Ulster Jacobean.

The oval houses of Ireland and the circular, thatched pepper-pot house, which is probably the heritage of an ancient form of monastic building, have all but departed from the Province. Dean Swift's house at Kilroot is still an example of the oval type, and, although 'pepper-pots' were common in the Irish and Scottish quarters of Carrickfergus down to the last century, they have now ceased to exist. I know of only one corbie-stepped gable in this town, where corbie-steps were once the rule.

In the Lagan Valley in and round Lisburn one can almost feel the English influence. Stand in the park of the town and see that charming row of red Georgian houses through the trees; the cathedral spire (one of the best examples of Planters' Gothic in the country); an old town-gate; some walls; a bastion; a fine Georgian cupola on the town hall; and it is not difficult to reconstruct the early setting of the Planters of Lisnagarvey, as the town was then named.

All through the Province there are remnants of seventeenth- and eighteenth-century rural industry, such as corn-mills with water-wheels, probably orange against a white wall, the whole fabric now being slowly devoured by greedy ivy and the death-watch beetle; but they still stand making a bold show beside a vivid blue cupful of water fringed with sedges, their tangled gables and sagging slates like the backcloth of a rural ballet. The scene is still enlivened by the quack, grunt, and gaggle of the farmyard, the heritage one thousand years of husbandry has bequeathed to us. Something dreadful will happen to the soul of the nation when, on the sites of such mills and barns, corrugated iron finally rises triumphant.

Newtownards, with its handsome town hall and market cross, betokens Scottish influence in its solid stonework and slate. The town had its origin in the fifth-century schools of St Finian, where Columbkille was educated. It passed into Norman hands and its centre was moved from Movilla down to where the abbey now stands. Behind this building may be seen to this day some medieval walls and corner defence towers, as well as a monks' fishpond. The 'Black Abbey', as it is called, is now in ruins and possesses one or two details of fifteenth-century carving which are typically Irish in style, as well as a few grave slabs of the tenth to fourteenth centuries. To Montgomery, Laird of Braidstane, who headed the Scottish Plantation in Ards in 1606, must be attributed the interesting Jacobean entrance to the abbey. The Jacobean town of the Scottish Planters centred round the Town Cross, with its ancient hostels and taverns, and the building which still incorporates the lower storey of Montgomery's castle in which he lived when he first came over. In the summers of 1605 and 1607 the harvests were good, and we read that Sir Hugh Montgomery's lady 'built water-mills in all parishes to prevent the necessity of bringing

225

meal from Scotland and grinding with quairn stones as the Irish did to make their gradden'.

In the eighteenth century a handsome plan for the town was evolved and the market house and square became the focal point of Newtownards. It was here that the Ards Door, a Georgian type of entrance, was introduced, possibly from England, although the Ards was a Scots-planted area, just as Holywood, in County Down, adopted a peculiar coach entrance, with the front door opening off it instead of being placed on the façade of the building. From the point of view of getting in and out of the coach dryshod, the idea was excellent, but the Georgians liked formal entrances, and, as this particular type tended to be dark and rather informal, it had few imitators outside the town where it appears to have been invented.

The Scottish Plantation never reached Belfast, which was English, but stopped with the high ridge of hills between that city and Newtownards and struck down by Holywood, which was on its extreme western boundary. In the seventeenth century the Holywood hills were wooded, and transport across them very primitive, so that towns like Newtownards and Belfast must have been separated in those days by several hours of travel. Be this as it may, the Scottish influence round Comber, Newtownards, and the northern end of Strangford Lough did not penetrate into the English Plantation of the Lagan Valley.

Ulster in the time of our great-grandfathers must have been architecturally beautiful. I say 'must have been', for today our heritage is much spoiled and in greater danger probably than that of any part of the British Isles. It is threatened now by prosperity and so-called improvement.

The Province possesses a virile Vernacular Georgian architecture. It stems upon the home of the yeoman farmer.

The formula for this is simple yet always alive and original – a fanlighted door or a window detail or some whimsical arrangement of fenestration. One would expect regional development in a country that for generations must have felt very remote from the capital, for in Georgian times Ulster was three days from Dublin, and it was not until the year 1788 that a stage-coach was first established between Dublin and Belfast, which reduced the journey to twelve hours. In spite of these difficulties, Ulster abounds in large Palladian mansions, some scarcely less ambitious than

226

those of Leinster itself. Florencecourt (1764), by John Cole, and Castlecoole (1788), the work of James Wyatt, senior, are among the most important, and in or round Belfast many fine Georgian homes are located, notably Hillsborough Castle, Mount Stewart, Greyabbey House, Castleward, Castle Dobbs.

In Ulster a type of farm building round a courtyard is sometimes seen. This arrangement was foreign to native Ireland, and is said to have come to us through French influence. Such farmyards usually have their dove-cote; and the outside steps leading to the barn-loft are a common feature all through the country, with native Irish, English, Scottish and French alike. Orange carts tipped up in the dark shadows of elliptical arches, on a floor of cobblestones, and beyond that a sky of blue with white cloud is a sight to remember. In the farm kitchen will be a large open grate, unless a modern cooker has recently been installed, but, if you are lucky, a pot and crane may be left. The china dogs on the mantelpiece there nearly certainly will be, while round the door you can count on proud, Hussar-like cockerels swaggering and strutting, and a County Down collie with a wall eye and a sharp, welcoming bark. No matter how far inland you may be, you will probably find seagulls contesting with rooks beside the pigs' trough.

No survey of the Renaissance in Ireland would be complete without mention of the Ulster Presbyterian Barn church. A fine example of this is the Non-Subscribing Presbyterian Church, Dunmurry, County Antrim (1779). You might expect to find it in Salem or Williamsburg, USA. It is essentially Puritan and Nonconformist. It, like Planters' Gothic, has no roots in the soil of monasticism. In scale and conception it is utterly foreign to the English church, and attempts on the part of misguided Gothic architects to pull the Barn church into ecclesiastical line have always met with dire failure. It is best left alone, for it readily wilts and perishes when snobbish hands are laid upon it. It has a domestic beauty far more in common with the farmyard than the church.

from 'Architecture in Ulster', from *The Arts in Ulster*, 1951

Fair Play for Dialect

W.F. MARSHALL

There are two good reasons why you should be fair to this kind of speech that we hear so often. One is that dialects are a great help in the study of English. The other is that most of us have something of this dialect in our speaking – no matter what we may have got in the way of education. Now if these two statements are true – as they undoubtedly are – surely our Ulster speech is worth examination.

...We didn't invent our Ulster English. How then did it come to be here? Well, the big part of our Ulster speech came here with the Planters, and the rest of it we took from the Gaelic.

Some of the Planters, as you know, were from England. They came here very early in the seventeenth century, and they occupied the country from Islandmagee to Belfast. They settled at Lisburn and Hillsborough and went up the Lagan valley. They were soon at Donacloney, and then along the Lough shore up as far as Killead, and they took with them, of course, their English speech.

It wasn't long, however, till the Scots settlers were at their heels. They were in the Ards from 1606, and by 1614 they mustered 2,000 fighting men. They spread very quickly through Newtownards and Comber, and across the northern half of Co. Down. They made their way from Islandmagee to Glenarm. They went west as far as Antrim town. They moved up as far as Ballymoney, and pushed the MacDonnells back again into the Glens. Everywhere they went they took with them their Lowland Scots.

So much for Antrim and Down. Remember, these two counties weren't in the big Crown scheme which is known in history as the Plantation of Ulster. That scheme covered, or was intended to cover, certain other counties of which we're only concerned with four: Derry, Tyrone, Fermanagh and Armagh. The settlers who came to Co. Derry were mostly Scots. Those who came to Armagh, Fermanagh and Tyrone (except North Tyrone) were mostly English.

Now, in a rough way you can still trace this distribution of settlers in the speech of Ulster. You can start in the Ards, and follow the Scots speech across North Down till you lose it in Armagh. You can trace it from the Braid to Ballymena and Ballymoney and Coleraine. In just the same way you can trace the English Settlements.

This doesn't mean, however, that the track of the Scots speech is equally firm all the way from Donaghadee to Dromore, or from the Braid to Donemana. Nor does it mean that the English you hear in Tyrone is uniform. It changes the farther you go south, and when you leave Tyrone and come to Newtownhamilton in Co. Armagh, or Garrison in Co. Fermanagh, you can hear in it most distinctly the *Irish brogue.*

This brings me to the third and last element in our Ulster speech, which is the Gaelic. When the Plantation came, the natives of Ulster were, of course, all speaking Irish. But all over, as the Planters made contact with the natives, they absorbed into their English a great many native words. In that way our speech was greatly enriched, especially in districts where the native population remained thick. The native Ulster people, too, had their part to play in this enrichment. They had to learn English at the outset as a foreign language, and they had to learn it, not from books, but conversationally, and naturally enough they stuck to many of their own idioms, merely translating them into Irish.

But what happened to the Irish brogue? We've no Irish brogue at all now in the six counties, except in parts of Fermanagh and Armagh, and perhaps a bare trace of it deep in the mountains. This is easy to understand. Where the Planters were numerous, their way of speaking prevailed and the brogue died. Where the native-born were more numerous and where they were not completely encircled by the strangers, the brogue lived and still lives.

Well, you see now the three elements in the Ulster speech. Elizabethan English, Lowland Scots, and Ulster Gaelic. These three and no more. And, as a matter of fact, there would be some point in saying that there are not even three, but only two. For Lowland Scots is old Northern English. What you hear in Donaghadee and what you hear in Armagh are not so different as you might suppose. They have a common ancestor.

Let's take a look, now, at Ulster English generally. There are some things about it that you notice immediately. For example, it's full of what you'd call bad grammar. But let us be careful here. Grammar isn't made, as I said before, by people who write books about it, or by the people who teach it. Good English writers and good English speakers – they're the people who in time make the grammar.

Shakespeare and Ben Jonson are full of what wouldn't pass as good grammar nowadays. But still it was the grammar that was used by the good writers and speakers of *their* day. When *they* used it, it was good.

Very few English writers have got more compliments than Joseph Addison. What could beat *The Spectator*? Well, *The Spectator* and all Addison's writings are just 'hoatchin' with grammatical mistakes. I once made out a list of over two hundred of them before I got tired of the job. If a boy made one of these mistakes now, there are schools where he would be asked to 'bend over', thus putting a strain on what Shakespeare and Dr Johnson would have called 'gallowses'. Indeed, most of our so-called vulgarisms are really survivals of the good grammatical forms of the past. When we talk about our 'childer' we are using a perfectly good Middle English plural of 'child'. This plural still survives in 'Childermas' Day, and in the First Prayer Book of Edward VI we can read about 'our childers children'. When a countryman refers to his wife as 'hir', and to himself and his wife as 'huz', he is again using forms that can be found in English authors from Chaucer to Spenser. At one time indeed, there was a regular distinction made between 'hir' as a feminine singular, and 'her' as a possessive plural, and it was only when 'their' came into general use that 'her' could be used as we use it now. Similarly with the pronoun 'hit'. We hardly ever misuse the letter 'h' as they do so commonly in many parts of England, but when we want to emphasize the word 'us', we call it 'huz' or 'hiz', and an emphatic 'it' is 'hit'. This was the usual nominative and accusative form in Middle English. Queen Elizabeth used it frequently and it was used by Shakespeare in *Macbeth* and *All's well that ends Well*.

We must be careful then, if we want to throw stones at the Ulster speech, to distinguish between bad grammar and grammar that is merely out-of-date. You mustn't judge it by present-day standards. It has quite a good pedigree.

The same thing can be said of many of our so-called Ulsterisms. Take the case of the beautiful and expressive Ulster phrase, 'to think long'. An English lady told me this was the funniest expression she had ever heard.

Well, at any rate, it was fun for me to hear her say that. Our own Sir John Byers thought that 'to think long' wasn't merely an *Ulster* phrase, and as proof of that, he quoted 'the thoughts of youth are long, long thoughts'. But we can do far better than that. Margaret Paston, writing to Sir John Paston in the fifteenth century, says, 'I thynk ryght leng tyll I here tydyngs from you.' In *Romeo and Juliet* Paris says, 'Have I thought long to see this morning's face?' In *The Rape of Lucrece*, Shakespeare writes, 'But long she thinks till he return again.' And if you turn up Swinburne's *Eton: an Ode*, written, remember, near the end of the nineteenth century, you'll read of:

> Lords of state and of war, whom fate found strong in
>   battle, in counsel strong.
> Here, ere fate had approved them great, abode their
>   season, and thought not long.

If that's not a good enough pedigree for anyone, I don't know what is.

Or take a farmer's direction to his servant man: 'Give that horse a lock of hay!' That word 'lock' meaning 'a moderate quantity' is in the English dialects. But a well-known English traveller and writer, Fynes Moryson, in his *Description of Ireland in the Seventeenth Century*, says about the Irish cattle that 'they have to stand or lie all night in a dirty yard without so much as a lock of hay'. You'll remember, too, that Shakespeare writes about 'a bottle of hay', and so does Ben Jonson in his play *The New Inn*. In *Henry IV*, I, you read about 'a power of English', which is exactly the same phrase as we use when we say there was 'a power of cattle' in the fair. There's the same use of 'power' in the Apocrypha, in I Maccabees, iii, 41. And you won't read very far in the stately Authorized Version until you come across ample justification for our fashion of saying 'for to'. 'He hired me for to lift corn.' 'He went into the synagogue on the Sabbath day, and stood up for to preach.' Some time ago, a writer defied me to justify our Ulster expression, 'be to be'. 'He be to be very busy, or he'd a come.' This, he maintained, was a vulgarism pure and simple. Well, I've got a lot to learn, even about this subject I'm dealing with, and there are conundrums in it that I've still got no answer for, but I would say about this person that he be to be too busy to read his Shakespeare carefully. When he gets time, let him open it at *Henry VI*, II, ii, and in the speech of Queen Margaret this is what he will read:

I see no reason why a king of years
Should be to be protected like a child.

The other day an Armagh man said to me, 'As Mat Mulcaghey says, "I was putt till a stan'." ' I can take that remark to illustrate my point. It is, of course, no product of Mat's rich invention at all. Sir Richard Petty, writing to Lord Southwell in 1685, refers to certain circumstances that will 'putt all Trade Improvement and Exchange to a stand'. Mat, however, says that he is '*putt* till a stan' '. Now, in the North of Ireland an educated person says 'poot' (put), unlike a dialect speaker who will say 'putt'. But in a game of golf an Ulster schoolteacher will say 'putt' without any thought of dialect. He will 'putt' (if he can) the golf ball into the hole. For golf is a very old game, and in the game we keep the old sound of the vowel. And the dialect speakers keep it too, not only in one use of the word but in all uses of it. But again, Mat didn't say he was 'putt *to* a stan' ', but '*till* a stan' '. 'Till' here is an old Norse word which means 'to', and I could fill pages with examples of its use by English authors in the fifteenth and sixteenth centuries.

Now let me say something about our dialect pronunciations. When you read the English classics of two and three hundred years ago, you don't see much difference between the spelling of that time and the spelling of today. So you're liable to think that because there's not much difference in the spelling then and now, there's not much difference in the way the words were spoken. But there's a big difference. How do we know? One of the ways by which we know is from the diaries and letters written in the past. There *was* a standard spelling and we have it in the books, but nobody bothered about it except the people who wrote books and those who read a good many books – what we would call the book-minded people.

But then there were other people who weren't book-minded, and there were far more of them. So when a nobleman of this type or his wife wrote a letter they spelled their words in a rough phonetic way, much as a child or a very uneducated person would do now, and by this spelling we can make a good guess at the pronunciations. We have the early grammars and pronouncing dictionaries to help us, and we have the rhymes of the poets.

232

But we have to go very carefully here. If Lady Wentworth writes 'Dartmouth' we are sure that she spoke the word as she wrote it. But if we see it as 'Dertmouth' in a book, we must not be misled by the spelling. Any writer who wanted to put down on paper the sound that you hear in 'Dart' would write it with an 'e' and not with an 'a'. The sound of 'er' written was 'ar'. Now, that's why our country people call 'terrible', 'tarrible', and 'servant', 'sarvant'. And don't forget that it's not so very long ago that polite people stopped saying 'sarvent' and 'tarrible'. They said it in the eighteenth century. Our people in the country still say it. They keep the good speech of a century and a half ago.

What I've been trying to show you is that the explanation of many of our mis-pronunciations in Ulster is that they are merely survivals of what used to be polite and correct speech.

from *Ulster Speaks*, 1936

233

FROM THE IRISH SHORE

DENIS IRELAND

Belfast. An industrial city at the mouth of the Lagan. Described by a French journalist who visited it during the troubles as *une ville sanglante* – referring, of course, to its red-brick villas, its (then) red tramcars, and the blood then running in its streets. Literal translation difficult. A red-brick city, with a forest of factory chimneys vomiting smoke, and sea-gulls screaming about its harbour gantries; forbidding for the stranger or the theatrical in third-rate lodgings; a *bleeding* city, perhaps.

Anyhow, at least in its own estimation, a thorn in the flesh of the Vatican.

In this city my father once flourished as a linen merchant and manufac-turer. The factory was at Lurgan, seventeen Irish miles away, in the Lagan valley, where as a child I remember watching the hand-loom weavers at work in their stockinged feet. Pictures cut from newspapers, emblems, and mottoes pasted on the framework of each loom told you what the religion of the weaver was.

Today the weavers are still at work, and still in their stockinged feet, but my father is in his grave on the mountain-side overlooking the smoke clouds of industrial Belfast.

In summer we went to a whitewashed meeting-house on Sundays. The meeting-house stood amongst the rocks on the seashore, so close to high-water mark that at full tide the thud and backwash of the waves mingled with the singing of the Psalms.

> O God, our help in ages past,
>   Our hope for years to come,
> Our shelter from the stormy blast,
>   And our eternal home,

we sang. Sometimes the head of a seal appeared as a black dot in the channel between the big rocks, and from the gallery on particularly fine

Sunday mornings you could look out through the small-paned windows clear across the Irish Sea to the tiny white farmhouses and the green squares of the fields on the Mull of Galloway.

The village shop had glass jars of sweets in the windows. At night it was lit by a single oil lamp that hung from the ceiling. Round the lamp clustered a conglomeration of boots, hams, tin-cans, and brushes, all hanging together in confusion. The door had a bell that rang with a faint *ping*. You then made out in the background, beyond the zinc-covered counter, a pile of small dark-wood drawers with glass knobs. These drawers contained, as we knew from experience, everything that a normal man could require, from fish-hooks to pills and plug tobacco.

Saturday night was the big night in the village. On Saturday nights the shop was crowded with women, all patiently waiting with their tin-cans concealed under their shawls and their pennies clutched in their hands. Then at midnight the bell would go *ping, ping, ping*, and the women would file out into the darkness to wait for their men outside the public-house. . . . Across the street in M'Gimpsey's the barman would fling out the last customer, remove the corks from the automatic bottle-opener, and swab up the bar with a damp cloth.

Then he would come and stand in the doorway in his shirt-sleeves, outlined against the brilliant interior, survey the crowd, spit once, with emphasis, into the street, and shut the door.

Then more and more lights would go out throughout the village, and more and more plainly the sound of the waves would come up the steep, narrow side-street that led down to the sea.

School. The school stood on a main thoroughfare in Belfast, with the statue of a famous Presbyterian divine overshadowing its railings. Outstanding memory, the heating system. Hot air was delivered into the class-rooms through huge pipes, and a dart cleverly thrown at the vent-holes would turn and sail above the heads of the class, descending from the most unexpected quarters – even, on red-letter days, from behind the master's desk.

Item. The playground was extremely muddy and covered with brickbats. *The Kingdom of Mourne*. Motor to Newcastle from Belfast via Hillsborough and Dromara. Hillsborough still drowsing in the eighteenth century, and a very good century to drowse in. Beyond Hillsborough the road grows narrower and begins to meander through hilly country, with scattered cottages standing back from the road, each planted on its green hillock with its surrounding plantation of trees, and ducks and geese sunning themselves in the meadows – prosperous little homesteads, glittering in immaculate whitewash. Here and there in this backwater of Down, on some of the narrower and less frequented by-roads, stand little white meeting-houses, with small-paned windows, that are gems of unpretentious architecture – the expression of Ulster Presbyterianism when it was still uncorrupted by Victorian commercialism and snobbery. Here also, in the village of Finnis, just beyond Dromara, I met a most interesting old priest, educated at Salamanca and a philologist of European reputation. He sat on the parapet of a bridge over the Lagan, smoking cigarette after cigarette – he told me that he habitually smoked sixty a day – and discoursing most learnedly of the affairs of Europe. He had lived already to a ripe old age, so his perpetual cigarette smoking doesn't appear to have done him much harm. It certainly had not dimmed the liveliness of his intellect.

Round Dromara the country grows wilder, and in some of the lonely mountain farms there are still recollections, handed down from father to son, of the rebellion of 1798, of the battle of Ballynahinch, and the time when a peasantry armed for the most part with pikes rose against the English regulars and the Irish militia. . . . Then keeping the road southwards from Dromara, the Mournes rise across the skyline like a barricade; the most dramatic mountain mass in Ireland, with the possible exception of the Twelve Pins of Connemara. Newcastle, nestling between Slieve Donard and the sea, was once overhung by heavy woods, but in wartime the trees were cut down and the young Douglas firs planted in their place are still only striplings, so that the lower slopes of Donard are not in the least like those depicted by the railway advertisement artists of the last century. I remember my rage and disappointment when I first saw Donard shorn of its trees, and how, curiously enough, this particular piece of sacrilege struck home to my bosom more than the destruction of the library at Louvain or the Cloth Hall at Ypres. The library at Louvain I had never set eyes on; the Cloth Hall at Ypres had never meant anything to me except a pile of ruins that you dodged past quickly lest worse might befall you; but those trees I had seen in their glory. Moreover, they were on *my* ground, the piece of earth where I felt profoundly at home, since nearly every man has an adopted as well as an actual birthplace. I was born, technically speaking, and following the location of my birthplace on the Ordnance maps, in Antrim, but the soil of Antrim has always seemed to me cold and forbidding compared with that of Down, and of all the arts and parts of Down the 'kingdom of Mourne' attracted me from the beginning. The valley opening from Bryansford, clothed by the trees of Tullymore Park and overshadowed at its upper end by Slieve Bearnagh, has always seemed to me one of the most beautiful, or perhaps, to be more accurate, one of the most gracious in Ireland; I know only one other that gives just the same impression of emerald softness on looking down into it from a height, and that is on the road from Glengarriff to Kenmare – seen from the winding turns that lead upwards to the rock tunnel at the summit of the pass. But Kerry and West Cork remain slightly alien for me, in spite of their beauty; there is a touch of something Iberian in their atmosphere – a cruelty that is altogether lacking in South Down; and if the fates are kind I hope to end my life somewhere within the kindly shadow of the Mournes. . . .

Belfast. Walk on the Castlereagh hills. A sunny day, the city, with its red tentacles of suburbs, sprawled below on the green floor of the Lagan valley, with the dome of the City Hall and the gantries of the shipyards rearing themselves above the smoke haze. Behind all this rises the Cave Hill, evoking memories of Wolfe Tone and Napoleon, or perhaps, for twentieth-century inhabitants, only of Napoleon, since they prefer, for the most part, not to think of Tone. And yet Tone once walked those streets, as large as life – the same streets where the worthy citizens whose sons and grandsons were to become the pillars of Victorian commercialism in Ireland were carrying Republicanism to the point of parading in uniforms fashioned on those of the French Republican Guard and celebrating the downfall of the Bastille by the waving of tricolours and the firing of cannon. But all this happened in the last decades of the eighteenth century, and with the coming of the Union in 1800, Belfast's history was changed. Tone had come to a bloody end in the Provost's prison of

Dublin barracks, and Ulster Presbyterianism, perhaps by force of example, had stopped fishing in the troubled waters of the French Revolution and had become respectable; the uniforms fashioned on those of the French Republican Guard disappeared from the wardrobes of prominent merchants, and no one thought any more of firing off cannon to celebrate the fall of the Bastille – so much so that by the middle of the new century it had become impossible to tell where a Presbyterian left off and a Churchman began. At the same time steam began to replace water power in the spinning and weaving of cotton and linen, and the stage was set for the appearance of that Belfast of the 'nineties where I was born – a strange, tough, hybrid town, with a forest of factory chimneys on both banks of the Lagan; a town which, paradoxically enough, regularly reared (and then promptly expelled) a host of writers, artists, and unpractical 'dreamers' of all kinds, spreading them with lavish generosity over the face of the earth and not being particularly kind to them when they made any attempt to return. . . .

Jubilee night. A bonfire on Collin mountain. This is the mountain I used to see standing mistily blue through the apple blossom in our orchard, the orchard that we mistakenly cut down in order to utilise the space for a vegetable garden. Now beside the bonfire a scoutmaster in *pince-nez* calls for hearty British cheers. Privates Compton and Carr should have been here. 'I'll wring the neck of any —— bastard who says a word against my —— —— king.' Far-away bonfires twinkle on the surrounding hills: Scrabo, Castlereagh, the Sperrin mountains beyond Lough Neagh. Then the heat mist comes down, obscuring everything except the lights in the valley below. Belfast glows like a jewel in the darkness, the long glittering lines of street-lamps radiating from the centre, set here and there with the red and green blaze of advertisement sky-signs, like the filagree of a diadem, with the floodlit dome of the City Hall floating triumphantly above what appears from the mountain-side to be a sparkling spider's web. Beyond all this illumination the lough lies dark and unresponsive, while from somewhere on the hills beside the Parliament House at Stormont the long white finger of a searchlight stretches up to sweep the skies. But there is no sign of the bonfires on the Scottish coast; we strain our eyes in vain towards where in daylight the

Mull of Galloway sometimes appears as a smudge on the skyline beyond the opening of the lough; a sea mist has come down and we are shut off here alone in our island in the Atlantic. Perhaps the mist is symbolical. . . .

We then motor down into Belfast to see the sights, a long swift rush down the mountain-side, past the City Cemetery, down the Falls Road, the area which in the extraordinary history of this extraordinary city has so often resounded to the rattle of rifle fire, past the stark chimneys of the silent factories, and out into Castle Junction, the centre of the web of light which we have just seen from above. It is after midnight, but Donegall Place is still jammed with sightseers, a slow black tide surging past the lighted shop windows. There is electricity in the air, and no one in this usually sober city seems to think of going to bed. At the upper end of Donegall Place the City Hall, flood-lit in layers of red, white and blue, towers like a gigantic tier cake – the reward of the good Victorian. . . . At one o'clock the black tides are still surging past the lighted shop windows and the trams are still running, nosing their way through the crowds that occupy the roadway. What a strange world it is! a world full of flood-lighting, cheap electricity, new clothes, cigarettes, silk stockings, sixpenny seats at the cinema, and apparently endless leisure. I think of my dead father, now three years in his grave on the mountain-side above the city: how he toiled and moiled through the gas-lit decades of the Victorian era, and now we are all walking about through brilliant clean-swept streets, wearing new flannel trousers and smoking endless cigarettes, criticising European pictures, listening to wireless bands from the ends of the earth – a bright, clean, hard world in which gifts are showered on us in endless profusion, in which everything behind the illuminated plate-glass windows of the shops steadily cheapens, but in which one has only to step out of main street in order to see the grey, pinched faces of men, women, and children starving in the back alleys. A mad world, for all its concealed lighting, flood-lighting, and electric profusion. And leaving the thronged streets about the city centre and the three-tiered cake of a City Hall behind me, I walk home at one-thirty in the morning through the deserted commercial quarter, past rows of linen warehouses every third one of which bears a to-let notice, past the building that was my dead father's life-work and eventually the mausoleum of his worldly hopes, and out

239

into quiet suburban avenues where the only sign of the junketings at the centre of the city is an ominous-looking glare in the lofty summer sky. . . .

Portaferry, Co. Down. To-day I rode from Belfast to Portaferry on a push bicycle, a splendid method of progression in that one can dismount, sit by the roadside, and spend hours looking back the way one has come. With a motor-car there is no looking back, whereas half the fun of progressing through life or anything else consists in orienting one's self with what has gone before; to tear blindly ahead is to lead only half a life, to go to the devil with all the other road hogs. And what a view there is to-day to look back at! A full tide has set the lough brimming with deep blue water; the green hummocks of the islands on the farther shore, with white farm-houses gleaming here and there in the sunshine, appear to be floating on the brimming tide; beyond them again, and apparently changing position as the road leads on, rises the dim blue outline of the Mournes. Backwards the road leads towards Belfast, smoking somewhere beyond the hills to the north-west, past Greyabbey and Mount Stewart, following the lough shore, with heavy woods crowding close to the water's edge. An attractive country, full of variety, with water, woods, islands, distant mountains, ploughed land, pasture land, and, close inshore, the surface of the lough white with wild swans. . . . As the road leads on towards the tip of the peninsula, the character of the country begins to change, grows hillier, not quite so *soigné*; loose stone walls appear here and there instead of hedges – a very different country this from the strip of coast fronting the Irish Sea at the upper end of the peninsula where I spent the summers of my childhood. There the farmers spoke broad Scots, as well they might, seeing that from their farm windows they looked across to Galloway; here one might be running into Catholic and Nationalist Ireland. I turn aside from the main road and climb on to the high ground above Portaferry, to see one of the finest views in Co. Down. The town itself nestles below, half hidden amongst woods, at the edge of the water. But it is to the east that the view is stupendous. Eastwards the North Channel of the Irish Sea appears, owing to some peculiar atmospheric effect, to have been narrowed to the width of a handsome river; a collier in mid-channel resembles a toy model stuck upon a narrow sheet of mirror. To the north-east, bordering the sheet of mirror, lies the Mull of

Galloway, then comes the long gap of the Solway Firth, then the twin humps of the Isle of Man, with, behind and appearing almost continuous with them, the dark mountain masses of Cumberland. To the south-west the Mournes rear themselves, a tremendous dark blue barrier, tempering down to the lower ranges of Slieve Croob and the Dromara mountains, beyond Ballynahinch. But it is the lough that is the centre of attraction in this landscape, the whole of it outlined below as on a map, from Scrabo to the sea, with its chain of green islands festooning the farther shore. This is the most important of the ancient seaways into Ireland, the landfall of St Patrick, and later of the Norsemen, who harried the monastery of Nendrum on Mahee Island, further up the lough. On the opposite shore of the narrow inlet through which the tidal waters ebb and flow, round Strangford, the woods of Cuan crowd close again to the water's edge, the woods of which Deirdre cried out:

> Woods of Cuan, O woods of Cuan,
> In which are the cold waters . . .

But not only the cold waters: noisy waters as well, for at certain states of the tide the roaring of Strangford bar can be positively terrifying. And beyond this narrow, mirror-like strip of swiftly moving water, beyond the dark woods of Cuan above which rooks are wheeling, begins one of the most fateful territories in Ireland, the fertile triangle between the Quoile river at Downpatrick, the outfall of Strangford Lough, and the long beaches of Tyrella: the land where St Patrick preached his first sermon at Saul, later to be studded with castles and ravaged with fire and sword by the Normans, and still marked on old maps as the barony of Lecale. Here, upon the wooded shores of this sea lough, the light of Christianity was caught and reflected back again into the darkness of Europe.

from *From the Irish Shore*, 1935

A Personal Digression

LOUIS MACNEICE

The week-end was all sunshine. I could not remember Belfast like this, and the continuous sunshine delighted but outraged me. My conception of Belfast, built up since early childhood, demanded that it should always be grey, wet, repellent and its inhabitants dour, rude and callous. This conception had already been shaken last night in the boat-train from London; a Belfast man sitting opposite me at dinner was nice to my little boy, said: 'A child should live a life like an animal till it's five.' This did not seem true to type. Belfast men were expected to be sadists whose only jokes are gruesome – *D'ye know what I saw yesterday – a boot floating down the river? There's nothing much in that. Nothing much in it! There was a leg in it.*

Breakfast in my family's house was as ample as always. The same porridge on the side table – each one helping himself – the same break-fast service, the same triangular loaves of shaggy bread. But the house was not the same. Since living for twenty years in an ordinary little house at Carrickfergus, ten miles down the lough (running the gauntlet daily of factory hooters), and before coming to this large, ugly but comfortable mansion on the Malone Road, my family had spent three years in a Queen Anne house at Waterford. This break had upset my view of the Black North.

I have always had what may well be a proper dislike and disapproval of the North of Ireland, but largely, as I find on analysis, for improper – i.e. subjective – reasons. A harassed and dubious childhood under the hand of a well-meaning but barbarous mother's help from County Armagh led me to think of the North of Ireland as prison and the South as a land of escape. Many nightmares, boxes on the ears, a rasping voice of disapproval, a monotonous daily walk to a crossroads called Mile Bush, sodden haycocks, fear of hell-fire, my father's indigestion – these things, with on the other side my father's Home Rule sympathies and the music of his brogue, bred in me an almost fanatical hatred for Ulster. When I

242

went to bed as a child I was told: 'You don't know where you'll wake up.' When I ran in the garden I was told that running was bad for the heart. Everything had its sinister aspect – milk shrinks the stomach, lemon thins the blood. Against my will I was always given sugar in my tea. The North was tyranny.

When I was older and went to school in England my dislike of the North was maintained. At school I felt among my equals, but when I came home I belonged nowhere. There was a great gulf between myself and the bare-foot boys in the streets. When I passed the men who stood most of the day, spitting, at the corners, I imagined that they were spitting at me. (I was the rector's son; they must think that I too disapproved of their swearing and censured the porter on their breath.) A perpetual embarrassment; I was the rector's son.

As for the gentry I did not like them. They were patronizing and snobbish, and it seemed to me, hostile. Hostile because they idolized the military and my father was a clergyman and a pacifist, because they were ardent Unionists, and my father a Home Ruler. This hostility I almost certainly exaggerated. They no doubt thought of me as a shy and gauche little boy, who being forbidden to play games on Sundays or bathe at the pier, was not over-good company for their own children. I still think, however, that the Ulster gentry are an inferior species. They lack the traditions and easy individuality of the southern Anglo-Irish landowners; comparatively new to their class, they have to keep proving that they are at home in it. A few may try to ape the *bonhomie* of the South, but most of them set out to be more English than the English. All the boys go to English public schools and any daughter is a failure who fails to marry a soldier.

I had only been back in the North twice in the last seven years. During most of that time I had lived in Birmingham and now, on this lucid weekend, I compared these two industrial cities and found that Belfast was, if only for the moment, preferable. The voices of Birmingham are flat, dreary, 'with the salt left out of the soup', as someone said to me. The voices of Belfast are harsh and to an English ear unintelligible, but one feels personality behind them. A harsh personality, but something at least to rely on.

Then Belfast has hills around it and shipworks. The town itself is built on mud, resting on thirty-foot piles, but it is at least a town in a significant position – commanding Belfast Lough. Whereas Birmingham commands nothing. Looking up from the tramway junction I saw the Cave Hill blocking the end of the street. And my family's house lay under the Black Mountain – not black, but a luminous grey-blue. There was no speck of wetness on the streets. The macabre elements seemed to have vanished – no El Greco faces under shawls, no torn feet of newsboys leaping on racing trams.

The house was full of azaleas and the long greenhouse of geraniums. Built in the last century by a tea merchant, it was a hideous house, but very comfortable – run by five maids who slept in a wing over the garage. The walls stiff with heavy anaglypta wallpapers, plaster vine-leaves grossly choking the cornices. The wooden panelling on the stairs ended at the turn to the second floor.

On these stairs, gloomy between dark walls under a stained-glass window, hung small engravings – the Bishops of Down and Connor, the Bishops of Dromore. Dr Percy of *Percy's Reliques*, in turban and bands, Dr Dickson with powdered hair and beau's eyebrows, Henry Leslie in a short beard and a ruff. In the dining-room were oil portraits in heavy gilt mitre-topped frames. Dr Hutchinson, of the early eighteenth century, self-possessed, in a heavy wig to his shoulders, a man who knew the world. Next to him Robert Knox of the middle nineteenth, youthful, poetic à la Romantic Revival, floating in lawn sleeves. Over the mantelpiece Jeremy Taylor, moon-faced, quill in effeminate hand, sensitively self-conscious.

In the afternoon we drove through County Down. Ballynahinch, Dundrum, Newcastle – drab rows of houses of dun-coloured or slate-coloured stucco. To tea with two elderly ladies under the Mourne Mountains. The spring had pampered their garden. All the trees were blossoming six weeks early – syringa, rhododendron, cherry. Enormous rooks exploded out of the tree-tops. Of six adults at tea three were deaf.

We drove back with the sun sinking on our left. The country was extravagant with gorse as if a child had got loose with the paints. Gorse all over the fields and sprawling on the dykes. Rough stone walls dodged their way up the mountain. A hill-side under plough was deeply fluted with shadows. The pairs of fat white gateposts with cone tops showed the small fields of small farmers. Brown hens ran through a field, their combs like moving poppies. Then Belfast again, swans on the Lagan, and home towards the Black Mountain, now a battleship grey, by a road called Chlorine Gardens.

On Sunday morning my father went off to preach at Ballymena and I went with my stepmother to morning service in the cathedral. Looking at the strictly vertical worshippers in front of me – women's hats level as inverted pudding basins, men's bald patches, red ears, gold spectacle clasps clamping the ears behind, I felt myself again a schoolboy, not at my ease, standing with my hands together and my elbows pressing on my hips, catching solitary phrases – the sea is His and He made it – remembering that it was in this cathedral that my father scandalized Belfast; he had refused to allow the Union Jack to be hung over Carson's tomb in perpetuity.

Religion in Ireland is, as everyone knows, still a positive influence and still inextricably fused with social life and politics. Few of the Protestants or Presbyterians can see the Cross merely as a cross. Like a man looking into the sun through half-shut eyes, they see it shoot out rays, blossom in the Union Jack. And the Son of God goes forth to war in orange.

Idling in the house on Sunday afternoon, eating chocolates from a box which had been a Christmas present, I noticed that though the house was a different house, the creation of the tea-merchant with his Victorian ideal of taste imposed on prosperity (a front door with polished granite pillars and Corinthian capitals: radiators throughout), my family had brought with them so much of the bric-à-brac of years that I still felt, as on my earlier visits to Waterford or Carrickfergus, suspended in a world without progress – eating chocolates left over from Christmas. Here were the same mats, only a little shabbier, floating at anchor in the passages, never quite level with the walls; here were the 'Grecian' black marble clocks, the same blue twine-box on the hall-table (which had cost, no doubt, ninepence but had survived since I could remember), the oil-paintings of the Shamrock Girl and the Cockle Gatherers, the small teak elephants from missionary exhibitions, the little calendars hanging in the lavatories on electric light switches, the solid pond of books of scriptural commentary, the flotsam of occasional literature. The old drawing-room carpet had gone to a top-floor bedroom. Glass cases contained presentation silver teapots, seashells, family photographs. In most of the rooms the blinds were drawn against the sun.

In this context I had to admit that I was not in touch with the North of Ireland or with Belfast. Who was I to condemn them? I was insulated with comfort and private memories. It was very possible that Ulstermen were bigots, sadists, witch-doctors, morons. I had seen their Twelfths of July. But I had always dramatized them into the Enemy. They were not really grandiose monsters. If they were lost, they were lost with a small 'l'.

When I was a little boy and my sister and I had to go to Belfast, we would sit in the train returning home, swinging our legs and chanting 'Belfast! Belfast! The city of smoke and dust!' Belfast was essentially evil – largely because it was new. Living in a town of Norman remains, I had held the doctrine that oldness was in itself a merit and new things *ipso facto* bad. This doctrine I no longer hold, so I must absolve Belfast on that score. For the rest I consider that Belfast politics are deplorable and the outlook of her citizens much too narrow. But that is not good enough reason for hating her citizens. If I hate, I only make them more hateable. And even if I had adequate grounds for hating them, I still ought to make sure that I am not hating them mainly because I identify them with the nightmares of my childhood.

The boat for Heysham left at 9.45 on Sunday night. A row of girls on the deck was singing 'When Irish eyes are smiling'. And before the gangway was loosened Lord Craigavon came on board. The eyes continued smiling and we left for England. One must not dislike people, I thought, because they are intransigent. For that would be only playing their own game.

The night was full of stars and a moon two-thirds full sat steadily above the funnel. Not having yet reached its brilliance it showed its features clearly, resembling the death mask of Dean Swift. The water was still and, as the boat moved gently out, a dark lead expanse, but lustrous, widened between the boat and the quay. The lights on the quay-side sheds were reflected in the water, but each reflection appeared to be two lights rather than one. From the Lagan bridge behind us the lamps plunged organ-pipe reflections deep into the river. The boat moved in its sleep. Gliding on a narrow channel through a jungle of steel.

As we went faster, crinkling the water a little, the reflections squirmed like tadpoles, the double reflections from the sheds regularly and quietly somersaulting. Two cranes facing each other conferred darkly. In the

246

widening channel the lines of reflected lights behind us stretched in un-certain alleys like the lines of floating corks set out for swimmers. A black motor-boat cutting across them threw out shooting stars behind it. A buoy skated rapidly backwards winking periodically red. Then the cranes and quays fell away and the channel opened into the lough – a single line of lights on each side – like a man stretching his arms and drawing a breath. Cassiopeia was tilted in her deck-chair over Antrim; Arcturus over Down.

I went into the smoke-room (the whole boat was luxuriously appointed). Tomorrow I shall be back in London, visiting a house-agent. It was he, himself an Irishman from Limerick, who said to me two days ago: 'The Englishman is bigger. He doesn't let things upset him so.' Yes, I thought, the Irishman, like the elephant, never forgets; it is time that I forgot my nightmares. Before going to bed I went out again on deck. The night was cold and clouding; the moon had a slight aura. On our right the Copelands lighthouse swept its light at intervals from west to east as if shooing us away from our country.

from *Zoo*, 1938

THE SENSE OF PLACE

SEAMUS HEANEY

I think there are two ways in which place is known and cherished, two ways which may be complementary but which are just as likely to be antipathetic. One is lived, illiterate and unconscious, the other learned, literate and conscious. In the literary sensibility, both are likely to co-exist in a conscious and unconscious tension: this tension and the poetry it produces are what I want to discuss. I want to consider how the different senses of Ireland, of Northern Ireland, and of specific places on our island, have affected poets over these last hundred years.

I might have begun the exploration much further back, of course, because in Irish poetry there is a whole genre of writing called *dinnseanchas*, poems and tales which relate the original meanings of place names and constitute a form of mythological etymology. An early epic like the *Tain bo Cuailgne* is full of incidental *dinnseanchas*, insofar as it connects various incidents on the journey of the Connacht armies from Cruachan to Carlingford with the names of places as we now know them, or at least as they were known in the Gaelic past. Ardee, for example, the town in Co. Louth. In Irish, Ardee means Ferdia's Ford, and it was at this point (at a ford on the River Fane) that Cuchullain and Ferdia, brothers in arms in their youth, fought their great single combat by day and tended each other's wounds by night until Cuchullain slew Ferdia with his magical weapon, the *gae bolga*. It is a story that would have been current in everybody's mind when Irish was the *lingua franca* and it is still one of the best-known and best-loved legends in the Ulster cycle. So the place name, Ardee, succinctly marries the legendary and the local.

It now requires some small degree of learning to know this about Ardee. We have to retrieve the underlay of Gaelic legend in order to read the full meaning of the name and to flesh out the topographical record with its human accretions. The whole of the Irish landscape, in John Montague's words, is a manuscript which we have lost the skill to read. When we go as tourists to Donegal or Connemara or Kerry we go with at best an aesthetic eye, comforting ourselves with the picturesqueness of it all or rejoicing in the fact that it is unspoiled. We will have little felt knowledge of the place, little enough of a sense of wonder or a sense of tradition. Tory Island, Knocknarea, Slieve Patrick, all of them deeply steeped in associations from the older culture, will not stir us beyond a visual pleasure unless that culture means something to us, unless the features of the landscape are a mode of communion with a something other than themselves, a something to which we ourselves still feel we might belong.

. . . [Once] the landscape was sacramental, instinct with signs, implying a system of reality beyond the visible realities. Only thirty years ago, and thirty miles from Belfast, I think I experienced this kind of world vestigially and as a result may have retained some vestigial sense of place as it was experienced in the older dispensation. As I walked to school, I saw Lough Beg from Mulholland's Brae, and the spire of Church Island rose out of the trees. On Church Island Sunday in September, there was a pilgrimage out to the island, because St Patrick was supposed to have prayed there, and prayed with such intensity that he branded the shape of his knee into a stone in the old churchyard. The rainwater that collected in that stone, of course, had healing powers, and the thorn bush beside it was pennanted with the rags used by those who rubbed their warts and sores in that water. Then on a clear day, out in the Antrim hills beyond Lough Beg, I could see the unmistakable hump of Slemish, the mountain where the youthful Patrick had tended sheep. That legend, and the ringing ascetic triumph of the lines in his *Confession* where he talks about rising in the frosts of winter to pray to his Christian God, all combined to give Slemish a nimbus of its own, and made it more potent in the mind's eye than Slieve Gallon, a bigger, closer mountain that we faced on the road home from school, and which took its aura from our song '*Slieve Gallon's Braes*'. On Aughrim Hill, between the school and the lough, somebody had found an old sword, deemed to be a Viking sword, since we knew those almost legendary people had sailed the Bann a thousand years before; and on a shelf in the master's room there was a bit of wood that had been turned to stone by the action of the waters of Lough Neagh.

There, if you like, was the foundation for a marvellous or a magical view of the world, a foundation that sustained a diminished structure of lore and superstition and half-pagan, half-Christian thought and practice. Much of the flora of the place had a religious force, especially if we think of the root of the word in *religare*, to bind fast. The single thorn-tree bound us to a notion of the potent world of fairies, and when my father cut such a thorn, retribution was seen to follow inexorably when the horse bolted in harness, broke its leg and had to be destroyed. The green rushes bound us to the beneficent spirit of St Brigid: cut on Brigid's Eve, the first of February, they were worked into Brigid's crosses that would deck the rooms and outhouses for the rest of the year. Indeed, one of my most cherished and in some way mysterious memories is of an old neighbour of ours called Annie Devlin sitting in the middle of a floor strewn with green rushes, a kind of local sybil, plaiting the rushes and plaiting all of us into that ritualized way of life.

Then on May Eve, the buttercups and ladysmock appeared on the windowsills in obedience to some rite, and during the month of May the pagan goddess became the Virgin Mary and May flowers had to be gathered for her altar on the chest-of-drawers in the bedroom, so that the primroses and the celandines also wound us into the sacral and were wound into it in their turn. Late summer, and my father plaited harvest bows from the new corn and wore them in his lapel. Hallowe'en, and the turnip, that homely and densely factual root, became a root of some kind of evil as the candle blazed in it from a gatepost in the dark. At the fireside then, the talk of old times when cows were blinked and men met the devil in the shape of a goat or heard him as a tinkle of chains on the road after dark, or saw him, or powers of some sort, in lights dancing in spots where no lights should be. Such naming of examples is a pleasure to me, and that is, I believe, itself an earnest of the power of place.

But of course it wasn't just the old religion that exhaled its fragrances in that place. The more recent sectarian varieties were also intimately bound up with different locales. The red, white and blue flagpost at the Hillhead, for example, was a totem that possessed all the force of a holy mountain, and the green chestnut tree that flourished at the entrance to the Gaelic Athletic Association grounds was more abundantly green from being the eminence where the tricolour was flown illicitly at Easter or on sports days. Even Annie Devlin's rich and overgrown garden, with its shooting leeks and roofings of rhubarb leaves, even that natural earth was tinctured with the worst aspects of our faiths, insofar as that lovely flower, Sweet William, became suspect in the imagination from its connection with William of Orange, the king we sent to hell regularly up the long ladder and down the short rope.

(Lecture given in the Ulster Museum, January 1977)

from 'The Sense of Place', from *Preoccupations*, 1980

Newtownards and Killyleagh

ROBIN BRYANS

I had already discovered transformations and reformations in Ulster and yet at Killaghy, only twelve miles from Belfast, the old Presbyterian ways kept their roots. As I continued my journey I tried to remember the verses County Down Presbyterians used to sing at their choir practices. Since the metrical Psalms were holy writ, the words could not be profaned at practice by the choir-master's directions and interruptions. Instead secular doggerel was inserted, such as

> In Ireland doth fair Dublin stand,
> The chief city therein;
> And, as is said by many men,
> The chief city for sin.

When he had a church living in the north and was having his *affaire* with Miss Jane Waring of Belfast, Jonathan Swift may well have heard this and similar rhymes. Swift did not take kindly to Irish Presbyterianism. He put his hatred of it into print and even when he rose to fame later in Dublin the bitterness remained. His *Polite Conversation* is thought to vent his feelings about the superficiality of Belfast society. But the antipathy may have been on both sides for the Presbyterians would hardly have approved the way in which this literary cleric involved himself with various women, and certainly would not have looked kindly on the cruel way he dropped them when the ladies no longer charmed him.

Swift's antics over his Ulster church must also have irritated the intensely serious Presbyterian brethren. On one occasion, Swift's jealousy at the emptiness of his own church compared to the fullness of the Presbyterian one led him to indulge in something very much like a modern publicity stunt. One Sunday, Swift began wheeling stones from the beach into his church. And so curious were the good people to see what the eccentric rector was doing on the Sabbath that they crowded into the church to find out, whereupon Swift locked the doors. He then conducted a full service, of the kind which his kidnapped congregation's ancestors had fled from in *The Eagle's Wing*.

Despite Swift's disapproval, the Presbyterians did much good and left behind some fine building in their farmhouses and churches, an example of which I saw later in the day at Killinchy, after leaving my old blacksmith friend Hugh Martin. The Presbyterian Church today is still a large and influential body in Northern Ireland and in a harmonious accord with the Church of Ireland which Swift would certainly have disliked. The biggest embarrassment today is not an entanglement with any Establishment but with a minority group who call themselves the Free Presbyterian Church, led by the Reverend Ian Paisley. These extremists recently picketed a meeting held by the ex-Moderator of the Presbyterian Church, because he had attended the World Council of Churches at New Delhi – which for the 'Frees' looks like another road to Rome!

On my travels, however, I was concerned with the road to Newtownards where, until a few years ago, Farmer Davidson used to come every Sunday morning with his pony and trap loaded with home-churned butter for sale in the town.

Possessing a more sophisticated eye than I had in my adolescence when I knew this part of County Down quite well, I saw now, on coming into Newtownards, that the town conformed to the pleasing and simple pattern of country towns common throughout Ulster. Old, higgledy-piggledy, thatchy and indoor-beamy villages beloved by motor coach tourists in England do not exist. Instead, even the smallest village has an imposed sense of order descended from the grand town planning of Georgian times.

Newtownards's regular, straight streets and its town square in which stands the white turret-topped town hall, looked somehow French. I almost expected to find bistros and pavement cafés and cheap wine. What I did find, however, just outside the town were some factories for newly established light industries. Blacksmith Martin had told me his grandson had come home from sea and had gone 'into the nylon' at Newtownards. The traditional skills of linen and hand embroidery were being absorbed by such modern developments.

An intriguing footnote to the town's history lies in the fact that it was here that an early idea of copyright came into existence. This was through St Columba who was educated at Movilla Abbey outside Newtownards.

The abbey was founded in 540 by St Finian who came back from Rome, where he paid his tribute to the Pope, bearing a copy of the Vulgate text as revised by St Jerome himself. Seeing this sacred document young St Columba set about making a further copy, for his own use. When this was done St Finian claimed that this copy of the copy was also legally his. He did not get it and so appealed to Diarmid, King of Ireland.

This king then gave his famous judgement – 'To every cow belongeth her little offspring cow, so to every book belongeth its little offspring book.' And so was established an early principle of copyright. St Columba smarted under this decision and the great 'Dove of the Church' went to war to uphold his claim on the copy he had made, and many were the souls which 'were sent to perdition'. It was because so many people went to perdition through this battle that St Columba set off for Iona to try and bring more men to Christ than he was responsible for killing. The disputed copy, however, survived the battle. And when it passed into the O'Donnell family they cased it in a silver shrine and carried it into all their clan battles. St Columba's copy survived even this, and then all the centuries that followed it until it was deposited in the Royal Irish Academy.

I wanted to get on to Comber and waited for the bus in company with two boys who had trout rods. Of course, they had no fishing licences but were cautious in talking about their angling exploits in case I might be a detective – despite my hitch-hiking appearance. They were off to the Carrigullion Lakes, they said, where the fishing was free and great pike were easily caught by a Colorado spoon.

However, having thoroughly catechized me as to my business in those parts, for Newtownards was small enough for a stranger to be conspicuous, they relaxed. One of them 'borrowed' tenpence and went off to buy another fly for his collection. He kept it in an old tobacco tin which was full of those trout-tempters with such mellifluous names, purple snipe, gold-ribbed hare's ear, Greenwell's glory, Wickham's fancy, boat-wing sedge.

Scrabo Hill brooded over the landscape, the highest point for miles, a rugged hill from which red sandstone used to be quarried when I lived in County Down. I used to pass the quarries on my way to the heathery top, not always alone and for more romantic pursuits than merely to enjoy the fantastic panorama of Strangford Lough. Scrabo – the Sod of the Cow –

did not have the holiness for me that sister hills had for St Patrick when he herded swine.

A square tower stands on the hilltop as memorial to the third Marquess of Londonderry whose home with its exquisite gardens is nearby. This nineteenth-century soldier and diplomat, despite his elevation, was over-shadowed on my bus-ride by the fame of another soldier – 'Ould Gillespie' as the boys with the fishing rods described him.

But they said it affectionately for Gillespie is still a kind of schoolboy hero. The thirty-foot high stone obelisk on which he stood in the little square at Comber does not diminish his dashing story. He remains a pre-celluloid Errol Flynn in spite of the titles and honours inscribed on his statue, 'Lieutenant-General Sir Robert Rollo Gillespie'. The most pompous memorial in the world could not dim the fact that he was the bravest man in the British Army.

He was born in Comber in 1766 and joined the army while still in his teens. After killing a fellow officer in a duel, 'across the handkerchief', young Gillespie left Ireland and joined the French in San Domingo. Having had the most swashbuckling of wide-screen adventures by shipwreck and bloody cutlass battles he turned up in India in time to take command of Arcot. And from there he rode out to the Indian mutineers at Vellore. During another epic drama he was hoisted into the besieged fortress by a rope, once more becoming a popular hero. All this was too good to last, and he was only 48 when he was killed in India, shouting his most famous command, 'One more shot for the honour of Down'.

'He must have been a terror,' my young friends said before they went off on their own piracy of high season trout and salmon.

General Gillespie appealed to a couple of girls who came to peer in my notebook. 'Och,' they said of the bronze soldier, 'what lovely legs he's got.' He had indeed, meaty thighs rising out of top-boots, though the girls soon lost their interest in Gillespie for the real thighs of a farm youth driving through the square on his tractor. When he had gone the after-noon quiet flowed back again and I was left alone in the square to reflect that Comber, like most places in the world, would be better without its modern improvements. The petrol pumps and neon signs and concrete lamp-posts had nothing to give the simple Georgian buildings which they did not possess before.

Comber was so rurally peaceful that not even a bus threatened its seclusion so I started walking again, in the direction of Killyleagh where I wanted to spend the night. The countryside now seemed to be heavily wooded, though this was an illusion created by fine ash and sycamore and beech left in the hedges by the farmers. The gardens beyond Comber were loaded like flower shows, and wild sweet-pea vied with honeysuckle for supremacy of the hedges where for miles herb Robert was truly jack-of-the-hedgerows. Herds of Herefords seemed also to be competing with red Devons for the heavy-weight contest as they went from one lush meadow to the next.

A grocer stopped his van and gave me a lift as far as Killinchy where I stayed long enough to admire the Non-Subscribing Presbyterian Church of 1845, a plain but dignified, pedimented building. Some of Northern Ireland's most interesting architecture of the Presbyterians belongs to the Non-Subscribing Church. Many of these simple, graceful buildings appear unexpectedly all over Ulster's countryside. They show how the Presbyterians hated the shams of the romantic revivals of bygone styles – an architectural activity associated strongly in their minds with the Church of Ireland. The qualities of these fine Georgian churches also clearly demonstrate the social differences, as well as ecclesiastical ones, between the two denominations at that time.

Swift was not the only member of the Established Church to attack the Presbyterians, who, along with all Nonconformists were made to suffer. Because of the 1704 Test Act many Presbyterians were obliged to resign from official positions, even though they represented the major Protestant denomination in the province. After this Act Presbyterians could no longer sit on the Town Council if they adhered strictly to the views of their fleeing fathers of *The Eagle's Wing*.

Matters reached a climax when a Belfast rector, William Tisdall, tried to have a substantial house tax imposed on everybody to keep his own church coffers full. Fortunately, people were so outraged that they brought Dr Tisdall to law. The result, however, did not mean that Presbyterians could hold public office – though George I had revived William III's *regium donum* grant of money to Irish Presbyterian ministers.

Faced with Rome on one hand and the Established Church on the other, Ulster Presbyterians soon had a revolution in their own ranks. The battle was over the question of assent to the Westminster Confession of Faith, an accepted procedure to orthodox Presbyterianism. This was no minor teacup affair but a major storm which went on for years and eventually led to a split and the founding of the Non-Subscribing Presbyterian Church of Ireland, whose distinctive early architecture is still such an adornment to the Ulster scene today.

While trying to get from Killinchy I was joined by a 17-year-old Sikh pedlar in a sugar-icing-pink turban. 'I've got something nice for you,' he said mysteriously as he opened his case and spread his wares by the road which was full of traffic going to and from Killinchy Dinghy Championship.

The water here was in fact another arm of the sea, though longer and more lonely than Belfast Lough. Norse invaders originally gave this long stretch of water its name, Strang Fiord or the Violent Fjord. Through the lough's extremely narrow neck, opening to the sea, hundreds of millions of tons of ocean rush up and down with every tide.

Earlier when I had reached the upper end of Strangford Lough the tide was out. And long before I could see, I could hear the cries of the wild-fowl delighting in the sloblands and rocks of the shallows. The lough is said to have three-hundred-and-sixty-five islands, great and small. Few of the islands were farmed and most were given over as haunts for Arctic tern and ringed plover, red-breasted merganser, sheelduck and oyster-catcher. Currents round the neck flow up to eight knots but this only adds to the sport of seals and porpoises.

It pleased me to know that at least one place in Northern Ireland had retained its original Norse name, for not many were left bearing traces of Scandinavian invaders. To find Strangford Lough with its ancient associations pleased me because the place reminded me very much of Roskilde Fjord in Denmark, a place where I had spent many hours among similar rafts of wildfowl and pagan and early monastic ruins and stories of buried treasure like Strangford's. And a further similarity was shown me by a family called Lyness who gave me a lift to Killyleagh on their way home from the dinghy racing. They took me out to their loughside house which stood looking out over the water and the islands exactly as the house of Bridget Swinton, an Irish painter, at Roskilde. The Lynesses' house was called Fool's Penny. An amusing story from the last century tells of a woman who sold stout to fishermen and sailors from the coal-boats, making a penny profit on each bottle. When sufficient pennies had been made from the fools she retired and built the house by the lough. I stood on the lawn of that penny-wise woman while my host talked about the grampus which came into the lough after seals. But my attention was taken by the stately flight of a heron as it disappeared into the gathering twilight on slow, powerful wing-beats. I remembered a line from James Hanley's *The Ocean* – 'From this silence he made walls.'

And it was from a rectory also built along the loughside at Killyleagh that the silence of the ancient walls of Egypt and Assyria again woke into speech after thousands of years, for in the rectory lived Edward Hincks, the greatest orientalist of nineteenth-century Europe. As Moses spent forty years in the wilderness so Hincks spent forty years in the obscurity of the loughside forging the keys which would open the hitherto unknown secrets of the East.

Casts of the ancient stones were sent all the way to Killyleagh for his use in deciphering. The principles Hincks laid down then still enable scholars today to translate the hieroglyphic and cuneiform scripts of the Nile civilization. I hope that Hincks's bust in Cairo has received more thoughtful treatment in recent years than did that of de Lesseps, the canal builder who was dishonoured in the first rush of Egyptian national pride.

As though the tiny town of Killyleagh had not given enough material to the Bloomsbury experts another local lad achieved fame by being the founder of the British Museum. Sir Hans Sloane, traveller and physician, was born in a small house in 1660 in Frederick Street, a house still standing and lived in today. There were people who believed that Hans may have been a 'wee love bird', born on the wrong side of the blanket to the Rowan-Hamilton family, overlords of the local estate. Hans Sloane might well have been illegitimate for the founder of the Killyleagh Hamiltons, the Reverend Hans Hamilton, was himself born on the wrong side of the ducal blanket. Sloane at any rate had his education in the magnificent library of Killyleagh Castle.

The town sprawled about the castle foot which rose, towered and turreted over its roofs and above its screen of trees for all the world like a castle in a German fairy story. From behind its high curtain wall the castle looked grim and forbidding, as though dark and bloody secrets lay buried behind its battlements.

I could hardly resist the desire to invest the castle with arms like a knight bent on rescuing a captive damsel. With imaginary accoutrement jingling in my ears I went up to this Rhine Valley fortress, having arranged a knightly hospice in the form of a bed at Killyleagh's ex-manse. But this poor knight, armed in reality with nothing more than his insatiable curiosity, found no breaches in the walls. There was no chance of a half-crown tour for the castle was still the private residence of its owner Mrs Rowan-Hamilton.

A strawberry ice-cream, bought from the man whose celeste music sent rooks squabbling about the chimneys and lodges and cottages built into the walls, did nothing to help. He could not tell me how to gain admittance. I looked up to the remote inner towers where the rooks settled again by a television aerial. The gate lodges were empty and locked. No bells connected the gates to the castle and I saw notices 'Strictly Private. Trespassers Prosecuted.' I began to think the only way in would be General Gillespie's – to be hauled up by a rope.

The postmistress in the little post office nestling under the walls saved the day. Only for one day in the year, she said, were the gates opened to the public and then in aid of a charity. But nevertheless a telephone call was put through and as a result Mrs Rowan-Hamilton, from somewhere in the depths of her castle, invited me to call the following morning.

With the rest of that evening to kill I went into the Dufferin Arms to be welcomed with friendly chaffing and inquisitiveness and forceful generosity by the local farmers who would hardly hear of me buying my own drink. A large whisky and a Guinness 'chaser' appeared and I tried to concentrate on at least one of the many threads of talk, for in their enthusiasm the farmers tended to talk and tell stories all at once.

I did disentangle the tale of Captain Blood and the ghosts of Moore Hall, a house which the owner's brother-in-law wanted me to visit. But I had to resist the invitation to 'Come over and see the wee grey lady' abjuring the supernatural for the supernormal in the form of more whisky and Guinness presented by another farmer. He was just getting over a bad dose of 'rat's disease', contracted through taking a horse to the Dublin Show, and rubbing an open cut against rat-infected straw.

The crescendo of talk and laughter increased, and I tried to discover who the 'blonde bastard' in the town was. This character intrigued me, for some avowed and some denied that the 'blonde bastard' appeared recently in a court of law. I asked somebody and discovered that the 'bastard', due no doubt as much to whiskies as to the richness of the Killyleagh dialect, was not a bastard but a barrister. It seemed high time to leave the proceedings though I almost had to use physical force to dissuade my new friends from walling me into my seat with fresh bottles and glasses. The publican's wife asked if I would like to go through the yard, not as a way of escape, but in order to see Sir Hans Sloane's house which was just outside the Dufferin Arms back gate. I was still capable of reading the date over Hans's house – 1637, and 1880 as the date of rebuilding.

Sitting on the window-sill of the house next door was Gordon, a youngster who had just come back from shooting hoodie crows.

'Have you seen the stile?' he asked.

I had not, but I knew what he meant, the one I knew of from childhood, the stile in Lady Dufferin's song *The Irish Emigrant's Lament*. She wrote it sitting in a window of Killyleagh Castle, looking out towards the meadows spreading below the castle walls.

from *Ulster: a journey through the Six Counties*, 1964

COUNTY FERMANAGH

FRANK ORMSBY

Fermanagh is in the news again. Fermanagh is always in the news. On the front pages and on the back pages, in the small print and in the large, among the football results and the nature notes. In books about fishing and pot-holing, agriculture and industry, drainage schemes, folklore, ancient monuments. In tourist brochures and National Trust pamphlets, in local histories, in development reports and among statistics about the unemployed. Like every other place I know, it ripples perpetually outwards in the memory and imagination, renewing and re-creating itself, familiar and elusive and forever strange.

So I read about the latest political squabble in the Council chambers, or the latest milk-churn bomb exploding in a culvert on a country road, or the inconvenience caused to the remoter farming communities by the authorities' decision to crater an unapproved border road, and the news is old news. Until I learn that the rare orchid *Spiranthes romanzoffiana* has turned up in a garden in Enniskillen, or that someone has spotted *Quercusia quercus*, the Purple Hairstreak butterfly, in Pobble Forest, or that a large bat, previously thought to be extinct, has come to light in the caves of Boho. And I'm willingly chastened again into seeing how presumptuous is the claim to 'know' any place.

For me the ripples started in the townland of Makeny, about a mile and a half from the village of Irvinestown, on the main Enniskillen road. We lived in what amounted to a valley. The road wound out of sight a few hundred yards away on either side. The three houses immediately visible from ours were on a higher level and formed a rough circle around us; and we did not own a car, so that family outings were unusual, if they took place at all. Lough Erne played no part in my early childhood. It was miles away and inaccessible. I was eleven before I saw Devenish Island, for example, and even then it was only the top of the round tower glimpsed daily from a bus window as I travelled to and from college in Enniskillen.

Meanwhile, the world in the vicinity of the house was manageable and its variety infinite, a world in which every field and landmark had its name – not 'Fermanagh' as yet, but the Brown Ground, the Brick Hole, Donnelly's Bog, the Long Bottom, the Green Lane, the Two Trees.

Directly opposite the zinc bungalow where we lived were the woods we called the Plantation, and a short distance away the mottled railings and dilapidated gate-lodge at the main entrance to the Castle Irvine or Necarne Castle Estate. Playing in those woods, or even venturing into the empty castle through an open window, had the appeal of the illicit. The castle grounds were, in fact, open to the public but it was more of an adventure to lie under the rhododendrons like trespassers as Captain Richard Herman's car glided over the pot-holes, or to duck behind the big chestnut tree at the sound of the gamekeeper's jeep.

The castle itself was history. It reached back to the days of the Lowther family, who had founded Lowtherstown, and the Irvines, who had changed the name to Irvinestown, its greystone battlements and coat of arms conferring an antiquity that was somehow both remote and satisfying. The remains of an American and British hospital camp from the Second World War were history too, but we never thought of them in that way. The circular, earth-covered burrows of the air raid shelters with their damp, vegetable darkness and dull echoes, the stone floors like a series of intersecting pavements where the Nissen huts had stood, the earthwork that might have been a trench or the site of a gun emplacement, the piles of rusted beer cans in corners of the undergrowth – these were special attractions of the natural playground that surrounded our house.

The estate had its characteristic sounds – the dangerous modulations of a chain-saw and the crashing of trees, the frantic gear-wrenching and gravel-rending of rally drivers time-trialling among red and white bollards, the yowling of hounds, the blattering and keening of beaters during the annual shoot, the panic-stricken explosion of pheasants across the main road. Most familiar of all was the sound of gunfire – the shotguns of the hunters, the gamekeeper, the clay pigeon shooters, and often, in the long evenings, the rifle-fire of the 'B' Specials practising in the castle grounds. There were characteristic sights and smells too – the grisly tree on which hung the rotting bodies of grey crows, magpies and other scavengers, the suppurating rabbits, blind and swollen with myxomato-sis, which crawled onto the avenue to die.

When we began to think of Fermanagh as an entity, one piece of the thirty-two-part jigsaw that was the map of Ireland, it seemed a peculiarly isolated place, one of those limbo-like, half-lost border counties, like Monaghan and Cavan, roughly equidistant from the centres of power. There were villages like Belleek, Pettigo and Belcoo, that seemed to straddle the border, and houses in the border sector which seemed to belong to neither Northern Ireland nor the Republic. To travel from one end of the county to the other was to hear people's accents take on a Donegal or Cavan or Monaghan twang. Yet, in spite of these shades and gradations, the political boundary was there, denied by the landscape and the dialects on either side of it, but visible as customs posts, road-blocks, the place-names in both English and Irish on the signposts in the Republic, and as palpable in our minds and imaginations as if it had been a broad white band painted across roads and farms. It was palpable too in the tension and division that permeated almost every aspect of life in Fermanagh. Among the lakes, drumlins and housing estates of that deceptively placid, postcard county, a defensive Unionist minority, who controlled local government, and a Catholic majority, resentful of discrimination against them in housing and employment, squared up to each other perennially, loathed each other's festivals and sometimes shed blood.

When I went to St Michael's College in Enniskillen in 1959, we were packed into St Michael's Reading Rooms, a parochial recreation centre attached to the school buildings in Belmore Street. Next door was the dark green hush of the snooker room. Outside the window the River Erne flowed under the East Bridge and the people of Enniskillen walked past above on the Queen Elizabeth Road. All around was a townscape that told a convoluted story. From the Forthill, General Galbraith Lowry-Cole, a hero of the Peninsular War, looked over the houses from his fluted Doric column. At one end of Belmore Street, in Gaol Square, was the obelisk commemorating the Inniskilling Regiment in the South African War and at the other, under the gable of the Reading Rooms, the Great War Memorial, a bronze soldier on a granite plinth with his head bowed in prayer. Here the ripples seemed both local and global. Here, too, on

Poppy Day 1987, the troubled history of a border county converged more devastatingly than usual, a variant of the history that had converged earlier on Ballykelly, Darkley and other places.

So Fermanagh is in the news again. Fermanagh is always in the news. I hear that the County Council has a scheme to plant willow forests for the production of methane. I read about the restoration of Castle Coole's Palladian grandeur, about the coming attractions at the Ardhowen Arts Centre, about Enniskillen Flying Club and Enniskillen Agricultural College, and about trampolining at the Lakeland Forum. I follow Lisnaskea Emmets and Lisnarick Rangers, Teemore Shamrocks and Irvinestown Wanderers up and down the league tables. I learn that the Remembrance Day bombing has given impetus to a new programme for mutual understanding in schools – and note, without surprise, that the programme has already been condemned as a plot to 'teach Protestant and Unionist children the tenets of Romanism and the political system of Irish Republicanism'.

Some day soon I'll make a trip to William Blake's pub in Enniskillen and the Clock Bar in Derrygonnelly, visit White Island and Davy's Island and Belleek Pottery, mingle with the continental fishermen, the tourists cruising the lough, the canoeists and water-skiers at Carry Bridge. I'll climb Topped Mountain for the first time, perhaps, and make my first descent into the Marble Arch caves.

And the ripples that have never stopped spreading will begin again – accumulating, accommodating, reflecting from a hundred angles that indefinable, irreducible, unforgettable place.

'County Fermanagh', from *Thirty-two Counties*, 1989

5

'Muddled Ulster'

JAMES SIMMONS

PREOCCUPATIONS

SEAMUS HEANEY

READING

When I was learning to read, towards the end of 1945, the most important books in the house were the ration books – the pink clothes coupons and the green 'points' for sweets and groceries. There wasn't much reading done apart from the deaths column of the *Irish Weekly* and the auctions page of the *Northern Constitution*. 'I am instructed by the representatives of the late John James Halferty, Drumanee . . .' My father lay on the sofa and rehearsed the acres, roods and perches of arable and meadow land in a formal tone and with a certain enlargement of the spirit.

On a shelf, behind a screen and too high to be reached anyhow, there were four or five mouldering volumes that may have belonged to my Aunt Susan from her days in Orange's Academy, but they remained closed books to me. The first glimpse I have of myself reading on my own is one of those orphaned memories, a moment without context that will always stay with me. It is a book from the school library – a padlocked box that was opened more or less as a favour – involving explorers in cork helmets and 'savages', with illustrations of war canoes on a jungle river. The oil lamp is lit and a neighbour called Hugh Bates is interrupting me. 'Boys but this Seamus fellow is a great scholar. What book are you in now, son?' And my father is likely wringing what he can from the moment with 'He's as bad as Pat McGuckin this minute.' Pat McGuckin was a notorious bachelor farmer – a cousin of ours – who was said to burn his scone like King Alfred every time he lifted a book. Years later, when *Death of a Naturalist* was published, the greatest commendation at home was 'Lord knows Pat would fairly have enjoyed this.'

Of course, there were always religious magazines like the *Far East* and the *Messenger* – Pudsy Ryan in the children's corner of the former was the grown-ups' idea of a side-splitting turn, but even then I found his misspellings a bit heavy-handed. Far better were the technicolour splendours of Korky the Cat and Big Eggo in the *Dandy* and *Beano*. The front pages of these comics opened like magic casements on Desperate Dan, Lord

Snooty, Hungry Horace, Keyhole Kate, Julius Sneezer and Jimmy and his Magic Patch and probably constituted my first sense of the invitations of fiction. They were passed round at school, usually fairly tattered, but every now and again my mother brought a new one from Castledawson, without a fold in it, its primary colours blazing with excitements to come. Occasionally, also, an American comic – all colour from beginning to end – arrived from the American airbase nearby, with Li'l Abner, Ferdinand and Blondie speaking a language that even Pat McGuckin did not know.

There was a resistance to buying new comics in our house, not out of any educational nicety, but because of a combination of two attitudes: that they were a catch-penny and that somehow they were the thin end of the wedge, that if you let them into the house the next step was the *Empire News, Thompson's Weekly, Tit-Bits* and the *News of the World*. Nevertheless, I ended up persuading my mother to place a regular order for *Champion*, a higher-class comic altogether, featuring a Biggles-rides-again figure called Rockfist Rogan and Ginger Nutt ('the boy who takes the *bis-cake*', in South Derry parlance) and Colwyn Dane, the sleuth. With the *Champion* I entered the barter market for the *Rover*, the *Hotspur*, the *Wizard* and any other pulp the presses of old England could deliver. I skimmed through all those 'ain'ts' and 'cors' and 'yoicks' and 'blimeys', and skimmed away contented.

So what chance had Kitty the Hare against all that? *Our Boys* appeared regularly, a cultural antidote with official home backing, healthy as a Christian Brother on a winter morning, the first steps towards *Ireland's Own*. Cultural debilitations! I preferred the japes of Ginger Nutt, the wheezes of Smith of the Lower Fourth, the swish of gowns, the mortar-board and the head's study to the homely toils of Murphy among the birettas. It would take Joyce's *Portrait of the Artist as a Young Man* and Kavanagh's *The Great Hunger* to get over that surrender.

My first literary *frisson*, however, came on home ground. There was an Irish history lesson at school which was in reality a reading of myths and legends. A textbook with large type and heavy Celticized illustrations dealt with the matter of Ireland from the Tuatha De Danaan to the Norman Invasion. I can still see Brian Boru with his sword held like a cross reviewing the troops at Clontarf. But the real imaginative mark was made with a story of the Dagda, a dream of harp music and light, confronting and defeating Balor of the Evil Eye on the dark fortress of Tory Island. Cuchullain and Ferdia also sank deep, those images of wounds bathed on the green rushes and armour clattering in the ford.

Yet all of that yielded to the melodrama of Blind Pew and Billy Bones, Long John and Ben Gunn. *Treasure Island* we read at school also and it was a prelude to the first book I remember owning and cherishing: there it was on the table one Christmas morning, Robert Louis Stevenson's *Kidnapped*. I was a Jacobite for life after that day. Instinctively I knew that the world of the penal rock and the redcoats – that oleograph to the faith of our fathers – was implicit in the scenery of that story. To this day, my heart lifts to the first sentence of it: 'I will begin the story of my adventures with a certain morning in the month of June, the year of grace 1751, when I took the key for the last time out of the door of my father's house. . . .'

As a boarder at St Columb's College I did the Maurice Walsh circuit – *Blackcock's Feather* remains with me as an atmosphere, a sense of bogs and woods – but again it was a course book that struck its imagery deepest. When I read in *Lorna Doone* how John Ridd stripped the muscle off Carver Doone's arm like a string of pith off an orange I was well on the road to epiphanies. Not that I didn't stray into the imperial realms of Biggles or the baloney of the William stories. But it is only those books with a touch of poetry in them that I can remember – all coming to a head when, in my last summer holiday from school, I sat up all night to finish Thomas Hardy's *Return of the Native*.

I missed Pooh Bear. I can't remember owning a selection of Grimm or Anderson. I read *Alice in Wonderland* at the university. But what odds? Didn't Vinny Hunter keep me in wonderland with his stories of Tarzan:

> 'When he jumps down off a tree
> Tarzan shakes the world.'
> So Vinny Hunter would tell me
> On the road to the school.
>
> I had forgotten for years
> Words so seismic and plain
> That would come like rocked waters,
> Possible again.

(*Education Times*, 1973)

A few months ago I remembered a rhyme that we used to chant on the way to school. I know now that it is about initiation but as I trailed along the Lagan's Road on my way to Anahorish School it was something that was good for a laugh:

> 'Are your praties dry
> Are they fit for digging?'
> 'Put in your spade and try,'
> Says Dirty-Faced McGuigan.

I suppose I must have been about eight or nine years old when those lines stuck in my memory. They constitute a kind of poetry, not very respectable perhaps, but very much alive on the lips of that group of schoolboys, or 'scholars', as the older people were inclined to call us. McGuigan was probably related to a stern old character called Ned McGuigan who travelled the roads with a menacing blackthorn stick. He came from a district called Ballymacquigan – The Quigan, for short – and he turned up in another rhyme:

> Neddy McGuigan,
> He pissed in the Quigan;
> The Quigan was hot
> So he pissed in the pot;
> The pot was too high
> So he pissed in the sky;
> Hell to your soul, Neddy McGuigan,
> For pissing so high.

And there were other chants, scurrilous and sectarian, that we used to fling at one another:

> Up the long ladder and down the short rope
> To hell with King Billy and God bless the Pope.

To which the answer was:

> Up with King William and down with the Pope
>
> Splitter splatter holy water
> Scatter the Paypishes every one

If that won't do
We'll cut them in two
And give them a touch of the
Red, white and blue.

To which the answer was:

Red, white and blue
Should be torn up in two
And sent to the devil
At half-past two.
Green, white and yellow
Is a decent fellow.

Another one which was completely nonsensical still pleases me:

One fine October's morning September last July
The moon lay thick upon the ground, the mud shone in the sky.
I stepped into a tramcar to take me across the sea,
I asked the conductor to punch my ticket and he punched my eye
  for me.

I fell in love with an Irish girl, she sang me an Irish dance,
She lived in Tipperary, just a few miles out of France.
The house it was a round one, the front was at the back,
It stood alone between two more and it was whitewashed black.

We weren't forced to get these lines by heart. They just seemed to spring
in our mind and trip off the tongue spontaneously so that our parents
would say 'If it was your prayers, you wouldn't learn them as fast.'

There were other poems, of course, that we were forced to learn by
heart. I am amazed to realize that at the age of eleven I was spouting
great passages of Byron and Keats by rote until the zinc roof of the Nissen
hut that served for our schoolhouse (the previous school had been cleared
during the war to make room for an aerodrome) rang to the half-understood
magnificence of:

There was a sound of revelry by night
And Belgium's capital had gathered then
Her beauty and her chivalry, and bright
The lamps shone o'er fair women and brave men.

> A thousand hearts beat happily; and when
> The music rose with its voluptuous swell . . .

I also knew the whole of Keats's ode 'To Autumn' but the only line that was luminous then was 'To bend with apples the mossed cottage trees', because my uncle had a small orchard where the old apple trees were sleeved in a soft green moss. And I had a vague satisfaction from 'the small gnats mourn/Among the river sallows', which would have been complete if it had been 'midges' mourning among the 'sallies'.

The literary language, the civilized utterance from the classic canon of English poetry, was a kind of force-feeding. It did not delight us by reflecting our experience; it did not re-echo our own speech in formal and surprising arrangements. Poetry lessons, in fact, were rather like catechism lessons: official inculcations of hallowed formulae that were somehow expected to stand us in good stead in the adult life that stretched out ahead. Both lessons did indeed introduce us to the gorgeousness of the polysyllable, and as far as we were concerned there was little to choose between the music with 'its voluptuous swell' and the 'solemnization of marriage within forbidden degrees of consanguinity'. In each case we were overawed by the dimensions of the sound.

There was a third category of verse which I encountered at this time, halfway between the roadside rhymes and the school poetry (or 'poertry'): a form known to us as 'the recitation'. When relations visited or a children's party was held at home, I would be called upon to recite. Sometimes it would be an Irish patriotic ballad:

> At length, brave Michael Dwyer, you and your trusty men
> Were hunted o'er the mountain and tracked into the glen.
> Sleep not, but watch and listen, keep ready blade and ball,
> For the soldiers know you hide this night in the Glen of Wild Imall.

Sometimes, a western narrative by Robert Service:

> A bunch of the boys were whooping it up in the Malamute Saloon.
> The kid that handles the music-box was hitting a ragtime tune.
> Back of the bar at a solo game sat Dangerous Dan McGrew
> And watching his luck was his light o'love, the lady that's known as Lou.

While this kind of stuff did not possess the lure of forbidden words like 'piss' and 'hell to your soul', it was not encumbered by the solemn incomprehensibility of Byron and Keats. It gave verse, however humble, a place in the life of the home, made it one of the ordinary rituals of life.

(*Worlds*, 1974)

from 'Mossbawn', from *Preoccupations*, 1980

CULTURAL IMPERIALISM: AN IRISH VIEW

GEORGE J. WATSON

We all live in actual places, but we all equally inhabit, imaginatively, countries of the mind. I was born in a small town called Portadown, County Armagh, and lived there until I was twenty-one. I want to talk about the various ways in which I have been possessed by imaginative senses of England, a country which in some ways seemed more real to me than the Northern Ireland I grew up in. Inevitably, I will be talking about the effects of cultural imperialism on me, as an Irishman, but I hope to avoid the Hibernian tone so deftly characterized by Evelyn Waugh when he spoke of the Irishman as 'carrying everywhere with him his ancient rancour and the melancholy of the bogs'. Perhaps, too, what I say may be of interest for the light it throws on the complexities of cultural arrangements and accommodations within the tiny archipelago which is called the British Isles.

Portadown is where the Orange Order was founded in the late eighteenth century, and it has remained a bastion of Orange bigotry to this day. When Sir John Lavery wished to paint the strange tribal rite known as 'The Twelfth', when the Orangemen parade on July 12 with their drums, bands, sashes, and banners through the streets in celebration of their domination over the sullen Papists, he chose – appositely – to site his picture on Portadown's main street. I could have been one of the small boys on Lavery's canvas, standing back on the edge of a Catholic street to watch the parade from a safe, discreet distance. Catholic adults stayed indoors, but even Catholic boys found it hard to resist the appeal of the bands – accordion, flute, and best of all, the pipes in the 'kilty' bands. And watching those parades as a very small boy was where I first encountered a sense of England. The Orange phenomenon might have been a purely indigenous growth, but its iconography asserted the might of England. The Union Jack was everywhere; the huge Lambeg drums which thundered ceaselessly the warning 'Catholics lie down' proclaimed 'God Save the King' on their gross swollen bellies; the banners portrayed the crown; on them King William of Orange urged his white charger across the Boyne to smash King James; on them, Queen Victoria, in full regalia on her throne, held out a Bible to a kneeling black African who kissed it, over the legend 'The Secret of England's Greatness' – a message easily translated and understood by Northern Ireland's negro population. The *Royal* Ulster Constabulary were out in force to prevent riot, revolvers in their shiny holsters and their oak-pale batons prominent, on their caps the insignia which emblematized our status – English crown above Irish harp. The Orangemen – and the whole state as well – were 'Loyalist'. Loyal to England. And the Orangemen hated us. So presumably England hated us too? I would never go to England: if it could be like this on its fringes, what must it be like at the centre?

In the home, however, things became more complex, and it was difficult to identify 'English Ulster' with 'England'. Every evening at nine, with the immutable regularity with which we said the family rosary, my father would switch on the wireless. And there would be a different England. The glorious solemnity of Big Ben filled our Irish kitchen: my very first sense of drama came from that moment of complete silence between the ending of the chimes and the first of the nine reverberating gongs. Then: 'This is the BBC Home Service, and this is Alvar Liddell with the nine o'clock news. Today, on Luneburg Heath, Field Marshal Montgomery accepted the surrender of all German forces. The war in Europe is over. . . .' The beautifully modulated voices, the rational moderation ('so far, these reports are unconfirmed' was a phrase which ran like a leitmotif through the news bulletins of my boyhood), the largeness of the issues, all seemed totally unrelated to the tight bigotries of Northern Ireland's streets. For me, the BBC was quintessentially English – those accents! – and provided an enormous sense of security. I remember how particularly I loved the shipping forecasts, especially on stormy nights, when the wireless would bring into the warmth of the kitchen a comforting sense of other men's danger, but danger, the smooth voice always implied, under control: 'The meteorological station issued the following gale warning to shipping at 0600 hours Greenwich Mean Time: "Gales are imminent in sea areas Dogger, Rockall, Fisher, German Bight, Lundy, Fastnet, Faroes, Finisterre. . . ." ' There was a kind of poetry in this; and also early on, I derived a strong sense of the poetry of English place names. I lived near

275

places with beautiful names – Tanderagee, Banbridge, Slieve Donard in the Mourne mountains, Slieve Gullion, Slemish (where St Patrick fasted and prayed), Ballynahinch, Magherafelt, Magheramore – but, of course, I didn't see anything special about them. The place name is without honour in its own country. There is a wonderful moment in Brian Friel's fine play *Translations*, which is about the imposition of English names on Irish places carried out by the Army Ordnance survey in the nineteenth century. One of the English officers falls in love with the music of Irish place names, and with an Irish girl. For her, however, his glamour is located, at least in part, in *his* places:

Winfarthing – Barton Bendish – Saxingham – Nethergate – Little Walsingham – Norwich – Norfolk. Strange sounds, but nice; like Jimmy Jack reciting his Homer.

My responses to English names originated less romantically, but in their own way, just as strongly.

Once again, it was the BBC which, at 5 p.m. every Saturday, opened a casement on a magic land: 'Here are today's football results: Tottenham Hotspur 2, West Bromwich Albion 0; Wolverhampton Wanderers 1, Manchester United 1; Blackburn Rovers 1, Accrington Stanley 2; Brighton and Hove Albion 3, Nottingham Forest 2.' Wolves did wander, I knew, and Robin Hood lived in a forest near Nottingham, but who was Stanley? And could anything hit the ear, let alone the imagination, more finely than the tripping rhythms of 'Tottenham Hotspur'? (Our local football team was called, prosaically, Portadown.)

And England was the home of cricket. My mother was born in the province of Connacht, in Connemara, on Ireland's western coast, a beautiful but barren, boggy, rocky, and mountainous region, its coastline deeply fretted by the huge Atlantic breakers which take their first bites at this last outpost of Europe on their voyage from North America. Like most people of that area at that time, she spoke the Irish language; and I know she never saw a cricket match – perhaps not even a cricket pitch – in all her life. The game's terminology – leg before wicket, silly mid on, long leg, the slips, the gully, the covers – remained obscure to her, as to me, for many years. Yet I remember our mutual raptness as the wireless transmitted commentary on the Test Matches, especially those between England

and Australia, from distant Lords or the Oval. I suppose it had something to do with the very mysteriousness of the arcane terminology. 'And Bradman has swept Bedser down to fine leg for two runs.' Certainly it had to do with the round gravelly tones of John Arlott, whose deliberation was a byword and who seemed to *relish* all those moments – frequent in cricket – when nothing is happening. 'And Edrich just gives a little tug at his cap, while a small boy moves behind the sight screen. Probably on his way to buy a bottle of pop. It's certainly a hot enough day here at the Oval, with the famous gasometer shimmering faintly in the heat haze.' Most of all, the appeal of cricket on the BBC was precisely due to its suggestion that a world of harmless ritual, of endless sunny afternoons, of soporific torpidity – all of which contrasted so appealingly with the tension and latent violence of our lives in the North. England, as refracted through the BBC, with its dignified voices which highlighted the more our spiky hard-edged local accents, with its romantic names and its calm, was – most confusingly for me – the great good place.

We could also receive, of course, and did, the broadcasts of Radio Eireann, the radio service of the Irish Free State, lying a mere twenty miles south, where the famous border runs from Crossmaglen to Bessbrook and Forkhill. But Radio Eireann was a sponsored service, and even as a boy I thought that some of the dignity of its news bulletins seeped away when they were followed by advertisements for Donnelly's Pork Sausages ('is it true they're the talk of the nation?') or for Galtee and Mitchelstown Cheese ('keeps you slim, trim, and brimful of energy'). Our relationship as a family with the Free State, which became officially the Republic in 1949, was in any case an uneasy one.

My father was born in Kilkenny in 1898, my mother in Connemara in 1900. Both Catholics. Both believed in Home Rule. Like many another Southern Irishman, my father saw no incompatibility between believing in Home Rule for Ireland and enlisting as an infantry private in the British Army during the First World War, where somehow he survived the carnage of Passchendaele. When he returned, lacking any real educational accomplishments, he joined the Royal Irish Constabulary. But the Ireland he returned to was a different place. In the aftermath of the Rising of 1916, Ireland had embraced the republican doctrines of Sinn Fein, and the IRA had begun a policy of harassment, intimidation – and indeed shooting – of members of the RIC, as these were seen as representative of the English Crown forces in the island. His family's house was burned down and many of his comrades shot. Coincidentally, my mother's house was burned down, too – her father was also a member of the RIC. And so, when the Treaty which partitioned Ireland was signed in 1921, they both came North to the new statelet, and my father made the worst mistake of his life – though what else could he do? – and joined the Royal Ulster Constabulary. His seven children were all born in the North. Externally, the conditions of our lives were not easy. It wasn't so much that we were poor, though we were (my father had a constable's wage); but we were Catholics in a Protestant state designed, as its first prime minister put it, for a Protestant people. (Indeed my parents gave themselves away every time they opened their mouths, because they retained their Southern accents.) Worse, our coreligionists regarded us with deep suspicion – the RUC was unquestionably a sectarian police force. My father wore his revolver and carried his baton as if the albatross were hung around his neck.

Internally, in terms of that imaginative sense of tradition and continuity which all of us need, I found it equally difficult. Even had I wanted to – for that matter, even had my father wanted me to – I could not identify with Northern Ireland as a state or polity. The Protestant boys whom we had to fight almost daily on our way back from primary school told us we were Fenian scum, and in a probably unconscious echo of Cromwell's words told us to get to hell back to Connacht. They were British, we were Irish.

Things improved slightly when I was sent to secondary school at St Patrick's College in Armagh, ten miles from Portadown (which did not, of course, have a Catholic secondary school). Armagh was a Catholic, nationalist town, and since the school served the archdiocese of Armagh, I was surrounded by boys from South Derry, Tyrone, Fermanagh, and even from across the border, from Dundalk and Dunleer and Ardee. For the first time in my life, I remember feeling that *we* outnumbered *them*, and that it was *our* Ireland. But ... while I learned Irish, played Gaelic football and hurling, and found it easy enough to identify with nationalist Ireland, I could never go the whole hog. Partly it had to do with differing attitudes to the Second World War. Southern Ireland had remained

278

neutral, and I knew Catholic boys from Belfast whose families deliberately left lights burning in skylights during the blackout in the hope that German bombers would spot them. As regards the war, I was firmly pro-British and even more so after seeing those first ghastly newsreels about the liberation of the concentration camps. But mostly my internal complications about nationalism centred on feelings about my parents and their history. A youthful idealism and a love of eloquence in me responded powerfully to the canonical texts of the Republican tradition – to Robert Emmet's speech from the dock in 1803 ('When my country takes her place among the nations of the earth, then, and not till then, let my epitaph be written'); to the proclamation of the Republic in 1916 ('Irishmen and Irishwomen, in the name of God and of the dead generations, Ireland through us summons her children to her flag and strikes for her freedom'); and above all to the graveside oration delivered by Patrick Pearse in 1913 over the body of O'Donovan Rossa: 'They think they have foreseen everything. They think they have foretold everything. But the fools, the fools, the fools! They have left us our Fenian dead, and while Ireland holds these graves, Ireland unfree shall never be at peace!' But these texts, learned lovingly at school, could not be uttered in my home. They would have affronted my parents, who had been driven into exile, in a very real sense, by the ideology which lay behind them. Indeed my father never referred to Patrick Pearse without appending the bitter phrase 'that squinting idiot'. (Pearse had a cast in one eye.)

I think all boys hunger for heroic models. I could find nothing heroic in Ulster Protestantism, save perhaps in the memorials to those killed on the Somme and in Flanders, and I didn't see why these memorials insisted on giving the impression that only *they* had fought there. I found plenty that was heroic in the long nationalist tradition, but my access to that was hampered and thwarted by family *pietas*. Perhaps inevitably – however paradoxically – the simplest solution for me was to go for *English* heroic models, which were, emotionally speaking, uncomplicated. This applied particularly to one Sergeant Matt Braddock, VC, the eponymous hero of a serial story that appeared in the boys' comic, *The Rover*, every week. Strong of chin, blue of eye, Matt Braddock was co-pilot of a Lancaster bomber of the famous Tiger Squadron. Only a sergeant, note – part of the great appeal was Braddock's ordinary background. He wasn't just co-pilot, either: on its bombing missions into Nazi Germany, the plane was attacked usually by thousands of Messerschmitts (their pilots saying over the radio things like 'Jawohl, mein Führer, the English *Schweinhund* will be brought down before Bremen'), and the flak was always most alarming. Matt therefore generally had to fly the plane single-handed – Squadron-Leader Neville 'Tufty' Tufnell having taken some shrapnel over the Ruhr – and navigate it, *and* act as rear gunner, *and* drop the bombs (always spot-on, and always on a factory making tanks for the Waffen SS), and nurse the crippled Lancaster – G for George – back to Lincolnshire before the chip shop closed. I loved it. I had not heard of Dresden. It was all so black and white – Nazi Germany *was* evil, it had to be beaten – and such a relief from the complexities of the home terrain. I think it was the very simplicity of English heroicizing that appealed. Even before I came to Matt Braddock, I had thrilled to the patriotic stanzas in the poems I found printed in Arthur Mee's *Children's Encyclopaedia* (a kind of hand-book of empire), poems like Sir Henry Newbolt's:

> The sand of the desert is sodden red, –
>   Red with the wreck of a square that broke; –
> The Gatling's jammed and the Colonel's dead,
>   And the regiment blind with dust and smoke.
> The river of death has brimmed its banks,
>   And England's far, and Honour a name,
> But the voice of a schoolboy rallies the ranks:
>   'Play up! play up! and play the game!'

I took that imperial England for a heroic dream. I could see no connection between it and the circumstances of my boyhood life. We were not, as it seemed, threatened by British soldiers or gunboats. The threat lay in the flintfaced Calvinism of Stormont, in the Orange bigot ranting his hatred, in the B-Special waving down your bicycle at night with his squat Sten gun.

In his famous essay 'Boys' Weeklies', George Orwell remarks that 'the worst books are often the most important because they are usually the ones that are read earliest in life'. Later in life, when I read English literature at Belfast University, I was to encounter the genuine cultural wealth of one of the world's greatest literatures. 'The gaunt thorns all bent one way as if craving alms of the sun' in *Wuthering Heights*, the district where the young Wordsworth was 'fostered alike by beauty and by fear', the heroic pathos of Milton's Satan ('If thou be'est he, but o! how fallen, how chang'd'), the creamy sensuousness of Hardy's Tess, the laconic effrontery of Jonson's knaves and Shakespeare's Edmund, and so much more, became part of my mental furniture forever. However, I think Orwell has a point. I was an avid reader of public school stories, my favourite being a book called *Teddy Lester and His Chums*. It was prototypical of thousands of pages I read of a similar kind. Teddy Lester himself was superb at all games, and preternaturally fair in competition, but with a disarming weakness at French irregular verbs. Conversely, Ivor ('Bat') Robinson was the school genius, absorbing vast amounts of knowledge through thick spectacles, completely uncoordinated at Rugby football, but with a special talent for bowling devilish googlies. Lord Edward Ponsonby was a real sport, and constantly treated the chums at the tuck-shop with fivers sent him by his 'pater'. And so forth, and so on.

Orwell suggests that the great attraction of the public school ethos lies in its snob appeal, the overall class glamour of the thing. This was not what appealed to me, and I doubt if any Irish boy would have felt that particular attraction – the niceties of the English social register were well beyond us. Mainly, I think, the appeal lay in the notion of codes and rules, especially as those applied to enmity. You might have to fight, that is, but if you did, it would be with boxing gloves in a ring, with a proper referee, and afterwards, hands would be shaken. Even the cads and bounders subscribed to the notion of 'fair play'. In that world, you would not see, with that sickening lurch of the heart, three shadowy figures detach themselves from a wall and saunter towards you, while you realized that your mental navigation – Matt Braddock, where you are? – had let you down and you had blundered into an Orange street. In Teddy Lester's world, you would not get a half brick on the head because you were a 'Papish'.

Orwell describes sardonically the mental world of the public school story. 'You are sitting down to tea in your study on the Remove passage after an exciting game of football won by an odd goal in the last half-minute. There is a cosy fire in the study and outside the wind is whistling. The ivy clusters thickly round the old grey stones. The King is on his throne and the pound is worth a pound. Over in Europe the comic foreigners are jabbering and gesticulating, but the grim grey battleships of the British fleet are steaming up the Channel and at the outposts of Empire the monocled Englishmen are holding the niggers at bay. Lord Mauleverer has just had another fiver and we are all settling down to a tremendous tea of sausages, sardines, crumpets, potted meat, jam and doughnuts. . . . Everything is safe, solid and unquestionable. Everything will be the same forever and ever.'

Exactly. As a boy, I would not have had had worries about the comic foreigners of Europe or the black or yellow peril. But what this England of the mind offered, in its atrocious way, was an image of security so powerful that the rubs of sad experience and the much greater literature I read subsequently could never quite expunge it. Perhaps it was because the Orangeman with the half brick was such an immediate danger; but there was also in that cosy study and that English public school world of *Teddy Lester and His Chums* a more metaphorical kind of security – a security of cultural identity. A complacency, even. Perhaps an arrogance: the English were so obviously the master race that they didn't have to argue about it: they had the effortless superiority of the Balliol man. How I envied that confidence! At a simpler level, the physical comforts were not to be sneezed at: one of the reasons why I enjoyed middle-class English children's fiction – from Enid Blyton's Famous Five Series through Richmal Crompton's William stories, to the works of Arthur Ransome where the girls were called amazing names like Titty – one of the reasons, apart from the fact that William and Co. had to *invent* their enemies, why I enjoyed them so much was that nearly everyone had a bedroom to himself or herself. And tents. And boats. And the church clock stood at 10 to 3 and there was honey still for tea. No world is as timeless as the world of our first reading, especially if that world is itself *deliberately* nostalgic, as I began to see that it was when I graduated to P.G. Wodehouse, in whose work the Drones Club, Blandings Castle, and Mr Mulliner's bar are simply immortal, places out of time.

I had, then, lived quite intensely in various Englands of the mind before I arrived in Oxford, aged twenty-one, to be a graduate student. Perhaps that almost farcically beautiful city is not the best place to begin an encounter with the real England; but so, for me, it was. The first shock to my system was to discover how completely secular a country England was, compared to my own. I remember my first Sunday walking to Mass and wondering where everyone was, until I began to notice various manifestations of the most sacred English religion of today: the Worship of the Car. Everywhere machines were being washed, polished, buffed, hoovered, dusted, adored. Religion in England had dwindled, I saw after a while, to what I might call secular rituals – the weekly car-wash, show-Saturdays, race-meetings, seaside outings, weddings at Whitsun: the secular rituals celebrated so beautifully, yet with such characteristic English agnosticism, in the poetry of Philip Larkin. I perceived this secularism with a kind of contempt; I was sufficiently Irish to consider the worship of material things vulgar. Furthermore, I could see that England had not really excised intolerance: there was no religious intolerance, true, but that was only because religion was a dead duck in England; what there was was plenty of racial intolerance.

The second major shock was to encounter, even in the sacred colleges of Oxford University – or perhaps I should say *especially* in the colleges of Oxford? – condescension and ignorance. The condescension was well meant in the sense that it was friendly, but all the more alarming for being so: one was made to feel like a monkey in the zoo. I would not have minded so much being a monkey in the zoo if I could have felt that the spectators were rather more informed about the monkeys. Precisely because I had lived imaginatively in England I expected (unreasonably?) that the English might have devoted a little thought, a little imagination, to their oldest colony. They hadn't – as was made quite clear in the desperate flailing scramble of the editorial writers to clarify fifty years of total neglect, when the Northern Irish time bomb finally exploded in 1968–69.

The wheel had come full circle. The trials and tribulations of life in Ireland, plus the proximity and sheer bulk of English culture, had helped to turn me into a kind of exile in my own country who responded to versions of Englishness. Living in England, explaining myself, and watching my little province tear itself apart, I found I was driven back on my Irishness.

Perhaps all I have demonstrated are some of the effects of cultural imperialism. Or perhaps it is a more personal, psychological thing –

perhaps I am naturally an exile, or marginal man. But there is more to it than that, I suspect, and I have asked myself: what does it all mean?

There is a famous paradigmatic moment in Joyce's *Portrait of the Artist* where Stephen Dedalus experiences the shadow of imperialism falling across his conversation with an English priest:

> He felt with a smart of dejection that the man to whom he was speaking was a countryman of Ben Jonson. He thought:
>
> The language in which we are speaking is his before it is mine. How different are the words *home, Christ, ale, master*, on his lips and on mine! I cannot speak or write these words without unrest of spirit. His language, so familiar and so foreign, will always be for me an acquired speech. I have not made or accepted its words. My voice holds them at bay. My soul frets in the shadow of his language.

Speaking the English language, listening to the BBC, reading English school stories, considering soccer and cricket superior to Gaelic football and hurling, being more interested in the Battle of Britain than in the Battle of Clontarf, wanting to go to Oxford rather than to University College, Dublin – I might be a perfect specimen of the colonized, if the index of that condition is the degree to which the colonizer's value system is internalized. But how intensely do I feel the 'smart of dejection'? Or, in general terms, how evil *are* the effects of cultural imperialism? To answer that question would require the best efforts of political theorists, sociologists, and anthropologists. Indeed, it may not be possible to give a comprehensive answer. That would be part of my point. For it is certainly easy to dramatize, sentimentalize, and over-generalize about the condition of the colonized.

Thus I can easily sympathize with, even identify with, those Irish writers who seek to restore in their art the consciousness of 'the dispossessed', the consciousness of the Gaelic civilization of Ireland which began to die in the eighteenth century, and which received its mortal wound in the calamity of the Great Famine. My sense of deprivation is there, and it is real, as I recall some of my mother's Irish phrases and turns of speech. But there is also the question of realism. I would agree with the Irish poet Thomas Kinsella's remarks on the vanished Gaelic world: 'The inheritance is mine, but only at two enormous removes – across a century's silence, and through an exchange of worlds.' The broken tradition, the fragmented culture is a reality, and it is only honest (if painful) to accept that this is so. To pretend otherwise, to imagine that the clock can be turned back, is a mistake; and the sterilities (and the dangers) of a strident assertion of the purity of the national identity – 'little Irelandism' – are sufficiently obvious in the island today.

I see now all the faults in my youthful embrace of the simplified stereo-types and clichés of Englishness, which the English manufacture with such facility and export with such success – what might be called 'Master-piece Theatre England' (*Brideshead* and all that) in all its ineffable silli-ness. But I must ask myself: was I wrong to feel that to respond to Eng-land's involvement in World War II with the traditional phrase 'England's difficulty is Ireland's opportunity' was to respond narrowly and myopi-cally? Would I have received a university education if I had not had the benefits of the British university grants system? Was it a bad thing to be opened to English culture and, through it, to the culture of the Anglophone world, whether American or Australian or West Indian? Was it not useful (it was certainly instructive) to grow up even in Northern Ireland, where I learned early the oppression, discrimination, and bigotry which is the fate (at more frightening levels) of so many peoples of the world? Cannot an admiration for Irish cultural traditions coexist with an admission of the relevance of the modern world? I learned many useful things from my encounter with 'Englishness'; and on balance, I would say the benefits outweighed the very real drawbacks: ethnic political resentment is a fact, but so is a sense of cultural enlargement.

I understand the feelings and motivation of those who would insist on the purity, or the purification, of their own cultural traditions. The ho-mogenization of the world – McDonald's in Munich, Coca-Cola in Khar-toum, 'Dallas' in Dublin – is not a pretty sight or a pretty prospect. But I have more faith in the unquenchable, individualizing diversity of cultures, despite the levelling forces at work in our modern world, than those who, even for laudable ends, would erect *cordons sanitaires* around their own ethnicities. And, as the history of the twentieth century shows with depress-ing clarity, cultural nationalism can be a very dangerous force indeed.

A final point. One of the dangers of cultural nationalism is its insistence on the absolute uniqueness of the cultural experience, whether German,

Japanese, Iranian, or Irish. But we who are modern live increasingly in a discontinuous, polyglot world, and what is now clear to me is that the experience described in this essay, of confused loyalties and uncertain identity, is not, as I once thought, aberrant. In a world often politically and culturally disrupted it is an experience which becomes increasingly typical. I end with part of a letter to Herbert Read, written by that great defender of tradition, stability, and continuity, T.S. Eliot:

> I want to write an essay about the point of view of an American who wasn't an American, because he was born in the South and went to school in New England as a small boy with a nigger drawl, but who wasn't a southerner in the South because his people were northerners in a border state and looked down on all southerners and Virginians, and who so was never anything anywhere and who therefore felt himself to be more a Frenchman than an American and more an Englishman than a Frenchman and yet felt that the USA up to a hundred years ago was a family extension. It is almost too difficult even for H[enry] J[ames] who for that matter wasn't an American at all, in that sense.

'Cultural Imperialism: an Irish view', *Yale Review*, 1986

A Christian Brothers Education

DENIS DONOGHUE

Girls: No grand passion occurred to me in their company, though I could feel that they were a different order of reality, and an infinitely higher one, than boys. I recall mainly their names and the opulent lapse of one syllable into another. Camilla, Madge Crawford, Aileen, whose surname I have forgotten, though I recall the colour and sweep of her hair. Isabel Bridges; but that was a different provocation. During my ill year the local authorities laid a new maple floor in the Town Hall and opened it for roller-skating. The air of the hall could not be regarded as fresh, but I was allowed to go skating and soon came to be good at it. So good that I could dance on skates as I never thought of dancing without them. Among the boys, I excelled. The best skater among the girls was Isabel Bridges, a girl who moved, at least on skates, like a queen. I wanted to dance with her, but it was out of the question. Her father was the local manager of the railway and a Protestant, so I could not think of speaking to his daughter. No matter now, but at the time it felt like deprivation. Not that in any formulated sense I disapproved of political or religious divisions. A Protestant was as alien to me as a Muslim, and Muslims had the merit that I didn't know any of them. It did not occur to me not to keep my distance. When we left Warrenpoint in September 1946 and went south, it was a new experience to cease distinguishing between Protestants and Catholics. I continued to know the difference and to deduce that Brian Boydell, say, was a Protestant, or at least not a Catholic. That was what a Protestant was to me. A Protestant was someone who wasn't a Catholic. In the South the distinction was and is a minor matter; it did not affect social life. . . .

There is a passage in the *Enquiry Concerning Political Justice* (1793) in which Godwin attacks the system of national education, on the grounds that it enforces the idea of permanence and unity, encourages a prejudice in favour of 'such tenets as may chance to be established', and tries 'to form all minds upon one model'. I'm not sure whether he had in mind only the British system of education or presumed that every system of national education had the same – or a similar – prejudice. It may be true that every school has an interest in giving its pupils a conviction of permanence: it would be hard to imagine a school founded upon Heraclitean principles of change. And even Heraclitus sought, in the end, some stable principle beyond or behind the irrefutable appearances betokening change. Unity may be another question. It would be possible to imagine a school devoted to the idea of making its pupils at-home in heterogeneity, teaching them to cope with differences and mobility. But I suppose most schools like to think of education as a comprehensive process, featuring at least an ideal unity of experience even if pupils mostly see indications of fragmentation. The division of knowledge into subjects isn't fatal to the inculcation of unity: if you divide something, you imply what you divide and posit it as unity.

In school at the Abbey I was aware of a certain social and political reservation, not in my mind but in the character of the school and the education it provided. The school was comfortable enough within the national system of education; it trained its pupils to sit for the state examinations and eventually for the Senior Leaving Certificate. It was not a private school; the teachers were paid by the State, and obeyed its instructions. On the other hand, the Christian Brothers did not feel any loyalty to Northern Ireland as a political entity. Government of the province was based on the propriety of 'a Protestant parliament for a Protestant people', as its most celebrated Prime Minister described his ideal institution. The Christian Brothers did not encourage us to become rebels, but they recognised that a Catholic growing up in the North must live by a certain stratagem, spiritual secrecy. Everything done in the school was legal, but it was accompanied by the conviction that as Catholics we were by definition Nationalists. Our relation to the government at Stormont in Belfast was bound to be a withholding one, maintained by practising a double consideration. The centre of our universe, as Catholics, was Rome, the Church, its visible head His Holiness the Pope. Our aspirations as Irish boys were most fully articulated by the government in Dublin, even though its writ did not run beyond the Custom Post at Carrickarnon. Our sense of Stormont was therefore ironic. We were entitled to the benefits of British citizenship, a boon we had not chosen, but the Brothers took it for granted that we must enjoy these satisfactions with mental reservations. The Brothers did not expect that we would grow up to kill British soldiers or bomb public houses in Belfast, but they encouraged us to be spiritually and silently insurgent.

The teaching of Irish and of Irish history provided the richest occasions of this practice. Irish was a fully recognised subject in the official curriculum, though in practice it was taught mainly in Catholic schools. Learning Irish was therefore a sign that one's kingdom was not of the Protestant, Unionist world; we lived elsewhere. That Irish and English were such different languages was a further token of spiritual secrecy: to speak Irish, it is necessary to speak differently, as if we were speaking French or Spanish; different pronunciation, intonation, cadence. It also entailed respecting and maintaining a form of social continuity which the British Empire and the Irish Famine of the 1840s had nearly ended. Under the Penal Laws in the eighteenth century, the Irish language was nearly defeated; it sustained itself only in remote communities along the Western seaboard. After the Famine, surviving parents knew that their children would have to leave the country or starve; and that if they left, they would have to speak English in their new countries: America, Canada, Australia. Besides, Irish was now associated with misery and defeat, the mark of a dejected people. In the middle years of the nineteenth century the British government did not have to destroy the language; it was already beaten. In the twentieth century those teachers who wanted to recover the Irish language taught it as a sacred trust, a difficult language, since its grammar and spelling were erratic and it existed in three main dialects. In Newry we learned the Irish of Ulster and spent a month in the summer speaking it and listening to it in Donegal.

Rannafast was the village in Donegal to which we were sent: it was and is a barren landscape, a stony place except for a few houses which survive largely upon the college. Every summer, hundreds of schoolchildren attend Coláiste Bhríghde, St Brigid's College, taking classes in Irish language and literature. They live in the houses of native families where Irish is the spoken vernacular. It is doubtful whether the language can sustain itself against the force of television and transistor radios: in principle, these villages in Donegal (or rather in the Donegal Gaeltacht, where Irish is the daily language, as distinct from the Galltacht, where English is spoken) are supposed to be protected communities. The Irish government gives the villagers money, grants for improving their houses and services, in the hope of keeping them in Donegal, Connemara, and Kerry, where they provide at least a residual context for Irish as a spoken language. But the lure of foreign places is keen. The next generation will probably leave these communities and find jobs in Dublin or abroad. But in my time Rannafast was still a genuine Gaeltacht, and to some extent it still is. The college provided formal classes and entertainment in the evenings. When I was a student there, I went round to the houses where the best storytellers, the breed of *seanchaidhe*, were known to live, and transcribed their stories into my copybook. Irish was one of my best subjects, the supreme moment of my achievement in it being the speech I gave, at an *Oireachtas* in Dublin, as representative of the North.

from *Warrenpoint*, 1991

The Procession

PEADAR O'DONNELL

Well, it was all fixed at last. The procession would come into Derrymore that day, and you never saw a morning break so clear-eyed out of mixed weather. There wasn't a wisp of mist anywhere around Slieve Gorm. The sky dripped its healthy blue down into the sunshine until puddles of blue shadow overflowed from hollows on the hillside. A light breeze toyed with shiftless patches of smoke. Rain was not far away, nor was storm, but the day would have all the more sparkle for being a pet.

The splendour of the day was not welcomed in Derrymore for it had been their one hope that rain might come to their rescue at the last moment. But now that ray was withered, and recklessness lashed out in the whistle of a youth here and there setting out to his work. Women whispering among themselves wondered if anything except prayer could have brought a day like this for the procession. As the morning increased in splendour a sense of unreality grew up in people's minds. Could it be that the whole parish was coming in to sing hymns around Phil Timony's? In dry and sober daylight grown-up men and women singing hymns around a neighbour's house. . . .

The first stir of anything alive within the Townland itself came from Mary McFadden; she came outside to feed the hens, wearing her Sunday neck shawl and black skirt. That little movement around McFadden's was like the stirring of a curtain when an audience is anxiously waiting.

But it was more than a mere sign that something was coming, it was one hint to the Townland how to behave. Women withdrew hastily and tidied their hair, giving themselves something of the appearance that was expected of them on a Sunday evening around their own houses; nothing so noticeable as Mary McFadden's dress, but still a touch of trigness, leaning them towards the procession; after all they were not heathens either.

And just when this setting for what was to come seemed wise, Nora Dan put a ladder against a gable and went up it to whitewash. This was war. There was no doubt in anybody's mind but that this was an open act of war against the whole procession. Ann Melly saw Nora Boyle on the ladder, an old check apron tied around her head, coarse sacking over an old skirt and a great heavy pair of brogues on her feet. Yonder was Mary McFadden walking about her own green in the clothes of a Sunday evening, and she wasn't even knitting, and now here was Nora Dan; this would tear the Townland in two. Women yawned nervously.

It was easier for the men. They were at their own work and nobody would put any heed on how they were dressed. Donal Breslin was walking around the bull like a man getting his first sight of a strange animal, but every now and then he would stop and look around, making a great show of perplexity. Nobody was in the least taken in, and anyway it was fine to have him there for all the neighbours need do is keep an eye on him and they would know when anything came into view on the road below. Denis Melly was drawing thatch. Briany McFadden was planting early potatoes. The whole Townland was subdued, soundless, uneasy.

Ann Melly stole up along a hedge to get within talking distance of Nora Dan. Nora saw her and tucked back the head-wrap to bare an ear.

'The devil is in you, Nora. Didn't we all agree to stay inside and take no side at all. Did Dan put you up to this in the end?'

'He did not,' Nora said, 'but it got into my own head this morning that if a woman's man is in a thing and she believes in it, the least she can do is to show the whole world what's in her mind. And if they come within reach of my whitewash brush I'll brighten their body more than all this play-acting will brighten their souls.'

'It would be better to stay inside,' Ann urged. 'It's not goin' to attack him they are, only to sing hymns and pray. It will look like we are all against you, if you do a thing like this by yourself.'

'Well, I got fair mad this morning when I got outside and looked around at us all. I got fair mad.'

'Aren't you the bully, Nora; it's what I'm all of a tremble,' Ann said. 'If I saw them coming up the road and me up there, I'd spill down off the ladder.'

Nora laughed, and then suddenly she jerked her head to look down the road. Ann Melly got up on a chair. Donal Breslin was up on a hillock running a few steps this way and that, undecided what to do with the news of what he was seeing. Ann Melly saw the tip of a banner, and then came the suffocating boom of a drum.

'Come down, Nora, come down,' Ann pleaded. And she ran for the shelter of her own house; the children might be frightened if they were left alone. From her own doorway she saw women race here and there, darting in short runs from point to point, snatching toddlers and carrying them inside. The drum was crushing tighter now and the flutes could be heard. They were playing ''Tis Heaven is the Prize'.

The procession came into view. Right in front marched John James Michael, his great expanse of rounded collar flashing in the sunlight to catch the eye more than the banner. Behind John James Michael walked four nuns, the white border to their pale faces glistening like a halo. Next to them marched the young ladies of The Town, all in white and wearing their Child of Mary medals on blue ribbons. School children followed – hundreds of them, drawn from all the schools around The Town. And then men and women. At the gate of Derrymore School there was a pause, while the children trooped out and took their place in the procession.

The pouring of their own children into the procession was something the Townland had not expected. The sight drew women from byre doors, the shelter of stacks and the inside of cottages. This very fact of their children being out there behind the banner with John James Michael and the nuns and the drums was in itself a kind of an absolution for them all. The Townland was not being attacked; all morning it had seemed as though they were all more or less under the lash. People came out openly on their own streets, women grumbling; mock grumbles that their children were not dressed for a display like this.

The drum ceased and John James Michael, walking backwards on the road and beating time with both arms, began 'I am a Little Catholic'. There were some fine voices among the girls from The Town. John James Michael had a good voice. But above all there was Smullen. Nature plants beauty in strange places, and people often wondered that such a voice should have been installed in a beer-swollen mound like Smullen. Anyway, there it was and the day was touched by its loveliness. Timony's house across the way, with its darkened walls and stumpy chimneys, looked drab and guilty all of a sudden.

Briany's field was wired off so the procession must approach Timony's across Donal Breslin's meadow; the laneway was only a water track. Donal Breslin, concealed between two cocks of hay, saw John James Michael motion the procession into his field. Andy the Post and one of the Garveys' shopboys, carrying the banner, entered first. Donal himself had helped to carry that banner to Land League meetings more than once. He couldn't make out which side of the banner was facing him; Wolfe Tone most likely. St Patrick would be looking down on the hymns and Wolfe Tone on Timony's. But Donal's mind didn't delay long on this. It had never entered his head that the procession might cross his land. The thing was would the Boyles blame him – would this be taking sides? It was all Briany's fault. If Briany had only given a hint what he had in mind putting up the wire. Briany was a botheration these days the way he was keeping his mind hidden. And the Boyles were hasty. As like as not the Boyles would blame him. Donal sweated standing there in his own garden.

The word that would go out would be, that Briany McFadden had shut them out but that Donal Breslin left his field open. The worst thing that could happen to any man would be to have the hungry beagles below in The Town on his side and have the neighbours against him. Donal got down on his hands and knees and made his way to the garden gate, sneaked back the bolt gently and let out the bull.

The procession was moving very slowly now. That low, thatched cottage, dark of wall, stumpy of chimney, cowering on the edge of the river just where the waterfall churned short-lifed bubbles, it was round that they must circle, sing their hymns and pray their prayers. Maybe John James Michael would curse him. The procession was tense with the sense of the threat it carried. In front of them St Patrick's face glistened in the sun, and his foot was on the neck of the snake. 'Hail, Glorious St Patrick.' What other hymn could you sing at a time like that?

Nobody noticed the bull, and the bull didn't lift an eye to the procession. He slunk along the broom hedge, drawn by a memory of a sweet moment recently snatched among Donal's cabbage plants. His grey-tinted back did not show against the grey broom rods. Maybe, it was the drum did the harm. The memory of the stolen moments snapped and a flash of annoyance swung the sniffing head into the clear air. The bull saw Wolfe Tone. And the bull let out a bellow.

Everybody agreed afterwards that it was a terrible roar. What was clear just then was, that the procession couldn't be in a worse fix to meet a bull. John James Michael and the nuns were behind the banner. They had reached a point where they should halt to let the procession swing to the right and left so that one vast chain might move forward to close around the devil-possessed cottage. For a second nobody thought it was a real bull. Even Andy the Post, that should have known better, had blessed himself before he could gather his wits. And then he flung the pole from him and ran.

The crash of the banner ripped the procession into screeching, racing confusion. School children, who had been in the lead, flung themselves back panic-stricken on the adults behind. Only the nuns stood their ground. Holding each other's hands, with somewhat of the courage of the gentle Christian martyrs, they stood trembling. And the bull, really incensed now, came for them bellowing.

Everybody's eye had been so much on the bull that Phil Timony and Dan Doyle had not been noticed as they dashed out of the store and tore along the hedge. It was only when Phil Timony burst into view through a gap, his bellow ringing above the bull's, that everybody's breath really tightened. It was a near thing. Phil's coat swept down on the bull's horns only when it seemed nothing could save the now fluttering sisters. When Phil Timony brought the enraged beast to his knees Dan Boyle was at his side.

For a space there wasn't a sound anywhere. And then Briany McFadden's voice rose in a crash of laughter, real laughter, crammed with joy and exultation. He lay against the hedge and banged round him with a cudgel he had snatched up. And Phil Timony found breath to spare to join Briany. All Derrymore found its lungs. Their laughter rose into cheers. Children, escaping from the tension of their scare, only knew that they too must make noise, and joined in the cheering.

from *On the Edge of the Stream*, 1934

MOVING HOUSE

MICHAEL MCLAVERTY

A week before the Easter holidays the fellows went around swaggering and pulling out everyone's tie. In the breaks between the classes they began singing:

> This day fortnight where will we be,
> Out of the gates of misery. . . .

Colm didn't join much in the jollity. Day after day he waited longingly for a letter with money to take him home. And then three days before the break-up he almost gave up hope. He had heard of fellows who had stayed on in the College for the Easter holidays, their parents wanting to save expense, and the fellows pretending that they'd rather stay than go home. He would have to make some excuse to Chit and Millar. But the arrival of a letter on the day before the holidays dissolved all his fears.

It was from his mother. He read it over and over again with a mixture of joy and sorrow; they were all leaving the island for Belfast: Alec had got his job back in the bakery, and, as Theresa couldn't get off, he would call for Colm to get the house ready. He put the letter in his pocket. It was the end of being a boarder anyway. He kicked a pebble going round the track, and when Chit and Millar saw him approach they shouted, 'Here comes the good MacNeill.' Colm stopped, pulled out their ties, and raced with joy round the track with Chit and Millar chasing him.

The next day Alec came for him and together they went in the tram to their new house. It was in the middle of a street of little red-bricked houses. There were two bedrooms, and downstairs a kitchen and a parlour. When they opened the back door they looked out upon a large stretch of waste ground: clothes-lines hung here and there; hens moved about; and boys were playing football, bundles of coats marking the goalposts. Opposite was a long black paling enclosing private grounds ringed with trees, and on the paling someone had scrawled in white letters, UP THE REBELS; REMEMBER 1916. At the top of the street were the brickyard and brickfields, and beyond that again more fields straggling up to the foot of a mountain. The mountain was so close they could see a few scattered houses at its foot and cattle in the fields.

Alec made up his mind to take Colm and Jamesy over the mountain and show them Lough Neagh, Belfast with its long tongue of a lough, and if the day was clear they'd see the hills of Galloway in Scotland. But Colm was disappointed when he was told that they wouldn't be able to see Knocklayde.

When they came in Colm wandered about the bare house. The walls were dotted with nails and where pictures had hung were square marks like sunlight. Between the floor boards match-heads and candle grease were stuck and in one place Colm saw a half-penny. He tried to lift it out with a pin, then he pulled the boards apart to get his fingers between them. His two fingers were on it when it slipped and fell. He got up from his knees. From the bedroom window he watched the boys playing football, and heard them shouting, 'Our out!' whenever the ball hit the paling.

Downstairs Alec was whistling and it sounded loud and deafening in the empty house. A cockroach raced across the red tiles towards the coalhouse and Alec cracked it with his boot: 'I hope there's not many of them boyos about. The smell of them would knock you down.'

They went out together, Alec to the station to collect the things they had taken from the island, Colm to Smithfield where Alec had bought secondhand furniture. Later in the evening they would both go to meet their mother, Jamesy, and Clare.

At Smithfield Colm helped the man to lift the furniture on to the empty coal-van: a yellow arm-chair, a black sofa with a spring bulging out of the bottom, a little bamboo table, a chest of drawers, and a deal table. When it was all safely on top, the man sat on the arm-chair in front of the van, reins in hand and a cigarette in his mouth. Colm sat at the back, one hand holding the bamboo table. They set off along King Street and turned on to the Falls Road. Boys at street corners laughed and joked at the man driving from the arm-chair. At Hughes and Dickson's Flour Mill Colm saw, through an open door, steel hand-rails and a man naked to the waist feeding a furnace, but when he raised his eyes to the top of the high building his head got dizzy, and he turned his head away until the cart had passed. All the narrow cobbled streets were filled with playing children. A man was writing on a shop window: EGGS DOWN AGAIN. In a doorway a woman with a shawl over her head blew her nose in the tail of her skirt. A tram passed with a little boy clinging on to the lamp.

When the mill horns screeched loudly girls in their bare feet and black slips with scissors dangling from a strap came flowing out of the doors. They were pale-faced and there was a smell of tow and oil off them. The driver winked at them and they shouted back. Then four girls passed linked together, swinging their tea-cans and laughing.

'Aw, Lizzie, luck at Lord Alphonsus!'

'Hello, daughters,' answered the driver. 'Do you want a lift?'

The driver slowed down and Colm blushed when he saw the four mill-doffers running towards the back of the van. They hopped up, two to each side of him, their faces smeared with dirt and pouse in their hair.

'All aboard, ladies . . . Gee up, Suzina!' the driver shouts at the horse, cocking his cap to the side of his head, and holding the whip as straight as a flag-pole.

'That's a quare nice wee fella!' says one of the girls.

'Are you the Duke's son?' says another, and snuffled loudly.

Colm didn't answer and the cart rattled and bumped over the hard road.

'Is that yer da?' says another.

'Ah, Mary, lave him alone; he's my boy. Aren't you, dearie?'

At that moment one of the wheels came off and girls, furniture, and all slid off in a bundle on to the road. Fellows cheered. But when the trams came up and clanged their bells for the cart to move off, and it on its three wheels, Colm was so ashamed that he stood afar off pretending that he didn't belong to the annoyance.

He was glad when he was back in his own street again. They were waiting for Alec to come with the key when a young boy offered to get his mother's key to open the door. He called himself John Burns. He helped to carry in the furniture and later brought Colm up to his house where his mother gave him a mug of tea and a bap.

When Alec arrived with the island furniture Colm had a few boys around him. They helped to carry in the pictures, the rolled-up mattresses, his mother's sewing-machine, a crock filled with delph, a wooden trunk, a statue of the Sacred Heart in a glass cover, and a few odds and ends.

Later they went to the station. The evening still held its light when the train came in.

Standing outside the ticket-barrier they saw their mother approach in a black plush coat and black hat, Clare holding on to her hand, and behind them Jamesy in grey knickerbockers and Rover on a rope jumping round him.

Alec and Colm had great welcome for them, and they passed out of the station, Jamesy and Colm together and the dog licking them and tossing its head with delight.

'He knows him, mother. Look, mother, he knows Colm!'

'He'd be a stupid dog if he didn't,' said Alec.

The noise of the city traffic made the dog squirm with fright, and Jamesy lifted him in his arms as they went into a tram and sat downstairs. The boys talked loudly and the people stared at them. They exchanged news, Colm of the street and Jamesy about the island, Uncle Robert, Paddy John Beg, and Father Byrne. Rover put his nose under Jamesy's coat and Clare held tightly to the seat of the tram.

Back in the house it was dark; Alec hadn't remembered to go down to the Gas Office to have the gas turned on and they had to move about by candle light and pin newspapers across the bare windows to keep the neighbours from looking in. It was chilly, and to take the frost out of the air and to boil the kettle Alec lit a fire of sticks and old felt that he had found in the bin.

They had to sleep on the mattresses on the floor and Rover was put into the yard, but he whined and barked so much that the mother came into the boys' room: 'Do you hear Rover, Alec? He's breaking his heart.'

As they listened, a man pushed down a window and shouted, 'Take in that dog to hell out o' that.'

Then a woman yelled, 'Take in your neb and let the poor people get into the house in peace!'

Alec stood at the window and was about to pull it down when his mother caught him by the arm, 'Don't say anything, Alec. God only knows what kind of neighbours we've got. Just let Rover in for the one night; he finds the place strange, poor fellow.'

When the dog got in he raced up the stairs and across the bed on the floor, whining and mad with joy. Colm and Jamesy covered themselves up with the clothes, shuddering with delight as the dog ran over the humped blankets. He licked their faces and Colm hugged him and then Jamesy hugged him saying,

'Aw, let him sleep between us!'

'Let him sleep between us!' shouted Alec from the head of the bed. 'D'ye want to have the bed a nest of fleas? He's lucky to get into the house itself without yez making an hotel for him.'

And in the darkness each would whisper to the dog and Rover would sniff at the corners of the blankets, Colm putting out a finger to feel the wet nose. Alec shouted to the dog to lie down and at last he went to a corner of the room and lay on a few newspapers.

When all was still again Colm stretched out his hand quietly and Rover sniffed at it and ran over the blankets.

'Now who's eggin' on that dog?' said Alec. 'It's you, Colm. . . . Lie down there, Rover, and don't budge or out you and Colm will go to the yard.'

There was peace after that and listening now to the groan of the last trams racing for the depot they fell into a deep sleep.

from *Call My Brother Back*, 1939

THE SHOP

JOHN O'CONNOR

The boys followed the score out, and got back to the Corner about 5 o'clock. A few old men were standing up against the Dining Room wall, smoking. Pachy and Johnny Kelly were standing with them, and down at their door was Johnny Kelly's donkey and cart. The donkey was munching hungrily at an armful of hay strewn on the ground.

'Hello, Pachy,' Neilly greeted, 'we were down at the score there.'

'Ah, were you? Where's the banty?'

'Who? Shemie?' Neilly glanced around him. 'I dunno. He must be round at the Bridge Wall.'

Pachy turned to the bullet men.

'Well, who won all the money?' he asked.

An argument then started up regarding the shots which had been played. Tommy Kelly, the losing man's marker, pointed out that, if his man had played the shots properly, the way he had shown, the score would have been a walk-over. He put his hands out, and began to illustrate his point.

'Now that shot from the pole on top of the hill –?'

The rest of the fellows tightened their lips at each other.

'Ah, now –' Neilly, too, smiled up at Pachy, anxious to share in their ironic tolerance. Just then he noticed the Preacher and the two other boys he had met, coming down along the Mill Yard wall. As the Preacher crossed over, he dropped again into his long, menacing stride, and lifted his hands, pointing out his forefingers.

'Don't make a move,' he called. 'You're covered!'

'Well, well,' said Pachy, 'by the blinking left! Look who's here. Buck Jones himself.'

'I ain't Buck Jones, pardner,' the Preacher snarled. 'I bumped that guy off weeks ago.'

The fellows laughed.

'Well, well, well,' Pachy mused. 'So poor old Buck Jones has bit the dust. What did you bump off a decent guy like that for? I hear Billy the

Kid's on the trail looking for the guy that done it.'

The Preacher made another lightning draw, and backed a few paces, his eyes glancing quickly from side to side.

'The Kid,' he grated, 'so the Kid's in town, eh? I'll give him to sundown to hit the trail. After that, there's liable to be a lot of lead flying around.'

He let out a shout, and galloped off down the Row, slapping his hand against his hip.

'Sundown! I'll give him to sundown.'

Pachy turned and laughed.

'Why don't you jump on your horse like that, Neilly, and away down and lift us a few old Woodbines? I'm choking for a draw.'

'What? Pinch them?'

'What d'you mean, pinch them? You don't think that Tom Mix there would ask a question like that, d'you? Throw your leg over your horse there.'

Neilly hesitated, torn between his desire to please Pachy and the natural prickings of his conscience.

'I was at Confession the day,' he demurred. 'Only for that –'

'Ah, what harm is there in a mingy Woodbine? Shemie would go if he was here. Where's Shemie? He'll go. Christ the night! A poor pal you're turning out to be.'

Neilly hesitated for a few moments longer. Then he cantered off uneasily.

'Tell Kitty they're for Ken Maynard, if she sees you,' Pachy called after him.

Some of the fellows smiled and shook their heads.

'You'll have Kitty out on the warpath. Wait'll you see, he'll be caught.'

Pachy watched Neilly disappear into the shop. He laughed again, but did not speak. About two minutes passed, and Neilly came shooting out again.

'Ah, good man,' said Pachy, 'here he is.'

But the next moment Kitty appeared in the doorway and shouted after him.

Neilly stopped, and the fellows saw him gaze despairingly up at them. Then, his mother called again: 'Neilly, I want you. Come back here this minute.' He turned and was hauled back into the house by the butt of the ear.

The fellows all began to move about very self-consciously, clearing their throats noisily and scraping their hands together.

'Why didn't he come on up?' said Pachy. 'The wee fool. He's destroyed now.'

'Why don't you go for a nice dander down the road, Pachy?' some wit suggested. 'God bless us, a lovely evening like that.'

But Pachy was unruffled.

'No-o-o! What do I want to go down the road for a walk for? I've been walking all day.'

At that moment Kitty reappeared in the doorway and shook her fist up.

'It's a wonder you aren't ashamed of yourself, sending the childer down to stale cigarettes. I'll get the police,' she called.

Pachy cast his eyes up.

'Ah, bould Kate there!'

Kitty withdrew again, and Pachy shrugged his shoulders.

'Well, I suppose I'd better go on down and see what all the blinking shouting's about. Kate takes these notions sometimes, you know.'

He stuck his hands in his pockets and sauntered down whistling, into the shop. Kitty came to meet him in the hall.

'Is this a new trick now? Well, a nice fellow you're turning out to be. For two pins I wouldn't think much of putting my coat on and getting you lifted. If this is all you're ever going to do with yourself –'

Pachy pursed up his lips, and juking through the curtains he saw Teasie sitting on the sofa. Malachey was leaning against the mantelpiece in his shirt sleeves, smoking. Pachy breathed a sigh of relief. He gave an innocent smile.

'Why, what's wrong? What's the matter?' He came on into the kitchen. 'Hello, Teress, you're a bit of a stranger. How's the old woman? – Malachey!'

Malachey tightened his lips at him, and shook his head. His expression said: 'Well, you've done it now. The fat's in the fire this time.'

The two packets of Woodbines were lying on the counter, and over by the window Neilly was standing, snuffling.

'What's up?' Pachy asked again. 'What's all the narration about?'

'Ah, now,' Kitty sighed, 'God help us! God help us. That's all I can say. When you have to send a young, innocent child down, to stale cigarettes for you, well – God help us! That's all I can say.'

Pachy rocked back on his heels, to and fro, gently.

'I'm afraid you've got things a wee bit mixed up, Kate. Neilly, did I send you down here to stale cigarettes?'

Neilly looked at him with his left eye covered by his fist.

'What did I say?' Pachy asked him. 'Who did I say they were for?'

Neilly hesitated.

'You said you wanted them for Ku – Ken Maynard.'

Pachy looked around him and spread his hands out.

'Well, what harm was there in that? I only asked him to jump on his horse and bring us up a loc of cigarettes. I didn't mean him to pinch them.'

'Well, there he stands,' Kitty said, shortly. 'And now he won't be able to go near the Altar in the morning. That's the Confession for you, and all about it.'

'Ah, sure let him say a good Act of Contrition, and God won't say another word about it. Sure he didn't mean anything. He only picked me up the wrong way.' Pachy moved over, and rubbed his hands over Neilly's head. 'Ah, he's not a bad fellow. The only kid in the house! What are you? Ha-ha! The only kid in the house!' He looked over at Malachey. 'Believe there was a good score there the day, Malachey. You didn't go? Blinking fool you, you might have lifted a few bob. How's Tommy keeping, Teasie? I haven't seen him for a couple of days.'

Teasie recrossed her legs.

'Aye, Tommy!'

Pachy moved out round the counter again.

'Coming up to the Corner, Malachey? Get on your coat there, man dear.' He reached over towards the cigarettes. 'Can you spare these, Kate? I'll bring you in an old rooster when it gets dark.'

Kitty went over and pulled the drawer open.

'Where's Kelly? Is he up there?' She threw out another two packets. 'I suppose he hasn't a butt either. Don't you be going too far now, Malachey, the tay'll soon be ready.'

'Aye, right,' Malachey grunted.

'Well, cheerio, Teasie. Tell the old woman I'll be over for a drink of her aleplant one of these days. Cheerio, Kate.'

'Aye, cheerio! Cheerio!'

'Cheerio!' Kitty repeated when they had gone. 'Cheerio, aye! That's the quare playboy for you! What in under God would you do with a fellow like that at all? I'm sick, sore and tired trying to talk some sense into him. But ah-h-h – I wish to God he'd stayed in the Army.'

'Ah, poor Pachy,' Teasie smiled. 'How do they knock it out at all? Him and that Kelly fellow and his ould donkey and cart and his rags and his jam pots. I feel it a great pity sometimes for Johnny Kelly. He's lost over in that ould barrack ever since poor Annie died, God rest her.'

'Annie was good to Johnny,' Kitty murmured.

'There must have been a brave squad of them Kellys. Is the other girl of them still living in England? There were only the two sisters, weren't there?'

'Aye! Eileen's getting on well over there, I believe. Her man is a manager of some big place. She sent Johnny his fare over, many's a time, but, heh – you can guess the way it went – there, where are you off to?'

Neilly was caught in the act of trying to edge round the counter. Kitty waggled her finger at him.

'Come on. In! In! Not another foot you'll stir outside that door the day. Sit down there and learn your Catechism, it'll answer you better. How you're going to kneel down at the Altar in the morning I do not know. Where's that other wee ottercop?'

'I dunno where he is.'

'You dunno where he is! You dunno nothing! I wish to God I had let you run on to the pictures, away from about the place.'

'Ah, let him alone, God help him,' Teasie interceded. 'He's only a child yet.'

'A quare child! He's big and ugly enough to know what staling is.' Neilly began to sob softly again. 'Are you starting again?' Kitty demanded, threateningly. 'Have done now, this minute, this very minute, or I'm telling you I'll give you something to cry for. God's truth, I think you got off very lightly indeed. Let me see you sitting down there now with your Catechism and – don't wipe your nose on the sleeve of your jersey. God bless us, but I hate to see anybody doing that. Where's your handkerchief?'

Teasie held her own out to him.

'Here, son, don't cry now, like a good boy. Ah, Lord, Kitty, you're too hard on them sometimes. That's the boy! Don't be crying now, sure there's nothing to cry about.'

Neilly went sniffling into the room and brought his school bag out.

'Well, look here,' said Kitty, glancing up at the clock, 'you can go out for half-an-hour, no more. Be back here at 6 o'clock.'

Neilly wiped his fingers across his eyes and hiccupped gently. Without speaking, he walked through the curtains round the counter.

'Six o'clock, mind you,' Kitty called after him. She raised her voice. 'And keep away from that Pachy fellow.'

Teasie rose up.

'Well, I'll have to be going now myself, Kitty.' Her lips moved bitterly. 'If I stay any longer that'll be another fault.'

'Well, mind now what I said,' Kitty advised. 'I know the old woman is hard to put up with at times, but sure she's the best in the world really. Sure I wouldn't take under my notice anything she says, that's only her way of going on. That woman couldn't live if she hadn't someone to fight and argue with.'

'Ach, I know, Kitty, I know. I've got nothing against the ould doll. That's only her nature, I know. It's Tommy I blame. Lord God, we all know how good his mother is to him – Oh, the sun rises and sets on Tommy – but, after all, I'm his wife, and he should think of my position once in a while. He could put an end to it all, you know, this very minute himself, if he'd say, "Well, look now, mother, I've married Teasie, and here she is, either for good or for ill, that remains to be seen, so why not try and make the best of it, and not be always bickering and –" But instead of that, he encourages her. Oh, maybe not on purpose! But he takes her part always, and you see, well, that makes her worse. Any argument that gets started – I'm the one who started it, and who the hell do I think I am, talking to his mother like that? His mother, his mother all the time. I'm telling you, Kitty, if it wasn't for the child I wouldn't stick it any longer. I – Who in the name o' God's that?'

A series of sharp kicks was suddenly delivered against the front door. Kitty opened it, and a little girl stumbled into the hall. She held up a penny in her grimy fist.

'A happorth o' sweets and a happenny back,' she chanted.

Kitty came back round the counter.

'What kind of sweets, daughter? Caramels?'

The child nodded gravely.

'A happorth o' caramels and a happenny back.'

Kitty put five caramels into a small paper bag and reached them over the counter. The little girl took them and held up her penny. 'And a happenny back.'

Teasie and Kitty followed her to the door, laughing.

They stood together for a few moments. Teasie was just about to move away, when a terrible outburst of crying suddenly sounded from up at the Corner. As they looked up, a young boy came round in the Row, hurrying through the crowd of fellows, howling piteously.

'Sacred Heart of Jesus!' Kitty exclaimed. 'It's Shemie. He's fallen into the river again.'

They heard Malachey call out to him, as his father recovered from his astonishment, but Shemie came tottering on heedlessly, roaring at the top of his voice, and the water running out of him.

Malachey, Pachy and Neilly started after him, and here and there along both sides of the Row, heads popped out over the half-doors. Old women clicked their tongues and murmured their sympathy as Shemie passed.

'Ah, God help him, he's drownded. Hurry on home, son, quick.'

'Bring him down, Malachey,' Kitty called, 'bring him on down. Jesus, Mary and St Joseph, that young fellow will be drownded yet. That's the third time this month. Now you see what I have to put up with, Teasie. What unlucky prayer was hanging round my head this day, that I didn't send them off to the pictures when I had the chance. Come on, come on! If I wouldn't be better off handcuffed to a ghost it's a quare thing to me.'

from *Come Day – Go Day*, 1948

THE BOYS OF SANDY ROW

ROBERT HARBINSON

'No Pope here', 'Not an inch', 'God save the King', and 'Remember 1690' were signs we saw every day. They appeared in huge permanently painted letters on the gable ends of the streets round about. Although our street lay midway between Falls Road, the centre of everything Catholic in Belfast, and Sandy Row, the strongest Orange quarter, we were staunchly Protestant. Even ruder slogans against His Holiness decorated some gables; together with elaborate paintings, some twenty feet or more high, of coronation scenes complete with flowering robes, regalia, and recognizable portraits of King George V and Queen Mary. The crossing of Boyne Water by King Billy, with flying banners and flashing swords, was, however, the favourite topic for these vast outdoor murals.

We had a mural too in the backyard of our house, but only a painted crown on the whitewash under the window-sill. Higher up, only just visible, remained the fragments of King Billy's charger, the open Bible, a lurid eye through the clouds, Jacob's ladder, the rainbow, and Noah's ark, painted years before by my father while in a mood of patriotism. Whatever they represented religiously and politically, the pictures added a dash of colour and life to the drab mien of the streets.

We tried to reckon how much an ordinary Mickey would have to pay at confession for a week's sins. It was our firm belief that every sin had to be paid for in hard cash, and that was why so many Catholics were publicans – unlike so many others their tills were always full of cash.

For one particular crime we could never forgive the Mickeys; their hatred of the Bible. All Catholics were under orders, we were told, to burn any scripture they found, especially New Testaments. The old song supported us,

> The intriguing Paypishes surround this loyal and ancient town
> They tried you know not long ago to pull the Bible down
> And to destroy it root and branch they often have combined
> But from Sandy Row we made them fly like chaff before the wind.

What pride we enjoyed for living so near to Sandy Row – the Boys of Sandy Row, stalwarts of our Orange Order.

We imagined also that newly dead popes were embalmed like Takabuti in the museum, and then put on display as human money-boxes; and that when they were stuffed so full that not another penny would go in, they were canonized and became saints.

Takabuti, the Egyptian mummy, a house-mistress of a priest of Amunre, reclined in a case at the museum not altogether without a vestige of former dignity. She could never have imagined, three thousand years before, the tiny faces that would press so often against the glass of her exhibition table. Her hair and teeth, whole though shrivelled and discoloured, and her delicate foot complete with flesh and toenails, attracted as much attention as perhaps they had so long ago. Certainly the priest of Amunre could not have paid her more attention than we did. However, much as we loved Takabuti and her wimple of blue beads, other kinds of priests occupied our minds – those of Rome.

Crowding out any other aspects of history, our schools dinned into us over and over again the Protestant story. On leaving school, and that none too early for my liking, I had no notion of the world's past other than a few prehistoric tales and dreary details concerning our Protestant faith and the unrelieved darkness of Rome. The particular rack on which they tortured us appeared in the form of a small, buff covered booklet entitled *How we differ from Rome.*

With what surprising, singeing pains my hands and fingers often smarted when a can or strap was administered because on being asked 'How does Pope Honorius, writing in 1221, refer to the entry of the English into Ireland?' I could not furnish the correct answer. 'Pope Honorius states that "the English entered Ireland by the authority of the Apostolic See and made it obedient to the Church of Rome".' Really! No excuse could be offered, they told me so frequently, probably every day, certainly every week; I had no reason, on being asked to 'Quote from Pope Adrian's letter to Henry II', for failing to report that 'Pope Adrian states: "While as a Catholic prince you intend to widen the bounds of the Church we are anxious to introduce a faithful plantation in that land" (of Ireland).' The complete horrid booklet had to be learnt by heart, before we could be upgraded to commit the Prayer Book catechism to memory, and finally present ourselves, suitably primed, for confirmation.

This picture appears black, but a lighter side did exist, a comic-relief provided by intimate details of the popes' private lives. Before we tumbled out of our cradles, we knew of the unspeakable behaviour by the pontiffs and their courts. The goings-on of the Borgias were as familiar as the affairs of the next-door neighbour.

Even proper history books, we were assured, disclosed the antics at the papal court, with Roman strumpets running round and burning their bare bottoms on the great lighted candles of the Vatican. Nuns undergoing initiation were sometimes forced to play the part of these naked shepherdesses – until too old for orgies. Then they were given the flowing habits to cover up the singe marks on their buttocks and legs, and sent back to Ireland or wherever they came from. No wonder our preachers referred in horror to Rome as the Scarlet Woman! And little wonder amongst our first nursery rhymes was,

If I had a penny
Do you know what I would do?
I would buy a rope
And hang the pope
And let King Billy through.

After all, our unswerving loyalty to the British crown was through King Billy – William of Orange, the man who defeated the Catholic Stuarts, the Irish and the French, in the famous battle at the Boyne river.

From these allegiances the greatest spectacular event of the Ulster year took place on the twelfth of July. How wise of William to win his battle at the height of summer, so that festivities in its honour through the centuries after could be held in sunshine and fine weather! How we children waited for that day, and for the day preceding, when the riot of decorations received finishing touches in the streets. A Union Jack hung from every house, and masses of bunting crisscrossed the street from upper windows; crowns and mystical triangles; crescent moons each with seven stars, and flaming suns with faces; the burning bush and David's sling and five stones; streamers; red, white and blue rosettes bloomed in a profuse garden of paper and linen.

Each street vied with the next in the splendour of the main piece, its triumphal arch. Spanning between two houses, bedizened with orange and purple streamers, the arch was studded with pictures of British royalty. The climax of these preliminaries to the Twelfth was the lighting of bonfires. In the manner of the English November Fifth, we had effigies of Catholic leaders, that had sat for weeks on street corners collecting pennies, and which were solemnly consigned to the flames like Guy Fawkes.

Before the ashes had lost their red hearts, the drums of Lambeg rolled like thunder through the summer night and ushered in our Glorious Twelfth. Day dawned; everyone was up early, ready to go out and see the sights and watch the traditional 'walk to the field'. It was a public holiday, as important to us as the Fourth of July in the USA.

For miles along the Lisburn Road, thousands waited to see the Orangemen walk in procession behind elaborate banners painted with symbols of their secret society. To us Belfast boys, the Black men we looked for in the procession were not negroes, but the most respected holders of the highest rank within the hierarchy of the Order. Purple men followed them in precedence and lastly the ordinary Orangemen, all three wearing sashes coloured after their rank and bordered with a heavy gold fringe.

Everywhere orange colour flamed in sash and banner, and in the lily which people wore. They twined in bunches with sweet-williams on top of the standards, for the orange-lily was as sacred to us as the shamrock was to the Mickeys or Fenians.

> Do you think that I would let
> A dirty Fenian cat
> Destroy the leaf of a lily-o,
> For there's not a flower in Ireland,
> Like King Billy's orange-lily-o.

Such sights! Such music, churning the Protestant blood in our veins! For my first eight Twelfths I had needs be content with trailing through the crowds, craning for a glimpse of glory, straining to see the cymbals flashing as zing-zing-zing they crashed in a flash of sun, pushing my way through a forest of arms and legs to catch the dozens of pipe-bands, the flutists, and the drummers. The drummers came between each Lodge, flaying the hides of the big bass drums from Lambeg, where, naturally, they made the finest drums in the world. The huge cylinders were painted and decorated in gold, red, and orange with figures and patterns, crests and royal coats-of-arms in a whirligig of colour and line. It was considered a point of honour by some Lambeggers to beat the great drums so hard, and for so long, that wrists chafed the drum's edge until the skin became sore or even until cuts and bleeding resulted.

As expression of loyalty to a Protestant throne it would have been hard to find anything finer. But as music the effect was open to question. Whether of pipes or flutes or brass, or simply four of the gigantic Lambeg drums, each band felt that responsibility for the day's music rested solely, and by no means lightly, on their shoulders. Consequently they blew, blasted, and banged as heartily as wind and muscle knew how. For a single band in isolation this would have been admirable, but since one band succeeded another long before the first one was out of earshot, closely followed by yet more, and all playing different music, the total effect was overwhelming.

Unsurpassable day! In the pomp's midst, we tried to see friends from our neighbourhood's Lodges, and waited especially for Nodding Will to come. He lived two doors away from us, was old and had a twitching, shell-shocked head. But he was also a Black man and because of this rode in state in an open landau, clad in his best dickie and Sunday bowler.

The very first time my mother allowed me to follow the Orange procession to Finaghy Field, where the brave followers of King Billy met, I lost myself. Holiday mood had seized everyone, money went like water, and so many lemonades and iced cakes were given to the lost boy that he was ill. But not so ill that he could not hear his name called over the loudspeakers, a thrill with an exquisite edge, the climax of climaxes, the gilding indeed of the orange-lily. The Field was Elysian for me on that first day, for I went round collecting hundreds of coloured bottle-tops, which I fastened to my jersey, so that by the time I arrived home, exhausted with excitement, I was as scaly as a crocodile.

But Orange celebrations did not occur only on the Twelfth, for later in the year children sat out on the backyard walls, singing Orange ballads as the trains went by crammed with Black men going to the traditional closing of the gates of Derry. Although we enjoyed these celebrations as much as the grown-ups, we knew that serious feelings underlay the festivities. We had odd ideas on many things, but not about the reasons for these demonstrations.

In school nobody ever told us about Marie Antoinette or Marshal Foch, but we knew Louis XIV and Robert Lundy the treacherous governor of Derry. We might not know the date of the French Revolution but we did know that in 1688, thirteen young men, apprentices in the city, closed the gates of Derry in the face of the Catholic soldiers. We would forget our avoirdupois tables, but we remembered well enough that during the famous siege a dog's head cost two-and-sixpence, a rat or a quart of horse blood one shilling, and a handful of chickweed one penny. Dogs were fattened on the dead, and sold for five-and-sixpence per quarter carcass. Our greatest bed-time story was of the fat gentleman who hid himself for three days because several of the garrison troops had looked on him with greedy eyes. It was our heritage, and we were proud of it.

Confident of the city's surrender, James II himself went outside the walls of Derry to receive it. Instead, the beleaguered Protestants lined the walls and shouted 'No Surrender', which we fancied still resounded in our own breast as we watched the Black men go off to the famous scene. On the gable walls, along with the murals of coronations and anti-papal slogans, 'No Surrender' was also painted. When we drank our lemonade we toasted,

> To the goose that grew the feather,
> To the hand that wrote No Surrender.

The passing of the years, which swept the heroic 17th century further and further away, also brought nearer the time when I could graduate from being a thrilled bystander to an actual member of the Orange Order. I joined a junior Lodge, a proud day indeed for it was the 'Loyal Sons of William', whose headquarters were in Sandy Row itself. To be reckoned amongst the Boys of Sandy Row who had made the Mickeys go 'like chaff before the wind', was high honour and laid grave claims on my own courage. And now I would most certainly get a good place in heaven and be able to see King Billy and the Protestant martyrs. Our Bible spoke of four-and-twenty elders before the great white throne, and we deduced that this meant King Billy and company, to whom also were given the key to the bottomless pit where the Mickeys would go.

At my Lodge enrolment ceremony I had to stand outside the sacred locked doors of the inner chamber, trembling and waiting in a gloomy passage. Then before the whole assembly wearing its glittering regalia my name was put forward and approved. The doors opened and my sponsors emerged to lead me in, keeping position on both sides of me. I was marched through the columns of Loyal Sons. I was now shaking physically and almost incoherent as I swore to keep the Lodge password.

A concert took place afterwards, and I won first prize for declaiming the tale of the boy who stood on the burning deck. The Lodge wanted threepence for enlisting me, and I had only a penny. A bad beginning, to fall into arrears, but nevertheless I left the hall with an impressive pen-knife loaded with unusual blades and gadgets which must have cost at least two-and-sixpence. Such a possession had no appeal for me, and I gave it to Gandhi in exchange for a tin of condensed milk.

Such a careless attitude could not be adopted towards the secret pass-word. This frightened me very much, for I reputedly talked in my sleep. And my fear of divulging the special word was not because of loyalty to the Lodge, but rather fear that my sisters, or people in the hospital when I went in, would hear it, and tell it to their friends. And eventually Catholic ears would hear it and this would bring catastrophe on us, and we would be hounded from Belfast for breaking so solemn a vow. The Order's shadow fell everywhere in the city, and I kept the wretched word and felt separated from my family by the Lodge.

When I got home from my enrolment, little Helen wanted to know everything that happened, especially if I had had to ride the goat. Until then we had been as thick as inkle-weavers. But now the hocus-pocus of secret societies inserted a wedge between us. Big 'Ina overheard us and gave me a meaning look to keep silence, and I knew the Lodge doings must burn unrelieved in my breast, and Helen be content with a slap for presuming to enquire into such things.

Junior Lodges had their big parade on a different day from the elders, normally on Easter Tuesday; and we made an excursion by train, assembling again at the other end. Nothing could quieten us as we waited at the station, milling chaotically in orange sashes, dashing madly all over the place, mixing ourselves up with banner-bearers and bandsmen, and finally falling into the train as the whistle blew. There were always saucy girls on the train encouraging us to go with them to the carriages where the 'big kilties' from the pipe-bands sat, to find out how many of them were wearing trews under their kilts.

Over the years, the riotous outings merged into a general blur without detail except for a few occasions, such as when I could hardly walk on the procession. On the previous day I had been surprised taking flowers from a preparatory school garden, and a master had chased me for the best part of a mile. He never caught up, but the flowers cost me dear in the form of terrible blisters on my feet. For the outing I could not wear shoes, and set out in white plimsolls. In the train, someone took my overcoat by mistake and left me theirs which was too big for me. When we reached our destination I joined the march in a garment that came down to meet my plimsolls. The onlookers laughed as I trudged along in the pelting rain, holding on to a thick orange rope to steady our banner of King Billy on his white charger.

A sneaking feeling began inside, that perhaps the crowd's derision was well-deserved, for my odd appearance could hardly do credit to our cause. I tried to take my mind off it by concentrating on holding the banner steady, and listening to the band in front as it changed from *The Sash my Father wore* to *Dolly's Brae*, while the band behind bombarded us with:

> On the green grassy slopes of the Boyne,
> Where King Billy and his men they did join,
> And they fought for our glorious deliverance
> On the green grassy slopes of the Boyne.

The parade always included some Orange champion dressed in 17th-century clothes and riding on a white horse to conjure before our very eyes a vision of King Billy himself. But on the Easter Tuesday when I limped along in plimsolls the day's rewarding feature was to see the white horse rear up on his hind legs and throw the rider. He was a little, wide-moustached man, rather like the one in the famous 19th-century cartoon of Lord Randolph Churchill as 'King Randolph crossing the Boyne'. Off he went tumbling to the ground, his elaborate peruke flying. While two St John's Ambulance nurses rushed to gather him up, we speculated on the certainty that the Mickeys had attempted an assassination.

315

Only one real assassination took place before my eyes on an Orange Easter outing. Some of my fellow Lodgemen from Sandy Row set fire to a hayrick and out of the holocaust dashed a rabbit. Better sport than hay-burning ensued, and in a few minutes the poor creature was dead, wounded from the things thrown at it and from the pursuers' boots. When the warm, furry football was left to go cold, and the louts went off in search of other fun, I gathered the rabbit up, happy to be alone so that I could bury it in a wood. I took the red-white-and-blue rosette from my lapel and gave the rabbit a good Protestant funeral. And in my heart I could not forgive the boys of Sandy Row for killing it.

Part of the day's thrill included leaning out of the train window to pick out which of the houses speeding by belonged to the Catholics. We could spot them easily enough for their gables, like ours, were painted. But the Mickeys' walls bore different signs – 'Up the IRA', 'Remember 1916', 'Silence is Golden'. The sign of the cross would appear on any blank space, and worse than any of them, 'God bless the Pope'.

The Pope! How we feared and hated him, we thought the Pope more terrible than Hitler when that German came to our notice, and certainly a greater evil than his disciple, Mr de Valera. From the safety of the passing train we could boldly hurl abuse at the Mickeys' houses and their papish murals. Pushing to get a space at the compartment window we shouted 'To Hell with the Pope', a devout prayer on Ulster lips and a favourite one. As late as 1951 a member of parliament built a climax into an election speech with 'God save the King, and to Hell with the Pope'.

But God had not left us defenceless against the dreaded Roman Pontiff. He had sent us Lord Carson to secure our Ulster freedom. Lord Carson was dead, and when the CLB parade brought me to St Anne's Cathedral, I sat with great awe near the new tomb. He was another of the four-and-twenty elders mentioned in the Book of Revelation, and would be found sitting on God's right hand at the Judgement Day. The least religiously or politically minded knew about Lord Carson as did the fervent, and all knew the song,

> Sir Edward Carson had a cat,
> He sat it by the fender,
> And every time it caught a mouse,
> It shouted, 'No Surrender'.

Our rhymes were like calypsos, endless, ingenious if monotonous, and dealing with everyday events whether political or not. Whenever anything new happened, then we found doggerel for the occasion. Mr Baldwin and an urging on to fight in Abyssinia appeared at one time. Mrs Simpson became the theme of endless variations. How our mothers had idolized the Prince of Wales! And although pictures of the Princesses, Elizabeth and Margaret Rose, with their corgies in 'Y Bwthyn Bach', the Welsh cottage, now filled the photograph frames in the parlour, we could sense the survival of the liking for Prince Eddie. Often the only contact maintained with the exile was through the medium of the Sunday papers. We scanned the pages for scandal or pictures.

Reaction to any incident concerning Protestant or Roman Catholic was always violent, nothing escaped notice and comment. When the new king ascended the throne his was our forsworn loyalty. And yet, in spite of such entrenched opinion, our ignorance of the Catholic world was profound. I, for instance, believed that Mickeys existed only in parts of Belfast and nowhere else except the Free State and Rome itself.

That many Catholics were living in London, or were allowed to live in London with our Protestant king, seemed impossible. The idea of a papist cathedral near the gates of Buckingham Palace would have been laughed at with scorn. So thought I, until coronation year. The celebrations burst over the city like a great coloured rocket, exploding in the drabness of our lives with a million sparks, a spectrum of excitement. Belfast went mad with patriotism. Even the Plymouth Brethren, so immured to anything but 'the word', published a coronation photograph on their Sunday tract.

Then we were presented with a magnificent coronation book, with close details of the ceremony, as well as pictures and diagrams of the important personages and Westminster Abbey, where it had all taken place. We prized the rare possession, and why not – for apart from religious story-books won as Sunday School prizes, hymn-books, and a vast collection of Bibles, New Testaments and Books of Common Prayer, it was the only real book in the house.

But through the coronation book I learned of what seemed a terrible betrayal. Included in the pictures of the royalty involved was one of the Duke of Norfolk greeting the two princesses. In a blood-curdling Orange sermon we heard about the subtleties of Catholic scheming, and the preacher had included Norfolk by implication. And there he was, a Mickey, shaking the hand of the heir to the Protestant throne, King Billy's successor!

But there were other, worse things of sinister import. Not only did he hold the office of Earl Marshal (we did not know what this was, but no matter) but he was the head of the nobility. If all the House of Windsor died, or were deliberately got out of the way, the Duke would be king, and the glorious freedom of Boyne Water would indeed be lost!

How I imagined Norfolk to be scheming and counterscheming to win the crown, and send the country back to the days of Bloody Mary, whose history besides that of Protestant martyrs we had heard in school. Perhaps Norfolk would one day buy the confidence of a Buckingham Palace servant, who guarded the King night and day, and persuade him to steal the crown. I could see the vast, richly draped bedchamber, the Yeomen of the Guard, and tall plumed soldiers standing round the sleeping monarch, and his crown hanging on the end of his bed, next to his long underpants. The crown gone, life for us would be over. Was not that the reason why my mother, every year when the backyard was whitewashed, got a neighbour to freshen up the painted crown on the wall?

Such a pity for the lovely book to be spoilt like this. We would have liked to rip out Norfolk's picture and burn it, but this could not be done for the Princesses were on the same page and the King on the other side, and to remove them would be disrespectful. In fact, reflection showed it would have been disloyal, just as disloyal as the Mickeys putting their postage stamps on letters upside down as an insult to the Protestant throne. Instead, we gave the Duke a pair of horns and a nice tail with an arrow point sticking outside his rich coronation robes.

'The Boys of Sandy Row', from *No Surrender*, 1960

AIR RAID ON BELFAST

BRIAN MOORE

Mr Burke, wearing the earphones of his crystal wireless set, sat by the sitting-room fire plainly excited by the six-o'clock BBC news. Old Mary had just brought in a full scuttle of coal and Gavin's mother, using the tongs, was rebuilding the dying fire. Kathy, home from work, was stitching the hem of a dance frock, and so, when Gavin ventured his head around the sitting-room doorway, nobody noticed him, at first. He had stayed in bed all day, hungover, and also to avoid the row he foresaw as certain. In half an hour, he would leave for night duty.

His father was the first to notice him, but his father, listening to the wireless, did not seem to be thinking of the previous night's happenings. 'Wait'll you hear this,' his father told the others, loosening his earphones, but still listening to the announcer's voice. 'The Germans have just marched into Greece. They went fifty miles in their first day. And the British are camped on Mount Olympus – isn't that marvellous – camped there, preparing for another of their "tactical withdrawals", I'll wager. You mark my words, what day is it – Tuesday? – well, by the end of the week, they'll be running for their ships, leaving another of their allies in the lurch. God help the poor Greeks.'

The Greek of last night danced, stately, grave, and solitary, into Gavin's mind. The Greek had wept on the way to Lili's. He must have known this news.

His father was listening again. 'Aha, the Yugoslavs,' he said.

Mrs Burke rose from her fire-making labours and turned to look at Gavin in the doorway. Her eyes threatened tears. 'I'm just going to pick up my sandwiches,' Gavin said hurriedly. 'Good night, everybody.'

'Don't you want any supper?' his mother asked.

'I'm not hungry.'

'You look like death.'

'I'm all right.'

He fled, escaping explanations and recriminations, knowing they were merely postponed, but sure that, in his present state, he could not endure them without a collapse into childish, hateful tears. Out into the rainy avenue, the day fading to night, running past the old waterworks where, as a child, he had spent long hours sailing his toy boat. Grown-ups, forgetting the servitude of children's lives, were fond of saying that one's school years were the happiest years of one's life, a statement which no child believed. But now, perhaps, he *was* becoming a grown-up, for, looking back at the bleak St Michan's days, he saw them in the fond forgetful light of an easier time. Life as an adult could be more terrible than anything a schoolboy might imagine. The Greek of last night danced into his mind, the weeping Greek whose mother, sisters, brothers, might even now be falling under Nazi guns. He felt sorrow for the Greek, and yet there was a shameful, guilty comfort in knowing that if he, Gavin Burke, was facing an ominous future, the rest of the world, whole countries, even, was in the same boat.

On the post, everyone was excited by the news of Captain Lambert's comeback.

'On my soul,' Soldier said. 'It just shows that what I always said is true. The gents look after their own. Ah, wait'll we slip this to Craig. 'Twill be a grand kick in the arse for him.'

'Which post is the Captain on?' Freddy asked. 'God, if only I could wangle a transfer.'

'Ah, the Lord love him, you can see him,' old Mrs MacCartney offered. 'Himself dead drunk in he's office, and every man and woman on the post asleep on their stretchers.'

The thought of the Captain's being in charge of others was irresistible. In a world where nothing happened, where the only battle was against sleep and Craig's drills, the Captain's elevation to power seemed a triumph against all those higher-ups, post officers, Local Authority inspectors, Control Centre and headquarters muckymucks, who, until now, had defeated the personnel as regularly as Hitler beat the Allies. A real excitement precluded the ten-o'clock drill. Wait'll they told old Craig.

'Bandages has not been folded properly. I said, bandages is a disgrace. Mister Bob Greenwood was in to see me tonight, and he has put the shaft in me. I said, he has put the shaft in me. He tells me his people is folding all bandages according to regulations, but that, when his people comes on duty in the mornings, the bandages left by our people is not properly folded.

'Now, I am not saying Mister Bob Greenwood is right, no, I am not saying that at all. But I address this, especially, to the ladies. I want them bandages just perfect. I said, perfect. I am excusing the ladies from drill tonight, because I want youse girls upstairs, folding the bandages. I want the bandages all correct and ready for inspection by me at eleven. I said, at eleven.

'Now, the ladies can fall out. The men, fall in.'

The whistle blew. Soldier, at the head of the line, squared off, straightening the line with an old soldier's efficiency.

'Now, tonight, we'll just run over the casualty clearing procedure.'

'Slip it to him, now,' Soldier whispered to Gavin.

'Hargreaves, I am asking you, what would you do if you had a casualty with he's left wrist fractured and, at the same time, a temperature of one hundred and five?'

'Excuse me, sir,' Soldier said. 'I just thought you'd be interested. Have you heard about Captain Lambert?'

'MacBride, I am asking Hargreaves a question.'

'Sorry, sir. But 'tis an extraordinary thing. Him getting that job.'

'What job?'

'Ah, you'll not credit this, sir. But the Captain's been appointed a post officer, the very same as yourself.'

'Your head's cut, MacBride.'

'No sir, 'tis true. Post 268, it is. Young Burke here met him last night.'

'He has no advanced certificate,' Craig said, his voice suddenly failing. 'You can't get no job like that without advanced certificates.'

But he did not sound sure. They watched him, delighted to be able to stick it into him.

'Ah, well,' Soldier said, 'it's different for gents. He knows a lot of higher-ups, so he does.'

Maggie Kerr, sallow-faced at the kitchen door. 'Mister Craig. Red alert.'

'Red alert,' Craig shouted. He blew his whistle.

'Ah, for crying out loud,' Soldier grumbled. 'Will they never let up?'

'Red alert, stand to your stations.'

Craig dashed back to his office. 'Well,' said Jimmy Lynan, lighting up his pipe, 'we got out of a drill, but, still and all, it spoiled the crack.'

'Did you see his face?' Wee Bates asked.

'Did he say *red* alert?' Big Frank Price asked. 'Why was there no yellow alert?'

'Red or yellow,' Freddy said. 'What does it matter? They just forgot to put the yellow through. No wonder. They're sick of these capers.'

Down the hall, the phone rang loudly in the office.

'All clear,' Soldier said, taking off his steel helmet.

'Right,' said Hughie Shaw.

Craig's voice, screaming: 'Burke and Hargreaves! In here, on the double.'

'Well, that's a new one,' Freddy said as he and Gavin left the kitchen.

In the office, Craig paced up and down. 'They're evacuating the Nurses' Home. The doctor in charge is short of firewatchers, and HQ has ordered us to fill in until replacements is sent. Youse two – over there and up on that roof. Incendiaries is expected.'

'It'll be nice to get a breath of fresh air,' Freddy said.

'Just a *minute*.' Craig's eyes were manic. 'This is no joke. German bombers is over the Irish Sea, they'll be here any minute.'

'Are you sure?'

'I have it straight from HQ!'

'In a pig's eye,' Freddy said, as he and Gavin went into the blackout.

Searchlights swept the sky. 'Look,' Gavin said. 'I never knew there were so many.'

'Maybe something *is* happening.'

In the blackout, they began bumping into nurses who were being evacuated from the Nurses' Home to the main hospital building. Harried by shouting old matrons, the nurses, some of them in their night clothes, some carrying suitcases and parcels, laughed and called to each other like schoolgirls on a picnic. Gavin went among them, hoping to find Sally, but in the darkness and in the rush of women, he could not discern individual faces.

'Come on,' Freddy said. 'Maybe there's some skirt still asleep up there.'

The thought of Freddy discovering Sally in her night clothes set off an instant rage. Keep your paws off her, do you hear? He found himself half running after Freddy, unwilling to let that old Plaza Dance Hall rake out of his sight.

'We're the firewatchers,' Freddy told the matron on the main door.

'You can go up the back stairs to the roof. And keep out of the dormitories. I have more girls to get out.'

'I'll bet we're the first men ever allowed in here at night,' Freddy decided, as they started up the back stairs, two at a time. 'Wonder which floor the dorms are on?'

'Oh, knock it off.'

'What's the matter with you? There's not going to be any bloody raid. But we might get a bit of a cuddle.'

'Jesus.' Gavin stopped on the landing. 'What's that?'

Over the noise of footsteps and the giggling sounds of girls, a sudden cough of explosions.

'Bombs?'

'Guns,' Freddy said. 'Ack-ack, behind Cave Hill.'

For a moment, coming up through the trap door onto the flat roof, they were blind mice, unsure in every direction. The first thing they discerned were two searchlights, circling across the semicircle of sky, intersecting, then falling, great white columns, down behind the black horizon. Tiny and sudden, flashes of light appeared on the far off hills, followed by the stammer of guns, which, like firecrackers, went off all around the perimeter of the city. Then, silence.

'Listen,' Freddy said. 'What's that? Do you hear?'

Did he? At first, Gavin could not be sure. But as he and Freddy approached the parapet of the roof, he heard it again, a distant grumble like the growl of a lion, a growl with grew to a loud, snarling roar: the sound of huge engines.

'Where are they?'

'Coming up from the Lough.'

'Going for the shipyards, I'll bet.'

The first bomb dropped. The explosion, far different from the harsh cough of the guns, preceded the faint red sheen which arose in the sky above the place of impact, then faded, leaving in the eye's retina a momentary afterimage of rooftops and church spires. The guns chattered like chickens.

'That was a bomb,' Freddy said, redundantly.

Two more explosions boomed on the far side of the city. The guns were silent. Then, beautiful, exploding with a faint pop in the sky above them, a magnesium flare floated up in the stillness, lighting the rooftops in a ghostly silver. Freddy was revealed, a few paces away from Gavin, his face uptilted, his glasses silvery opaque as they searched the sky. And in that moment, within Gavin there started an extraordinary elation, a tumult of joy. He felt like dancing a Cherokee war dance on the edge of the parapet. The world and the war had come to him at last. Tonight, in the Reichschancellery of Berlin, generals stood over illuminated maps, plotting Belfast's destruction. Hitler himself smiled in glee, watching the graphs of the planes' progress. Tonight, history had conferred the drama of war on this dull, dead town in which he had been born. And what about your parents? asked the White Angel. What about Kathy and Owen, down there in the darkness. And you. You too can be blown to smithereens.

But there, there was the joy. He had no fear: he did not care. He was actually smiling, impervious to his danger, enjoying the bombing as though it were a military tattoo, put on for his benefit.

'We'd better find some sandbags,' Freddy said. 'It looks as though they're dropping incendiaries.'

On a rooftop across the street, flames grew with startling suddenness, licking across the slates, exploding from an upper-storey window. In the reflected light of the flames, Gavin saw that Freddy seemed nervous.

'Hey, see over there.' His own voice was elated. 'Look. That one's on the Ormeau Road, I'll bet.'

'Maybe on Reverend Batshaw's house,' Freddy said. 'Go on. Blow up old Baldy Batshaw.'

The Reverend Batshaw, an archenemy of Freddy's, had once threatened to put the police on Freddy for going around with the Reverend's underage daughter.

'Do you hear, me, Batshaw?' Freddy shouted. 'This is the bloody revolution, Batshaw, you praying mantis, you. It's the end of your whole bloody world. Come on, Hitler. Blow up his bloody church.'

'Yes, and blow up St Michan's,' Gavin shouted, prancing in his war dance on the roof.

'Blow up City Hall.'

'And Queen's University.'

'Blow up the Orange Hall.'

'And the cathedral and the dean.'

'Jesus, what a show.'

But the next bomb fell quite close. The roof shook. Gavin was thrown to his knees.

'Are you all right, Gav?'

'OK'

'Let's find those sandbags.'

'I saw some behind you.'

A high, ominous whine sounded above them, and, instinctively, the heroes of a moment ago crouched down, hands over their necks. A second explosion shook the street, and they heard, in delicate counterpoint, the tinkling, rending smash of windows in their own building. They stood, ran to the parapet and looked over. 'Blew out every window in the place,' Freddy announced, triumphantly. 'That was close, let me tell you.'

'I wonder are all the nurses out?'

'Maybe we'd better look.'

Back down through the trap door to the sound of the ack-ack guns. The lights had gone out inside the building and, instead of the giggles and footsteps of ten minutes ago, there was the black silence of an empty loft.

'Hey, nursies,' Freddy shouted down the stairs. 'Nursies,' echoed back. A bomb fell. The staircase shook. 'Let's go back up,' Gavin suggested. Somehow it seemed safer on the roof than in here, in this black emptiness, knowing that bricks and marble and concrete could tumble down and bury you.

Up on the roof again, they had a clear, fire-lit view of the city. 'Flaming, by Jesus, all over the place,' as Freddy put it. 'Except here and in the Antrim Road.'

'Blow up a few capitalists,' Freddy shouted, suddenly.

'And the Bishop of Down and Connor,' Gavin yelled.

'And Stormont Castle and Lord Carson's statue and the houses of bloody Parliament.'

'Not with a whimper, but a bang.'

They stood for a moment, drunk with the bombers' power. 'Say, Gavin, do you smell something funny?'

Smoke drifted over the parapet of the roof. 'Maybe the hospital's on fire. Let's have a look.' Gingerly, they approached the parapet. The hospital was invisible in the blackout. But two streets away, a house blazed with flames, illuminating smaller fires all along a row of working-class dwellings. The smoke, however, came from somewhere closer. They began to cough and choke. They moved to the other side of the roof. 'Hey, Freddy?'

'What?' Freddy's myopic eyes blinked and watered as he peered out across the city.

'Look down below. Do you see?'

Two floors beneath them, smoke and flames were coming from one of the windows of the Home.

'Christ, we're on fire.'

'Get a couple of sandbags.'

Carrying two sandbags, they went down through the trap door into the blackness of the building. Gavin led the way, his hand on the stair rail. The fire was on the fifth floor, in a room at the end of a long corridor. They approached it through a thick swirl of smoke and, when Freddy opened the door, saw that it was a nurses' dormitory, its window frames, beds, chairs, and rugs all garlanded by long ribbons of flame. They retreated at once, pulling the door shut.

'An incendiary must have come in through the window,' Freddy said. He dropped his sandbag.

'I suppose we should phone the fire brigade.'

'OK.'

Freddy remembered that there were telephones in the lobby. Down on terra firma was where they both wanted to be. To ease their conscience, they stopped on each landing on the way down, calling out: 'Nurse? Nurse? Anybody there?' Luckily, no one answered. They reached the lobby and struck matches to find the phone booths.

The phones were dead.

'What'll we do now?'

'Better tell them at the hospital. No point in hanging around here any longer.'

'Anyway, every fire engine in the city must be out on call.'

'OK, then. Let's cut on over to the hospital.'

They went out, leaving the front door open. 'Makes it easier for the firemen,' Freddy said, although, as he spoke, they both sensed their failure and avoided each other's eyes. They stood in the courtyard of the Home and looked up. The whole of the fifth floor was ablaze. Above them, in the cloudy night sky, they heard, once again, the dull roar of bomber engines. The roar was ominous. Aye, said the White Angel. You know what I'm thinking, don't you? Say an act of contrition, and be quick about it. You may not get another chance.

'Come on.' Freddy had found and opened the courtyard gates. A magnesium flare burst in the sky, lighting the street. A policeman in a steel helmet was coming toward them, helping an old woman in a black shawl. The old woman's face was bleeding. 'Hey, you,' the policeman called. 'Are you First Aid?'

'Right.'

'This woman needs to go to the hospital.'

'Come on, missus,' Freddy said, putting his arm around the old woman's waist. The policeman let go and, turning, hurried back across the street. 'Our first job,' Freddy said. 'Gav, get on the other side of her.'

Half dragging, half carrying the old woman, they set off up the street. The anti-aircraft guns set up a fresh chatter.

'Them sons of whores,' the old woman groaned. 'Them bastards done it on purpose. They brought the German.'

'Who?' Gavin asked, staring at her bleeding brow, mater martyr, a face from a Dürer triptych.

'The Fenians, the IRA, them's the ones who done it. They should be hung, every one of them, aye, and a fire lit beneath them.'

'Come on now, missus,' Freddy said. 'Save your breath.'

'A fire lit beneath them, hell roast them.'

'Let's take her over to the extern department.'

'I can't see a thing,' Gavin said. The flare's light had died. Two cars passed, their masked headlamps almost invisible in the blackout.

'I suppose everybody's trying to get out of town.'

'Wouldn't you, if you could?'

327

The old woman, her feet dragging, her breathing stertorous, rallied herself and began to sing:

> Do you think that we would let
> A dirty Fenian get
> Bespoil the Royal Orange Lily-O!

'Shut up, mother,' Freddy said. 'Come on now, we're nearly there.'

'Nearly where? Is it the papist hospital youse are taking me to?'

'Yes, mother.'

'Well, youse can let me die in the street, so youse can. If you think I'm going into any Fenian hospital run by them nuns to get myself poisoned and kilt, then youse have another think coming. Take me to the Royal Victoria, boys.'

'But that's on the other side of town. Now, come on, have a heart.'

'Let go of me. Are youse Fenians?'

'Come on, Gav,' Freddy said. 'Lift her up.'

Arresting officers, they carried the old woman, kicking, through the extern department entrance. The waiting hall was crowded, mostly with people who had come in to take shelter from the bombs. A young girl, her face smeared with dirt, came running out of the huddle of people in the doorway. 'It's my gran! Oh, Gran, what cut you?'

'Fenian gets,' the old woman muttered. Weeping, she put her arms around her granddaughter. Freddy and Gavin, glad to be shut of her, went into the extern surgery to report on the fire. A bomb fell close by, a big one. At the sound of the explosion, the herd of people in the extern hall crouched down, heads bowed. Some made the sign of the cross. Doctors and nurses paused in their work of bandaging and suturing, as though arrested in some private moment of reflection. It was as though everybody waited for the next bomb, the one they would not hear, the one which would bury them. Gavin and Freddy, nonchalant, kept on walking, officers going along the top of a trench. They spotted old Dr MacLanahan, the medical superintendent, coming down the corridor from the main hospital building, accompanied by a staff sister. He wore slippers, tweed trousers, a white coat over his striped pyjama top. A stethoscope dangled from his neck. 'What, what?' he snapped, as Freddy went up to intercept him.

328

'Sorry, sir. The Nurses' Home is on fire. We couldn't get the Fire Brigade.'

'Any nurses there?'

'No, sir.'

'All right. You men help with those stretchers.'

'Excuse me, sir, but shouldn't we report back to our post? We're supposed to be on ambulance call.'

'There's plenty of work for you here.'

The staff sister whispered something in Dr MacLanahan's ear. 'Hmhmhm,' he hummed, impatiently. 'All right.'

'You two follow me,' the staff sister said. 'Pick up a stretcher over there. I have a job for you.'

Carrying the stretcher, they went into a small rest room behind the surgeries. An old man sat on a straight-backed chair, his head lolling against the rest room wall. His face was a purplish colour: his eyes were open.

'Heart attack,' the sister said. 'Cover him up and take him around the back to the morgue.'

Clumsily, they took hold of the corpse and carried it to the stretcher. As they laid the old man's head down, his mouth opened and his false teeth fell out. Freddy put the teeth in the old man's jacket pocket. They covered him up in a blanket, then carried him out, past the crowds. At the back entrance, a policeman held the door open for them. 'Where's the morgue?' Freddy whispered.

'Up the yard, mate.'

At the morgue entrance a light shone, defying the blackout. A man in a long rubber apron held the door open for them. 'That a corp?' the man asked.

'Yes.'

'Bring it in here.'

There were several morgue tables inside, but only one of them contained a sheeted body. The morgue man beckoned them on, into a back room, bare as a garage. There, on a concrete floor, a middle-aged woman, a young girl, a baby, and a sailor lay in the lax postures of death. 'Put it down there on the end of the line,' the morgue man said. 'Do you have his name and address?'

'No. He died in the extern.'

'That's all right, then. He was admitted.'

The morgue man lit a cigarette. 'Did you notice?' he said. 'The bombs have stopped.'

'Have they?'

'Listen.'

An ambulance backfired in the yard outside. Somewhere, a child wailed. Then there was silence, the silence of death. The morgue man puffed on his cigarette. 'I hope it *is* over,' he said. 'We only have room for fifteen bodies in here, that's why I'm stacking them in the back. I expect we'll have fifty before the night's out.'

Outside the main morgue room, a familiar voice bellowed: 'First Aid party with one dead.'

Freddy pushed open the swing doors. Craig, his battle-dress chalky with dust, stood at attention among the morgue tables. Behind him, lowering their stretcher were Wee Bates and Jimmy Lynan. Freddy explained about the fire in the Nurses' Home.

'And youse didn't put it out?'

'We couldn't.'

'Right then, youse will have to fill in a report. Get back to the post on the double.'

'A report. Now? Dr MacLanahan told us to help with stretchers.'

'Dr MacLanahan has no call giving youse orders. I'm in charge here. Who does he think he is?'

'Simmer down, will you,' Freddy said.

The morgue building shook. 'I was wrong,' the morgue attendant said. 'They're still at it. OK. Put that corp in the back room.'

As Bates and Jimmy Lynan passed by with their burden, Jimmy favoured Gavin and Freddy with an exaggerated wink and jerked his head meaningfully toward Craig. For a moment, his mind confused by the excitements of the night, Gavin found himself puzzled as to the meaning of the wink. Then, in a brutal image, he saw Craig lying on a concrete floor in the back room, blood congealed on his brow. No, that was rubbish, there was enough real death around here without giving in to schoolboy fantasies. Yet Lynan looked serious. You've got to separate Lynan from Craig tonight, the White Angel warned. Otherwise –

330

'Come on, get the lead out,' an ambulance driver called, coming in at the main door. 'I have a call up the Antrim Road.'

The Antrim Road. 'What about me and Freddy taking a turn on the ambulance?' Gavin said.

Craig, flustered by the ambulance driver's shout, nodded agreement. 'All right, get moving.'

Outside, in the hospital yard, the clouds had parted, allowing a sinister moon to shine down on the city. 'Antrim Road,' Freddy said. 'Isn't that where your people . . . ?'

'Yes.'

The ambulance raced out of the gates, turning into a deserted street. The moonlight showed broken window glass, glittering like rhinestones on the pavement. There was no noise, other than the sound of the ambulance motor. 'The bombing's stopped,' Freddy decided.

'You should have seen the one I seen,' the driver said. 'The soldiers told me they call it a land mine. It come down on this parachute and blew up a whole row of houses in one go-off.'

'Whereabouts?'

'Over in the Shankill.'

'Where else have you been tonight?'

'No place. This is only my second call.'

The ambulance swung into the rotunda of Carlisle Circus, passing the pigeon-spattered statue of a Protestant divine. As it turned into the Antrim Road, Gavin saw three boys coming out of Mullens' Sweet Shop. The shop-windows were broken, and the boys carried boxes of chocolates, which they were eating in gluttonous haste. When they saw the ambulance approach, they ducked back into the shadows of the doorway.

'Whereabouts in the Antrim Road is this call?'

The driver had no time to answer Gavin's question. The ambulance shook violently and, without any of them being aware how it happened, the ambulance was on the far side of the street, but still moving.

'Holy God.'

'A bomb?'

From behind them came a sudden, deafening roar. They looked back and saw a huge sack of dust swell up behind the dwellings in the nearby side street. Fragments of brick and glass fell on the ambulance roof.

331

'Did you see that? That bomb blew us right across the street.'

'And we kept going.'

'Suffering J.,' said the driver. 'Wait'll I tell about this, nobody'll believe me.'

'The Germans are still on the job.'

'Too right, they are. We're not home yet.'

Guns rattled defiance off the slopes of Cave Hill. Gavin, sitting between Freddy and the driver, looked in turn at each of their faces. Was Freddy afraid? There was no question about the driver's fear. He said, 'Let's pull in a minute. We don't want to be blown off the road.'

'Keep going,' Gavin said. Freddy looked at him strangely.

'What's your hurry, Gav? It's bloody dangerous driving in the middle of these bombs.'

'We're getting paid for it.'

'Aye, paid heroes,' the driver grumbled. 'And dead heroes.' But he kept the ambulance moving.

The driver was afraid. Freddy was afraid. Why wasn't *he* afraid, then? Why was he filled with excitement, with a feeling that, tonight, nothing could kill him, that, like the knight in some ancient romance, he carried a shield which stood between him and all harm? He did not know: he *did* know that, given the chance, he was capable of dashing into a burning building, snatching a girl from beneath a tumbling wall, walking among explosions, anything.

As they reached the Lyceum Cinema, people began appearing from the streets which converged there, people who tried to flag the ambulance down, calling. 'Hey, wait a minute. We have a sick woman here.'

'Are youse going out of town? Give us a lift, please.'

'Hey, mister, take these kids and me as far as Glengormley.'

'Please, mister.'

The driver, his finger jabbing at his horn, kept the ambulance moving through the crowd. Gathering speed once more, it turned up the Cliftonville Road. At the corner of the road was a Presbyterian church which Gavin used to pass each day on his way to and from school. Tonight, all was changed. The church was without its steeple. Bricks and rubble were strewn on the lawn of the adjoining manse. The steeple lay, like a great tree, amid the headstones of the old church graveyard.

Light shone from the windows of a pub called The Swan. There was the sound of a shot. The light went out. A policeman came out of the pub into the moonlight street, holstering his service revolver. He waved at the ambulance as it passed. He was smiling.

A moment later, the ambulance passed the avenue where Gavin lived. All seemed quiet. Had his family taken refuge in the shelter in the street, or were they huddled in the coalhole beneath the stairs? Was his father still applauding Hitler's deeds?

And then, turning into an avenue, two streets up from his own home, the ambulance was flagged down by a stout old warden, who waited in the middle of the road. 'There's two casualties in the back entry,' the warden told them, as Gavin and Freddy jumped down, carrying their folded stretcher. The warden's torch guided them. Arms straining, they lifted a very fat man onto the stretcher. The warden's torch showed the fat man's left leg, broken below the knee, turned sickeningly around so that the man's shoe seemed to be on back-to-front. Arms straining, stumbling in the rubble, they carried the fat man to the ambulance and, returning, were guided toward an injured child. Gavin applied the first real tourniquet of his life in an effort to stanch the bleeding from the child's mangled arm. Uneasily, he remembered his inattention in all those months of first aid classes.

Two old ladies had climbed into the ambulance, believing it to be leaving the city. They wept as Freddy and the warden forced them out. As the ambulance turned back down the Cliftonville Road, a bomb fell two streets away, the force of its explosion spinning the vehicle around in a wild skid, ramming its bonnet against a lamp-post. The motor stopped. The driver stamped on his dead accelerator pedal, pulled out the choke, hammered his fist in anger against the dashboard. 'Holy God!'

Gavin and Freddy got out and pushed the ambulance bonnet free of the lamp-post. 'If I could get her on the hill, going down,' the driver said. 'I might get her running. We need a shove.'

Just then, two English air force sergeants emerged from a doorway. They had been taking shelter on their way home from a dance. They offered to shove, in exchange for a lift. With Gavin and Freddy, they ranged themselves behind the ambulance and, all four straining, managed to push the ambulance back onto the road and point it downhill. The driver called out: 'All together now. Push hard!'

They pushed. The ambulance began to gain momentum, but the motor did not catch. Suddenly, the engine began to splutter, and, at that moment, Freddy and the two air force sergeants jumped on the tailboard. The engine caught, the ambulance accelerated, and Gavin was left alone in the middle of the road. He continued to run, expecting that, once the engine was firing properly, the driver would apply the brake and wait for him to climb aboard. But the ambulance did not stop. Gathering speed, it shot off down the Cliftonville Road, turned a corner and was gone forever. He was stranded.

from *The Emperor of Ice-cream*, 1965

334

SAVAGE MARY

JOHN MORROW

In the much-Oscared film *Network*, a demented TV presenter, played by the late Peter Finch, marks the zenith of his dementia by urging his viewers to shout in the streets as a protest against the regimentation of life, an assertion of their individuality. And in case they can't think up anything themselves, he tells them what to shout – which they all do, to the exact syllable, in what seems to me to be a complete negation of all that shouting in the streets is about.

Of course, it could be that the fellow who wrote the book of the film came from a good home in a nice suburban area and really thought that he had come up with something new. Not at all: nocturnal shouting in the streets was as traditional as hopscotch or wife-beating in the old working-class honeycombs of our industrial cities, and it had nothing at all to do with orchestrated, chorused frustration; it was the heart-cry of the special individual, ranging in degree from the homeward-bound drunk raving obscene longings to the sleeping street – a sort of pre-telephonic heavy-breather – to that pride of the shouter's aviary, the full-throated gossip-monger, as loved and feared by the bedded denizens of humble terraces as are the Paul Slickeys of Fleet Street by upper-class night prowlers in London West One.

Oh, the pre-television delight of lying snug in bed on a calm summer's night, waiting for the scrake of Savage Mary's ill-fitting front door, prelude to an hour of entertainment and revelation! Mary was the prime night-singing bird in my native kraal, a scrawny, beady-eyed brown hen who strutted the streets by day, one stiff leg and stick tapping, accompanied by an ancient diseased dog. At her approach every child ran to the other side of the street, and when she passed all knew to spit three times – if you didn't you'd be dead by morning. For Mary Savage was a witch, a fortune-teller and a reader of tea-cups. Her real name was Marie Savage, the legend went, and she'd been left on an orphanage doorstep by a troupe of gipsy circus performers. Her great hooky nose, brass earrings

335

and dark pigmentation seemed to bear out the foreign extraction – until soon after her death, when the undertaker's sponge eroded a fair chunk of the myth . . .

Mary lived in a small, dirty terrace, its two windows blinded by hessian spud bags. When you passed, if the door was open, the stink of old dog and paraffin oil was overwhelming, for Mary would have no truck with anything as new-fangled as piped gas. But neither dirt, stink or gloom deterred her clientele. Her main source of income was the girls from the local mill who paraded down every pay night for a glance into their romantic futures. They queued up the hallway with ready-used cups clutched in their hands, the queue sometimes spilling onto the street. After being done, they deposited a coin in a big soup plate on the hallstand beside which crouched Scamp, Mary's mangy dog, watching. And woe betide the ankles of any girl who didn't make sure that Scamp saw the flash of a silver sixpence.

The girls said that Mary at work spoke in a deep voice, almost like a man's, with a trace of a Charles Boyer accent. Otherwise the only sound ever heard from her was a high-pitched screech, whether it was calling Scamp, cursing children or performing in the small hours, when it could carry three streets away even above the nightshift clattering in the nearby foundry or a passing cattle train on the Central railway line.

Her prologue varied little . . . 'Oh, yis needn't think I don't know yis are all there with yer lugs cocked . . . Oh aye, I know yis – nice God-fearin' folk all tucked up after sayin' yer prayers . . . But I'm the one that knows the other side of yis, y'load of durty, two-faced gather-ups yis . . .' Here there'd be a short pause, nerve-racking for those with something to hide, for all knew that nothing was safe from Mary. You could guard against the ordinary gossip, but against Savage Mary, who had never been known to speak a civil word to anyone, let alone gossip, there was no protection. All of which leant an aura of the occult to her revelations. And it could be anyone, any night . . . 'Are ye listenin', Ellie Smith? Gittin' to be a big girl, aren't ye . . . Yi'll soon have to let out a seam or two in that sausage skin you've bin wrigglin' about in. Eh? An' you needn't tell me it's because you've bin atein' fresh bread, for I'm the one that knows who you've bin goin' down the railway with . . .' Ellie was on the first train to her aunt's in Lurgan the following morning. Mr and Mrs Smith didn't need a second opinion: Savage Mary had spoken. She had a particular down on the righteous . . . '. . . oul skinny-ma-link McNabney, the select vestryman. Oh yer there all right, Wullie John. Butter wudn't melt in yer mouth. Mister Holy Joe McNabney, the master plumber that niver served an hour to the trade. Eh, Wullie John? They give you a quare groundin' up in Borstal that time you robbed the widda's gas meter in 1919 . . .'

She had competitors, of course . . . Granda Skillen, ex-welterweight boxer, who had a strong line in aggressive abuse and whose speciality was punching holes in neighbouring front doors prior to wrecking his own house. Early in their marriage his wife had had all the furniture sectionalised, so that it would disintegrate easily and be as easily put together again, in much the same way as houses are constructed in the earthquake regions of Japan. And then there was wee Mr Brophy, known as 'Sean-Sean the Leprechaun'. One of a tiny minority in that Protestant stronghold, Sean-Sean gave vent only at certain festive times, his sole message conveyed in a spoken ballad concerning the Reformation and the debt it owed to the sexual appetites of Henry the Eighth . . . A brave wee man, Sean-Sean. But he and Granda were clowns, mere patter-merchants, compared with Savage Mary. Only fear of the vindictive Dark Powers she represented preserved her for an over-ripe old age and a natural death.

But there came a time every year when the subjects of her harangues had the opportunity of venting at least some of their spite. On the night of the eleventh of July the traditional bonfire was always sited directly opposite Mary's house. And in the small hours of the Twelfth, as the flames mounted roof-high and the Dutch courage sparkled in the veins, everyone cheered as the Witch's windows cracked audibly and the paint bubbled on her front door. Mary herself was always there, full of Red Biddy, lashing about with her stick and screeching resumés of her next season's programme. A few days later two or three decent men in the street would club together and re-glaze her windows and re-paint the front door . . . But don't let them think for one minute that it would save them from her tongue, as Savage Mary never failed to tell them even as they went about the job with Scamp snarling at their heels. And it never did.

from *Northern Myths*, 1979

THE MILL VILLAGE

MAURICE LEITCH

Kildargan isn't any different from any of the other mill villages which you see in this part of the North. They were all built about a hundred or so years ago and their sites chosen for hard-headed, money-making reasons when the linen bubble was at its fattest and most iridescent. For a start, they were placed as close to a river as possible; our Row have their privies on stilts out over the water, which is a good idea when there's a flood on but not so good in a July and August heatwave. All the houses suffer from damp and there's a cold river mist which wraps itself lovingly around you as soon as you open the back door.

The Dargan slides along fast and rounded and the same colour as a gun-barrel too, in the straight, dangerous stretch behind the houses. Young Tommy Scullion from Number Seven was drowned there in the school summer holidays last year. Four miles further on the spate of water spearheads a way out into the big Lough, then loses thrust, merges into the buff, turgid waters and dies. It is twenty-eight miles in length, and there are derelict basalt-built mills on its banks and on the banks of its tributaries for most of that length. The black walls merely get blacker with age but the softer, less durable insides have rotted long ago. Each mill has its Row or rows or square of houses and these are still occupied, although any life centred around the Mill has long lost any meaning. They are ugly, depressing places to live in. There are about three mills left which are still in operation. Kildargan is one of them.

Some of the older people, like 'Dixie' Dean in Number Five, and my old friend Tom Snoddy one door up, talk about the days when the place hummed and seven hundred hands worked from early in the morning until late at night, six days a week. Now, my father – he's a foreman in the Works – tells me there's only about forty left. And, as each month passes, the noise of the machines gets less and less, as one by one they change overnight from oily, rhythmic monsters to silent heaps of scrap. I can

338

remember the time when you ate, slept and breathed against the low background rumble. Now you catch yourself listening to the quiet.

Our mill is going through what is known in the Trade as a 'recession'. I say *our* mill, but, frankly, I couldn't care less what happens to it. It never did the workers any good – it just gave them rheumatics through working in the steamy damp, stripped to their semmits and long drawers. The Spences who own it, and the houses, and at one time the workers too, from all I hear, got the profits, some of which should have been ploughed back but wasn't.

I was standing up on the grass verge of the High Road looking down on all this. The flat valley-bottom's narrow at that point – just enough room for the Mill buildings and the houses and not much else. The High Road is built on the first shelf above the river, and on the opposite shelf runs the railway and the main Belfast to Derry road. They converge on Annagh.

Away on the furthest, highest side of the valley rim facing me, Knockaddy Mountain, covered almost to its knob with regular afforestation, rose above the lesser, bluer Antrim hills.

Up there the roofs of the cottages are of bleeding, corrugated tin, and the people who live under them – large families packed into two–three, small, low, thick-walled, dark rooms – are as hard as the stones that break through the soil every time you strip off a sod. They haven't changed since their ancestors first arrived from Ayrshire and the other depressed Scottish shires three centuries ago, not to better themselves, as it turned out, but to mark time, strugglingly. Hill folk. The same as the other side of the valley too, behind me. In the valley, living *on* the valley, people of the same stock, but not so elemental – farmers with Land-Rovers and a new bright red or blue Fordson Major every other year. And then *us*, neither one or the other – the industrials . . .

It was twenty past ten by my watch now, and the smoke from the Row's chimneys was rising straight and true into the light, cold air. There was still a wisp too of mist clinging to the river. An occasional car or lorry slipped past on the road behind me. Most of the cars were going up in the direction of Belfast – young country couples and families intent on getting the town's shopping done before the big shops closed. It looked like a grand day ahead, crisp and clean, the best kind of tail-end of February day.

from *The Liberty Lad*, 1965

A BOGSIDER'S EDUCATION

EAMONN MCCANN

When I was a very small boy we used to sing at passing Protestants:

> Proddy, proddy dick
> Your ma can't knit
> And your da
> Won't go to bed
> Without a dummy tit.

We might meet Protestants on the way to school because our school was outside the Bogside. No Protestant lived in the Bogside. The Unionist Party had seen to that. Not that the absence of Protestant neighbours was regarded by us as any deprivation. We came very early to our politics. One learned, quite literally at one's mother's knee, that Christ died for the human race and Patrick Pearse for the Irish section of it. The lessons were taught with dogmatic authority and were seemingly regarded as being of equal significance. Pearse ranked high in the teeming pantheon of Irish martyrdom. There were others. They had all died in the fight to free Ireland from British rule, a fight which had paused in partial victory in 1922 when twenty-six of our thirty-two counties won their independence. It was our task to finish the job, to cleanse the remaining traces of foreign rule from the face of Ireland.

No one was explicit as to how this would be done. Some said that Catholics, because of their higher birth-rate, would one day out-number Protestants in the Six Counties and that we could then vote ourselves democratically into an all-Ireland republic. Vague confidence was occasionally expressed that eventually the Protestants themselves would re-discover their Irish national heritage. And there were always those who said that sooner or later we were going to have to fight for it. We recognized that it was not an immediately attainable object, that it was not going to happen tomorrow, but no one ever doubted that some-day, somehow, it would come, and at moments of greater patriotic fervour we sang of it; that Ireland, long a province, would be 'a nation once again'.

We learned of the United Irishmen, the Fenian Movement, the Easter rising; of Emmet hanged, and Tone who had cut his throat in his cell to cheat the English executioner; of Connolly who was wounded in the leg and could not stand up so they strapped him to a chair to be shot; snatches from Pearse's speech at the grave of O'Donovan Rossa: 'The fools, the fools, the fools, they have left us our Fenian dead . . .' There were men in the area who embodied the tradition – Paddy Shiels, Neil Gillespie, Sean Keenan, Old Republicans who had fought in the past and been jailed and whose suffering represented a continued contribution from our community to the age-old struggle. They were regarded with guilty pride by the great majority as living out too urgently the ideals to which, tacitly, we were all committed. When Paddy Shiels died everyone said that he was a 'Great Irishman'.

Frankie Meenan was of the same stamp and always resented the fact that he had to speak English to make himself understood in the area. He ran classes in Gaelic for local children in a disused billiards hall in Chamberlain Street. Rows of children, few of whom would ever progress beyond primary school, would sit reciting in unison, '*Ta me, Ta tu, Ta se, Ta si* – I am, you are, he is, she is', and wrestling with the intricacies of the vocative case. Women in the street would ask Frankie: 'How's he getting on at the Irish?', to which he always replied: 'Oh, coming on, coming on.' Few ever became fluent, but it was felt right to make the effort. Frankie probably paid for the hire of the hall himself. He bought about thirty hurling sticks once and on Saturday mornings would take a crowd of us up to a field behind the Rosemount School, distribute the sticks and try to teach us the national game. The instructions were shouted in Irish, '*Anois, Buail e, buail e!*' and '*Ach, amadan,* bloody *amadan*' (Now hit it, hit it! Fool, bloody fool!) when one missed the ball completely for the *n*th time. There were always those who, privately, affected amusement at Frankie's activities, but no one openly denied him respect.

The Irish lessons and the hurling classes ended when Frankie was arrested one night in 1957. It was during the IRA's border campaign. He was coming home when a police car stopped and he was asked his name. He could have said, 'Frankie Meenan' but, being what he was, he said, '*Proinsias O'Mianain, ta me ag dul abhaile*' (I am going home), for which piece of bilingual impertinence he was taken to Crumlin Road jail in Belfast and held without trial for seven months. No one came out to riot about it – there was no point. He was released for his father's funeral and in an outburst of humanitarianism the then Minister of Home Affairs, Brian Faulkner, did not order his rearrest. Some months later Frankie went to live in Dublin. . . .

Religion and politics were bound up together, were regarded, indeed, as being in many ways the same thing. The oppression against which the political heroes of the past had fought was, we learned, primarily oppression of the church. Children would be taken by their parents to see Father Hegarty's Rock, outside Buncrana in Donegal, and told how Father Hegarty had dived from there into Lough Foyle to escape from the Redcoats, how the Redcoats had shouted to him that he would be guaranteed safe passage if he came back, how they had bayoneted him to death when, believing them, he had returned to the shore. It probably happened. We knew all about the Penal Days, when Catholics were not allowed to become lawyers or doctors or to own a horse worth more than five pounds, when every priest had a price on his head and people were burned to death for going to mass. Masses had to be said away deep in the hills, the people gathered around flat rocks, 'altar rocks', with sentries posted to watch for the Redcoats. During the Famine the English had offered food to anyone who would agree to change his religion, but through it all the people stayed faithful. The most rousing hymn in our repertoire was 'Faith of our Fathers':

> Faith of our Fathers, living still,
> In spite of dungeon, fire and sword.

An essential part of the Irish Freedom for which patriots had fought through the centuries was, we understood, the freedom to be Catholic. Priests themselves had often taken up the sword to lead the people in the fight. 'Father Murphy from old Kilcormack' who had 'spurred up the rock with a warning cry' in 1798 was among the most celebrated. . . .

Some of this one learned at home, a lot of it at school. The church controlled our education. At infants' school we were taught by nuns, who were kindly and dedicated. One learned the prayers and the catechism

343

answers by rote, how to salute a priest in the street, and what to do if one was ever introduced to a bishop. The three Rs were not neglected, but there was never any doubt about the priorities. After infants' school everything was geared towards passing the 11-plus.

The 1947 Education Act made a great difference to places like the Bogside. It created an educational obstacle-course which, if one could negotiate it, opened the way to grammar school and even university education – and Catholics had no handicap. Those who passed went to St Columb's College. Catholic Derry is steeped in the influence of St Columb's. Almost every Catholic teacher, Catholic doctor, Catholic solicitor, Catholic architect, accountant and businessman in the city was schooled there. The headmaster of a local intermediate school has no one on his staff whom he himself did not teach when he worked at St Columb's. Before the introduction of state scholarships St Columb's was the preserve of the Catholic middle class and, until the school got used to it, Bogsiders who arrived were made aware that they were intruding. Priest in a maths class: 'Where do you come from?' 'Rossville Street.' 'Oh yes, that's where they wash once a month.'

St Columb's described itself as a 'junior seminary' and one of its main functions was to supply candidates for the priesthood. Its other aim was to turn out upstanding Catholic citizens. About half the teachers were priests. Only the priests were eligible to become principal or vice-principal. Some of the priests interpreted their role in an eccentric fashion. Father D. could come into class and pick on a pupil in the front row: 'Kearney, think of a number.' 'Two, Father.' Then, starting with the boy sitting next to Kearney and counting: 'McLucas one, Patton two. Come out here, Patton.' Patton was given a beating with a strap and told, 'Don't blame me. Blame Kearney: he chose your number.' In later years Father D. explained that this was designed 'to encourage respect for your betters'. Dr M.'s favourite technique for inculcating love of the Latin language was to invite a boy to kneel on a platform in front of the class with hands stretched out in front and the feet, behind, raised off the ground. This is a very difficult thing to do. The boy was then made to open his mouth and a chalk duster inserted into it. If he fell forward on to his hands or relaxed backward so that his feet touched the ground he would be beaten around the head. Thus balanced precariously on the fulcrum of his knees and emitting animal grunts he would be invited to agree by a nodding of the head that he was a rogue, a ne'er-do-well, a stupid oaf who ought to be out digging roads and not wasting teachers' time and taxpayers' money here in St Columb's. Outside class Dr M. walked quietly and read his breviary. He was said to be an extremely clever and a very saintly man. Not all techniques were quite so sophisticated. Father F. might simply knock a boy unconscious and tell two of his class-mates to 'cart him outside. I'm not having him here, lying about in my classroom.' These were exceptions, but exceptions which were tolerated, in no way regarded as outrageous. Had lay teachers behaved so, there might have been protest from parents, but one did not question the activities of priests.

History lessons did not always rigidly follow the curriculum laid down by the Northern Ireland Ministry of Education. One teacher, admittedly regarded as something of an eccentric, was at pains to discredit English propaganda, such as that which suggested that Charles Stuart Parnell and Mrs Kitty O'Shea had been anything more than good friends. At the beginning of a new school year he would lead the class through the set text-book instructing them to tear out passages of fiction, such as those alleging that the Papal states had played a reactionary role during the Risorgimento. That done, lessons could begin.

Between a quarter and a fifth of the students at St Columb's were boarders. They were the sons of farmers and rural businessmen from Donegal and Counties Derry and Tyrone, and they were reckoned to be altogether more solid and sturdy than the tatty products of the Bogside who went to dances at night and consorted secretly with females. The boarders all played Gaelic football. Everyone was supposed to play but most day-boys dodged it. The priests, most of whom came from the same milieu as the boarders, were fanatical about the game and scornful of those whose distasteful origins placed them outside its fraternity. Which is not to say that the boarders had a good time. They were not allowed to go outside the school grounds and spent much of their free time walking around the paths in the grounds, which were known as 'the walks'. They did not have a great deal of free time anyway: there were four hours of compulsory study each evening.

Recreational facilities consisted of two gravel football pitches and two handball alleys. There was no gymnasium. Until the middle-fifties, all newspapers were banned. It was a punishable offence to possess a comic-book of any description or any book which had not been obtained from the school library. One was not allowed to have a radio on the premises. In so far as it could be organized and enforced, nothing alien was allowed to penetrate the defensive walls of the school grounds, nothing which might disrupt the educative process designed, in the words of Archbishop John Charles McQuaid, 'so to train the child entrusted to us that supernatural habits may become more firmly and more deeply rooted in its soul'.

One was taught to respect the authority of the church in all things. 'Catholic Social Science' provided a framework for industrial relations, of which 'doing a fair day's work' was a vital component. 'Catholic Apologetics' armed us with the answers to demolish anti-Catholic arguments from atheists, Protestants or any other errant individual. 'Church History' detailed the struggles of the church from the time of Christ to the present and proved the apostolic succession of the Pope. We were warned against 'modern errors' and told that undoubtedly we would come up against these in the future. In the late fifties Mr Bertrand Russell and his writings and activities were the subject of especial execration.

By 'ordinary' educational standards St Columb's was quite a successful school, yearly notching up the average number of state exhibitions and university scholarships. But this, one was told repeatedly, was by no means the only or most important aspect of its work. In the end we had been involved in an intellectual package deal, and had been given a complete set of ideas, attitudes and pieces of knowledge and urged to understand that these were adequate to equip one for any human situation in which it was proper ever to find oneself. One sensed that it was suspected that we were not properly grateful. In our own area St Columb's boys were seen in a different light. We were the first generation ever given the opportunity to climb out of our condition, and much was expected of us.

The church's insistence on controlling the education of Catholic children affected not only those directly at the receiving end. Through the parish Building Fund it involved the whole community. The price of opting out of the state system was that the church authorities had to find thirty-five per cent of the cost of school buildings. In a depressed community with a high birth-rate and a thirst for education this was a considerable problem. It was answered with sales-of-work, jumble sales, Christmas bazaars, lotteries, Sunday night concerts, silver collections on the third Sunday of each month, pantomimes, door-to-door collections, and much else besides. All these required volunteer workers with high motivation. For some, the parish Building Fund became not so much a spare-time activity as a way of life. The collection of money and articles for sale and the selling of tickets for weekly functions kept every household in almost daily contact with the church, provided the occasion for constant, repeated renewal of commitment to it.

The intellectual diet served by the church, the schools and the Nationalist Party was supplemented by the local paper, although not to the extent of providing any variation. Everyone in the area read the *Derry Journal*. The *Journal* appeared thrice weekly until 1958, when it became a bi-weekly, published on Tuesdays and Fridays. The harmonizing voices of the church and the Nationalist Party spoke to us from its editorial columns. These were couched in a curious, florid style which may be peculiar to Irish provincial newspapers. The word 'forsooth' was commonly employed to indicate emphasis. The *Journal* was, and is, bitterly anti-Unionist, passionately pro-Fianna Fail, reverently Catholic and hysterically anti-communist. It never wrote 'Northern Ireland', always ' "Northern" Ireland'; never 'Londonderry', always ' "London" derry'. Even the punctuation was patriotic.

from *War and an Irish Town*, 1974

BELFAST BUILDINGS

C.E.B. BRETT

In the years since 1966, the architectural character of Belfast has changed utterly: and not for the better. It has been a sobering experience to re-perambulate its streets (or such of them as still exist) carrying the same notebook in which I started work more than a quarter-century ago, on the first of January, 1959, on the first edition of this book. Then, and still at the time of publication, Belfast was (as I wrote) 'a very individual city, with a pronounced character all its own'; a character made up of an uncommon combination of Georgian, low and high Victorian, and Edwardian, buildings, with – at any rate in the city centre – only a tolerable sprinkling of incongruous later ones.

In fact, a surprising number of the best individual buildings recorded in 1966 are still there; it is their surroundings rather than themselves which have mostly deteriorated. But the overall effect has nonetheless been horrifying.

Four principal causes have contributed to this. Three of them – the property boom of the sixties and early seventies; the inexorable processes of inner-city decay; and the constant growth in the demands for space of cars, vans, lorries, containers, and juggernauts – have, in varying degrees, exerted similar pressures on almost every other city in the western world. The fourth cause, the so-called 'Troubles' of Ulster, has been purely local. And in my view the compound fractures so inflicted have been aggravated by the unsympathetic fashions of the day amongst architects, engineers, and town planners.

The property boom, which lasted from the mid-sixties until the mid-seventies, struck all too damagingly at the dignified mercantile heart of Victorian and Edwardian Belfast. Many fine buildings were lost, and many greatly inferior ones were substituted for them. Few of the new buildings, even when tolerably good in themselves, were in scale or sympathy with their neighbours; although in this respect there has been some improvement in the eighties. Happily, many office blocks of this period are already suffering from the defects of their shoddiness, and, it may reasonably be hoped, will fall down soon.

There is no lack of egregious examples: one of the most striking was the destruction of the very fine warehouse block in Bedford Street and its lesser but worthy neighbours in Franklin Street and James Street South, despite loud cries of protest, to make way for the 23-storey Windsor House. This was doubly tragic: for an insurance company had been found, able and willing to restore and modernise the existing buildings, until deterred by the unrest in the city; moreover, it is now widely acknowledged to have been a grave mistake to have allowed so exceptionally tall a building to over-shadow the City Hall and the heart of the city.

Another case where developers and bombers between them brought about disaster was the Ulster Club in Castle Place, an imposing building by Sir Charles Lanyon. After it had been vacated by the clubmen, it lay vacant for many months, indeed years, and suffered bomb damage which was allowed to go unrepaired; on my last visit to it, in company with Philip Goodhart (then minister at the Department of the Environment), whom I still hoped to persuade to refuse consent for demolition, we had both to wear gum-boots even in the ground-floor rooms, so deep was the litter of soaked plaster and reeking pigeon-dung which, along with wet rot everywhere, had resulted from holes in the roof and broken windows left unmended. Alas, even I was forced to conclude that it was a hopeless case for restoration and it seemed not right to demand a replica.

The record of public bodies in the field of office design is no more creditable than that of the private developers: Churchill House, River House, Telephone House, the Post Office slab fronting Donegall Quay, the Ministry of Commerce block in Chichester Street: none of these is a loved or loveable ornament to the landscape. Most of the new office-blocks, public or private, are in the faceless international style, and could be anywhere in the world: whereas the banks, warehouses and offices they replaced were richly carved and detailed in an individual and inimitable style more characteristic of Belfast than of any other city.

The population of the city has fallen quite sharply from a peak of 443,000 in 1951 to an estimated figure, at the date of writing, of 305,000, notwithstanding the boundary extension of 1971. In some ways this fall of well over 25% of the inhabitants of a formerly greatly overcrowded city has been a good thing, though of course it has brought some awkward problems in its wake. What brought it about? Partly it has been due to slum clearance, euphemistically called 'redevelopment', and the far higher space standards required for the replacement dwellings. Partly it has been due to a contraction in the traditional inner-city industries, combined with the establishment of new industrial estates in a twenty-five-mile ring all around the city; followed by a general recession affecting all manufacturing. Partly it has been due to the flight of warehousing and wholesaling to the outskirts, because of the difficulty of handling large container loads in congested streets and loading-bays. Partly it has been due to changes (very regrettable ones, many people feel) in the pattern of shopping: the closure not only of the hundreds of small uneconomic back-street shops, but also of traditional general or specialist emporiums in the city centre (such as Robb's, Arnott's, Robinson & Cleaver's, the Bank Buildings); and the growth of shopping centres, served by acre upon acre of car-parks, around the periphery. Partly it has been due to the natural wish of young householders to bring up their families in pleasanter surroundings than the old narrow streets, their still narrower back alleys, and their overcrowded parks and playgrounds; not to mention the vandalism and violence endemic in so many districts.

As the human population has dwindled, so the pressures of road traffic and the demands for parking have increased. It must be acknowledged, however ruefully, that action had to be taken if the whole city was not quickly to become clogged up. In the late sixties, ambitious road plans, involving extensive demolition, were drawn up. There was, in particular, much debate on the scheme for a six-lane Urban Motorway, to cut a broad swathe right through the northern sections of the inner city. Several alternative routes were canvassed; one political party came up with a particularly ingenious route which would have meant the demolition of the headquarters of all its rivals! In the end, the original scheme was abandoned on grounds mostly of its phenomenal cost; and the Westlink, a comparatively narrow four-lane roadway, in parts sunken, without hard shoulders or extravagant landscaping (but also without separation of levels at several busy junctions) was built instead.

The combined effect of the opening of this new road, and the closing to through traffic (for security reasons) of the former main axis of the city through Donegall Place and Royal Avenue, has wrought the single largest change from any cause in the character and structure of Belfast. The inner and outer roadways (still far from complete) which have accompanied it have had almost equally devastating effects. Vast dreary car-parks, still inadequate to the demand as they are, have finally broken up the city's streetscape and pattern.

This is not all loss, of course; traffic jams and parking problems in Belfast are very much less severe than those in Dublin, where (rightly or wrongly) much less attempt has been made to tame the motor-car. But unhappily, however technically proficient they may be, roads engineers seem to be rather an insensitive body of men. Countless good buildings, and a few exceptionally fine ones, have been swept away; wide acres of tarmac and cement, retaining walls, ugly street furniture, railings and the all-pervading invasion of space-leftover, have replaced a formerly digni-fied and coherent townscape with a kind of vast, straggling, unworthy no-man's land.

Many visitors to Belfast have been appalled by the wide acres of waste-land and devastation, which they have been too hasty in attributing en-tirely to the Troubles. Yet the Troubles have caused damage enough. The bombing campaigns, at their worst in 1970–3 but flaring up again from time to time ever since, have been for the most part aimed at 'economic targets' – warehouses, shops, public-houses, offices; or at public build-ings; or premises used by the police or army. In some instances the targets have been very deliberately selected, but probably more often the sites have been chosen just so as to inflict a maximum of damage. Great quan-tities of explosives have been used, often in car-bombs. It is not to be overlooked that, for every building actually destroyed, very many others – within a radius as great as a quarter of a mile – may suffer serious injury. Window-sashes, doors, slates, skylights, roof-timbers, chimneys, have of-ten been destroyed, over a wide area, and by no means always replaced. Incendiaries and fire-bombs have had on the whole slightly less extensive effects, though a fire may spread from the building attacked to its neigh-bours; and gutted buildings are seldom capable of reconstruction.

In the residential parts of the city, though indeed bomb-damage and fire-damage have not been unknown (as witness the burning of whole terraces at Bombay Street in 1969 and Farringdon Gardens in 1971), the pattern of damage has been somewhat different. Here, rioting, street-fighting, barricades, and gunfire between the 'defenders' of adjacent but mutually hostile areas, have led to massive population movements: the first wave in the autumn of 1969, the second in the summer of 1971. Since then, each community has retreated into its own territory, and derelict strips of uninhabitable no-man's land mark the dividing-lines between the zones.

In physical terms, the visible consequences of this unrest have been striking: but they have also changed progressively over the troubled years. At quite an early stage, the whole central shopping area of the city was ringed with steel railings and security gates, of great ugliness, designed to exclude the bombers. (It is a remarkable fact that these railings followed almost exactly the line of the long-demolished 17th-century town ramparts.) The area within the barriers became an at first involuntary, but later a popular and highly successful, large-scale pedestrian precinct. Metal barrels or concrete tubs filled with cement were placed around likely targets so as to make impossible the near approach of car-bombers. Booms, locked at night, were placed across the roads at the principal crossing points between the territory of one faction and the other. Windows were first criss-crossed with adhesive tape, then treated with shatter-proof film; or covered in steel grilles; or, following the invention of the grille-bomb using a butcher's double hook, covered altogether in steel plate. In the working-class streets, screens of corrugated iron were at an early stage erected by the army along some of the most violent boundaries of confrontation, and wryly christened 'Peace Lines'. (It is a remarkable fact that the barrier between the Falls and Shankill Roads follows, to within a few inches, the dividing line recorded by the Commission of Inquiry into the Belfast riots of 1886.) Police stations and army posts in central and outer areas alike were increasingly heavily fortified with sandbags, tall wire-mesh screens, 'sangars', pill-boxes, humps in the roadway outside, and chicanes.

To an astonishing extent, the city has now assimilated, and even come to take for granted, these extraordinary adjuncts to urban life as it is mostly lived elsewhere. The railings and security gates have been 'prettified': they have today something of the look of ornamental garden wrought-iron gates. The tubs and barrels have largely been replaced by elegant

352

cast-iron bollards with an ornamental sea-horse (from the city's coat of arms) picked out in a contrasting colour. The peace lines have been rebuilt in brick, sometimes with decorative insets and graffito repellent. (Incidentally, the M1 Motorway and Westlink roadway serve as another rough and ready peace line along some parts of their length.) Pill-boxes are fetchingly disguised as *cottages ornées*; new police stations are designed to be defensible in the most tasteful way possible. The pedestrianisation of the city centre has proved a blessing in disguise; the suspicious shopkeepers would never before have agreed to it, but now the lunchtime crowds in Ann Street, Cornmarket, Castle Lane and Donegall Place on sunny days have brought back prosperity from the shopping centres of the outer suburbs. There is a sort of grim realism about the design of new buildings of every kind, including public and private houses: security considerations are seldom left altogether out of account: but then, security from robbers and vandals is a material consideration elsewhere, too.

. . . Georgian, Victorian and Edwardian Belfast derived its character to a great extent from the seemly terraces which lined all its streets and radial roads: fine tall buildings in or near the centre, slightly less tall ones further out, but still coherent and dignified on frontages such as those of University Road, the Antrim Road, the Ormeau Road. Not only do people not want to live in tall houses like these today, they do not much want to live facing the noise, smells, vibration and pollution generated by heavy traffic on the main roads. (Horses were smelly, carts and carriages were noisy, and traffic accidents not infrequent, a century ago; but that is by the way.) So what is to be built along these road frontages? No so-called barrier block yet designed is visually satisfactory. The Housing Executive has made valiant efforts to develop a new formula, particularly the three-storey dwellings it has built on the Antrim Road and the Donegall Pass; but it is only in rare cases that the commercial frontages to main roads fall within the remit of the Executive. Unless means can be found of providing suitably scaled and proportioned buildings to front onto the main roads of the city (not to mention the Westlink), the appearance, character and integrity of Belfast will continue to degenerate as they have done over the past two decades.

from Introduction to *Buildings of Belfast 1700–1914* (revised edition), 1985

Crossing the Lisburn Road

Michael Longley

Because of our reduced circumstances my parents could not afford to send Peter and me to one of the posher preparatory schools. (They were both old-fashioned Tories.) We attended the local Public Elementary School where, out of a large class of nearly forty pupils, we were almost the only middle-class children. Most of the others lived on 'the wrong side' of the Lisburn Road. Their clothes were different from ours – woollen balaclavas, laced boots with studs in the soles. Alongside them Peter and I must have appeared chubby and well-scrubbed. I noticed at once the skinny knees and snotty noses, but most of all the accent, abrasive and raucous as a football rattle. This I soon acquired in order to make myself less unacceptable. 'Len' us a mey-ek' – 'Lend me a make' (a ha'penny). At home I would try to remember to ask for 'a slice of cake' and not 'a slice a'cey-ek', to refer to the 'door' and the 'floor' rather than 'doo-er' and 'floo-er'. By the age of six or seven I was beginning to lead a double life, learning how to re-create myself twice daily.

I made friends with the other pupils and started to explore the Lisburn Road. Belfast's more prosperous citizens have usually been careful to separate themselves safely from the ghettoes of the bellicose working classes. An odd exception is the Lisburn Road which runs south from the city centre. Intermittently for about three miles workers' tiny two-up-and-two-down houses squint across the road at the drawing-rooms of dentists, doctors, solicitors: on the right, as you drive towards Lisburn gardenless shadowy streets, on the left rhododendrons and rose bushes. Belfast laid bare, an exposed artery.

I spent much of my childhood drifting from one side to the other, visiting the homes of my new friends: the lavatory outside in the yard, stairs ascending steeply as you entered, low ceilings and no elbow-room at all. My first tea at Herbie Smith's was fried bread sprinkled with salt. Herbie came to our house and gasped when he saw the size of our back garden. For the first time I felt ashamed of our relative affluence.

Our separate drawing and dining-rooms, the hall with its wooden panelling, the lavatory upstairs were all novelties to Herbie. He seemed curious rather than envious. Every corner of the home I had taken for granted was illuminated by his gaze as by wintry sunlight.

Another pupil John McCluskey was often caned for being late. He delivered papers for Younger the newsagent. If the *Belfast News-Letter* was delayed, John without complaint or explanation would be standing at 9.30 in front of the class, his hand presented to the whistling cane and then hugged under his armpit as he stumbled over schoolbags to his desk. Should I have told the teacher that he delivered papers to *our* house? Sometimes, as though to drown his sorrows, John would swig the blue-grey sludge from one of the small white inkwells. Every December my father gave me a half-crown as a Christmas box for the paper boy, as he called him. I never told my father that the paper boy was in my class. On the doorstep John McCluskey and I behaved like strangers and avoided each other's eyes as the half-crown changed hands. Later in class the transaction would not be mentioned.

John and Herbie shared with me their mythology which was mostly concerned with Roman Catholics. Did I know why Taigs crossed themselves? What dark practices lurked behind confession and Mass? Didn't the nuns kidnap little girls and imprison them behind the suspiciously high walls of the big convent at the top of the Ormeau Road? The Orange Order and the B Specials marched through our conversations. The son of English parents, I was, at nine, less politically aware than my classmates. A photograph at home of Grandpa George lording it in his Mason's apron prompted me once to speak with snooty disparagement of the less dignified Orangemen. I was sent to Coventry until I apologised. To secure the conversion two friends smuggled to me under the desk pamphlets which purported to describe Catholic atrocities from the twenties and thirties. Every page carried blurred photographs of victims who, it was claimed, had been tortured and mutilated, their brains or hearts cut out, their genitals chopped off. Forgeries? Adaptations of photographs of road accidents from forensic files? Or real victims? This vitriolic propaganda burned deep into my mind, and I perused those grim pages with the same obsessiveness that I was later to devote to *The Red Light* and nudist magazines. I craved the bond of shared fears and superstitions.

At primary school (and later at grammar school) there was little on the curriculum to suggest that we were living in Ireland: no Irish history except when it impinged on the grand parade of English monarchs; no Irish literature; no Irish art; no Irish music. When we sang in music classes we mouthed English songs. One inspector criticised our accents and forced us to sing, 'Each with his bonny lawss/a-dawncing on the grawss'. Our teacher in Form Three, an affable man who coaxed us through the Three Rs with care and skill, became tense when for one term we were joined by a boy from Dublin – a Protestant but still a focus for our suspicions. Having flirted for a while with the unfortunate nine-year-old's political ignorance and his own paranoia, the teacher eventually decided to confront this embodiment of menace and treachery. It was a crude question.

'Niall, who owns Belfast?'

'Dublin, sir.'

'Who? Who?' This was much more than he had hoped for. 'To the front of the class, boy.'

'Who owns Belfast?'

'Dublin, sir.' A slap in the face.

'Who told you that?' Another slap. A spittly crescendo of hatred.

'My granny, sir.' More slaps. And Niall in tears.

We were invited to correct the error, to put down the rebellion. We did so and felt frightened and exhilarated.

With its dozens of little shops and the Regal Cinema where entrance to the front stalls cost threepence, the Lisburn Road became my hinterland. The cinema was demolished not so long ago, and many of the shops have now been transformed into Chinese restaurants and fast food takeaways. But the rows of back-to-back houses remain, the homes of Herbie Smith, John McCluskey, Norman Hamilton, Sally Patterson, John Boland, Alan Gray, Helen Ferguson, Norma Gamble.

from 'Tu-penny Stung', *Poetry Review*, January 1985

6

'The sticks and stones of an old grudge'

MICHAEL LONGLEY

MEMORIES OF ULSTER

CAROLINE BLACKWOOD

And for all that I found there I might as well be
Where the Mountains of Mourne sweep down to the sea.

Many people from Ulster have always felt that the man who wrote that song was a liar. 'If the fellow once managed to get himself out of Northern Ireland,' a woman from Belfast once said to me, 'it's a bit hard to believe he's all that sincere when he pretends he was always fretting to get back. But the tune's all right, and the sentiment is all right. And in Ulster, of course,' she added, 'the tune and the sentiment have always been the thing.'

That was long ago. But I still feel surprised whenever I hear Ulster mentioned in the news. It always used to seem like the archetypal place where nothing would, or could, ever happen. For as long as I can remember, boredom has seemed to be hanging over Northern Ireland like the grey mists that linger over her loughs. Boredom has seemed to be sweating out of the blackened Victorian buildings of Belfast, running down every tram-line of her dismal streets. Now, when Northern Ireland is mentioned, the word 'internment' rattles through every sentence like the shots of a repeating rifle. And yet for years and years so many Ulster people, both Catholic and Protestant, have felt that they were 'interned' in Ulster – interned by the gloom of her industrialised provinciality, by her backwaterishness, her bigotry and her tedium.

In 1940, war was seen as a solution. 'All the American troops will liven things up a bit round here.' But the last war never broke the back of Ulster's boredom. Everyone kept predicting – almost with pleasure – that the Belfast docks would be a prime German target, that Hitler would almost certainly launch his invasion via Northern Ireland. All the sign-posts were swivelled round in the Ulster lanes to trick his troops, and force tanks which had hoped to roll towards Ballynahinch into ending up in Ballygally. However effective all these crafty precautions would have been in the event of a full-scale Axis landing, they turned out to be

359

needless. There were very few raids, and one of these by error bombed what Protestant Northerners called 'collaborationist' Dublin. This was said to be an act of God.

The American troops livened things up very little in Ulster. They hadn't much to do except hand out chewing-gum to the kids. They slouched miserably through their 'duration' – and then they were gone. The few bonneted black faces which appeared in Ulster prams were the only memorable trace that they left of their unenjoyable stay.

And day after day – post-war, just as they had pre-war – in the grey squares of the Ulster villages groups of men in tweed caps, most of them toothless and out of work, went on standing around in huddles. They would rub their hands and mutter, and sometimes have a smoke, like people on a platform waiting endlessly for some cancelled train. And day after day – post-war, just as they had pre-war – in the wealthy suburbs of Belfast the wives of industrialists went on reading the Bible, drinking their sherry and eating scones. In those days all their houses were meant to contain that most curious of rooms known as 'the parlour'. The parlour was always musty and unused. There every stick of silver, every horse-show trophy and spoon, every candelabra and christening-cup, that the family had ever acquired was always laid out day and night, as though in defiant display of the rewards of Protestant virtue. Far too valuable to be used, and very heavily insured, there used to be a desolation to all this silver, which was polished daily by the maid and seemed to be perpetu-ally waiting on its mahogany table as if in preparation for some longed-for, but never-arriving occasion. And very much the same effect used to be created, in the rooms which were in use for entertaining, by all the plaster Peter Scott geese, which were nailed so that they appeared to be flying past the photograph of the Royal Family in a freedom arc up the side of the wall. Sometimes one had the feeling that these status-symbol geese themselves secretly knew that their flight was an illusion: that they were just as static as their owners, that they would never fly out of these stifling, expensive interiors, where the light could hardly penetrate all the Gothic-cathedral stained-glass of the windows.

Then there were the Ulster Sundays. Post-war, there were still the Ul-ster Sundays: the war changed them not at all. On Sundays all the towns were still closed down, so that they seemed like the ghost towns of Colorado, and the Day of Rest went on being so well-observed that the serving of a cup of tea was still damned as a violation. When anyone died, people still went on saying that they feared it was a 'judgment': that the dead one must have gone out driving, or drunk a Guinness, or read some novel on a Sunday.

And the war never changed the sermons which were preached on those Ulster Sundays, and the families still trailed off to listen to them. They would go all dressed up with hats and gloves and coins for the collection, taking their bored and dressed-up children. One particular sermon I heard in Ulster has always stayed with me. It was delivered on a Christmas Day, and the minister preached it from a pulpit decorated with holly. He said that on this special day he would like to start by quoting 'the most beautiful words in the English language'. His choice was curious: 'The womb of a virgin hath he not abhorred.' In his own terms, it was a daring choice. And some puritanical hesitation seemed to panic him, forcing him into a slip. He paused dramatically before delivering his words, and then boomed them out in ringing church-chant tones: 'The worm of a virgin hath he not abhorred.' I looked round his congregation. Surely they would have some reaction to this most unusual Christmas Day text. But all the scrubbed faces seemed to be in their usual trance. Glazed eyes just went on staring despondently at dusty hassocks, at the bleakness of the altar, stripped of all ornamentation to make a contrast with the idolatrous churches of the Papacy. Not one single person reacted to the minister's beautiful words – for not one person had heard them. His congregation had been interned by his sermons for far too long for his words to have any more power to penetrate the defensive depths of their devout deafness.

'Do you come from Northern Ireland?' I remember Foxy Falk barking the question at me years ago at an Oxford dinner. I was used to contemptuous responses from English people whenever I answered this question. 'The South of Ireland is very nice,' was all they would usually say. Or else, making one feel like some kind of mongrel impostor: 'Oh, then you are not even proper Irish at all.' But I felt that the question, when asked by Foxy Falk, was going to lead to something a little different. A collector of Ming vases, Cézannes and Persian carpets, he was a man who said that he believed in 'the rule of the élite and the artist'. He was tyrannical, reading Keats's letters aloud to people who had little desire to hear them, forbidding anyone in his household to use the telephone because he felt that it had ruined the art of conversation – and thereby creating daily difficulties as to grocery orders etc. He would intimidate by his spluttering rages, which made one fear that the boil of his anger would crack his arteries. He was famous for the fact that he had once been Pavlova's lover.

'Do you come from Ulster?' I saw that the charge behind his question had already turned his whole face to a tomato-coloured balloon. Then his fist came smashing down on to the table so that the knives went shivering against the glasses. 'All I can say is that the place where you come from ought to be blown up! It ought to be blown skyhigh, and wiped from the face of this earth!' If he felt like that . . . I found myself staring blankly at his poor old turkey wattles, which were wobbling with agitation as they dripped down over his high Edwardian collar.

Then he calmed a little and explained that Pavlova at the height of her fame had danced in Belfast, and that the theatre had been totally empty except for two people. He claimed that she had never felt so insulted and distressed in her whole life – that Belfast was the only place in the world which had ever given her such a criminal reception.

Maybe because of the bombastic way the whole subject had been approached, and because I felt I was being personally blamed for the disastrous unsuccess of her visit, all I could feel was a sudden impatience with both Pavlova and her lover. Why were they so astounded by what to me seemed to be so very unastounding? What could have made them think that her dance could ever set the grimy dockyards of Belfast dancing? When had the most austere of cities ever pretended for one moment that its prime interest was the dance?

I thought of the Ulster Protestants. Surely they had enough problems without having to be 'wiped from the face of this earth' for being a poor audience. A fear of Catholics bred into them from childhood until it became instinctive like a terror of spiders. Their lifelong drill of eccentric Ulster commandments. 'Never drink from the same glass that a Catholic has drunk from. Any such glass should be broken immediately.' And then their feeling of always being beleaguered, with the enemy pressing its full weight against the feeble ribbon of the border. Their suspicion that the

362

enemy's prohibition on birth-control was a crafty long-term plan to out-breed them. Finally, their way of seeing the enemy – it's a very common way of seeing enemies – as dirty, lazy and cruel, plotting and promiscuous, and with one extra unforgivable vice – prone to dancing on a Sunday.

What happened? Everyone asks this as they look at the rubbled streets of Belfast and Londonderry on the television. The question never seems to be well answered, and only leads to more questions. If there had been no Catholics, would the Ulster Protestants have found it necessary to invent them? Certainly for years and years they provided the only spark of thrill and threat which could blast the monotony of the Ulster everyday. Month after month I remember listening to the same repeating rumours that the Catholics were marching up from Dublin – 'mustering' on the border – and infiltrating industry. Did all those interminable Ulster sermons seem less tedious when it was envisaged that iron-handed Papists might very soon try to put a stop to them? Did the polluted belch of Northern industry seem less hideous if it was felt that greedy Papal fingers were tentacling out to grasp the factories?

Can there be a boredom so powerful that it finally acts like an explosive? Marx said that the cottage must never be too near the castle. If England was the castle, was the provincial cottage of Ulster just a little bit too near?

'Wouldn't you think that people might be less bigoted in this day and age?' English people keep on asking me that. 'You certainly would think so,' I answer. And immediately I find myself doing a double-take. 'Why would you think that they might be?' I wonder. 'What reasons are there for thinking so?'

Every day the Ulster victims are flashed on the British television screens. They stutter out their tragedies in accents so unintelligible to the English that they might as well be speaking Swahili, and then they are cut off in mid-sentence for lack of television time.

When the Reverend Ian Paisley makes an occasional BBC appearance he seems awkward, oafish and provincial. He seems to lose all his rhetorical teeth when he is speaking to an English audience. He needs the roll and rattle of the Orange kettledrums to accompany his impassioned and oracular calls to duty. He needs to have his fanatical congregation, and King Billy of the Boyne, and The Lord, behind him. To see him on the BBC, who could believe that he could be idolised in Ulster? Who would ever think that he was an innovator – that back home in his Northern Irish church he has invented something quite as new as the 'paper collection'? For Ian Paisley has said that the Lord wants no more coins. . . . During his services, when the collection plate is passed round the congregation, the pounds pile up on it like great mounds of crumpled Kleenexes. But then when the plate is handed in to him, Dr Paisley refuses to bless it. He just looks at it in sad silence and he shakes his enormous head. 'The Lord,' he says, 'is not going to be very pleased with this.' And the plate is sent back to the congregation for another round.

And while the Reverend's collection plate is circulating, the IRA seems less and less heroic as they blow the legs and arms off typists, and plant their gelignite wires across the routes of the school buses. And yet Ulster's rate of mental disease keeps on dropping as the troubles persist. Doctors claim they have never known it so low. All the while the Ulster Defence Association, dressed up like Ku Klux Klansmen, like Knights Templar from Outer Space, are drilling, and recruiting from the Orange Lodges of Scotland. They too set up their 'no go' areas and their kangaroo courts. Last week I spoke to a Protestant who lives in County Down. 'You don't like to go out at night,' she said. 'You feel that you might run into some roaming regiment of UDA with all their guns, and their goggles, and fishnet stockings over their mouths. And you feel that they might not like the look of you. They might set up a kangaroo court, and you'd be tried in their pouch.' War games . . . And on both sides how many really want them to end one can sometimes despondently wonder. Has the whole province become intoxicated with its new-found power to seize the international headlines from its ancient overshadowing and world-important sister, England? Does it now feel some perverse and destructive terror of sinking back into a humdrum and peaceful obscurity in which the individual Ulsterman will no longer feel the superiority and glory of springing from a world-famed trouble-spot?

'Why not move all the Protestants out?' English liberals keep suggesting. 'Why not move all the Catholics out?' Another common, and less liberal, suggestion. Both suggestions make it all sound so easy, like moving pinned flags on a staff map. Families, farms, occupations, the tie to

364

the place of birth – all these things are made to seem like trifling, selfish quirks, which should be sacrificed for the greater good of the community. But who is going to decide which community most deserves this greater good? Then you are back again with an 'Ulster problem'.

'Why can't they all just get on with one another?' The English can seem very smug at the moment. . . . If the IRA started hurling high explosives into the shopping-centres of Maidstone or Colchester, how long would it take before Catholic families living in the areas began to feel afraid of reprisals?

'Memories of Ulster', from *For All That I Found There*, 1973

COMMONPLACE EXPERIENCES

C.E.B. BRETT

On the evening of 28 May 1972 my wife and I dined with friends near the south shore of Belfast Lough, some seven miles from the centre of the city. Sound travels far over water; as we were sitting talking after dinner, we heard a series of heavy explosions – nothing unusual about that, of course, in 1972 or since. Wryly I remarked that somebody was getting a battering tonight, and the conversation continued. We reached home about midnight. Soon afterwards, the telephone rang; it was one of my partners; 'You've heard by now, I suppose?' 'No, what?' 'The office has been blown up.' There was nothing more to be done that night, except to awaken our architect and arrange to meet him there at first light to assess the damage.

A stolen car, with an extremely large bomb in it, had been left in the narrow lane behind our office. No warning was given. It blew up (to quote the police report) 'at 8.56 p.m.', causing 'extensive damage over a wide area', and 'extensive structural damage to property near the seat of the explosion'. The lane is like a canyon, closely hemmed in by buildings on both sides, which magnified the effects of the blast. Our poor care-taker was blown right across his basement kitchen, but was fortunate enough to escape worse injury than shock, scratches, and bruises. I have no reason to think that the bomb was particularly aimed at us; the firm employed Catholics and Protestants with impartiality; many neighbours suffered equally; it was simply a place to achieve the maximum damage with the greatest economy of means.

Next morning was Bank Holiday Monday. It was a heart-breaking day, though it closed with the comforting advice that the main part of the building, farthest from the bomb, was not so unsafe that it must be de-molished. My own room had come off comparatively lightly, shielded in part by the stable-block at the rear. Of course the window had been blown in, and sharp fragments of glass had scarred the furniture and walls; the door had been blown off its hinges. The damage was much worse upstairs. All the back windows, and their slim Georgian astragals, had been blown in; most of the panes at the front had been blown out; internal doors and partitions had been wrenched from the main walls; one of the two great beams carrying the roof had cracked and sagged; many slates were off; chunks of plaster had fallen from the ceilings: the whole building had been lifted a few inches into the air and then dropped again a fraction out of true; the staircase and the polished mahogany banister-rail were sadly scarred and battered; files, documents, papers, had been thrown into confusion; dislodged dirt and fragments of glass had been scattered everywhere.

The former stable-block at the rear took the full force of the blast. The car-bomb had been placed some eighteen inches from the outer wall of the strong-room; which, designed to resist fire, did not prove strong enough to resist fifty pounds of high explosives. The whole wall was blown in: one of the wheels of the car was found, a week later, blown some fifteen feet into the wreckage. The concrete slabs of the ceiling were canted crazily, many now resting only on the buckled remains of the steel shelving with which the strong-room had been lined. The rooms above were, of course, completely destroyed. Beyond the strong-room, a little further from the bomb, was the ground-floor office used by my father since his semi-retirement. That morning the back wall to the lane had wholly disappeared, leaving the ceiling unsupported; but to my astonishment, the inlaid eighteenth-century grandfather clock, though scarred by glass, was still ticking, and showing the correct time. Alas, I made an incautious movement in the doorway: at 9.30 a.m. precisely the ceiling collapsed in front of me, and the poor clock disintegrated into hundreds of fragments under a pile of chalk and laths. (The pieces were collected, reassembled, and the clock painstakingly restored: it now keeps perfect time once again.)

It took a week before we knew how much, or little, had been lost. The beams of the strong-room ceiling had to be shored up individually and the steel shelving (which had saved us from fire) laboriously cut away, section by section, with hammer and cold chisel. Within the pigeon-holes, deeds and documents had been compressed together like fish fingers as the shelving was hurled across the room; japanned tin deed-boxes had been twisted and crumpled; some bundles of papers were damaged by the rain that drove into the wreckage during that unhappy week: but only a few of the precious documents were lost or destroyed. Teams of us worked in our oldest clothes, filthy and often bleeding from scratches made by slivers of broken glass, to clear up the mess; to sort and label the papers; and to pack them into tea-chests for transport to the basement vaults of a neighbouring insurance company.

It took three years to settle our claim for compensation: since the building was an old one, the amount of the eventual award fell far short of the cost of replacing old with new.

It took almost five years to complete the rebuilding. We are now nearly, though not quite, back to normal. Some changes were unavoidable. There is no resident caretaker now: today I have a gas fire in my room instead of the fire of coal and turf that used to be laid and lit each morning in winter until 1972.

On the first working day after the explosion, I took a break for lunch, dirty and angry and dressed in my old clothes; at the table I met a Belfast business-man, a prominent Unionist and an Orangeman. I have never forgotten, and am unlikely ever to forgive, his first words to me: 'Well, sorry about your bomb, but it serves you right for your years in the Labour party.'

On the evening of 13 June 1974 I arrived home from work as usual around six o'clock. 'Home' was a comfortable foursquare former manse in the Malone Road area of Belfast. It was a very pleasant summer evening; the long avenue of lime trees was in full leaf. The children were away. My wife was waiting for me with the news: 'They say there's a car-bomb in the park behind us.' This was the parallel avenue some 75 yards away. Somebody had shouted a warning over the hedge; the ends of the avenue had been sealed off by the police, and the houses fronting it cleared. There had recently been a good many bombs in the city, mostly in commercial buildings, but there had also been a vast number of hoaxes and scares. 'I don't believe it,' I said; 'let's sit down and have a glass of sherry. But we'd better keep away from the windows.' (There is always a quandary in a bomb-scare: if windows and doors are opened, the damage is minimised, for the blast-wave can travel freely till it spends itself: but anyone in the process of opening windows when the explosion comes may be dreadfully mutilated by flying glass.) We decided to leave the windows alone, poured ourselves sherry, and sat down in our usual chairs on either side of the fireplace in the sunny drawing-room.

Five minutes later, as we were sitting peaceably chatting and sipping, there was the loudest explosion I have (yet) heard; a sucking wave of blast; and all the glass in every window in the room fell shimmering and tinkling to the ground. By good fortune, it was the secondary inward wave, not the initial outward blast, that broke the windows; so that most of the fragments fell harmlessly onto the window-sill or into the rose-bed outside.

When we had collected ourselves – it took a little time – we went outside and joined our neighbours on their lawn; the police were afraid there might be another bomb, and had ordered everybody out of doors. We lay on the grass for three-quarters of an hour before the all-clear was given. Then we dispersed to assess the damage. We were lucky. We had lost many window-panes; several doors and door frames had been broken or displaced; a ceiling was cracked; a great many slates (as we were to discover next winter) had come loose. Our next-door neighbours had fared much worse: their roofs and ceilings were severely damaged. The house in the avenue behind us, outside which the car had been left, was almost completely destroyed: the owners (friends of ours) lost nearly everything they possessed.

That summer, each time I mowed my lawn, the blades of the motor mower would give a crunch and a shower of sparks when they struck some brown and mangled piece of metal hidden in the grass; these were fragments of the car that had been blown up.

I do not recount these experiences because they are other than commonplace. Few people in Ulster since 1969 can have escaped happenings of this kind. Very many people suffered far more and far worse. Friends, colleagues, or acquaintances have had their homes or businesses burnt out, or totally destroyed; have been shot or shot at; one died of burns received when the bus she was travelling on was set on fire; one was murdered when he opened the door, as he thought to the postman, while cooking the family breakfast; another was killed outright by bomb-blast. None of these things has – yet – happened to me, or to any close friend or near relation.

The most frightening thing is the extent to which one becomes hardened. This is neither insensitivity nor cynicism; it is a necessary mechanism of self-defence. In the first year of the Troubles, one listened intently to every news bulletin, and to the broadcasts of Orange and Republican free-lance radio stations. One's heart turned over at the account of each new horror. One rushed to look at each new wall-poster – some of them, derived from the Paris student uprisings of 1968, were brilliant – I have still an illicitly obtained copy of a poster that read 'Malone Road fiddles while Falls Road burns'. One stood in the garden on summer evenings listening to fusillades of shots a mere mile away, wondering whose bullet had found what billet this time; watching the palls of smoke and sometimes the glare of flames from burning buildings, and wondering whose; listening to the windows rattle at the sound of unidentifiable explosions.

But after a year, still more after eight years, one no longer responds in the same way. The extraordinary has come, inevitably, to seem almost ordinary. When the morning news bulletin reports no bombs, no fires, no murders, no riots, no hijackings, then it has been a quiet night, and it is that that seems extraordinary (and in a depressing way, a little flat). The illegal radio stations have long since closed down: no more Free Belfast, no more Orange Lily at the record turntable. Such posters as now appear, and they are few, are dreary and uninteresting. Even the graffiti are uninspired, and rarely raise even a tired smile: as did the sudden rash of 'F.T.P.', which appeared all over the Protestant districts in 1970. (As Lord Hailsham remarked at the time, to Fuck the Pope remains an anatomical impossibility.) Today, when there is a bomb alarm, one evacuates briskly but with resignation, and tries to get on with one's work elsewhere till it is over. There is a traffic bollard near the City Hall that has often served me for an open-air desk. When there comes the crump of an explosion – unless it is very close – one perhaps looks at one's watch, so as to find out later which particular bang that had been; but work is not interrupted for more than a moment or two. And one comes almost to ignore the sinister bells and sirens, heard many times on most working days, which indicate that police cars, ambulances, fire engines, and the armoured cars of the bomb squad are galloping to an alarm.

As I have said, this is a necessary mechanism of self-defence: the protective scab that grows over even a deep wound. But I acknowledge, with distress, that it is inevitably accompanied by a coarsening of sensibility; a lessening of anguish; a deadening of humanity. One has heard now a thousand times the words of condemnation, certainly sincere and heartfelt, employed by politicians, clergymen, and other public figures when something particularly revolting has happened. They have become almost meaningless: the vocabulary has been exhausted. 'Terrorist', 'murderer', 'diabolical', 'dastardly outrage', 'cowardly crime': what other words can the poor men use? But the currency has been devalued; not just the currency of the words; the currency of the concepts, too. I am sure this is so of the individuals who commit the murders, who plant the bombs; otherwise no degree of idealism, whether in the cause of 'a Free Ireland' or in the cause of 'our Protestant heritage', could allow them to persevere without falling victims themselves to nausea, hysteria, and collapse. There is a protective mechanism for them too. Unhappily, if the rest of us are to survive without losing our reason, we must allow our own emotional reactions to be devalued. It is possible that all those who survive the Ulster Troubles of the 1970s will be morally or emotionally crippled for the rest of their lives. But I hope, and choose to believe, otherwise; just as a whole generation could return from the slaughter of each of the world wars without (as it seems to me) any perceptible loss of humanity, so (it seems to me) when this plague has passed by – and sooner or later, somehow, it must – the survivors will return to a more human level of sensibility.

from *Long Shadows Cast Before*, 1978

A TV CONFRONTATION

NAOMI MAY

'That's John Mulholland!' A group of people turned to stare at him as John entered the television studio. He had persuaded an acquaintance of UTV to allow him to take part in a discussion group titled 'The Way Ahead'. There were three other men on the panel, a Republican, a social worker and Roger Benson, a member of the Alliance party, whom he had met before.

The interviewer, Joseph O'Brien, seeming to take it for granted that his face was well-known, shook them in turn by the hand without bothering to introduce himself. He had long hair, a straight black fringe and a drooping moustache and his modish clothes had been carefully chosen to look well in colour. It was the controversial programmes, he explained, that he enjoyed the most; the Troubles had made his job more exciting. Encouraging them not to feel inhibited when expressing their different views, he said that it was usual for people nearly to come to blows in front of the cameras and then to return to normal, joking and on good terms, as soon as the show was over. John looked round at the other members of the team, all of whom were wearing suits except Paddy Hennessy, the Republican, who had shown his contempt for the system by turning up in an open-necked shirt and a cardigan with a hole at the elbow; although he was already voluble, he was chain-smoking, while Roger Benson had begun furtively mopping his forehead.

'No need to be so nervous!' O'Brien seemed amused by their discomfiture in a scene where he, himself, was at ease. 'Just work out what it is that you want to get across. We've got fifteen minutes so that should give each of you time to have a fair crack of the whip.' He turned to John: 'You're being very quiet, but I suspect that you're the man who's really got the most to say. You asked to be put on this, didn't you?' John nodded. 'Well, perhaps you'd like to go over it with me – I understand you feel that the ruling caste in Ulster has become demoralized?' From the way he pronounced the word 'caste' John guessed that he had a chip on his shoulder. He was incensed to find himself being patted familiarly on the cheek: 'Watch it! You're the one I'm going to gun for!'

When they went into the make-up room John was surprised to find that the girls not only knew who he was but were competing to do his face. 'You've got presence – that's very important.' They laughed coquettishly when he grumbled that they had put mascara on his pale eyelashes: 'See how pretty we'll make you!' He noticed that O'Brien spent a long time in front of the mirror and was snappish with the assistants.

In the studio, in spite of the powdering, their faces began to shine while they waited under the heat of the arc lights and large drops of moisture appeared on Roger Benson's forehead; he was so agitated he was unable to keep still. John leaned forward, thinking that O'Brien wished to speak to him; it took him a time to realise that he was talking to himself, rehearsing aloud his introduction: 'In Ulster today . . .' Gesturing and raising his eyebrows, he was actually practising his expression. When the warning light came on he hissed at them: 'When I ask you a question you must answer at once – say anything you like – but keep talking!' Then they were on and, using exactly the same expressions, even the hand movements, he was explaining to the viewers that, joining him in the studio to discuss the problems of Ulster today were members of two political minority parties and, from the social and economic sphere, Gordon McMahon, who had first-hand knowledge of the troubled areas and John Mulholland, representing industry – and the interests of the privileged sector. From this John suspected that whatever he tried to say would be misinterpreted. Whispering under his breath, 'Call me, Joe!' the interviewer started with Benson: 'Well, Roger, now what's the main obstacle as you see it?'

Stammering pitifully, the Alliance man began a speech about the need for conciliation and a better spirit of harmony between the two communities.

Obviously bored by his timid sincerity O'Brien turned to the social worker to ask with a facetious grin: 'What hope of harmony, Gordon, in Sandy Row?'

His cheeriness had misfired: Gordon solemnly described the bitter prejudices of people brought up on legends. 'The irony of it,' he said, 'is that the working classes in the Falls and Shankill have a great deal in common with one another in their general way of life.' He scratched his head, correcting himself without a smile; 'Though it's misleading to refer to them as the working classes when so many of them are unemployed. . . .'

'And now, John, you're the man with a positive solution to offer!' Confronted by his suave smile, John shifted uneasily. 'I take it you follow the Faulkner line that there's no sense in talking politics until the violence has been stamped out?' He frowned, as if in an effort to present fairly his own version of John's views. 'And to achieve this you would like to see a ruthless deployment of the armed forces – quite regardless of the casualties among innocent civilians that this would involve?' When John did not reply, he prompted: 'Have I got it right?'

'That's one way of putting it.' John knew he must commit himself, but he could feel his hands becoming clammy through a fear of being tripped up by his own words. 'Yes, that is right,' he looked firmly into the camera: 'I think the violence must be stopped – and, of course, the only people who can do this are the Army. As our politicians have been dismissed it is my hope that members of the business community will join together to put pressure on the British Government to see that a determined – and final – effort is made.'

'Your hope, John?' the interviewer had dropped his voice, his eyes crafty. 'This is wishful thinking?'

John refused to address him by his Christian name. 'No, it is my intention to try to bring it about. The reason for my coming here this evening . . .'

'It's people like the Mulhollands,' Paddy interrupted, 'who are the cause of the disturbances in this country. Everyone knows they're partisan – they've never employed a Catholic! It's because of him,' he pointed accusingly, 'that the boys are in the camps. . . . And it is my hope that they shall be set free as soon as possible! There can be no justice while internment lasts and no peace until the Army is withdrawn.'

Now it was John's turn to interrupt: 'Those are the demands of the IRA!'

'The IRA?' Derisively Paddy tossed back his hair. 'Who's wasting their breath on them when the real danger comes from the gangs of Prods marching about wearing,' he circled his fingers over his eyes, 'goggles and stocking masks and frightening the populace out of their wits!'

'If the IRA had been dealt with they'd be off the streets. They're only there because the security forces give them no protection.'

Paddy slammed his hands down on the table, shaking the glasses of water. But, before he could object, O'Brien intervened: 'Gentlemen, please!' Delighted that the show was progressing stormily, he returned to John: 'Perhaps we could hear your views on the Protestant menace – or don't you see it as a menace?'

'I do indeed! It is one of my main complaints against the new regime that it should have been allowed to take shape. The UDA ought to have been proscribed!' The camera rested on John's face.

'Those are forceful words,' O'Brien drawled, playing for time: this he had not expected. 'A provocative statement at the very least in these days. . . .' He managed to insinuate a sense of danger. 'So I would be correct in quoting you – a member of the Protestant establishment – as saying that in your opinion the UDA ought to be outlawed?'

'You would.' John glanced at Paddy who was lighting a cigarette from a stub. 'When Whitelaw first came over here he seemed somehow to close his eyes to the fact that there was a problem of law and order – it was nearly three months before he visited the Army Headquarters in Lisburn!'

'Is that so?' O'Brien was interested. Trying to catch him out, he asked: 'So it's on Mr Whitelaw that you lay the blame?'

Again the camera lingered on John while he paused, clearing his throat before replying in the affirmative. One of his golfing friends, a surgeon in the city's principal hospital, had written to the Secretary of State, sending him a photograph of a heap of severed limbs, in order to bring home to him the urgency of the situation; in reply he had received a note from a girl in the office informing him his communication had been filed. 'Yes,' said John, 'I do personally blame him for the worsening of the Troubles.'

The others glared at him in astonishment. The Alliance member stammered a defence of the Supremo, but the interviewer cut him short and turned to the Republican:

'Well, Paddy, as a representative of Catholic opinion could you be said to share this view?'

'Ah, now,' Paddy tilted his head to one side, 'you pose me a ticklish one.' He leaned his elbows on the table, resting his chin on his hands, and stared moodily into the camera. 'No, it couldn't be said that I was satisfied – but for the opposite reason. Mr Whitelaw, he seems to me to be far too slow and grudging – he's not been liberal enough, not by a long way. When the internees . . .'

'How can you describe a man as a representative of Catholic opinion when he's a known sympathiser with the IRA?' John refrained from adding that, as such, his presence in the studio was an affront. 'The bulk of the Catholic population is as desperate for peace as anyone else. The only trouble is that many law-abiding Catholics, while they deplore the violence, are reluctant to raise their voices against it because of a whimsical nationalist sentiment that they knew perfectly well had nothing to do with the reality.' As the camera closed in on him, John became aware that the nearer he came to the truth the more unacceptable his views would be. He tried to fix his gaze on the centre of the lens: 'And it is to those people, you who are watching this programme now, that I appeal. . . .'

'I must remind you, Mr Mulholland,' the camera shifted to the stern face of the interviewer, 'that this is a discussion, not a political platform!' The camera travelled slowly over the members of the panel, ending with John. Then the programme was over. 'That was great!' O'Brien jumped up from his chair: 'What timing!' The others rose to their feet, blinking now that they were no longer under the lights, and Benson wiped his moist brow. 'I pride myself on producing something lively. It's when the insults start flying that the thing makes an impact – that was a fun show!' O'Brien shook John warmly by the hand: 'A very good first performance! We'll see you here –' his sharp eyes were asking beyond the question: 'You may have cause to visit us again, I hope?'

John tried not to appear too uncivil as he made his escape before he could be further interrogated. He had taken such a dislike to the man, with his fancy hair-cut and tricky manner, that he felt humiliated to discover how nervous he had been when he clasped his fingers. He went to the wash-room and scrubbed his hands as if they had been contaminated. A clown's face looked out at him from the mirror. He found the make-up girl and asked brusquely:

'Can you get this muck off me?'

'Sure,' she simpered at him. 'Just sit you down and lean back your head. Now close your eyes. . . .'

'No, no! I'll do it myself!' Feeling suddenly that he could not bear to be touched, he dabbed at his face, thinking fleetingly of the corpses that had

had their eyes torn out. But the girl seemed unaware of his aversion. Her friends clustered round his chair with teasing offers of help and compliments on the way he had stood up to O'Brien: 'He'd said he was going to make it hot for you before you came in!' Flattered by their attentiveness, he left feeling less dissatisfied.

But, once he was in his car, he felt ashamed at losing his temper and for allowing himself to be manipulated into saying things that were indiscreet: he had attacked the man whose influence was all-powerful and, by his criticism, had probably antagonized the people he hoped to woo. He had behaved with the lack of sophistication typical of Protestant politicians who showed themselves at their worst when harried by hostile interviewers. When it came to publicity, would it be best to leave it to the professionals – presumably they, or their advice, could be hired? As he drove through Belfast and saw the grim messages scrawled all over the boarded windows, he wondered if it would be worth investing in posters, propaganda on the walls. . . .

His agitation lessened and he felt more optimistic after he had left the city and was driving through the countryside with its long shadows. He re-enacted the interview, wording it with greater eloquence and planning how he would restate his case given another opportunity. For a moment he felt elated by the limelight, the sense of power; even the little girls, flirting with him as they applied the cosmetics, had made him feel important. Perhaps his regret at having been so outspoken was merely a loss of nerve. . . .

I'm becoming an exhibitionist, he thought, as his car rose over the crest of a hill and a wide view of the landscape was spread out for him: is it egotism that deludes me into leading a one-man crusade? So far his efforts had been discouraging, his main support coming from a group of Jewish businessmen; some Presbyterians, whose views were hard-line but who did not want to be associated with formal politics, had promised to back him, and one exuberant Catholic who had made his own fortune. But he had failed to attract the moderates from either side. A couple of large concerns had offered to help financially provided their names remained anonymous and there were others who, while sympathetic, preferred to wait till he was seen to succeed. More often, however, his plans would be greeted with coldness and it seemed to him that those who could be most effective were more interested in their summer holidays. Such is the force of rumour in a small place that nowadays when he entered the Ulster Club he would find himself being regarded with antagonism by Protestant and Catholic alike and, when he sat down at a table, his companions would appear uncomfortable; he had overheard complaints that he was a meddlesome fool heading for trouble.

from *Troubles*, 1976

Meeting Brookeborough

POLLY DEVLIN

One hot still July when the boats were all out and the graveyard was deserted save for the watcher with the spy-glasses up on the Point keeping a look-out for the King, Eiram and I slid down the secret path to the shore to be about our business. She was skimming stones over the water and counting the triumphant skims when there was, sudden, amazing, an invasion.

Down the lower path which skirts the Cross and graveyard comes a crocodile of children neatly dressed and carrying baskets, the procession headed by a Vicar. We are put out to see a man in a dog-collar wearing grey clothes and not the black of our priests, but it is the shiny neat children, so precise, so beautifully uniform, that hold us. They might have been a dragoon of Hussars clattering past the sloe-trees from the way we stare. A Sunday School outing. We have never seen so many shiny children before, although I have met individual children like them, friends of my aunt and uncle who live in Warrenpoint. This town has an enormous fascination for me, partly as a place of excavation of my mother's past, partly because it is so utterly different from where we live, and partly because so many apocalyptic events take place there in my young life; because I suppose I have ventured out of my own territory and am subject to chance and change. It was in Warrenpoint that I first perceived Eiram as another person; and in Warrenpoint I commit sin.

It is a pretty Edwardian seaside town, with bay-windowed boarding-houses, a proper sea-front with breakwaters and boats for hire and bandstand and a large open air salt-water swimming-bath painted white and green with cabins and canopies and high white railing jutting out into the sea. It is utter, utter glamour. Part of this glamour comes from the aunt with whom I stay, my mother's sister; she is witty, humorous, with plenty of time, and her slender blonde body is quite unlike the bodies of women at home – hers looks like that of a young girl and she wears swimsuits and tailored suits. She treats me with delicacy and love, and I respond with such a passion that, although I crave home, I long to stay with her: her son Maurice – 'Whiteskull' – is my first real sexually-based love and I observe his life with an astonished curiosity. But the other people we meet there seem alien, especially the children, and it is through them that the first intimation that we are inferior is subtly brought home to me.

These children are casually engaged in activities that previously I have encountered only in library books. They arrange meetings in each other's houses by telephone, hold parties with conjurors who perform magic tricks, they ride, swim, play tennis, join the Girl Guides or Boy Scouts, go camping with rucksacks and tents. Their parents meet for meals, for drinks, for coffee, to play golf or bridge, or to arrange fund-raising events to help deprived children overseas. They lead, in other words, a perfectly ordinary mid-twentieth-century, middle-class existence.

My life at home and theirs seem to have little connection and I wonder and ponder on the discrepancies. Years later I realized that our worlds were anthropologically apart, that we came from different time-zones and different cultures; but by then it hardly mattered. I thought then, though, that there was a manifest physical difference. Certainly those children in Warrenpoint did not possess that placating look that we all had in those old photographs. Those children seemed shiny, as though the very process of being cared for had polished up their soft skin, buffed to shine by the lovely rub of affection. (Reading Tolstoy later I was amused and delighted to find his descriptions of a loved and cared-for and well-satisfied prince – 'He looked as fresh as a big glossy green Dutch cucumber.')

Looking at our old photographs I know now that we too were shiny; but I thought then that we were rickety, our bones joined carelessly, without grace, our skins thin and pallid. Many Catholic children then did look undernourished; and Protestant children, I believed, never looked anything other than cucumber-glossy. It was only when I went to Belfast, and saw in the traditionally Protestant areas children playing who had the same narrow limbs and white faces which I associated with the children of my own faith that I realized these were the physical marks and characteristics of the poor.

Later still, when living in New York in the late 1960s, I read of the fluttering astonishment and dismay among sociologists when they discovered the low self-image black children had of themselves and of each other, revealed to observers by the distorted, spidery self-portraits traced tentatively along the bottom of the page. When the same children were asked to draw white people, they drew large colourful portraits, centred on the page. No one who had been a member of an oppressed minority would have felt any surprise at those results.

Warrenpoint was then, and may still be, a segregated town. In the big houses along the sea-front, in the tree-lined streets, around the handsome square, lived the Protestants who ran the businesses and composed the professional classes. The golf club outside the town was exclusively Protestant. The Catholics lived in the back streets near the railway sidings, and when I went to Mass at the Catholic church I was always amazed at how many Catholic children there were – the church was full to overcrowding yet I never met any elsewhere. Later I recognize those I kneel among at Mass, shabbily dressed, playing in the back streets and down by the sea, beyond the point where the series of jutting breakwaters, seaweed-encrusted and barnacled, come to an end, marking the boundary of the beach as a social meeting-place.

Those children play in an anarchistic way there, pushing each other into the water, shouting and screaming and making a disturbance. Many wear old knickers instead of swimsuits. I lean over the high promenade wall and stare down at them, both repelled and drawn, for I should be down there with them and not up here with the gentry. The children look up and seeing me begin to shout catcalls. I am thrilled at their courage, feel a traitor and see how clearly they could be labelled sluts and outsiders; I am like a quadroon who in earlier days and other eras, hoping to pass for white, might shudder at a black person. It is a self-protective gesture.

In Warrenpoint too I commit the first mortal sin. It happens when I am with one of those shiny girls, the one who is my accredited official friend, and who is as suspicious of me as I am of her. Walking back from Alexander the baker's where they sell individual meringues, she bites into one and asks, 'Are you a Roman?' I do not know the term but I know instantly what she means. One moment I am pondering on the mystery of meringues – what they can possibly be made of, this crispy white exotic stuff so redolent of Warrenpoint, and how the word is spelt – the next a question has been asked to change my world. 'Are you?' she persists.

I know I must confess to being a Catholic, but I long to be accepted, to be like her, conforming, confident; and I know that she is that safe thing, a member of the Church of Ireland. I shake my head. 'What are you then?' There is a silence. 'Methodist,' I say, inspired, and wait to be struck down. Nothing happens. She looks doubtful but cannot gainsay me. The meringue turns to ashes in my mouth and I go back to my aunt's house with a heavy heart, thinking of the gospel that has been read to us so often of how when Jesus had been arrested after his night in Gethsemane he had already prophesied that his friends would deny him, and how although Peter had been most vehement and angry in his denials, it was he who before the cock crowed twice had denied Him thrice.

I thought of the hymn I carolled so fervently at October Devotions: 'How sweet would be thy children's fate, if they, like them, could die for you. . . .' And I had thought as I sang of how I would have stood up straight and confessed my friendship, boasted of it. It is a bitter lesson to find I have denied Him under the quizzing of another girl. I think of the Christian martyrs, delivered to us daily in sermons and homilies as supreme examples of human endeavour, and the deaths they suffered, the endless mutilations described with such relish in our religion lessons and shown so graphically in the statues in the chapel. Lucy with her eyes torn out, Cecilia with her breasts cut off, Bartholomew displaying his flayed skin over his arm, Lawrence being grilled; and I know I can never join them in their maimed Heaven. All I can really think about is whether to confess to my aunt and see if she will back me up about being a Methodist. I incline to confessing – it's a habit, and I like the wonderful sticky glue that spreads through the veins after I have dumped the guilt.

'Do you remember that line of children?' I ask Eiram thirty years later.

'That was a most significant moment for me,' she says, her voice angry. 'I hate that memory passionately because I betrayed myself, and because of it I think I understand the thing of racial self-hatred, where a race turns in on itself, and feeds on the memories of inferiority, of others being superior. We hate ourselves both for letting it happen, for being inferior, and for allowing ourselves to become so. But how could we not? It's where the IRA get part of their angry energy. We all know how you can demoralize an Irishman. Nobody is easier to demoralize by parading manners and social graces, and by making him feel socially ill at ease.

That way you can make almost any Irish person feel uneasy or inferior. But touch him, lay a finger on him and he'll kill you. And somewhere now that is my own reaction. People can demoralize me. But let them violate me physically, show even a hint of aggression and I'm at their throats. It's a reaction from the gut. Oh, I remember that scene so well. Their bus was parked upon the New Road – and we had never seen a bus down there before, the roads were too narrow for buses. That rector in his grey suit. When they arrived where we were playing, and had always played, they spread themselves out and we shied away apologetically. We, who had spent all the days of our living memory on that shore, crept off.

'But why blame them? Blame ourselves, blame our upbringing, blame our religion, blame most of all our history. But I *do* blame them. We went further along the lough shore and went on playing and paddling and one girl followed us, pursued us. She said: "C'mere you two, are you two papishes?" I knew there was something amiss, and so did you, but I tried to answer the question, I said, "What are papishes? Papishes?" "You're papishes," she said. "Come on over here."

'We were scared, but her companions were with her, watching us, waiting, and we went over to her. "She said Say the Lord's Prayer. Go on say it, at once."

' "Our Father Who art in Heaven," I said. But you wouldn't say it. You wouldn't. You stood your ground. But I did, and when she heard "Who art in Heaven" instead of "which art" which is how they said it, she said, "You dirty wee papishes, you wee bitches, get on home." And we ran home crying, and said to Daddy, "What are papishes Daddy? They called us papishes."

'He was murderous. He got up and began to walk around the room, agitated. He knew we'd been defiled, and he's always been, you see, so unprejudiced, so unbigoted. I remember me saying to him about Wilbur who never went to Mass, "Daddy, Wilbur is he a Catholic or Protestant?" and him replying, "Eiram, what does it matter? It doesn't make a bit of odds." '

The thing that any outsider witnessing or listening to this story might find curious is how those children knew with such certainty, on the instant, that we were Catholics. We felt then that it was because of our appearance. But we know now that it had to do with language and words, still so potent in Ireland; and in so small a difference as Catholics using the form 'Our Father Who art in Heaven' and Protestants the form 'which art' lies a vast division. The very pronouns in speech are used to widen gaps between people who have nothing different about them but whose common history has made them enemies.

Almost every sentence we speak contains a word or expression, a twist or a phrase, a rearrangement of order, an irony or a bitterness which gives our speech great potency. The number of violent words, flashing angry imagery, and grotesque threats used in everyday speech reflects our history and condition. The strength of the oath, the fear of the curse, the belief in the efficacy of the prayer, the respect for words, for poetry, the quickness of wit, the flashing repartee, the fast outpourings of scorn – this verbal facility so characteristic of the Irish is bred deeply into us and the people around us. For when oral communication carries a whole heritage and becomes the only way to bequeath a culture to your descendants, then it must needs become the art of a nation. In secret Ireland the spoken and sung word has had to carry everything that painting, sculpture, scores, books, libraries, the museums and acknowledged repositories, the fruits of centuries of encouraged and open culture, carry in other countries.

The words we use are important. Our antique daily vocabulary seems to hang with more freight and meaning in each sentence than the pale nimble English we hear when we go out of the district to gentler or future places. We use a dialect studded with words and phrases that are either a literal translation from the Gaelic or are unchanged in pronunciation and usage since the enforced conversion of the Irish-speaking population to the English language.

The fear of the word, of humiliation and ridicule, is deeply inlaid in us, bred from the time when satire was the ultimate deterrent, used by bards as inescapable punishment and judgement against wrong-doers, especially those so powerful as to be inviolate from most other forms of violence. Certain words – amadan, kitterdy, tackle – are genuinely humiliating, and hoarded as though to preserve their venom. Their despatch through the air towards their target is laden and accurate. All the words to do with physical contact have a strange ambivalence. The word 'touch' is interchangeable with the word 'hit'. 'Don't touch her' means 'Don't beat or hit her', never 'Don't caress her'. To dote on, which in ordinary English means you love someone, especially a baby, means in our vocabulary that you are wandering in your mind or are senile. And words more suitable for describing a hunt or to call down damnation are used almost casually in everyday speech. 'I'll slaughter you' is an ordinary threat from one of our teachers, and 'You'll go to hell if you do that' is a standard warning. Many an adult discovering some small offence will, as often as not, say 'I'll kill whoever did it', and we in turn use these threats to each other as familiar utterances; in using them our voices take on a vehemence and passion that gives a dangerous edge to ordinary communications. Certain problems arise (which one might call overkill) – for how is authority to find more powerful deterrents, to preempt more serious offences, when you have been told you will be massacred for stepping in a puddle, or for not having done your homework?

When we leave Ireland we find that people are bemused or threatened or appalled by the passion and exaggeration in our speech. But such passion is a legacy of our history. The constant use of violent imagery and threat in the Irish version of the English language reflects the damage done to Ireland, and the ravages to the Irish spirit, through centuries in which the country and its people have suffered invasion, decimation, starvation, brutality and brutalization, contemptible legislation, eviction on a massive scale, emigration and religious persecution and savagery. If you mention memories and history as reasons for the language, outlook and behaviour of the Irish today, you are treated with contumely, as though you were trying to keep old hatreds alive by digging deep into some musty mausoleum for an obscure tract lost to human memory. But in the places where such things happened the memories are bitterly alive. We remember, for why should we forget. To forget is to stop lamenting those children whom Arthur Chichester saw in 1597 running naked across the burnt and scorched earth which his soldiers had devastated, towards the heat and warmth of the fire that had been lit expressly to lure them there for sport and slaughter.

Memory is re-enacted desire, and Ireland lives in the bones and flesh of her citizens. In that sense Ireland has no history, since the past is as real as the present and continues to happen and we all remain emotionally entwined with it in an apparently necessary conjunction of pain. The psychic violence done to the native Irish is so profound that the living perspective makes the history, rather than the actual old event. Incident after incident lives on in our memory. Here is one such, recorded by Isaac Butt:

> On the estate of the Marquis of Lansdowne there lived, a few months ago, a man and his wife, Michael and Judith Donoghue; they lived in the house of one Casey. An order had gone forth on the estate (a common order in Ireland) that no tenant is to admit any lodger into his house. This was a general order. It appears, however, that sometimes special orders are given, having regard to particular individuals. The Donoghues had a nephew, one Denis Shea. The boy had no father living. He had lived with a grandmother who had been turned out of her holding for harbouring him. Denis Shea was twelve years old – a child of decidedly dishonest habits. Orders were given by the driver of this estate that this child should not be harboured upon it. This young Cain, thus branded and prosecuted, being a thief – he had stolen a shilling, a hen, and done many other such crimes as a neglected twelve-year-old famished child will do – wandered about. One night he came to his aunt Donoghue, who lodged with Casey. He had the hen with him.
>
> Casey told his lodgers not to 'allow him in the house', as the agent's drivers had given orders about it. The woman, the child's aunt, took up a pike, or pitchfork, and struck him down with it; the child was crying at the time. The man, Donoghue, his uncle, with a cord tied the child's hands behind his back. The poor child after a while crawls or staggers to the door of one Sullivan, and tried to get in there. The maid of Sullivan called to Donoghue to take him away. This he did; but he afterwards returned with his hands still tied behind his back. Donoghue had already beaten him severely. The child seeks refuge in other cabins, but is pursued by his character – he was so bad a boy, the fear of the agent and the driver - all were forbidden to shelter him. He is brought back by some neighbours, in the middle of the night, to Casey's where his uncle and aunt lived. The said neighbours tried to force the sinking child in upon his relations. There is a struggle at the door. In the morning there is blood upon the threshold. The child is stiff dead – a corpse with its arms tied; around it every mark of a last fearful struggle for shelter, food, the common rights of humanity.

Irish history is littered with such charred emaciated corpses. Their stoor still chokes us, and because of the continuity with the past we know intimately in the spring of our blood who those children were. They were the makings of each one of us, and that part of me which is still connected with their sufferings makes me want to turn on my rational present educated other part and rend myself in half, or tear one part from the other so that one part of me can wholly hate.

Self-esteem, that fragile and necessary attribute, is easily enough removed from vulnerable people and individuals of any tribe living under official contempt. In their subsequent loss of confidence they will turn on themselves, become fiercely protective, and yet find little that is lovable among or about themselves. Part of this bequest is the self-hatred and dolorousness that poisons so many of the lives around us. In seeking a means of escape from this coil some terrible injuries are self-inflicted, although a person who is scorched while escaping from a burning house can hardly be said to have inflicted his injuries on himself.

All children born in segregated places are born with a dark caul, a web of ambiguities around them, from which it is difficult to struggle free. But the Roman Catholic children of the province of Northern Ireland have a darker, stronger birth-membrane imprisoning them against which they have to struggle, since the loyalties and love we feel towards our putative nation and powerful religion are subversive. Loyalty towards the idea of Ireland and love for Mother Church are inextricably entangled, yet neither feeling can be open, proud or free, since neither religion nor country has status, official sanction or respect. The feelings we have or cultivate for these important influences in our lives are something akin to the love we feel for the women round us – protective, fierce, yet contemptuous, because they are not powerful, and not respected or even recognized by the powers that we know to be.

Northern Ireland for us is neither one thing nor the other; in it we are neither English nor Irish. We are taught English history as the record of our past, and whenever the history or culture of Ireland is mentioned it is presented as arcane, obscure, and unconnected with the country in which we live and the people to which we belong. We read English literature and recite English poetry without anyone making the point that many of the writers and poets we study have come from our country. We study natural history, but it is all done from reference books dealing with the English countryside. No reference is ever made to the lough, just beyond the school-yard, and its unique shoals of fish. At school we sing English folk songs, and warble *Greensleeves, Barbara Allen* and *Scarborough Fair*. At home my father sings *My Lagan Love* in his cracked and off-key voluptuous voice, but I never hear his song as a distinct expression of a nation's voice and memory.

From my earliest days I know I am a member of the national Irish family, and in the same way that I am linked by such strong blood-ties to my own family that my membership of it is taken for granted, that I move only within its stretch and shelter, I am also linked to Irish history; and my perceptions and awareness of our past brings that forgiving knowledge that members of a family have of each other, an awareness of early hidden reasons for behaviour which to the less affected or engaged observer might merely appear as aberrant, or unreasonable. Old issues and grievances that in other circumstances could and would have sunk into history are living and unrepentant in our history still. We are bequeathed this nervous interest and enmeshment in our past as our best inheritance, entrusted with it like a sacrament.

We are reminded at every turn of our oppression and are reinforced in an idea of our true native Irishness – not by our parents who are not at all fanatical, but by our neighbours, by the songs that are sung, by the words and expressions we use and by many of the young men who nurture a heavy rage against the oppressor – that is, anyone who is not a Catholic, from the local police sergeant to the Sovereign of England; and for these men and many Republicans of that period, the Catholic religion and patriotism are so linked they are as one.

The fact that many of the heroes of the 1916 Rising, the pinnacle of heroic achievement in their eyes, were Protestant or Anglo-Irish is ignored or disbelieved. The religious crusading aspects of the Republican cause, the sexist theology, the belief that the real Irishman can only be a hero ready to die for his country (and that country having always been symbolized as a female) seem to produce a pathologically masculine Irishman whose idea of masculinity is a kind of disease connected with bloodshed, violence, valour. 'Bloodshed', wrote Padraic Pearse, one of the leaders of the 1916 rebellion, who indeed died for his adopted country, 'is a cleansing and a sanctifying thing and the nation which regards it as the final horror has lost its manhood.' The effective heroes of Ireland, the men who did so much in getting legislation passed to lighten the lot of the Irish, like Henry Grattan – whose famous assertion that 'the Irish Protestant could never be free till the Irish Catholic had ceased to be a slave' showed both camps how closely they were hoist – or Daniel O'Connell, whose courageous determination to avoid bloodshed is interpreted by many as demonstrating a final lack of courage and commitment to the cause of Irish nationalism, are not revered in the same way in public memory, are not what the Irish call 'real' heroes, heroes as national monuments.

These endless reminders of our past are not tendered to us as forms of atonement, or of ritual, but in order to keep the idea of a future revenge uppermost in our minds. Somewhere, those who speak so continuously of a United Ireland in this semi-religious way believe they can overturn the society in which they live without overturning themselves. Burke reflecting on the Revolution in France wrote: 'They should not think it amongst their rights to cut off the entail or commit waste on the inheritance by destroying at their pleasure the whole original fabric of their society, hazarding to leave to those who come after them a ruin instead of a habitation.'

In most of the houses up and down the road to the Cross there are relics and mementos of the 1916 Easter Rising in Dublin which began the war that eventually led to the founding of the Irish Free State. The Irish tricolour flag is more often than not tucked behind the framed text of the famous speech from the dock made by Robert Emmet who was executed for his part in a revolution in 1803 that was doomed to failure from the start. It is quoted to us so often we know it by heart:

I have but one request to ask at my departure from this world; it is the charity of its silence. Let no man write my epitaph; for as no man who knows my motives dare now vindicate them, let not prejudice, nor ignorance asperse them. Let them and me rest in obscurity and peace; and my tomb remain uninscribed and my memory in oblivion, until other times and other men can do justice to my character. When my country takes her place among the nations of the earth then, and not till then, let my epitaph be written.

It was a speech that inspired the people of Ireland when it was first uttered extempore at his trial, and it continues to inspire – although by

389

this time it is as much an inspiration towards hatred as towards the fulfilment of the ideal that Emmet died for. 'I acted as an Irishman,' he said,
'determined on delivering my country from the yoke of a foreign and
unrelenting tyranny and the more galling yoke of a domestic faction which
is its joint-partner and perpetrator in the patricide. . . .'

There is a feeling of anger and resentment underlying the apparently
calm political exterior of our parish, an anger kept alive and bubbling by
the system of discrimination that drifts like spore from Stormont, the seat
of government where the Unionist Party is in power. It is an organized
official system of discrimination built into the state of Northern Ireland,
from its very inception, and any attempts to remedy the situation are met
by fierce opposition and venomous provocation from the establishment
and political leaders at every level, all of whom are members of the
Orange Order. Indeed this secret Order and the Unionist Party are inextricably linked, and it is virtually impossible to rise in the Unionist Party
without being a member of the Orange Order.

Called Orange to commemorate the victory of King William of Orange
(whom Ulster Loyalists supported) over James II (the Catholic contender)
at the Battle of the Boyne, its members are a powerful freemasonry dedicated to helping each other, to continuing the exclusion of Catholics from
any passage to power, and to keeping partisan issues alive. 'In times of
tension', wrote Charles Brett, an eminent Belfast leader and lawyer, in his
book about Northern Ireland, *Long Shadows Cast Before*, published in
1978, 'the Orange Order becomes a secret society, not merely, as its members claim, a society with secrets; it acts as a focus for bigotry and extrem-
ism; it invites onto its platforms and to the pulpits at its religious services,
only those Protestant clergy who can be trusted to be outspoken in their
hostility to Rome. The connection between Orangeism and the Protestant
paramilitary armies of the present day is unproven; it is probably untrue
that a majority of Orangemen are paramilitaries; but I suspect it to be true
that a majority of Protestant paramilitaries are Orangemen.'

Soon after the State of Northern Ireland was founded the then spokesman for the Unionist Party, Sir George Clark, said: 'I would draw your
attention to the words civil and religious liberty. This liberty we know is
the liberty of the Protestant religion.' And these attitudes had not changed
much among the establishment in the intervening years. Discrimination

was manifested in almost everything; it was part of the hierarchy, the job-structure, the social services, in the continuum of the political life of the province. We met with discrimination in everyday life and we know we will meet it in the limits to our future; and our parents have to live in an irresponsible democracy based on the system of gerrymandering. The basic ploy of the gerrymander is to draw constituency or ward boundaries so as to spread the desired support over as many seats as possible and crowd opponents into as few as possible. In most constituencies with Catholic majorities boundaries were drawn so that two Unionist MPs could be returned with narrow majorities for one massively supported non-Unionist MP.

The system of representation means that for the twenty years between 1943 and 1963 so overwhelmingly Unionist was the establishment that there was no Catholic in the Northern Ireland cabinet; Lord Brookeborough, who during these years was Prime Minister of Northern Ireland, boasted that he would never employ a Catholic on his staff, and that he had never crossed into the Republic of Ireland. In 1971, Terry Coleman recorded in an interview this remarkable statement from a man who was head of a state in which there were over half a million Catholics in a population of over one million people:

'You see this argument that's going on why don't you have Roman Catholics in your cabinet, well to me that would be exactly like the British Government during the last war having a German in the Admiralty and a German in the War Office.'

But surely, Coleman ventured, surely he would not go so far as to call Roman Catholics traitors? 'Well, needn't use the word traitor I suppose.'

In 1971 when Brookeborough was asked in a newspaper interview about gerrymandering, he said, 'I really don't know that one. I never came up against it.'

The journalist Harold Jackson, writing about Brookeborough's long administration, concluded: 'The iron rule of Lord Brookeborough ensured that a surface tranquillity pervaded and no one in Westminster felt inclined to poke a stick into the mess bubbling underneath.' The more militant among the Catholic population did, however, and the Irish Republican Army, an illegal underground organization, tried to stir the mess by launching in 1956 a campaign of guerrilla activities against the state.

They hoped to galvanize the Catholic population into beginning a definitive struggle, but the vast majority of Catholics preferred to live under a system of injustices so long as it was tolerable; and it was only when the intolerance became intolerable and the grievances unbearable that enough Catholics finally felt impelled to try to change things. Analysing what had happened, the lawyer Charles Brett wrote: 'I think the Unionists could, without the slightest risk to their entrenched positions of power, have met these Catholic grievances with a spirit of fairness and generosity. Had they done so, I do not believe that any of the Troubles of the years since 1969 need have occurred.'

Years and years after that revelation on the lough shore I sat beside Lord Brookeborough at a dinner party. I was alarmed and rather flattered to find myself next to him. I was young, and uneasy. I was there because I was writing a story for a magazine, and so I already felt in the position of a governess – neither with the servants, nor with the guests, but posed uneasily between the two. It is perhaps to my hostess's credit that she put me beside the guest of honour, regardless of my ambivalent position. She may only have seen a *placement* that needed to be done and imagined, I suppose, that any young woman eager to please and ready to sing for her supper would make an agreeable dinner companion for the old man.

The dinner progressed. He treated me with a heavy-handed flirtatiousness. I tried to regard him objectively, this man who personalized bigotry for me, who by his actions and attitudes had exacerbated the divisions in the community of which he was the leader, and who had contributed to the ruination of many of my contemporaries' lives.

At the end of the meal he said: 'Tell me – I didn't quite hear your name . . .?'

'Devlin,' I said, looking at him; and seeing his face shiver and pinch inwards I said again more clearly, 'Devlin.'

I might have hit him across the face. The name could only be that of a Catholic. His long head swivelled away, his hooded eyes grew more blinkered.

'Devlin,' he said and fell silent. And then he turned back. He said, 'You've come far.' And turned away, nor spoke to me again that evening. I sat winded, my anger bubbling under my stricken heart. I had betrayed myself, but what was I to do? I hadn't come far enough if I had arrived at a seat beside him. Sitting at that table a scene came into my mind, erupted into it, perfect, sudden, like a shaken scene in a crystal ball.

We have been out with our father for a drive in the old Austin to visit Coalisland where Ellen lives, and where the pots and crocks we use in our dairy are made in a small pottery, and thence we have driven towards Dungannon. It is a hot July day and the car windows are open and as we get near the town an extraordinary noise comes rolling down the hill and buries us in a throbbing, pounding rhythm, erotic in its beating intensity. As the astounding and primaeval noise cascades down through the air over us I know the message it is pounding out is directed against *us*. But what have we done? My father stops the car and says quietly, 'There are some bad boys up there.'

It is my first real experience of the dramatic and coarse expression of religious intolerance which is so much to the taste of the people of Ulster; but it is only now sitting beside Brookeborough that I can reciprocate the hatred that those men, beating their drums in their black tattoo on that July morning years before, feel towards us. I can taste it, the voluptuous hatred bubbling down in my veins, a rich seething mixture of anger and frustration, spite and impotence, a rage that I didn't know I had, a hatred that is like a plague, a plague that my parents with their care and liberalism had tried to inoculate us from, but which too many others had already caught for us to escape infection. As I sit silent and isolated at that table I become for myself a parable for the situation of all of us Catholics in Ulster. I remember the hill and the noise, and it is too painful to bear and I leave the table.

from *All of Us There*, 1983

WHY BOGSIDE?

SEAMUS DEANE

We were born and educated in a ghetto. Catholics were so separated from Protestants geographically, and even more socially, that we scarcely knew of one another save by fearful reputation. Separation did not cause the hatred we had for one another. Hatred caused the separation. Integration, at school or elsewhere, will be the result not the cause of a change of heart in the North.

Even within our ghetto there were severe distinctions. Secondary schools stamped them indelibly upon us. I, like every Catholic who could manage it, went to St Columb's College. The welcome was not exactly stunning. I discovered that I was an eleven-pluser, and even, in the opinion of some teachers, a low type. Later we, as a group, became more popular as we began to win prestige for the school with university scholarships, State Exhibitions and a thickening of the stream toward Maynooth and other seminaries. But in those opening years especially, the unofficial but widespread snobbery was a hurdle to be crossed. Quite a few were brought down by it.

There was one priest who obviously felt he had fallen among savages. He carried his *Times Supplement* about like a caste mark, and assumed that we spent our grubby evenings glued to the cheek of a factory girl in a dimly lit dancehall in the heart of Bogside. (I wish we had.) Another ordered chosen victims not to pay attention in class, and punished them if he caught them listening. This particular man, however, taught us the valuable lesson that the psychotic in authority infects his subjects with the same or allied diseases. The political applications came later. Strangely, we assumed that appeals were pointless, partly because of the risk involved. If your Education was Finished, you were too.

Here was the other side of the coin. The dignity so admirable in our parents carried with it a deep reverence towards Authority. It was a traumatic shock for us to discover how unfair and corrupt Authority could be, even on our side of the fence. We were utterly fooled by the cult of manliness which went with all forms of punishment, a cult which blended Christian Brothers' nationalism, Jansenism and dregs of the English public school spirit. It declared that the 'manly' man played no foreign games, never cried, thought of all women as he thought of his sister (!), never told tales, and eventually, I suppose, died for Ireland or on the missions. We swallowed this mouthful whole. No matter what you got at school from layman or priest, you didn't tell. Nor did you cry. Once when I did, I was told I should be down in Foyle College with all the namby-pamby Protestant boys who had soft hands (since they were not slapped) and nice mammies. So much for our notion of today's Young Unionists.

It was stranger still to realise that if we were more 'manly' than the Protestants, we were less so than the St Columb's boarders. They rarely got out and they naturally played the school sports; Gaelic football, Gaelic football and Gaelic football. Fine, except that we were expected to do so as well, and on Sunday mornings too. We were punished if we did not, but we preferred the punishment.

When we had snow, the boarders used to keep a huge swarm of day boys returning for afternoon classes pinned down at the main gate under a storm of iced snowballs. The street outside was a mess of slush and hooting traffic. The boarders had a wide lawn laden with snow and an hour's preparation behind them. Yet this was cited as an instance of the superior manliness of the boarders over the suspect Bogside types who met girls after school (contamination will ruin our nation), played billiards and soccer and neither looked nor acted like Irish muscular Christians. Neither did the boarders when they got out, but that was seldom.

Of course, this boarder–day-boy distinction had no official status and the more intelligent teachers had no time for it. But like the snobbery, it was there and it too was an isolating force. Teachers prone to either notion leant heavily on those who contradicted their idea of what a schoolboy should be. As a result, many dropped out of school into the squashy lap of the dole. They hated the Unionism which refused them jobs and housing, they hated the Irish Catholic mystique which treated them from the beginning as misfits. They walked the streets and had faith in no one.

It may seem strange to those who think of Northern Ireland, and Derry in particular, as areas plagued by history, but the truth is they have neither of them a tradition to live by. There are multiple traditions to die for and loyalties to hold to, but together or apart, these do not constitute a way of life. Usually they make one impossible.

The standards we had were the same age as ourselves. We picked them off the cinema screen and combined them with what we learned for ourselves. Obviously religion gave, if in a bleak fashion, some basic rules. But few practised the virtues they preached; not priests, not teachers, not Catholic businessmen who refused to pay trade union rates in a market flooded with labour. Not (need I say it?) politicians. I suppose when you get down to it, the only heroes we had were footballers and film stars. Parents yes, not for public idols. In compensation for the lack of positive example, we did have one negative focus of attention – the police, and its thug cohort, the B Specials. They almost demanded the hate we had in such abundance to give.

During the IRA campaign of the fifties, the pressure was really turned on in Northern Ireland. Policemen had up until then been noticeable for the way they harried us off the street when we played football or for the clumsy way in which their plainclothesmen lounged at street corners asking sly questions and being fed some uproarious information. (One should remember that the great characteristic of the RUC after brutality, is incompetence.) But the IRA campaign was a farce. It got a lot of innocent people thrown into jail without trial, it gave Faulkner the propaganda he wanted, and it thereby deepened the Northern Irish sickness to a point where recovery became unlikely. We sympathised in a general way with the overall aim of the IRA, but knew its means were stupid, its timing wrong and its inefficiency an embarrassment. (Any 'army' which can be seriously troubled by the B Special patrols should be in opera.) And yet, through it all, we felt the reckoning had to come. The police had to be driven off the streets some day. At any given point, people would want to start breathing again.

Why did we hate the police so? Partly because they were the most visible reminder of a repressive regime. Partly because in any ghetto situation there is police hatred. Partly because we knew what sport they had in the barrack interrogations. There was no appeal against them. Magistrates revered them, the State lauded them, a vast weaponry protected them. In tiny incidents their brutality was incredible and sickening.

In 1957 in William Street I saw six young policemen baton two aged meth drinkers up and down the pavement until their sticks were shining with the dark blood. Military policemen from the British naval base, who witnessed the incident, intervened and took the victims away in their own vehicle along with some very sobered British sailors.

There was no redress. They rubber-truncheoned young boys in barrack interrogations late at night, they baton charged the home crowd at Derry–Linfield soccer games, they baton charged on St Patrick's Day, they raided houses for guns at midnight, and if they wanted the man badly enough, planted what they could not find.

As for the B Specials, they nervously pranced about dark country roads, red lanterns swinging, loaded sten guns at the ready, buoyed by the thought of the next Fenian car they could wreck under the pretext of searching it. If you didn't see the light, or if you thought it denoted a moving cow (a pardonable error), they fired. If you were so unfortunate as to work in a civilian job with one by day, he would not recognise you when he stopped you by night. So the love relationship grew.

Watching the police and listening to the politician, we learned, strangely, that hope need not be surrendered. In many ways Ulster Unionists are a comic bunch. They are stupid in a profound, bovine and solemn manner. By brute force and sheer luck they had landed themselves in an unbeatable position. With the help of the IRA, they maintained it. But the dullness, the crawling inanity of Unionism, epitomised so perfectly in the Brookeboroughs, father and son, gave us heart. If the situation ever loosened sufficiently, we knew we could overcome their narrow cunning by intelligence. The police and the B Specials, being so intimately part of the political structure, would crumble with it. The distraught provincialism of our rulers, neither Irish nor British, plausible nor effective suddenly revealed itself. What we had not bargained for was an intelligent Unionist. When he appeared in Captain O'Neill we sat back and waited for his political execution. Now it's time for political suicide. The Unionists don't need enemies.

The resemblances between the North and the southern states of the USA stem from the fact that in each area a single institution – slavery, sectarianism – became the basis of social privilege for a few, economic security for many, and a sense of superiority for all not condemned by it. This gave the opponents of this system a ready-made moral base for political attacks be they on State Rights or on Partition. Moreover, just as most Northern Protestants have no direct profit from sectarianism, few Southerners ever profited directly from slavery.

Only 3,000 owners had more than 100 slaves; three-quarters of the white people had no connection with slavery. Those slave-owners stood in the same relation to the poor whites as the thirty or so landed families of Northern 'gentry' now stand to the mobs of the Shankill Road. The only dignity a working-class Protestant has is his conviction that he is superior to any Catholic, even a prosperous one. If civil war ever does break out in the North it too will be, like the American 'a rich man's war and a poor man's fight'. The landowners have until recently had no fear of the Catholic niggers; they have always feared the illumination of their own poor whites.

As soon as sectarianism is seen to be the basis upon which many Protestants accept unnecessary poverty (and thereby also uphold the grotesquely large property holdings of this small group of families), then the feudal basis of Unionism will have vanished. Even Paisley and Bunting got to the point of saying this dangerous truth in their campaign to get rid of O'Neill.

But above all, this is the threat posed by Civil Rights eventually and by Socialism immediately. October 5 was the moment of truth, a Civil Rights march organised by a Socialist (Eamonn McCann). It was a moment of outrage too, but, in experiencing that outrage I also felt a certain satisfaction. The Diamond has traditionally been an arena for outrages (look at the architecture). Remembering some of them I saw, for the first time, a clear and terminating connection between them.

My parents remember the hiring fairs of the 1920s. They took place in the Diamond, and were apparently a sight to make anyone with a conscience wince. Children who spoke no English were hired out to farmers and householders who spoke no Irish for £6 a year, payable on completion of the work. I remember the fifties and one St Patrick's Day in the Diamond when Eddie McAteer and the Nationalist Councillors turned down Shipquay Street, tricolour aloft, to face a brutal baton charge which sent us all catapulting through the streets. Then came October 5.

What had these incidents in common? People bartered, people battered. The first, a custom, no voices raised. The second almost a custom, publicity of the sort to raise eyebrows but no voices. The third was televised, and outrage was widespread. But television, although it helped, was not the separating element. What worried the bosses was the revealed connection between bartering and battering. Politics, said the October march, do not serve either a political or religious ideal, although that is the pretence; they serve a reality, social privilege, a system which has as its necessary victims the servant girl of the twenties, the nationalists of the fifties, the Derry workers of the sixties hired out to the BSR or Dupont, or wasting away in a demoralising unemployment. But the crucial victim is the policeman, who upholds in the name of communal law and order the interest of a selfish few.

Unionism is one of those systems which so disguises its purpose that its practices (hiring, batoning) come to be taken as 'natural', as the decreed order of the universe. Any form of degradation continued for long enough becomes customary to both victim and agents. Protestants have been degraded by their willing agency in this respect, Catholics by their apparently eternal role as victims.

And they are victims. To live in a ghetto is to live in a strange homely and lethal climate. You can see people becoming rapidly distorted by the invisible pressures. The national euphemism for such people is 'characters'. They can be comic or tragic. They are part of an endless social problem. Derry, for instance, has a pretty bad drink problem, but it has a fearsome gambling neurosis. The compulsive gambler is less identifiable than most obsessives. No matter how poorly dressed, ill-fed he or his family may be, he puts all his money on the horse or dog of his choice and all his winnings on the next favourite and so on until he's cleaned out. Gambling is a rapacious pastime at best; when you see someone using it to quench a craving, it is unendurable. 'It does me good', they say. This is true. Obsessions are, and feel like cures for the moment they are indulged.

To the compulsive, on a winning streak the racing card is a series of suicidal jumps in one of which he will always hit bottom. This is the subtlest form of barter. Because all visible hope is denied in the sectarian society the man has sold himself to a visionary one. Between him and his desires is the pound note dangling on the end of a baton. That's the ghetto situation. October 5 began the revelation to the Bogside. The Shankill will have to learn it even more painfully.

from 'Why Bogside?', *Honest Ulsterman*, January–March 1971

IMAGES OF BELFAST

ROBERT JOHNSTONE

'I have forgotten something,' says Ciaran Carson's poem, 'I am going back.'·Smithfield might be an ecologist's paradise, where consumer goods are recycled for further use. It might be a ruminant stomach from which objects at the edges of our lives are regurgitated and chewed over. I prefer to think of it as a nexus of nerve-endings in some obscure corner of a collective geriatric brain, a tangle of memories that meant something to somebody once upon a time.

Smithfield Market used to be a single entity, a covered square with a warren of little shops that set out their goods so that you had to step round them, like the souk in an Hibernian Casablanca. You could pick up bargains in second-hand furniture or cheap clothes, but the special thing about Smithfield was its oddity, all the strange little shops that you saw nowhere else. Everything you never thought of was there.

My parents took me one day to the magic shop. I didn't know what I wanted, so the proprietor put on a show for me. There were most of the practical jokes I had seen only in the small ads at the back of *Batman* comics (soap that turned your skin black, foaming sugar, itching powder), but better were the magic props: a cup under which a ball would appear and vanish; a tiny wallet that stole your ten-bob notes; two hinged plastic blocks through which a string could be pulled – you put them together, cut the string, showed the cut ends, closed the blocks again and pulled the string through as if it had been restored. It was essential of course to say the magic words. My father must have gone back to the shop on his own, for every so often odd things would turn up in the house, like the sugar spoon with a hole in the middle, a fork which was hinged (pre-Gellerised cutlery to deposit your food in the wrong place), the rubber pencil, or the cigar which squeaked and shot out a pink worm.

Then there was the pet shop with cages and aquaria outside the door. I remember a tortoise like a waddling stone, snakes in glass cases, none of these like animals at all, more like plastic toys; the budgies' manic choir; lizards – dapper, nervous little men darting around as if they had something important to do. World is crazier and more of it than we think.

Once we schoolchildren could take frogspawn and sticklebacks from the burn at Finaghy. Nowadays that would be an antisocial act. Besides, the place is so built up now I doubt if I could find the stream. What do children miss, when they can't see that speckled pudding change to tadpoles in the classroom?

Childhood is fuelled by exotica, and Smithfield was its temple. There were places selling religious fancy goods, and religious bookshops beside shops that seemed to specialise in naughty magazines (hard to find in the Fifties, I imagine). In King Street, Gass the cycle shop, selling everything to do with bicycles, from pumps to racing gears or the plastic bottles road racers clipped to their handlebars. Maguire's, the boxing barber, is still there, where the fight stars got their crewcuts and where Van Morrison's first band got their Tony Curtis style. Posters for big fights are up in the tiny square window.

My friend Sam bought his first electric guitar in a second-hand shop in an obscure corner of the arcade. We had to clamber over three-piece suites and washing machines to get at it, a rudimentary but impressively shaped red guitar that pretended to be a Fender, made in Japan. Being in the forefront of fashion in the late Sixties, we bought our combat jackets – now making a comeback – in the shop that specialised in army surplus clothes.

The first one I tried on was so tight I couldn't move my arms.

'It's a bit tight,' I suggested.

'Ah, but you wouldn't be wearing a pullover underneath,' said the assistant.

I tried a second. It had obviously belonged to Orson Welles or someone similar.

'This one's too big.'

The assistant was unperturbed. 'Well of course you'd want to have a big thick pullover.'

He was so convincing and helpful I hardly noticed what he was doing. But I did get one that fitted eventually.

Another fixture of Smithfield was Havlin's, the locksmith, 'The KEY people in the SAFE business'. Once I went in there on an impossible quest. I had the handle of a key – the serrated blade had broken off and been lost. It was for an Italian car which had been out of production for about ten years. Could they cut me a new one? I was deeply impressed when they were able to reconstruct my original from the number alone. What's more, it worked.

Most or all of these shops are still there, but the main arcade has been lost, burned down and replaced by prefabricated buildings round the edge of the square. Smithfield looks no more tidy or reputable than before, just more ordinary. Thankfully the shops themselves are just as outré as ever. There are a few additions that mark changing times: Andrews, the big Yamaha motorbike dealer in Gresham Street, where bikers come to find the hardware for their mechanical romance, front fork oil seals or dogleg levers marked with tiny Japanese characters, or to ogle the gleaming new machines hot from the Orient; a little store selling videotapes, allowing people to be horrified in the privacy of their living rooms; Just Books, the anarchist bookshop in Winetavern Street, offering all that the well-read radical needs, from the Fabulous Furry Freak Brothers to the thoughts of Michael Bakunin.

Smithfield started life as a cattle market, situated as it was in the 1750s on the edge of the city, between the butchers of Hercules Street (now Royal Avenue) and land where cattle grazed. By the 1820s the square had been covered to make a shed for dealing in hides and skins, and Smithfield became a place of popular entertainment on Friday nights, with clowns, military recruiting bands and numerous liquor stores. In *As I Roved Out* Cathal O'Byrne paints a colourful picture of the bustle: the Punch and Judy, the peripatetic waxworks that would be set up in vacant premises, Mrs Davis's handball alley, the ballad singer Alec McNicholl, and Peter Maxwell, who 'told lugubrious stories of his mother, and shed copious tears while engaged in their telling'. Winetavern Street, until the 1930s, was a centre for clay pipe making, selling its wares all over Ireland and even supplying Wannamaker's Stores of New York and Philadelphia, which gave its employees a new clay pipe made in Belfast and a sprig of shamrock on St Patrick's Day.

My father bought supplies for his shop – fruit, vegetables, flowers, fish – several times a week from the old markets near the Law Courts and close to the docks. I often went with him, relishing the chance to enter an adult world of expertise and specialisation where, ostensibly, a huge casual structure of relationships and customs had evolved around the process of buying and selling perishable goods.

The very names of the merchants were sonorous. There was Jack Horner, a small quick man with black-framed spectacles, selling flowers; for fish, Owen O'Hagan, relaxed and friendly; Devine's, the big fruit and vegetable firm.

The flowers in all their colours, pristine as the blocks in a new paint-box, were set out in tubs, bordering a narrow pathway to Jack Horner's little office. Like a daily spring in the tundra they arrived and left rapidly, and appeared in such abundance, yet each bloom was precious and delicate. Professionals often handle their tools, even their animals, with rough familiarity. Sometimes they appear to take pride in doing so. But no one treats flowers with less than respect. You cradle a bloom in cupped hand as you test its perfume. The dandy lifts his carnation from the bunch with a flourish, but delicately, holding the stem between finger and thumb, twirling it perhaps, snapping the stem with efficiency, and looking down to admire the effect once it is threaded through his buttonhole.

There might be tulips from Holland, flown in like news of life or death, as if it were vital that supplies get through to Belfast. Some flowers came not in bunches but in long cardboard boxes, wrapped in tissue paper and separated with cardboard struts. Lifting out the long flowers was like finding an expensive new dress that had just arrived from a swanky store in a presentation package. Once or twice there would be an orchid – a single orchid –to remind us how impossibly extravagant nature could be. My father had some glass phials with pierced rubber stoppers, so that the orchids could be preserved like strangely living specimens.

How ephemeral it was. The huge chrysanthemums, big as the globe lights at school, dropped their petals in showers at the slightest touch. It was hard to believe there would be anything left of them by the time they reached the customers. We would usually come in the early morning when the place was crowded with colour. By late morning it was almost bare. The flowers were like ice that had melted away to every shop in Belfast.

The fruit and vegetables were piled high on either side of the narrow roadways that ran through the markets. There would be walls of oranges a couple of storeys high and big red lorries would nose in between them to load or unload. The drivers decorated their trucks with white heather or photos of busty girls, or fixed elaborate chromium hubcaps on their radiator grilles. One would tell you how his potato lorry had burned off a private motorist who had fancied himself.

I remembered from school how the port of Belfast both exported and imported spuds – we grew the seed potatoes, sent them to Cyprus and Egypt, then brought them back when they were grown. Potatoes came from Cyprus not in plastic bags but in boxes full of soft black humus, the potatoes clean like white pebbles in the spongy soil, wrapped in crinkly brown paper. Potatoes in colours like jewels or varieties of gold – white, blue, purple, brown and subtle red.

Sometimes I would try to count the countries that sent their food to us. There were all the different sorts of oranges, from Israel, South Africa, Morocco, Spain, oriental names. They might be big and pale or small and oily, with skin like coloured, polished hide. The apples came in cardboard boxes from the four corners of the globe, and with the most frivolous names – Mac Red, Golden Delicious. Those from Canada were packed in cells of impregnated cardboard, each waxy scarlet apple all the way from Canada in its individual cube of air. The Dayglo green apples from France arrived in refrigerated trailers that had driven all the way from Avignon. Then there were the lemons from Famagusta, each one wrapped in tissue paper, each wrapper with a gold motif of the Venus de Milo.

Grapes would come in barrels full of cork. You split the lid with a crowbar and lifted out a bunch like a dripping, dusty chandelier. Melons came in flat wooden crates, wrapped in woodwool. Lying cushioned there, they were like a drawer from a giant's collection of blown eggs. The peaches lay in dimpled polystyrene trays covered with cellophane, downy as a girl's neck, coloured as richly as amethysts or opals. Onions were in sacks of red netting tied with hemp, their loose skins crackling like dry paper, thin as gold leaf. So much trouble had been taken to pack these things, to keep them in perfect condition on their long journeys, it was difficult to look upon them as mere items of commerce. They were more like presents from abroad. In a crate holding twelve melons, there might be nine pieces of wood, two or three metal bands, and at least thirty-six nails, as well as the bed of woodwool.

Deals would be done at the side of the produce. Buyer and seller would discuss the quality of the goods, the price would be mentioned, a quantity noted down on a clipboard, as casually as if they were discussing the weather. My father might taste a plum with the critical air of a wine-taster, or weigh a melon in his hands, probing it like a doctor for ripeness.

The market was airy and open, its gates were never closed during the day, and there were always lorries edging in and out and people rushing to and fro. The aromas of every continent hung about – the acid tang of citrus, the musty smell of apples, the winey bouquet of grapes in cork – and even the faint odours of decay, from a pile of fallen cabbage leaves or a rotten lemon, purply-white, squashed like a cushion at the corner of its box, were intriguing.

It was almost as if the sea reached into the fish market, for it was always wet and cold, salt, seminal-smelling. I shared my father's romantic fascination with the life of the sea – fish were the only food Western men still went out to hunt in the wild. They went in their little trawlers to win their living from the oceans off Iceland, the Faeroes, the North Sea, and sent their catches to us. Filleted on board or at the dockside in Aberdeen, it would arrive in little wooden boxes lined with a single sheet of white paper and stuffed with snow. Or there would be white polystyrene boxes or big aluminium trays. A man in rubber boots and an oilskin apron, bare-armed, would stir a huge sink of herring, oily, their scales encrusting everything like transparent sequins. We would be shown any oddities: a couple of stray dogfish like miniature sharks, or the biggest cod, too long to fit any of the trays, which I preferred to think had been captured on the Grand Banks. Occasionally there would be lobsters, monstrous living things that waved their pincers in a tired gesture of dismissal when you lifted them up.

Since this was Belfast, I have to mention that the fish merchants were Catholic. Most fish was sold on Fridays because of the Catholic custom of refraining from meat on that day. Many Protestants had the same habit, though I think it has declined latterly. When the present troubles started, the Catholic fish merchants painted out their name on their vans, whether for their own safety or to avoid embarrassing their Protestant clients I am not sure.

The old wholesale markets were mainly about business, and Belfast had nothing as picturesque as Billingsgate or Covent Garden, but I felt that there was some sort of communal liveliness there. It had its own characters: tramps who might wander in looking for rotten fruit or maybe just a piece of cardboard to make a bed; old women looking for bargains; the labourer with the long blond hair who was known to everyone as Gloria; the flower sellers from outside the City Hall, a contrast with the solid small shopkeepers. The markets might have been awkwardly situated, causing problems as you dodged the heavy traffic with your head buried in bunches of flowers to get to your car, but they were busy and part of the city's texture. Now, in common with Covent Garden and Les Halles, they have been moved out of town, to Boucher Road beside the motorway. That was after my father's time, but I doubt if the new markets, in their modern advanced factory-style home, are as much fun, however efficient they are.

The fish and livestock markets remain across the road, but the City Council has promoted a Variety Market on Tuesdays and Fridays in the old St George's Market. The vast halls are filled with stalls: where once the lorry-loads of crates, boxes and sacks were piled high, small retailers operate within their corrals of fruit and veg. Signs advertise Ballynahinch eggs (is that good?) and fish fresh from Portavogie. On one long row of stalls is a communal grave of ghostly white chickens, gutted and dressed. An old-fashioned caravan dispenses old-fashioned hot sweet tea in old-fashioned white mugs.

The stallholders each have a style appropriate to their métier. Those selling vegetables are the most lively. A man with a woollen cap studded with metal badges calls out to the contemplative throng, 'Who's next, ladies?' more in encouragement than interrogation. Neighbours shout their competing claims: 'Fresh red tomatoes only thirty pee a pound', 'Spanish onions ten pence a pound' and so on. (Do the onion-advertiser's tomatoes cost more than 30p?) They flick open their brown paper bags with a flourish, check the desired weight, which they have guessed with uncanny accuracy, and thrust the bag at the customer in a fluid movement.

Much of the market is taken up with second-hand clothes. So much that one imagines that all the clothing in Belfast must sooner or later come here to die, or rather to be reincarnated. These stallholders sit patiently behind their wares, beside huge piles of old shoes – can you find a matching pair? – that remind me of a photograph from a prison camp.

Those selling the cheap new clothes walk up and down their stalls rearranging trousers and cardigans, folding them neatly flat. An old woman sells attractive patterned pullovers. 'These are quality garments you're looking at, girls, all at half price!' The 'girls' are mostly elderly women. The Sikh looks like a man dedicated to his calling. From the neck down he might be anyone, except that he wears so many clothes: a blue nylon anorak over the jacket from a light summer suit, a heavy pullover and a loud shirt. But his face has a full beard and magnificent mustachios, and his turban is a riotously printed length of fabric, quite in keeping with his cheap but cheerful goods.

A row of flat glass-topped cabinets hold jewellery and digital watches. This stall looks overmanned: what must be a family of stallholders discussing with every customer the intricacies of the digital alarm chronograph or the carats of the red and yellow gold bracelet. Disturbingly a sign announces 'Ears Pierced'. While-you-wait, no doubt. I do not witness this gory public spectacle being performed.

A large proportion of the shoppers are elderly ladies, hunting with the fascination I remember my mother had in the Fifties for bargains. The white plastic bags rustle like grass as they thread their way through the throng. Young mothers cause bottlenecks as pram and pushchair meet in the narrow spaces. One woman, who must be in her sixties and doesn't look like a football supporter, stuffs items into a bag with the legend 'Northern Ireland – Spain 1982'. A superb young girl – pink glasses, hair bleached and dyed in contrasting colours and pointing in several directions – examines the racks of second-hand clothes for additions to her exotic wardrobe.

On the way back from the Variety Market it is *de rigueur* to call in to Dowds Aquatics in Victoria Street. Unfortunately for me and the schoolboys who were there, we were five minutes late for the feeding of the piranha – rather inoffensive in his gentle colours – and the bird-eating spider was skulking halfway under a bit of wood, ignoring the doomed but cheerful grasshopper in his tank. Equally impassive were the tangle of yellow rat snakes ('Do not tap on the glass: these animals are wild and easily alarmed' – an irresistible temptation to my browsing companions). But I did make acquaintance with the hordes of red-eared terrapins and the snapping turtle, who lolled among the shreds of a hasty meal. And with the blue trigger fish and the golden angels and the black moors, more like bug-eyed spaceships decorated with feathers, the goldfish vibrating in their tiny voids: all so extravagant and outlandish it required an effort of imagination to remember they were part of the animal kingdom like ourselves.

Outside again in the unextravagant Belfast streets with their familiar concerns, ordinary life seems more colourful rather than less. We are amazed that natural wonders should exist at all, while the strangest constructs of the human mind are taken for granted.

from *Images of Belfast*, 1983

PAISLEY'S PROGRESS

TOM PAULIN

In 1969, while he was serving a prison sentence for unlawful assembly, Ian Paisley sent this message to his congregation:

> I rejoice with you in the rich blessings of last weekend. I knew that our faithful God would pour out His bounty. In prayer in this cell I touched the Eternal Throne and had the gracious assurance of answered prayer. What a joy to hear from Mr Beggs of a £1000 gift for the pulpit. Hallelujah! May that pulpit be the storm centre of the great hurricane of revival. Oh for a tempest of power, a veritable cyclone of blessing. Lord, let it come!

Eight years later, the preacher rose up in that enormous pulpit and waved a copy of a historical study which had just been published. 'Brethren and sisters in Christ,' he shouted, 'here is a great book that tells the Truth about Ulster. Go home, friend, and read it.'

The book was *The Narrow Ground* by A.T.Q. Stewart and until I heard of that Sabbath review I'd believed that historians were a type of Brahmin – pure vegetarians who existed at a level of consciousness far above that of politicians and other carnivores. I'd believed in their disinterestedness, their objectivity, their lack of axes to grind. Now I began to understand what F.H. Bradley meant when he said that we reflect 'in general not to find the facts, but to prove our theories at the expense of them'. In that moment of discovery historiography appeared like an ascent towards the Supreme Fiction, and among the mountaineers were Daniel Defoe, Wallace Stevens, Edward Gibbon and A.T.Q. Stewart – all imaginative writers with a style and vision of their own, but none with a style that was any 'truer' than another's.

Historians may be disinterested – some of them certainly like to congratulate each other on their disinterestedness – but they are doomed to be read by an *interested* audience. And many people must recall the comic sequel to the two televised accounts of Irish history in which an earnest Ludovic Kennedy asked Paisley what he'd learnt from the programmes and a group of Irish historians back in the studio held their noses at the whole enterprise. Inevitably, historians are drawn into politics – E.P. Thompson, for example, has an audience which supports both the Campaign for Nuclear Disarmament and the Labour Party, while historians in the North of Ireland have power-bases or followings on the Republican side or in the Democratic Unionist Party. How far historians are able to free themselves from the simplifications which their readers visit on them is problematic, but as far as the writing of Irish history is concerned I'm convinced that it is now, and will be for the foreseeable future, inescapably *political*. Those historians who are bored or embarrassed by the version of history offered in the schools and elsewhere in the Irish Republic may believe that it is possible to escape from that version into a sophisticated objectivity, but as far as I can see they simply become trapped in a rival simplification – the Unionist version of history. In either case, the embarrassment of, in that well-worn phrase, 'legitimising' a particular cause is bound to result.

The question that concerns me initially is this – where does the imaginative inspiration for a historical argument come from? Did *The Narrow Ground* inspire Paisley, or did the voice of Old Ravenhill inspire *The Narrow Ground*? Accompanying this question is the problem of the relation of middle-class Unionism to working-class Unionism, or – to put it in cultural terms – the relation of establishment and anti-establishment ideas within Unionism. As Unionism cracks and splinters a form of class politics begins to emerge – a populism in the case of Paisleyism and a form of socialism in the Ulster Defence Association.

For the UDA the problem is essentially one of identity: 'The Prods have been brainwashed into believing that they were strictly a British Community, have no Irish or Ulster traditions and therefore didn't need to learn Irish dancing, Gaelic, or folk music.' Thus Andy Tyrie, the leader of the UDA. Tyrie supports this view with a historical argument to the effect that there was an ancient British people ('British' in the non-imperial sense) who were called the Cruthin and who existed in Ulster long before the seventeenth-century settlement. He also emphasises his Ulsterness by having a photograph of the statue of Cuchulain in the GPO above his desk. Cuchulain is therefore an authentically *Ulster* hero in a way that Carson – a Dubliner who privately despised the province – can never be.

Where James Joyce offers a definition of Irish identity which is non-sectarian and truly republican, and which exists somewhere in the future, the UDA looks back to a dreamtime occupied by aboriginal ancestors in order to affirm an identity which is both epic and provincial. At the moment the UDA has stepped aside from the conflict and is insisting that it is a socialist and non-sectarian organisation composed of forward-looking people who are 'tired of being classed as Neanderthal bigots'. They may draw their inspiration from a form of atavistic energy, but they are also modern in their outlook and they are opposed to the link with Britain. They have parted company with what is now termed 'Official Unionism'.

Although the UDA has now distanced itself from Ian Paisley, he more than any other Unionist politician appears to belong to a dreamtime of Presbyterian aborigines – giant preachers who strode the Antrim coast long before the birth of Christ. He is a complex and protean personality who imagines cyclones of blessings, compares himself to the diminutive figure of a famous Brahmin called Mahatma Gandhi, and probably nurses a secret admiration for Parnell on whose parliamentary tactics some of his own appear to be modelled.

Ian Paisley was born in Armagh in 1926. His father, James Paisley, came of a Church of Ireland family who had lived in Co. Tyrone for many generations. In 1908 his father was 'saved' by an evangelical preacher and became a Baptist. In a memorial sermon, the son describes how his father went down to a frozen River Strule one Easter Sunday morning with a pastor who first broke the ice and then put him under the water:

> My father tells when he went under the waters of that river he identified himself with his Lord in death, in burial and in resurrection. When he came out that day he had lost many of his friends, he had lost many of the people that once associated themselves with him in the gospel. He realised that there was a reproach with the gospel. My father as I told you, was uncompromising in his character. He did not care. The more he was opposed the more he preached and the more he was persecuted the more he excelled in evangelism. God blessed him and eventually he went to Armagh to business.

This is a characteristically Protestant piece of writing: there is the assertion of uncompromising principle, a strong self-justifying theme which runs throughout the sermon, an affirmation of the work ethic (that brutal

412

verb 'to business' echoing the anti-Home Rule slogan, 'Ulster Means Business'), and finally there is the idea of being born again. In a very fundamental sense it is a description of revolutionary commitment because this is, imaginatively, a seventeenth-century world where religion and politics are synonymous. And so on Easter Sunday 1908 the puritan revolutionary rises out of the deep, having rejected friends, family, leisure and the private life. The old life of compromise, scepticism and individual personality is set aside in the moment of commitment. And that commitment is made out in the open air, as compared with, say, T.S. Eliot's Anglican and institutional commitment which is a 'moment in a draughty church at smokefall'.

Paisley senior later broke with the Baptists because of their ecumenism and set up his own Independent Fundamentalist Church. The son has inherited this characteristic of breaking with established institutions and he has a Cromwellian scorn of formalism, an instinctive libertarianism which conceals, or creates, a monumentally dictatorial personality. It appears that the alternative to compromised institutions could be a series of pyramids dedicated to his version of the egotistical sublime, to his relentless monomania. . . .

In 1949 Paisley began a mission in Belfast's dockland and he also joined the anti-Roman Catholic National Union of Protestants. Somewhere about this time there is a moment outside the printed record where he appears to have been snubbed by a member of the Unionist establishment. That establishment regarded him as a working-class rabble-rouser and his outspoken unrestrained bigotry threatened and parodied its defter sectarianism. The rebuff demanded vengeance and Paisley began the long march which was to bring him to the walls of the Unionist establishment, to the barrier around the demesne.

The Paisley of this period is partly modelled on the Reverend Henry Cooke, a reactionary and highly influential nineteenth-century preacher who did much to counter Presbyterian radicalism. This Paisley is an autochthonous bigot who once organised a mock-mass on the platform of the Ulster Hall. Patrick Marrinan, his biographer, describes the sinister shabbiness of this occasion, the nervous fascination of the audience laughing at a renegade Spanish priest reciting unfamiliar Latin words, the canny showmanship, the plastic buckets brimming with money.

Paisley's particular kind of puritan egotism is voracious in its subjectivity and for all its insistence on sincerity is in practice highly theatrical. He is a compulsive role-player and is fond of dressing up in other people's personalities. After the Almighty, after St Paul – for whom he confesses 'a strange liking' – his most influential model, or imaginative ikon, is John Bunyan, whose life and work obsess him. He calls Bunyan a 'poor unschooled tinker' who became 'the most prominent man of letters as far as English literature is concerned'. Bunyan is this 'dreamer and penman' who had 'the tinker's power of reaching the heart' – there is a hint of rural superstition and natural magic here. He admires Bunyan for his 'strong doctrinal preaching', his opposition to the civil and ecclesiastical authorities, the enormous crowds he drew, and for his prose-style. Bunyan's appeal is theological, social and aesthetic – he *is* culture and tradition. It's here that we enter a time-warp and see that the world of Ranters, Fifth Monarchy Men, Levellers and millenarian preachers which E.P. Thompson and Christopher Hill describe in their work. For Thompson, *Pilgrim's Progress* is one of the two 'founding texts of the English working-class movement' (the other is Paine's *Rights of Man*). And so to admire Bunyan is by definition to be a dissenting radical, a nonconformist and a republican – Bunyan was a soldier in the Parliamentary Army.

Bunyan was also imprisoned for twelve years for preaching without a licence, and in 1966 Paisley was imprisoned for three months for demonstrating outside the General Assembly of the Presbyterian Church. In a statement he said, 'it will take more than Captain O'Neill's nasal twang to defy us' – the class grudge is clear, even though class politics was an impossible concept then. O'Neill warned of the dangers of alienating 'our British friends' and with an unconscious dismissiveness referred to Northern Ireland as 'this small corner of the British Commonwealth'. Angered by this diminution, Paisley retorted: 'To Our Lord, puppet politicians are but grasshoppers with portfolios.' Like any republican he refused, in one of his favourite phrases, to 'bow the knee' to the colonial authority and its deputies. And so, in a small corner of the British Commonwealth, Ulster's Bunyan was imprisoned by a grasshopper with a portfolio.

While he was in prison Paisley wrote the most substantial of his four books. It is an exposition of Paul's Epistle to the Romans cast in the form of a puritan journal. Each section is dated and the *Exposition* ends with this dramatic, deadpan postscript: 'This section completed in the dawn of the eighty-third day of imprisonment: Tuesday, 11 October 1966.' It is the dawn of righteousness, conviction and inspiration, and it looks forward to Paisley's second prison term, three years later, when he sent this letter to his congregation:

Beloved in the Lord,

The day which we have prayed for and longed for has dawned. Captain O'Neill the tyrant is no longer the ruler of our country. We, who have suffered under his tyranny and wrath can surely sing Psalm 124. The Lord has wrought for us a great deliverance, and to His great Name we ascribe the glory. Let us be careful to return our heartfelt thanks.

I heard the news here in my cell, No. 20 (B2), as prisoner 636, at approximately 4.30 on Monday afternoon. Immediately I sang the doxology and fell upon my knees to give God thanks. We have had a long and bitter struggle. As a people we have suffered. As your minister I have been maligned and persecuted, and you have all shared the maligning and persecuting. We have been in the depths together. Every effort has been made to smash the testimony of the Church and the credibility of me, the minister of the church. THEY HAVE FAILED, FOR GOD WAS OUR HELPER. We are just a lot of nobodies, and the enemy thought he could trample us out, BUT GOD DELIVERED US.

Like some Luddite pamphlet, this message rises up from the very depths of popular culture, and that phrase 'We are just a lot of nobodies' concentrates much of the emotion which Paisleyism draws on and expresses. The plain, strenuous, autodidactic atmosphere that clings to Paisley's published works – a combination of earnest assertive pride and a deep lack of confidence – tells of a disadvantaged population which feeds its persecution complex by reading the Psalms and which dreams of emerging from the underground status of subculture into the light of power and society.

It is impossible to nourish such an ambitious dream and to see yourself as a grateful inhabitant of a small corner of the British Commonwealth, and Paisley's rejection of that dependent status is formulated in a theological argument. Commenting on Romans 1.1 – 'Paul, a servant of Jesus Christ, called to be an apostle, separated unto the gospel of God' – Paisley notes, 'Paul was a separatist.' This idea of separation is one of his major themes and in his commentary on Romans he is forming an idea of

Ulster nationalism which entails separation from both the United Kingdom and the Republic of Ireland. . . .

There is an epic moment in one of Paisley's published sermons where he insists obsessively that *'the sea speaks of separation'*:

> I stand at the edge of the sea. I look over its waves, and my loved ones are across in another continent. Between me and them stretches the waves of the briny depths. I know what it is to be separated from them. Nothing separates like the sea. What a barrier the sea makes. What a terrible barrier the sea makes. Separation.

The word obsesses him and in a cassette recording entitled *Separation*, which was released in 1980, he explains that Moses 'chose the affliction of the people of God' and rejected 'the beggarly elements of Egypt'. Here, Egypt is the United Kingdom – Ulster under Direct Rule from Westminster – and Paisley is offering a Pauline separatist argument: 'May God make us a separated people.' By 'us' he means the Protestants – there is a tribal exclusiveness central to this definition – and he sees himself as Moses leading his people out of bondage to the Promised Land. . . .

Paisley's political ambition and his motivating fire – a fire he has stolen from the Unionist establishment – are sometimes transparently evident in his scriptural exegesis. Commenting on the phrase, 'for it is the power of God' (Romans 1.16), he remarks:

> Gospel preaching is charged with the dynamic of heaven. Dynamite to be displayed in all its mighty potency must have the fuse and the fire. When the fuse of true prayer is set alight with the fire of the Holy Ghost and thus the gospel dynamite is exploded, what tremendous results occur. Then do the strongholds of Satan topple. Then do the bulwarks of idolatry collapse. Then do the towering walls of sin suddenly fall. Then is the enemy dislodged. Then is all opposition blasted and the power of truth is proved to be more than a conqueror. Oh for a day of real gospel preaching and gospel power! Lord let me witness such a day.

This prayer for power was offered in the prison cell in 1966 and three years later, in April 1969, there were a series of explosions which were blamed on the IRA, and which helped to bring about O'Neill's resignation. Though no one had accused them, the Ulster Volunteer Force denied responsibility for the explosions and it's generally accepted that they, or freelance Protestant terrorists, were responsible. Puritan metaphor is a form of irony which has a habit of becoming literal: a dynamic millenarian rhetoric can inspire men to place actual dynamite under the status quo.

Paisley's theological argument is that 'righteousness without the law' must be received by Faith and he explains that the seed of Abraham are not heirs of the law but heirs by the righteousness of faith without the law. According to the Anglican *New Commentary on Holy Scripture* Paul argues that an 'act of faith' procured Abraham's acquittal and by 'faith' Paul means 'the whole act, or attitude, of surrender to Christ, intellectual, moral, and emotional'.

The idea of an act of faith is fundamental to Paisley's thought, and from time to time it is given calculated existential expression – as, for example, his demonstration in the House of Commons after the assassination of the Reverend Robert Bradford and his subsequent call for a campaign of passive disobedience to force the British out. Of necessity, the leap of faith is intensely subjective and assertive, and it is informed or sustained by an idea of martyrdom. Paisley comments that Christ makes frequent references to his death as 'the culminating act of his ministry on earth', and this inspires his projection of himself as an exemplary figure, ready to stake all and do or die for his faith and his people ('sell our lives dearly', as he put it outside the House of Commons).

Although Paisley resembles De Valera in the theological cast of his mind, the religion he subscribes to is an apparently unstructured, intensely emotional experience. 'Justification,' he argues, 'is heart work as opposed to head work.' This assertion of emotion over intellect is both authoritarian and romantic, and Paisley finds its dogmatic justification in Romans 10.10: 'For with the heart man believeth unto righteousness; and with the mouth confession is made unto salvation.' . . .

Terence O'Neill dismissed Ian Paisley's chiliastic rhetoric and his political demonstrations as 'mindless', and the establishment view of him is expressed in two later remarks of Brian Faulkner's. When the British Government suspended Stormont, Faulkner accused it of reducing Northern Ireland to 'a coconut colony'. Later, when the power-sharing Executive fell, Faulkner called Paisley 'this demon doctor'. This habit of drawing analogies – whether with Hungary or Algeria – is a deep-seated Irish characteristic and the parallel here must be familiar to anyone who

417

has read the novels of V.S. Naipaul. It invites us to imagine a West Indian island, drums beating, the governor's mansion, a messianic revolutionary leader, riots, carnival and independence. Indeed, Paisleyism is curiously similar to reggae music – both are assertions of post-colonial identity, though reggae is much more advanced, sophisticated and culturally eclectic.

In 1970 Paisley became a Stormont MP, then a Westminster MP. In the following year Brian Faulkner introduced internment, and towards the end of 1971 Paisley emerged as a kind of republican statesman. With the SDLP, he opposed the introduction of internment 'in principle', though he had favoured it at first. At the end of November he suggested that if the constitution of the Irish Republic were amended then 'good neighbourliness in the highest possible sense' might prevail between the Republic and Northern Ireland. He said:

> I would like to see anything done that would be for the good of all the people of Northern Ireland and all the people of Ireland. I believe it could deal with the cancer and the cancer is not the 1920 Act and not the partition of the country but the cancer is the 1937 Constitution and the domination of the Catholic Church through it. I would like to see the whole thing thrown out.

When asked if he would favour a united Ireland if the Republic were to remove Protestant fears by amending its Constitution, he replied:

> If you ask me whether I can see at some time some way, somewhere in the future a united Ireland, that is a question I cannot answer because I cannot now say what will happen in the future and, anyway, I cannot answer the question because I am too much of a realist and such a question is really not even worthy of consideration now.

The establishment Unionists were quick to exploit this apparent rejection of the old anti-Home Rule slogan, 'We won't have it', and they accused Paisley of being prepared to sell out to Republicanism. He quickly drew back and claimed he'd been misquoted.

Three months later he emerged as a total integrationist in a pamphlet called *The Ulster Problem, Spring 1972: A Discussion of the True Situation in Northern Ireland*. This pamphlet contains a section called 'A brief history of Ireland' which is an interesting example of Unionist historiography.

All mention of the 1798 rebellion is carefully avoided and we are moved briskly from the plantation of Ulster to the year 1800:

> ... the Irish Parliament decided for legislative union or parliamentary union with Great Britain; and there was passed the Act of Union. The Irish Parliament was abolished, and from 1800 the members of Parliament from Ireland had their seats in the mother of Parliaments – the British House of Commons at Westminster.

Later in the pamphlet Paisley insists on the necessity of 'the complete union of Northern Ireland and the United Kingdom'. He wants 'full legislative union'. This appears straightforward – it was for a long time the policy of Enoch Powell and the Official Unionists – except that that favourite word 'separated' appears three times in his brief history of Ireland. He describes Daniel O'Connell and Parnell as separatist leaders, and the wish to equal them in stature is not beyond his ambition – he is a natural overreacher who has no regard for the ideas of balance, decorum and limitation which are such strong features of English culture.

In order to 'separate' he has had to appear to be leading his people back into Egypt, and it is now clear that Britain has absolutely no intention of granting Northern Ireland full, permanent legislative union. Paisley therefore understands Austen Chamberlain's remark that Northern Ireland is 'an illogical and indefensible compromise', and his policy can be interpreted as an ironic double bluff which invites both Britain and the Republic to lay their cards on the table. British policy may now be defined as 'get out' – the phrase hurled at Paisley, McQuade and Robinson by angry Westminster MPs – while the policy of the Irish Republic has recently become clear in the New Ireland Forum Report.

If total integration is a dead duck (and everyone recognises that it is), and if a United Ireland is an impossibility, then the only alternative is for Northern Ireland to secede and go independent – to 'separate'. Ultimately – and tragically – there never is any choice between this, that, and a something else which is neither this nor that. However, the idea of Ulster independence does express a conflict which is other than the Unionist/Republican conflict. Southerners appear to regard Northerners as incomprehensible savages, while Northerners look South and see, in the words of Henry Joy McCracken, 'a set of gasconaders'. At a deep level there is a

419

shared perception, a common bond, between the minority and majority populations in the North, and this bond is altogether other than the sentimental concept of 'ould dacency' purveyed by writers like Benedict Kiely.

It emerges, for example, in a speech which Paisley made in 1973, the year the House of Commons approved a White Paper for a Northern Ireland Assembly. During the Commons debate, Paisley said this:

> For too long the representatives of Northern Ireland have been asked: 'Who do you speak for?' It is important at this juncture that the people be given the opportunity to speak by the ballot box. In many senses we have been caught up in a struggle that goes far beyond the basic differences between two sections of the community. There are other elements in the situation that do not want a settlement of any kind, that are purely and utterly destructive, that want to see the destruction of Northern Ireland not merely as an entity in the UK, but as part of the Western democratic system. This House must face up to the fact that these forces in Northern Ireland care not about any Government White Paper or the democratic vote. They believe that violence in the end shall pay. It is sad but in many degrees violence has paid off in Ulster. Throughout this debate there has been the dangerous suggestion that if the elections throw up a group in Northern Ireland which this House does not like, then, with a stroke of the pen, they can say on 31 March next year: 'fare thee well'. When we say this makes us feel like second-class citizens, we are telling the truth. I would not like to see Northern Ireland ever going outside the Union, but there is a section there who are feeling restless with the attitudes of the members of this House and the Government.

Perhaps this was the first time that a Unionist stated in public that he felt like a 'second-class citizen'. It marks a significant movement of the spirit and helps to define the difference between official and unofficial Unionism. The majority of the constituents of Fermanagh and South Tyrone will hardly have needed to recall the phrase when the House of Commons simply ignored their wishes in a dangerous display of near-unanimity, or 'me-tooism' as one dissenting Labour MP courageously defined it.

Here we arrive at something hard and fast – a principle which unites Paisleyism and Republicanism. We come up against the collision between that principle and the sort of eyes-averted Burkean shuffle which characterizes British policy towards Ireland. The principle of one-man-one-vote is a great leveller and it has even prompted one Burkean commentator to suggest that Fermanagh–South Tyrone should become United Nations territory.

The complication in Paisley's attitude to this principle lies in his perception of himself as British. It is an intermittent and fluctuating perception (for the *Sunday Times* he is a 'defiler of the British way of life'), and it was expressed forcibly during a meeting Paisley had with Bernadette Devlin in 1968. She suggested that the Unionist state had been unjust and unfair, and although he conceded that there might have been injustices Paisley insisted, 'I would rather be British than fair.' In Ulster, the condition of being British is that you somehow believe in one-man-one-vote but are selective about its implementation. And so it is possible to have a situation where a group of demonstrators waves a placard saying ONE MAN ONE VOTE and a rival group waves either a Union Jack or a placard saying BETTER BRITISH THAN FAIR.

Because he possesses a theological temperament, Paisley is as opposed to liberalism as any Marxist. In one sermon, for example, he attacks the 'sinking sands of an easy believism' – he means ecumenism, liberal theology and politics. In another sermon he begins by stating, 'Ours is a Laodicean age', and in another he says, 'make sure of this, there will be no neutrals in this service. There will not be a man or a woman go down the stairs today, out onto the streets of Ballymena who will not have made a vital and a terrible decision.' This is the Baptist doctrine of total immersion or complete commitment, and anyone familiar with the ideological temperament will recognise it here in an earlier, theological form. It's a temperament dipped in icy, not lukewarm, water, an urgent single-minded attitude which says that the 'only minute you can be sure of is this minute' and which states that it's 'now or never'.

This tremendous leap of faith is directed both at personal political power and at an idea of God, and Paisley's God resembles a cross between Judge Jeffreys and Albert Pierrepoint. This 'God of inflexible justice' is described in a sermon called 'After This Judgment' in which Paisley gives a relished description of a court 'in the old days' where the chaplain comes and gives the judge 'the black cap'. He then states, 'Some day Jesus will put on the black cap.' . . . Somewhere deep in his personality there lies a fascination with judicial murder which involves a contradictory identification with both the victim and his executioner.

In a published sermon, 'Richard Cameron: The Lion of the Covenant', there is a stark and savoured quotation from the sentence of hanging and disembowelling which the 'Council of Blood' passed on one of the Covenanters. Here Paisley appears as a Scottish Nationalist laying the 'tribute wreath' of his sermon on the memorial to a Protestant martyr (his mother was 'born into a Scots Covenanting home' and he makes much of his Scottish inheritance). This is apparent in two cassette sermons on the Covenanters which are awash with cries of 'blood' and whose delivery at times resembles the intonation necessary to a reading of the closing lines of Yeats's 'Easter 1916'. Although Paisley doesn't write the sacred names out in a verse, he does recite them in a rolling, drawn-out, ululating intonation which elevates the 'Covenanting martyrs' and affirms their holiness. These almost forgotten historical figures are invested with a vocal halo by the preacher and so are changed into transcendent heroes. This is a Protestantism which is pushing deep into the territory of mystery and mythology; it is a celebration of chthonic forces and a rejection of secular and utilitarian values. . . .

When heaven was opened, Paisley says, the Covenanters hoped to see Christ 'on his white horse coming forth to put every enemy underneath his feet'. Here, Christ and William of Orange, the Second Coming and the Glorious Revolution, melt into each other. The Day of Judgement is a gable-end in Sandy Row and the white horse becomes the pale horse of Revelations. Paisley is an amateur and obsessive numerologist and he has a particular fascination for the apocalyptic vision of Revelations. In another Covenanting sermon he explains the symbolism of the fifth seal in terms which echo his discussion of grace and law in the *Exposition*. Five is the 'number of grace' and this is the 'mighty sovereign free grace of God' which enabled the Covenanters to 'stand true and uncompromisingly'.

In this sermon, metaphor and substance become confused: blood is both symbol and reality. The preacher shouts out:

> . . . all the attributes of God flow in the bloodstream of Calvary . . . we're under the blood-stained banner of the Cross . . . must sail through bloody seas . . . blood . . . blood . . . blood . . .

The sermon lurches towards a Churchillian rhetoric – 'there's a storm coming that will try all our foundations' – and it also has moments of bloody and paranoid dementia. At times it sounds a note of bitter failure, at others it is fired with a notion of glorious martyrdom. It looks beyond this world to the resurrection, yet it is also directed towards this world in its imagination of a radically new, radically changed society. It is part Protestant triumphalism careering off into heaven, part an attempt to heal the puritan split in consciousness by summoning a millenarian vision of a new heaven and a new earth. This sermon offers an essentially Lawrentian ethic – blood consciousness and the healing rainbow at the end.

This apocalyptic vision is given an antiquarian treatment in Paisley's book *The 'Fifty Nine' Revival*, which is an account of the revolutionary 'flood time of revival' which swept parts of Ulster in 1859. F.S.L. Lyons discusses this movement briefly in *Culture and Anarchy in Ireland*, though he sees it – wrongly I think – as an almost exclusively emotional and psychological phenomenon. His understanding of Presbyterianism is limited and inadequate, and this is because historiography – at least in the North – is still at the polemical stage. Future historians will have a mass of pamphlets, tracts, sermons and journalism to draw on. Lyons has failed to commence this excavation and this may explain why his discussion of northern culture is so unsatisfactory.

In his conclusion, Lyons states that between the fall of Parnell and the death of Yeats there was an anarchy

... in the mind and in the heart, an anarchy which forbade not just unity of territories, but also 'unity of being', an anarchy that sprang from the collision within a small and intimate island of seemingly irreconcilable cultures, unable to live together or to live apart, caught inextricably in the web of their tragic history.

Despite the counterbalancing quotation from Yeats with which he caps this, Lyons's Arnoldian terminology is unhelpful, and it could be argued – indeed it *was* argued long ago by George Birmingham in *The Red Hand of Ulster* – that Irish culture is really unified at its extremes. An example of this can be found in Paisley's historical study, *The Massacre of St Bartholomew*, where he explores the doctrine of martyrdom. He believes that 'true faith is a martyred faith' and argues that the blood of the martyrs is the 'seed' of the Church. This is close to the phrase 'elect seed' which he employs in his *Exposition* and it resembles Pearse's notion of martyrdom.

Does this mean, then, that it is Paisley's ambition to take over the GPO in Belfast and give his life for Ulster? Will there be a generation of Democratic Ulster hunger-strikers? Will there be a civil war of the kind Paisley describes in his history of the Huguenots? Will a shrunken, independent Northern Ireland barricade itself against an enlarged Republic? And will an ambitious group of Ulster Nationalists demand the return of Cavan, Monaghan and Donegal, as well as the counties lost from the six? Or will there be negotiation, argument, compromise, a new constitution, a parliament in Armagh and the beginnings of a way of writing history that is neither Orange nor Green, but is instead as white as the middle band of the Irish tricolour?

History, by its very nature, has no answers.

from 'Paisley's Progress', from *Ireland and the English Crisis*, 1984

*

QUESTION TIME

CIARAN CARSON

A native of Belfast, writes George Benn in his 1823 history of the city, *who had been brought up in one of the best streets which it contained, lately came over from America, after nearly a life-long absence, to visit the home of his youth. He could hardly find it. An immense place of business occupied its site, and he compared Belfast to an American town, so great was its progress in his absence, and so unexampled the growth of its population.*

That disorientation, that disappointed hunger for a familiar place, will be experienced all the more keenly by today's returning native; more than that, even the little piggy who stayed at home will sometimes feel lost. *I know this place like the back of my hand* – except who really knows how many hairs there are, how many freckles? A wound, a suture, and excision will remind us of the physical, of what *was* there – as the song has it, *you'll never miss your mother till she's buried beneath the clay.* For Belfast is changing daily: one day the massive Victorian façade of the Grand Central Hotel, latterly an army barracks, is *there,* dominating the whole of Royal Avenue; the next day it is gone, and a fresh breeze sweeps through the gap, from Black Mountain, across derelict terraces, hole-in-the-wall one-horse taxi operations, Portakabins, waste ground, to take the eye back up towards the mountain and the piled-up clouds.

The junk is sinking back into the sleech and muck. Pizza parlours, massage parlours, night-clubs, drinking-clubs, antique shops, designer studios momentarily populate the wilderness and the blitz sites; they too will vanish in the morning. Everything will be revised. The fly-specked gloom of The Elephant Bar is now a Winemark; Mooney's Bar is a denim shop; The Gladstone has disappeared. The tangle of streets that was the Pound Loney is the Divis Flats Complex, which is also falling apart, its high-rise Sixties optimism sliding back into the rubble and erasure. Maps and street directories are suspect.

No, don't trust maps, for they avoid the moment: ramps, barricades, diversions, Peace Lines. Though if there is an ideal map, which

425

shows this city as it is, it may exist in the eye of that helicopter ratcheting overhead, its searchlight fingering and scanning the micro-chip deviations: the surge of funerals and parades, swelling and accelerating, time-lapsed, sucked back into nothingness by the rewind button; the wired-up alleyways and entries; someone walking his dog when the façade of Gass's Bicycle Shop erupts in an avalanche of glass and metal forks and tubing, rubber, rat-trap pedals, toe-clips and repair kits. Or it may exist in photographs – this one, for example, of Raglan Street, showing

> *... a sight that was to become only too common to a generation of British soldiers as rioters stone 'A' Company, 2nd Battalion, The Queen's Regiment, during the savage Lower Falls riots of 3–5 July 1970 which left five civilians dead and eighteen military casualties ...*

But the caption is inaccurate: the camera has caught only one rioter in the act, his stone a dark blip in the frizzly air. The others, these would-be or has-been or may-be rioters, have momentarily become spectators, as their protagonist does his David-and-Goliath act; some might be talking about the weather, which seems unusually grey for July, or maybe this is a bad print; some others are looking down Bosnia Street at what is happening or might happen next. The left-hand frame of the photograph only allows us the 'nia' of Roumania Street, so I don't know what's going on there, but I'm trying to remember – was I there that night, on this street littered with half-bricks, broken glass, a battered saucepan and a bucket? In this fragment of a map, here is the lamp-post where I swung as a child, there is Smyth's corner shop; I can almost see myself in the half-gloom and the din. From here – No. 100 – I would turn into Leeson Street, on up to the Falls Road, across to Clonard Street on my way to St Gall's Primary School; at least, that was how I was told to go, and generally I did, but remember, *Never go by Cupar Street*, my father would warn me, and I knew this was a necessary prohibition without asking why, for Cupar Street was one of those areas where the Falls and Shankill joined together as unhappy Siamese twins, one sporadically and mechanically beating the other round the head, where the Cullens, Finnegans and Reillys merged with Todds and Camerons and Wallaces. One day I did come home by Cupar Street, egged on by a fellow pupil. Nothing happened, and we felt the thrill of

Indian scouts penetrating the British lines, the high of invisibility. We did it again; it became addictive, this perilous sin of disobedience and disappearance. We crept along in the dark shadow of the Falls Flax Spinning Mill, becoming bolder day by day in our deceit. For who knew what we were, who could tell? The forays ended when we were stopped one day by four boys about our own age. One of them had fashioned two little charity-type flags from paper and pins: he held a Union Jack in one hand, a tricolour in the other. He eyed us slyly, knowingly: *See them flags?* We nodded nervously. *Well, which of them would youse say was the best?* He had us cornered. If we chose the Union Jack, we were guilty of cowardice and treason – and he would know we were lying anyway; if we chose the tricolour, we would get a hiding. So we ran the gauntlet, escaping with a few bruises into the unspoken force-field of the Catholic end of the street. My father knew something was up when I got home; I broke down under questioning, and got a real hiding. I had learned some kind of lesson. So I thought.

I was reminded of this today, when I went out for what I imagined was a harmless spin on the bike. A showery day, blowing warm and cold – past the west side of Girdwood Barracks along Clifton Park Avenue – a few inhabited houses in a row of derelicts backing on to Crumlin Road Jail – up the Shankill; I come to the Shankill Road Library on the corner of Mountjoy Street (the name of yet another jail), remembering how I used to go here as a child in search of Biggles books because I had exhausted the entire Biggles stock of the Falls Library – I was older then, and was allowed to go, I think – how was it, across Cupar Street, up Sugarfield Street? I see the green cupola of Clonard Monastery towering high, almost directly above me, it seems, and I realise again with a familiar shock how little separates the Shankill and the Falls, how in the troubles of '68 or '69 it was rumoured that this monastery tower was a sniper's nest – so yes, I think, why not re-trace the route of all those years ago, 1959 or 1960. I turn idly down Mountjoy Street, Azamor Street, Sugarfield Street. Dead end. Here is the Peace Line, a thirty-foot-high wall scrawled with graffiti, mounted with drab corrugated iron; Centurion Street; Battenberg Street; dead end again. Where I remember rows of houses, factories, there is recent wasteland, broken bricks, chickweed, chain-link fencing. Eventually I find a new road I never knew existed – or is it an old street deprived of all its landmarks? – which leads into the Springfield Road. Familiar territory now, well, almost, for going down the Kashmir Road into Bombay Street – burned out in '68, some new houses there – I come to the other side of the Peace Line, which now backs on to St Gall's School – still there, graffiticized, wire mesh on the windows, but still the same, almost; the massive granite bulk of Clonard is still there; Greenan's shop is now a dwelling; and the west side of Clonard Gardens, where the Flax & Rayon mill used to be, is all new houses; Charleton's shop is bricked up; Tolan's the barber's is long since gone, I knew that; this side of the street is all derelict, breeze-blocked, holes knocked into holes; so on to the Falls. I go down the road a bit, almost as far as the library, then stop; I'd like to go down the Grosvenor Road, so I make a U-turn and stop at the lights at the Grosvenor Road junction, and I'm just wondering what's the point, it's Sunday and there's no traffic about, and certainly no policemen, when somebody mutters something in my ear, I turn, and I'm grabbed round the neck by this character, while someone else has me by the arm, twisted up my back, another has the other arm and I'm hauled off the bike, *Right – where're you going? Here, get him up against the railings – what do you think you're at?* – Legs kicked apart, arms slapped up, *Right, here, get him here – come on, MOVE* – and I'm dragged across the road into what used to be McQuillan Street, only it isn't there any more, into one of these hole-in-the-wall taxi places, arms up against the breeze-block wall, legs apart, frisked, and all the time,

You were seen coming from the Shankill.
Why did you make a U-turn?
Who are you?
Where are you coming from?
Why did you stop when you seen the car?
You know the car.
The car. Outside Sinn Féin headquarters.
You looked at it.
You looked at it.
You were seen. You were seen.
Coming from the Shankill.
Where are you from?

Where is he from?
The Falls? When? What street?
What was the number of the house?
How far down the street was that?
When was that?
What streets could you see from the house?
Cape Street? Yeah.
Frere Street? Yeah. Where was Cape Street?
Again. Who lived next door?
Next door again.
Why did you stop when you seen the car?
Why did you turn?
So you moved up the road? When?
How old were you then?
Where was that? Mooreland?
Where is that?
Stockman's? Where is that?
What's next?
Casement? Right. What's next?
You were seen.
Where do you live now?
Where's that?
So where did you live again?
Yeah, I know it's not there any more.
You just tell me what was there.
Again. No. 100. Where was that?
You were seen.
What's the next street down from Raglan Street?
Coming from the Shankill . . .

The questions are snapped at me like photographs.

The map is pieced together bit by bit. I am this map which they examine, checking it for error, hesitation, accuracy; a map which no longer refers to the present world, but to a history, these vanished streets; a map which is this moment, this interrogation, my replies. Eventually I pass the test. I am frisked again, this time in a regretful habitual gesture. *A dreadful mistake*, I hear one of them saying, *has been made*, and I get the feeling he is speaking in quotation marks, as if this is a bad police B-movie and he is mocking it, and me, and him.

I am released. I stumble across the road and look back; they have disappeared. I get on my bike, and turn, and go down the Falls, past vanished public houses – The Clock Bar, The Celtic, Daly's, The Gladstone, The Arkle, The Old House – past drapers, bakers, fishmongers, boot shops, chemists, pawnshops, picture houses, confectioners and churches, all swallowed in the maw of time and trouble, clearances; feeling shaky, nervous, remembering how a few moments ago I was *there*, in my mind's eye, one foot in the grave of that Falls Road of thirty years ago, inhaling its gritty smoggy air as I lolled outside the door of 100 Raglan Street, staring down through the comforting gloom to the soot-encrusted spires of St Peter's, or gazing at the blank brick gable walls of Balaclava Street, Cape Street, Frere Street, Milton Street, saying their names over to myself.

'Question Time', from *Belfast Confetti*, 1989

The Literature of Trouble

DENIS DONOGHUE

In January 1919 when Yeats was writing 'The Second Coming', his mind was recalling a rather dull passage from Shelley's 'Prometheus Unbound' and turning it into a series of cultural generalisations:

> Things fall apart; the centre cannot hold;
> Mere anarchy is loosed upon the world,
> The blood-dimmed tide is loosed, and everywhere
> The ceremony of innocence is drowned;
> The best lack all conviction, while the worst
> Are full of passionate intensity.

I shall not refer again to these lines, except to say that they were in Donald Davie's mind when, perhaps in 1952 or 1953, he made a trip to Belfast and wrote a poem called 'Belfast on a Sunday Afternoon'. It is useful to know that the Orange Order is a fellowship of extreme Unionists or Loyalists in the North of Ireland who celebrate, every year on 12 July, the victory of King William over James at the Boyne. On a summer Sunday afternoon in Belfast, it would be normal to see and hear the Orange bands practising for the great day, marching up and down their famous Shankill Road, or going further afield if they wanted to taunt the Catholics. Here is Davie's poem:

> Visiting Belfast at the end of June,
> We found the Orange Lodge behind a band;
> Sashes and bearskins in the afternoon,
> White cotton gloves upon a crippled hand.
>
> Pastmasters pale, elaborately grim,
> Marched each alone, beneath a bowler hat:
> And, catapulted on a crumpled limb,
> A lame man leapt the tram-lines like a bat.

And first of all we tried to laugh it off,
Acting bemusement in the grimy sun;
But stayed to worry where we came to scoff,
As loud contingents followed, one by one.

Pipe bands, flute bands, brass bands and silver bands,
Presbyter's pibroch and the deacon's serge,
Came stamping where the iron Maenad stands,
Victoria, glum upon a grassy verge.

Some brawny striplings sprawled upon the lawn,
No man is really crippled by his hates.
Yet I remembered with a sudden scorn
Those 'passionate intensities' of Yeats.

Davie's scorn is directed against those whose passionate intensities are automatic, unearned, the routine excess of the mob. The poem was published in Davie's little volume *Brides of Reason* (1955). If he were to visit Belfast again now, I don't think he could register an emotion as secure and distanced, as secure in its distance, as scorn. It is twenty years too late for that.

On 17 February 1978, a bomb which exploded in the La Mon Hotel near Comber, County Down, killed twelve people and injured many more. The bomb was placed, it appears, by members of the Provisional Irish Republican Army. There were about 500 people in the hotel at the time, most of them attending the annual dinner of the Northern Ireland Junior Motor Cycle Club; these included several boys who attended to receive their prizes. Other people were in the hotel as members of the Irish Collie Dog Club. A warning was received in the hotel by telephone just as the bomb was about to explode, but too late to do anything about it.

My theme is the literature of such trouble; more especially, the poetry which has been provoked in one way or another by passionate intensities in the North of Ireland since 1968, when violence again became commonplace. But I must begin further back. I shall assume that it is not necessary to say much about the English presence in Ireland for the past seven hundred years, except to remark two facts – that the English and Scots who colonised the country, especially in the first years of the seventeenth century, established themselves most firmly in the north-east; and that the history of Ireland has been taught in Catholic schools as a story of national feeling expressing itself in virtually every generation since the eighteenth century as a revolutionary act to drive the English out of Ireland.

In the past few years, as a reaction to the violence in the North, we have seen a waning of this tradition in many Irish schools. Our children are now told, some for the first time, that Irish history is plural rather than singular, that our country is the result of mixed parentage, that Catholics and Protestants equally share the fate of being Irish. The historical archetype of this sentiment is Wolfe Tone, now regularly quoted in that spirit. . . .

It is well known that much of modern Irish literature has been provoked by violence, and that images of war soon acquire a symbolic aura in this country. Our traditions are histrionic and oratorical. The themes of Irish literature are few: if we list childhood, isolation, religion, and politics, we come nearly to the end of them. R.P. Blackmur once argued that 'the politics of existing states is always too simple for literature; it is good only to aggravate literature'. The institutions of a state, of any state we think of, are never sufficiently complex to animate the difficult purposes of literature. But when he allows that the politics of existing states is good only to aggravate literature, he makes an allowance good enough for Irish writers. It is simple fact that Yeats, O'Casey, and a dozen writers up to Francis Stuart, Brian Friel, Thomas Kinsella, and Seamus Heaney have been aggravated by Irish politics to the point of turning their aggravation into verse and prose.

In August 1915, Yeats told Henry James that he did not feel inclined to write a war poem, even on Edith Wharton's invitation, and he sent James a few verses in that spirit, including the famous disclaimer, 'I have no gift to set a statesman right.' The plain fact is that Yeats did not feel inclined to put his genius to work in England's cause; but he never thought himself incapable of setting statesmen right if he felt sufficiently exasperated by their follies. A few months later the Easter Rising set his verses astir; he saw no reason to silence himself on that occasion.

Walter Benjamin once wrote that 'all efforts to render politics aesthetic culminate in one thing: war'. The remark occurs in an essay of 1936 when Benjamin was pondering the Fascist way of organising the proletarian masses without affecting the property structure which the masses, in principle, strive to eliminate. Fascism saw its salvation, according to Benjamin,

433

in giving these masses not their right, but merely a chance to express themselves. Hence the rigmarole of public displays, marches, celebrations, anniversaries, those secular rituals by which thousands of men are given the illusion of living a dramatic life in common.

The introduction of aesthetics into politics is a perennial theme; to consider politics as entertainment, or to ponder the aesthetic aspects of war, blood, and death, is not necessarily self-indulgence, it may be a crucial aspect of modern society. Indeed, modern Irish literature has often been animated by the aesthetic aspect of violence. Padraic Fiacc's recent anthology *The Wearing of the Black* contains many poems, most of them bad in nearly every respect, which testify to the thrill of blood and sacrifice. But it also contains a few poems in which the transfiguring power of violence is recognised, its way of turning boredom into drama; and in one of these poems the poet is tender toward the desire and the need. He virtually withholds his irony from it, while allowing the reader's irony to assert itself. The poet sees how naturally a young man wants to become a dramatic figure in an otherwise wearisome and characterless time. The poem is 'Bogside, Derry, 1971':

Shielded, vague soldiers, visored, crouch alert:
between tall houses down the blackened street;
the hurled stones pour, hurt-instinct aims to hurt,
frustration spurts in flame about their feet.

Lads who at ease had tossed a laughing ball,
or, ganged in teams, pursued some shouting game,
beat angry fists against that stubborn wall
of faceless fears which now at last they name.

Night after night this city yields a stage
with peak of drama for the pointless day,
where shadows offer stature, roles to play,
urging the gestures which might purge in rage
the slights, the wrongs, the long indignities
the stubborn core within each heart defies.

It is common for war correspondents to speak of a theatre of war. The aesthetic form most pertinent to war is theatre with its terminology of action, gesture, role-playing. John Hewitt's poem is perceptive in recognising the fact that people can deal with nameless fears only by finding a name for them and objectifying them in a hostile presence; in this case the British Army. He comes close to sentimentalising those stone-throwing youths, I suppose, but he narrowly avoids the temptation. There are many poems which do not scruple to avoid it.

Some poems, like Thomas Kinsella's 'Butcher's Dozen', and some plays, like Brian Friel's *The Freedom of the City*, have emerged far too readily from the events that provoked them. It is hard to deny a poet the right to cry and rant and rage when an act strikes him as peculiarly outrageous, as the events of 'Bloody Sunday' struck Kinsella and Friel. Yeats spoke of the will trying to do the work of the imagination, and he thought the effort misplaced; but it is hard to be patient.

There is further exorbitance: that of direct, apparently unmediated feeling which has not reached the stage of being either will or imagination; demanding to leap into expression without any mediation. We are told, and we believe, that there is no such thing as unmediated feeling; that the feeling is already inscribed, as if in invisible ink, and that we are never spontaneous. But it is a hard linguistics to act upon. Kinsella's poem and Friel's play come from the primitive demand, the insistence upon unmediated rage. The crudity of these works is not the price these writers willingly pay for the semblance of spontaneity, it is a sign of their rage with everything that stands between them and the feeling of the moment, everything that offers itself as form but could as well offer itself as delay or patience. It is natural for a writer to resent, on such a violent occasion, the admonition that his art is bound to be indirect in its effect and slow to act upon its cause. That poetry makes nothing happen is normally a tolerable fact; but there are occasions on which a poet feels that he must respond to one act with another similar in character and force.

Even in a quieter poet, like Heaney, there are moments of impatience. One of his Northern poems is called 'Whatever You Say, Say Nothing', a satirical piece, not one of his better poems but a minor essay in observation. His theme is the Northern habit of keeping one's counsel, saying nothing, intoning the clichés of communication for safety's sake. Heaney recites many of the currencies of such conversation, but at one point he breaks through them into an apparently direct speech of his own:

435

Christ, it's near time that some small leak was sprung
In the great dykes the Dutchman made
To dam the dangerous tide that followed Seamus.
Yet for all this art and sedentary trade
I am incapable.

'This sedentary trade' is a phrase from Yeats's poem 'The Tower', and Heaney's use of it brings him in under Yeats's shadow for the moment, the theme being the poet's general predicament, the gap between writing and action. But the reference to incapacity comes immediately after an outburst of political rhetoric; it's nearly time, Heaney says, the Unionist structures were undermined, and he goes back to the Dutchman William's victory over James at the Boyne in 1690 and the Orange Ascendancy in force in the North since that day. Heaney is more patient than Kinsella and Friel, but there are moments in him, too, when he chafes under the constraints of his trade. Not surprising in an Irish poet. . . .

The troubles in the North have been with us now for ten years. Everything that can be said has been said, though much of it has then been forgotten or ignored. So long as the present balance of forces continues, there is no clear reason why the troubles should ever stop. I have long thought that the British Government should make a declaration of intent to withdraw, and ease the transition to the next phase of Irish history. That would mean an end to the British guarantee, regularly given to the Unionists, that the position of Northern Ireland within the United Kingdom will remain intact unless and until a majority of the people in the North want a change. It would also mean either the unification of Ireland or the establishment of an independent Northern Ireland, independent of Britain and of Dublin alike. It is hard to say whether the majority of us in the South genuinely want the country to be united or not; a referendum would return a loud 'yes', but in the meantime a common sentiment in the South would say, 'Lord, let us be united . . . but not yet.'

I have implied that Yeats was not alone in Irish poetry in his ambivalence toward acts of violence. Conflict as such was dear to Yeats because it was the readiest form of his energy: he was more in need of conflict than of the peace that brings it to an end. He feared peace because he feared inertia. I do not mean that he was a propagandist for murder or that he condoned the Civil War; but he was afraid his poetry would stop if conflict stopped within himself; the grappling of opposites kept his art in force. This motive is still active in Irish poetry, but on the whole our poets have been turning their rhymes toward some form of transcendence.

Heaney is the most telling poet in this respect, and the success of *North* makes his case exemplary; it is clear that thousands of readers have found their feelings defined in that volume more than in any other. I shall maintain that Heaney's readers do not see themselves as lords of counterpositions, commanding a perspective in which all forms of conflict are held in poise. Rather, they find release in an area of feeling somehow beneath the field of violence and ideology; or imaginatively prior to such a moment. Heaney's poems in *North* point to such an area. The dominant analogy for his verses is archaeology, not history; his sense of time circumvents the immediacies of historical event by recourse to several different levels of experience, the accretion of cultures. He is, in *North*, a poet 'after Foucault', his knowledge archaeological rather than linear or sequential. In the poem 'Belderg' he writes of quernstones, millstones discovered in a bog, the hole in the middle of the stone like an eye, a pupil:

> To lift the lid of the peat
> And find this pupil dreaming
> Of neolithic wheat!
> When he stripped off blanket bog
> The soft-piled centuries
>
> Fell open like a glib.

A glib is a thick mass of matted hair, as the *Oxford Dictionary* reports, 'formerly worn by the Irish'. It is typical of Heaney to represent the experience of the archaeologist as a human discovery arising from a discovery of earth. Archaeology represents for him, paradoxically, the dream of full and immediate presence, time at once historical and perennial, in which the dichotomy between self and other is obliterated. The reconciliation which other poets represent as a vision of landscape is available to Heaney as meaning and value lying under the skin of the earth, waiting to be discovered. Heaney's desire is predicated upon the depth of earth, the levels and sites waiting, like the eye of the quernstone, to be found and seen. And the feeling goes both ways. In 'The Digging Skeleton', pictures in medical textbooks are called

> Mysterious candid studies
> Of red slobland around the bones

presumably because the tissue seems alluvial. And generally Heaney's imagination turns toward the bogland which contains and preserves the human past in forms deeper and more secret than history.

The word 'bog', Heaney has remarked, is one of the few English borrowings from the Irish language. In Irish, the word means soft and wet, and survives in Hiberno-English in the phrase 'a soft day', meaning a wet day, gentle, not cold. He has also reported that in Derry they call a bog a 'moss', a word of Norse origin probably carried to the North of Ireland by planters in the early seventeenth century. So he finds in the two words the record of invasion, colonisation, and shift of language in which the Irish word, for once, has held its place. There is a poem, 'Kinship', which ponders these affinities. But I think the pondering might go further. It strikes me that bogland, for Heaney, is the meeting-place between mineral and vegetable life, a state of nature which is soft, yielding, maternal, and full of secret lore. He has referred to 'images drawn from Anglo-Saxon kennings, Icelandic sagas, Viking excavations, and Danish and Irish bogs'. In 'Viking Dublin', he says:

> a worm of thought
> I follow into the mud.

As a motto for the procedures of *North*, the lines would answer very well. Many of the poems in that volume follow those worms of thought into soft bogland. In the poem 'Belderg', talking to the archaeologist:

> So I talked of Mossbawn,
> A bogland name. 'But *moss?*'
> He crossed my old home's music
> With older strains of Norse.
> I'd told how its foundation
>
> Was mutable as a sound
> And how I could derive
> A forked root from that ground

And make *bawn* an English fort,
A planter's walled-in mound,

Or else find sanctuary
And think of it as Irish,
Persistent if outworn.

Bawn can indeed mean a walled-in fort, if you take its meaning from the
English or Scots planter; or it can mean a place for milking cows, if you
leave its meaning in Ireland, especially the South. Heaney takes pleasure
in these matters, as a poet should.

He also likes to think of his language as issuing from the accretion of
centuries. In the poem 'Bone Dreams' he writes:

I push back
through dictions,
Elizabethan canopies.
Norman devices,

the erotic mayflowers
of Provence
and the ivied latins
of churchmen

to the scop's
twang, the iron
flash of consonants
cleaving the line.

'Scop' means a poet, minstrel, or satirist in Old English, so Heaney is
invoking the two strongest traditions in the forked tongue of English: the
Anglo-Saxon and the Latin. He puts the two dictions side by side in the
poem 'Kinship':

This is the vowel of earth
dreaming its root
in flowers and snow,

mutation of weathers
and seasons,

439

a windfall composing
the floor it rots into.

I grew out of all this
like a weeping willow
inclined to
the appetites of gravity.

It is common to think of vowels as the pleasure principle of language,
and of consonants as the reality principle; a thought congenial to Heaney,
who writes in the poem 'Aisling':

He courted her
With a decadent sweet art
Like the wind's vowel
Blowing through the hazels.

But Heaney likes to play off vowel against consonant, Latin pleasure
against Anglo-Saxon reality, within the grand allowance which is Language
itself, a concessive, permeable medium. So the topics or commonplaces
on which his language relies are those in which nature and culture meet
so harmoniously that we are not aware of a distinction between them.

I think this goes some way to account for the appeal of Heaney's poems.
His poetry as a whole gives the reader the satisfaction of believing that
nature and culture are not, as he feared, split apart once for all, or that
one term has overwhelmed the other. Make a short list of Heaney's themes:
salmon-fishing, the blacksmith's craft, the eel's journey, the thatcher's art,
threshing corn, pumping water, digging potatoes, water divining. Think
of water divining; an ancient skill, beneath or beyond explanation, requiring
nothing but a forked stick, two hands, and the gift of divination. As a
parable of the still vivid relation between man and nature, it is complete.
Writing a poem about it is hardly necessary, since it is already a form of
poetry, at once craft and gift. These motifs in Heaney's poetry make a
natural symbolism; or rather, testify to the continuing life of such processes.
He turns to them as Yeats turned from the reality of civil war to the
honey-bees of generation and creative force:

The bees build in the crevices
Of loosening masonry, and there

The mother birds bring grubs and flies.
My wall is loosening; honey-bees,
Come build in the empty house of the stare.

The sweetness of the honey-bees represents everything in Yeats's feeling that longs to move beyond the arguments and counter-arguments that make civil wars and keep them brutal. They speak of a natural world prior to history and culture and indifferent to their terrible possibility. Heaney's version is an appeal to those parts of human life which are still part of natural life. In the poem 'At a Potato Digging', from *Death of a Naturalist*, the gestures of the potato-diggers are assimilated to the seasons:

Processional stooping through the turf
Recurs mindlessly as autumn.

'Mindlessly' is a word of ease and satisfaction in this poem because it points to a custom, a way of work and life, so deeply grained in the lives of farmers that it does not need to be enforced by mind; the 'thinking of the body' is enough.

The welcome extended to Heaney's *North* has been remarkably profuse. Part of the explanation is probably the consolation of hearing that there is a deeper, truer life going on beneath the bombings and torture. There are levels of action and responsiveness deeper than those occupied by Protestants and Catholics; there are archaic processes still alive despite times and technologies.

It is a comfort to receive such news, especially in poems such as Heaney's. The outrage of an obscene act such as the bombing of the La Mon Hotel is indeed the denial of humanity which it entails, but it is also its immediacy. What the act gives, without our asking, is immediacy, a quality which we are ready to accept when it comes as an attribute of chance and misfortune but which leaves us baffled when it comes with human motive. This outrage is not diminished by anything we can say of it. Heaney's poems are as helpless in this respect as any editorial after the event in a newspaper or the standard expressions of sympathy from politicians and bishops. But the archives presented as an archaeological site in Heaney's poems offer a perspective of depth upon local and terrible events. Precisely because he does not present history in linear terms,

Heaney offers the reader not a teleology implicit in historical interpretation but a present moment still in touch with its depth. The procedure has the effect of releasing the reader – for the moment, God knows, and only for that – from the fatality which otherwise seems inscribed in the spirit of the age. There is little point in fancying ourselves free in space if we are imprisoned in time, but there are signs that poets and readers are turning away from time, having made such a mess of it, and seen such a mess made of it.

The immediate source of Heaney's bog-poems is P.V. Glob's book *The Bog People*, which contains descriptions and photographs of the Tollund man, who died 2,000 years ago, hanged in Tollund Fen in Denmark; his body was thrown into a bog and it has been preserved to this day by some chemical quality in the bog water. There is little consolation to be found in these facts, but Heaney's poems invoke them, I think, to release the reader's mind from the immediacy of his experience. I find the same motive in many of Donald Davie's poems, and in the poets he especially admires: poets of place and space rather than of time; or poets who find time resumed in space. Davie has argued that modern poets have made a mess of their politics because they have misunderstood their history; history and time have formed an extremely dangerous element which they could not negotiate. Davie has turned from history to geography, to the history that extends from the geographer–historian Herodotus to the geographer–morphologist Carl Sauer and the 'archaeologist of morning', Charles Olson, who wrote as the first sentence of his famous meditation on Melville, *Call me Ishmael*, 'I take Space to be the central fact to man born in America from Folsom cave to now.'

So what am I saying? Only this: that Heaney is the first of the poets of the North who are turning away from the terminology of time, with its claim to recognise the spirit of the age and to see a divinely inscribed teleology written in what they say is the past. I think I understand the motives at work, and some of their probable consequences. A vision founded on space, depth, archives, levels of soil is likely to emphasise continuity rather than change, and therefore the universality of human life. What his poems mainly give is the sentiment of that universality. But they do not guarantee that we will get our politics right, when it comes to the time in which we have to get them right or wrong. It means that the relationship between history and politics can be disconnected for a while and that this may be a prudent as well as a consoling thing to do. But beyond that, I am not sure. The evidence is not decisive.

from 'The Literature of Trouble', from *We Irish: selected essays*, vol. 1, 1986

BIOGRAPHICAL NOTES

SAM HANNA BELL

b. 1909 in Glasgow of Ulster parentage and brought up in County Down. Features producer with BBC Northern Ireland region, 1945–69. A novelist and short story writer, he also edited *The Arts in Ulster* (1951). Died 1990.

GEORGE A. BIRMINGHAM (pseudonym of Canon James Owen Hannay)

b. 1865 in Belfast. Church of Ireland clergyman and author of popular novels, including *Spanish Gold* and the satirical *The Red Hand of Ulster*. Died 1950.

CAROLINE BLACKWOOD

b. 1931 in County Down. Short story writer, essayist and novelist, whose *Great Granny Webster* (1977) is grimly humorous about the decaying Irish great house.

C.E.B. BRETT

b. 1928 in Belfast, and educated at Rugby and Oxford University. A solicitor, conservationist and pioneering architectural historian whose *Buildings of Belfast 1700–1914* was first published in 1967.

ROBIN BRYANS *see* Robert Harbinson

SHAN F. BULLOCK

b. 1865 in County Fermanagh. Worked as a civil servant in London. His novels include *Dan the Dollar, The Squireen* and *The Loughsiders*. Died 1935.

THE REVEREND SAMUEL BURDY

b. *c.* 1760. Rector of Kilclief parish, County Down, and author of some light verse. He is best known for his biography of the Reverend Philip Skelton. Died 1820.

WILLIAM CARLETON

b. 1794 in County Tyrone. A novelist and short story writer whose eye for social customs and the political abuses of the day compensates for his often melodramatic approach. Best known for his *Traits and Stories of the Irish Peasantry*. Died 1869.

CIARAN CARSON

b. 1948 in Belfast. Literature and Traditional Arts Officer with the Arts Council of Northern Ireland, he is also a poet, whose latest collection, *Belfast Confetti*, was published in 1989.

JAMES STEVEN CURL

b. 1937. An architectural historian and writer who is best known for *A Celebration of Death* and *Victorian Architecture*.

SEAMUS DEANE

b. 1940 in Derry. Professor of Modern English and American Literature at University College Dublin, his *Celtic Revivals: essays in modern Irish literature 1880–1980* was published in 1985. General editor of the three-volume *Field Day Anthology of Irish Writing* (1991).

MARY DELANY

b. 1700 in Wiltshire. Wife of Dr Patrick Delany, Dean of Down, she was an assiduous letter writer. Died 1799.

POLLY DEVLIN

b. 1944 in County Tyrone. A journalist and short story writer, she has also published an autobiography, *All of Us There* (1983).

DENIS DONOGHUE

b. 1928 in County Carlow. A distinguished critic and man of letters, he has written many works of literary criticism. Currently holds the Henry James Chair of English at New York University. *Warrenpoint*, a memoir of his Northern Irish childhood, was published in 1991.

WILLIAM DRENNAN

b. 1754 in Belfast. A doctor, poet and man of letters, he was also a founder of the Society of United Irishmen. *The Drennan Letters* – selections from the correspondence between Drennan in Dublin and his sister Mrs McTier in Belfast – provide some interesting details of the social life of the period just before and after the 1798 rising. Died 1820.

MARIANNE ELLIOTT

b. 1948 in Belfast. A historian, her *Wolfe Tone: prophet of Irish independence*, was published in 1989.

E. ESTYN EVANS

b. 1905. A geographer and pioneering anthropologist, he was also director of the Institute of Irish Studies at Queen's University Belfast. His publications include *Irish Heritage* (1942), *Mourne Country* (1951) and *Irish Folk Ways* (1957). Died 1989.

KATHLEEN FITZPATRICK

Had only one book published, *The Weans at Rowallan* (1905); it was reissued in 1938 and 1953 (as *They Lived in County Down*) by the Hogarth Press, with introductions by Walter de la Mare and C. Day Lewis, respectively.

JOHN GAMBLE

b. *c.* 1770 in Strabane, County Tyrone. He was a United Irish sympathiser and an informed travel writer. Died 1831.

DENIS O'D. HANNA

b. 1901 in Holywood, County Down, in a house designed by his father. An architect, he died in 1970.

ROBERT HARBINSON

b. 1928 in Belfast. He has given a vivid account of his upbringing in the four-volume autobiography beginning with *No Surrender: an Ulster childhood* (1960). Also an informative and inspired travel writer.

ROSEMARY HARRIS

b. 1930. She is a Reader in Anthropology at University College London.

SEAMUS HEANEY

b. 1939 in County Derry. A poet whose work has attracted international acclaim, he has also been Boylston Professor of Rhetoric and Oratory at Harvard University and, since 1989, Professor of Poetry at Oxford University.

JOHN HEWITT

b. 1907 in Belfast. Poet, man of letters and man of the Left. On the staff of the Belfast Museum and Art Gallery, 1930–57. He was Art Director of the Herbert Art Gallery and Museum in Coventry from 1957 until his retirement in 1972, when he returned to Belfast and went on to publish seven collections of poetry. Died 1987.

DENIS IRELAND

b. 1894 in Belfast. Served with the Royal Irish Fusiliers in the First World War. Later joined the family linen firm before becoming a freelance writer and broadcaster. A liberal–nationalist in politics, and author of *From the Irish Shore* and *From the Jungle of Belfast*. Died 1974.

ROBERT JOHNSTONE

b. 1951 in Belfast. A poet, he is also the author of *Images of Belfast* (1983) and *Belfast: portraits of a city* (1990), and co-editor of the *Honest Ulsterman*. He now lives in London.

BENEDICT KIELY

b. 1919 in Omagh, County Tyrone. Novelist, critic and author of a study of William Carleton, *Poor Scholar*. Best known for his ebullient collections of short stories, including *A Journey to the Seven Streams* and *A Ball of Malt and Madame Butterfly*.

MAURICE LEITCH

b. 1933 in County Antrim. A teacher, radio producer and novelist, his first novel, *The Liberty Lad*, was published in 1965. He now lives in London.

C.S. LEWIS

b. 1898 in Belfast. A Fellow of Magdalen College, Oxford, then Professor of Medieval and Renaissance Literature at Cambridge. A critic and Christian apologist/popular theologian, he also wrote the 'Narnia' series of books for children. His autobiography, *Surprised by Joy*, was published in 1955. Died 1963.

MICHAEL LONGLEY

b. 1939 in Belfast. Educated at the Royal Belfast Academical Institution and Trinity College Dublin. Combined Arts Officer with the Arts Council of Northern Ireland until his retirement in 1991. Author of five collections of poetry, of which the latest, *Gorse Fires*, won the Whitbread Poetry Prize in 1991.

ROBERT LYND

b. 1879 in Belfast. A distinguished man of letters, he was also a long-time contributor to the *New Statesman and Nation*, and his weekly essays for this periodical were issued between 1908 and 1945 in thirty volumes. Died 1949.

EAMONN MCCANN

b. 1943 in Derry. Socialist, journalist and broadcaster, his *War and an Irish Town* was published in 1974.

FLORENCE MARY MCDOWELL

b. 1888 in County Antrim. She spent all her working life as a national schoolteacher and was in her seventies when she began work on *Other Days Around Me* (1966). *Roses and Rainbows* was published in 1972. Died 1977.

MICHAEL MCLAVERTY

b. 1907. A novelist, short story writer and teacher, he is associated with Rathlin Island, west Belfast and the Strangford Lough area of County Down. His first and best novel, *Call My Brother Back*, was published in 1939. Died 1992.

LOUIS MACNEICE

b. 1907 in Belfast. Educated at Marlborough College and Oxford University. A poet associated with Auden, Spender and Day Lewis during the 1930s, he was also a producer and scriptwriter for the BBC. His *Collected Poems* was published in 1966. Died 1963.

W.F. MARSHALL

b. 1888 in County Tyrone. A Presbyterian minister, author of a good deal of light verse – he was known as the 'Bard of Tyrone' – and broadcaster, he was also a Lecturer in Elocution at Magee University College in Derry, and an authority on local dialect and culture. Best known for *Livin' in Drumlister*, his collected ballads and verses. Died 1959.

NAOMI MAY

b. 1934 in Scotland but lived in Northern Ireland for a number of years. A novelist and short story writer whose novel *Troubles* (1976) encompasses the 'liberal Protestant' viewpoint.

T.W. MOODY

b. 1907 in Belfast. Was Professor of Modern History at Trinity College Dublin and co-founder of the journal *Irish Historical Studies*. His publications include *The Ulster Question* (1974) and *A New History of Ireland* (1976). Died 1984.

BRIAN MOORE

b. 1921 in Belfast. One of Ireland's most distinguished novelists, he has lived in Canada and the United States since the late 1940s. Nevertheless, his Belfast novels – starting with *Judith Hearne*, published in 1955 – are among his most vivid works.

JOHN MORROW

b. 1930 in Belfast. He left school at fourteen to become a shipyard worker, moving on to work in insurance, and he is currently the Combined Arts Officer with the Arts Council of Northern Ireland. A racy and distinctive short story writer, humorist and social commentator.

JOHN O'CONNOR

b. 1920 in Armagh. A local journalist and short story writer, he wrote one novel, *Come Day – Go Day*, which describes his upbringing in Mill Row, Armagh. He emigrated to Australia in the early 1950s. Died 1960.

PEADAR O'DONNELL

b. 1893 in County Donegal. A novelist, trade-union organiser and socialist agitator, he fought on the republican side in the Irish Civil War. Continued campaigning against various forms of social injustice up to the age of ninety. Died 1986.

FRANK ORMSBY

b. 1947 in Enniskillen, County Fermanagh. A poet, teacher and anthologist, his most recent collection, *A Northern Spring*, was published in 1986, and he edited *The Collected Poems of John Hewitt* (1991).

TOM PAULIN

b. 1949 in Leeds, but brought up in Belfast. A poet, critic and Lecturer in English at the University of Nottingham, his *Ireland and the English Crisis* (selected journalism) was published in 1984, and he edited *The Faber Book of Political Verse* (1986).

ROBERT LLOYD PRAEGER

b. 1865 in Holywood, County Down. A geologist, geographer and editor of the *Irish Naturalist*, he also wrote *The Way That I Went* (1937) and *The Natural History of Ireland* (1950). Died 1953.

FORREST REID

b. 1875 in Belfast. A novelist and critic, his publications include *Peter Waring* (1937), *Young Tom* (1944) and two volumes of autobiography, *Apostate* and *Private Road*. Died 1947.

AMANDA MCKITTRICK ROS

b. 1865 in County Down. 'The world's worst novelist', she is famed for her alliterations and malapropisms. Author of three eccentric novels (the last, *Helen Huddleson*, published thirty years after her death), and some very peculiar verse. Became something of a cult figure in London literary circles during the early part of the century. Lived most of her life in Larne, County Antrim. Died 1939.

PATRICK SHEA

b. 1908. He was one of only two Catholics in the history of the Northern Ireland Civil Service to attain top rank as permanent secretary. Author of *Voices and the Sound of Drums* (1981). Died 1986.

A.T.Q. STEWART

b. 1929. Research Fellow at the Institute of Irish Studies at Queen's University Belfast and author of *The Narrow Ground* (1977).

GEORGE J. WATSON

b. in Portadown, County Armagh. Lecturer in English at Aberdeen University, and critic. Author of *Irish Identity and the Literary Revival* (1979).

MAX WRIGHT

b. 1932 in Bangor, County Down. Lecturer in Philosophy at Queen's University Belfast and author of *Told in Gath* – an account of a Plymouth Brethren upbringing.

BIBLIOGRAPHY

Bell, Sam Hanna. *December Bride*, London, Denis Dobson, 1951; republished
  Belfast, Blackstaff, 1974
  (ed.), *The Arts in Ulster*, London, Harrap, 1951
Birmingham, George A. *The Red Hand of Ulster*, London, Smith, Elder, 1912;
  republished Shannon, Irish Universities Press, 1972
Blackwood, Caroline. *For All That I Found There*, London, Duckworth, 1973
  Great Granny Webster, London, Duckworth, 1977
Brett, C.E.B. *Buildings of Belfast 1700–1914*, London, Weidenfeld & Nicolson,
  1967; revised edition published Belfast, Friar's Bush Press, 1985
  Long Shadows Cast Before, Edinburgh, John Bartholomew, 1978
Bryans, Robin. *See* Harbinson, Robert
Bullock, Shan F. *The Squireen*, London, Methuen, 1903
Burdy, Revd Samuel. *The Life of the Late Reverend Philip Skelton*, Dublin,
  William Jones, 1792
Carleton, William. *Autobiography of William Carleton*, London, McGibbon &
  Kee, 1968 (first published 1896)
Carson, Ciaran. *Belfast Confetti*, Oldcastle, Gallery Press, 1989
Curl, James Stevens. *The Londonderry Plantation 1609–1914*, Phillimore,
  Chichester, 1986
Deane, Seamus. 'Why Bogside?', *Honest Ulsterman*, no. 27, January–March 1971
Delany, Mary. *The Autobiography and Correspondence of Mary Granville, Mrs
  Delany*, ed. the Rt Hon Lady Llanover, 6 vols, London, Richard Bentley,
  1861–2
Devlin, Polly. *All of Us There*, London, Weidenfeld & Nicolson, 1983
Donoghue, Denis. *Warrenpoint*, London, Cape, 1991
  We Irish: selected essays, vol. 1, Brighton, Harvester Wheatsheaf, 1986
Drennan Letters, The. ed. D.A. Chart, Belfast, HMSO, 1931
Elliott, Marianne. *Wolfe Tone: prophet of Irish independence*, London, Yale
  University Press, 1989
Evans, E. Estyn. *Mourne Country*, Dundalk, Dundalgen Press, 1951
  Northern Ireland ('About Britain' series no. 13), London, Collins, 1951
Fitzpatrick, Kathleen. *The Weans at Rowallan*, London, Methuen, 1905;
  republished 1937 by Hogarth Press as *They Lived in County Down*
Gamble, John. *A View of Society and Manners in the North of Ireland*, London,
  C. Cradock & W. Joy, 1813
Hanna, Denis O'D. 'Architecture in Ulster', in Sam Hanna Bell (ed.), *The Arts in
  Ulster*, London, Harrap, 1951

Harbinson, Robert. *Ulster: a journey through the Six Counties* (written under the name Robin Bryans), London, Faber, 1964; republished Belfast, Blackstaff, 1989

No Surrender: an Ulster childhood, London, Faber, 1960; republished Belfast, Blackstaff, 1987

Harris, Rosemary. *Prejudice and Tolerance in Ulster*, Manchester, Manchester University Press, 1972

Heaney, Seamus. 'Mossbawn' and 'The Sense of Place', both in *Preoccupations*, London, Faber, 1980

Hewitt, John. 'No Rootless Colonist', in *Ancestral Voices: the selected prose of John Hewitt* (edited by Tom Clyde), Belfast, Blackstaff, 1987

Ireland, Denis. *From the Irish Shore: notes on my life and times*, London, Rich & Cowan, 1935

Johnstone, Robert. *Images of Belfast*, Belfast, Blackstaff, 1983

Kiely, Benedict. 'The Night We Rode With Sarsfield', in *The State of Ireland*, Boston, David R. Godine, 1980

Poor Scholar: a study of William Carleton, London, Sheed & Ward, 1947

Leitch, Maurice. *The Liberty Lad*, London, McGibbon & Kee, 1965; republished Belfast, Blackstaff, 1985

Lewis, C.S. *Surprised by Joy*, London, Geoffrey Bles, 1955

Longley, Michael. 'Tu-penny Stung', *Poetry Review*, vol. 74, no. 4, January 1985; reprinted in Frank Ormsby (ed.), *Northern Windows*, Belfast, Blackstaff, 1987

Lynd, Robert. *Irish and English*, London, Francis Griffiths, 1908; reprinted in Sean McMahon (ed.), *Galway of the Races*, Dublin, Lilliput, 1990

McCann, Eamonn. *War and an Irish Town*, London, Penguin, 1974; republished London, Pluto Press, 1984

McDowell, Florence Mary. *Other Days Around Me*, Belfast, Northern Whig, 1966; republished Belfast, Blackstaff, 1972

McLaverty, Michael. *Call My Brother Back*, London, Cape, 1939; republished Swords, Poolbeg, 1979

MacNeice, Louis. *Zoo*, London, Michael Joseph, 1938

Marshall, W.F. *Ulster Speaks*, London, BBC, 1936

May, Naomi. *Troubles*, London, Calder, 1976

Moody, T.W. and J.C. Beckett (eds.). *Ulster Since 1800*, London, BBC, 1954

Moore, Brian, *The Emperor of Ice-cream*, London, Deutsch, 1965

Morrow, John. *Northern Myths*, Belfast, Blackstaff, 1979

O'Connor, John. *Come Day – Go Day*, Dublin, Golden Eagle Books, 1948; republished Belfast, Blackstaff, 1984

O'Donnell, Peadar. *On the Edge of the Stream*, London, Cape, 1934

Ormsby, Frank. 'County Fermanagh', in *Thirty-two Counties*, London, Secker & Warburg, 1989

Paulin, Tom. *Ireland and the English Crisis*, Newcastle, Bloodaxe, 1984

Praeger, Robert Lloyd. *The Way That I Went*, Dublin, Allen Figgis, 1937

Reid, Forrest. *Apostate*, London, Constable, 1926

Ros, Amanda McKittrick. *Helen Huddleson*, London, Chatto & Windus, 1969

Shea, Patrick. *Voices and the Sound of Drums*, Belfast, Blackstaff, 1981

Stewart, A.T.Q. *The Narrow Ground*, London, Faber, 1977

Watson, George J. 'Cultural Imperialism: an Irish view', *Yale Review*, Yale University Press, 1986

Wright, Max. *Told in Gath*, Belfast, Blackstaff, 1990

ACKNOWLEDGEMENTS

Grateful acknowledgement is made to:

ALLEN FIGGIS AND COMPANY for permission to quote from *The Way That I Went* (1937) by Robert Lloyd Praeger;

BBC BOOKS for permission to quote from *Ulster Since 1800* (1954), edited by J.C. Beckett and T.W. Moody;

FERGUS BELL for permission to quote from *December Bride* (Denis Dobson, 1951; reissued by Blackstaff Press, 1974) by Sam Hanna Bell;

THE ESTATE OF GEORGE A. BIRMINGHAM for permission to quote from *The Red Hand of Ulster* (Smith, Elder, 1912; reissued by Irish Universities Press, 1972);

CAROLINE BLACKWOOD for permission to quote from 'Memories of Ulster' (in *For All That I Found There*, Gerald Duckworth and Company, 1973); for permission to quote from *Great Granny Webster* (Gerald Duckworth and Company, 1977);

BLOODAXE BOOKS for permission to quote from 'Paisley's Progress' (in *Ireland and the English Crisis*, 1984) by Tom Paulin;

SIR CHARLES BRETT for permission to quote from *Long Shadows Cast Before* (John Bartholomew and Son, 1978); for permission to quote from the Introduction to *Buildings of Belfast 1700–1914* (revised edition, Friar's Bush Press, 1985);

J. CALDER PUBLICATIONS for permission to quote from *Troubles* (1976) by Naomi May;

CAMPBELL THOMSON AND MCLAUGHLIN for permission to quote from *Other Days Around Me* (Northern Whig, 1966; reissued by Blackstaff Press, 1972) by Florence Mary McDowell;

JONATHAN CAPE for permission to quote from *Warrenpoint* (1991) by Denis Donoghue; for permission to quote from *On the Edge of the Stream* (1934) by Peadar O'Donnell;

CHATTO AND WINDUS for permission to quote from *They Lived in County Down* (1937 and 1953; reissue of *The Weans at Rowallan* [Methuen, 1905]) by Kathleen Fitzpatrick; for permission to quote from *Helen Huddleson* (1969) by Amanda McKittrick Ros;

SEAMUS DEANE for permission to quote from 'Why Bogside?' (*Honest Ulsterman*, 1971);

ANDRÉ DEUTSCH for permission to quote from *The Emperor of Ice-cream* (1965) by Brian Moore;

POLLY DEVLIN for permission to quote from *All of Us There* (Weidenfeld and Nicolson, 1983; Pan Books, 1988);

DUNDALGAN PRESS for permission to quote from *Mourne Country* (1951) by E. Estyn Evans;

FABER AND FABER for permission to quote from 'Mossbawn' and 'The Sense of Place' (both in *Preoccupations*, 1980) by Seamus Heaney; for permission to quote from *The Narrow Ground* (1977) by A.T.Q. Stewart;

GALLERY PRESS for permission to quote from 'Question Time' (in *Belfast Confetti*, 1989) by Ciaran Carson;

ROBERT HARBINSON for permission to quote from *No Surrender: an Ulster childhood* (Faber and Faber, 1960; reissued by Blackstaff Press, 1987); for permission to quote from *Ulster: a journey through the Six Counties* (Faber and Faber, 1964; reissued by Blackstaff Press, 1989);

HARPERCOLLINS for permission to quote from *Northern Ireland* ('About Britain' series, 1951) by E. Estyn Evans; for permission to quote from *Surprised by Joy* (1955) by C.S. Lewis;

HARRAP PUBLISHING GROUP for permission to quote from 'Architecture in Ulster' (in *The Arts in Ulster*, ed. Sam Hanna Bell, 1951) by Denis O'D. Hanna;

HARVESTER WHEATSHEAF for permission to quote from 'The Literature of Trouble' (in *We Irish: selected essays*, vol. 1, 1986) by Denis Donoghue;

H.M. IRELAND for permission to quote from *From the Irish Shore: notes on my life and times* (Rich and Cowan, 1935) by Denis Ireland;

JOHN JOHNSON LIMITED for permission to quote from *Apostate* (Constable and Company, 1926) by Forrest Reid;

ROBERT JOHNSTONE for permission to quote from *Images of Belfast* (Blackstaff Press, 1983);

MICHAEL JOSEPH for permission to quote from *Zoo* (1938) by Louis MacNeice;

BENEDICT KIELY for permission to quote from 'The Night We Rode With Sarsfield' (in *The State of Ireland*, David R. Godine, 1980); for permission to quote from *Poor Scholar: a study of William Carleton* (Sheed and Ward, 1947);

MAURICE LEITCH for permission to quote from *The Liberty Lad* (McGibbon and Kee, 1965; reissued by Blackstaff Press, 1985);

MICHAEL LONGLEY for permission to quote from 'Tu-penny Stung' (*Poetry Review*, January 1985);

THE ESTATE OF ROBERT LYND for permission to quote from 'The Orange Idealist' (in *Irish and English*, Francis Griffiths, 1908; reprinted in *Galway of the Races*, ed. Sean McMahon, Lilliput Press, 1990);

MANCHESTER UNIVERSITY PRESS for permission to quote from *Prejudice and Tolerance in Ulster* (1972) by Rosemary Harris;

THE ESTATE OF W.F. MARSHALL for permission to quote from 'Fair Play for Dialect' (in *Ulster Speaks*, BBC Books, 1936);

DR KEITH MILLAR for permission to quote from 'No Rootless Colonist' (*Aquarius*, 1972; reprinted in *Ancestral Voices: the selected prose of John Hewitt*, ed. Tom Clyde, Blackstaff Press, 1987) by John Hewitt;

JOHN MORROW for permission to quote from *Northern Myths* (Blackstaff Press, 1979);

THE ESTATE OF JOHN O'CONNOR for permission to quote from *Come Day – Go Day* (Golden Eagle Books, 1948; reissued by Blackstaff Press, 1984);

FRANK ORMSBY for permission to quote from 'County Fermanagh' (in *Thirty-two Counties*, Secker and Warburg, 1989);

PHILLIMORE AND COMPANY for permission to quote from *The Londonderry Plantation 1609–1914* (1986) by James Stevens Curl;

PLUTO PRESS for permission to quote from *War and an Irish Town* (1984) by Eamonn McCann;

POOLBEG PRESS for permission to quote from *Call My Brother Back* (1979) by Michael McLaverty;

EITHNE SHEA for permission to quote from *Voices and the Sound of Drums* (Blackstaff Press, 1981) by Patrick Shea;

MAX WRIGHT for permission to quote from *Told in Gath* (Blackstaff Press, 1990);

YALE UNIVERSITY PRESS for permission to quote from *Wolfe Tone: prophet of Irish independence* (1989) by Marianne Elliott; for permission to quote from 'Cultural Imperialism: an Irish view' (in *Yale Review*, 1986) by George J. Watson.

The Blackstaff Press Limited regret they have not been successful in tracing all copyright holders. They apologise for any errors or omissions in the above list and would be grateful to be notified of any corrections that should be incorporated in the next edition or reprint of this volume.

INDEX OF AUTHORS

Bell, Sam Hanna 168–71
Birmingham, George A. 132–9
Blackwood, Caroline 172–80, 359–65
Brett, C.E.B. 348–53, 366–71
Bryans, Robin 252–60; *see also* Harbinson, Robert
Bullock, Shan F. 101–3
Burdy, Revd Samuel 71–4
Carleton, William 90–7
Carson, Ciaran 425–30
Curl, James Stevens 29–36
Deane, Seamus 394–400
Delany, Mary 65–70
Devlin, Polly 379–93
Donoghue, Denis 287–90, 431–43
Drennan, William 75–9
Elliott, Marianne 37–44
Evans, E. Estyn 209–14, 215–17
Fitzpatrick, Kathleen 107–12
Gamble, John 80–9
Hanna, Denis O'D. 218–27
Harbinson, Robert 308–18; *see also* Bryans, Robin
Harris, Rosemary 152–7
Heaney, Seamus 248–51, 267–73
Hewitt, John 121–31
Ireland, Denis 234–41

Johnstone, Robert 401–9
Kiely, Benedict 98–100, 158–67
Leitch, Maurice 338–40
Lewis, C.S. 200–4
Longley, Michael 354–6
Lynd, Robert 113–17
McCann, Eamonn 20–8, 341–7
McDowell, Florence Mary 118, 205–8
McLaverty, Michael 296–300
MacNeice, Louis 242–7
Marshall, W.F. 228–33
May, Naomi 372–8
Moody, T.W. 45–50
Moore, Brian 319–34
Morrow, John 335–7
O'Connor, John 301–7
O'Donnell, Peadar 291–5
Ormsby, Frank 261–4
Paulin, Tom 410–24
Praeger, Robert Lloyd 183–96
Reid, Forrest 197–9
Ros, Amanda McKittrick 104–6
Shea, Patrick 51–3
Stewart, A.T.Q. 15–19, 54–62
Watson, George J. 274–86
Wright, Max 140–51